The Roots of Rural Capitalism

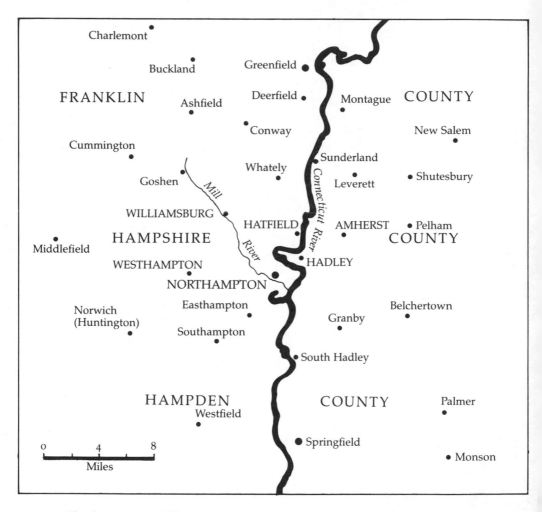

The Connecticut Valley in Massachusetts, with the location of towns mentioned in the text. The six towns that are the basis for this study are shown in capital letters. Franklin and Hampden counties were set off from "old" Hampshire County in 1811 and 1812.

THE ROOTS OF
RURAL CAPITALISM

Western Massachusetts, 1780–1860

CHRISTOPHER CLARK

Cornell University Press

ITHACA AND LONDON

First published 1990 by Cornell University Press.

International Standard Book Number 0-8014-2422-4
Library of Congress Catalog Card Number 89-46177
Printed in the United States of America
Librarians: Library of Congress cataloging information
appears on the last page of the book.

⊗ The paper used in this publication meets the minimum requirements of the American National Standard for Permanence of Paper for Printed Library Materials Z39.48–1984.

To my mother and father

Contents

Acknowledgments   ix
Abbreviations   xii

PART I
INTRODUCTION

1   Interpreting Rural Economic Change   3

PART II
INVOLUTION: 1780 TO THE 1820S

2   Households and Power in the Countryside in the Late
   Eighteenth Century   21
3   Households, Farming, and Manufacturing   59

PART III
THE BOUNDS OF INDEPENDENCE

4   Family Burdens and Household Strategies   121
5   Merchants and Households   156

PART IV
CONCENTRATION: THE 1820S TO 1860

6   "The Advantage Their Pay Demands": Morality and Money   195
7   Capital, Work, and Wealth   228
8   Farmers, Markets, and Society in Mid-Century   273

PART V
CONCLUSION

9   The Connecticut Valley in Perspective   317

Appendix: Population of the Six Towns, 1790–1860   331

Index   333

Acknowledgments

Margaret Lamb has given me her love and support, encouragement, advice, and assistance of many kinds during the years this book has been taking shape. I only hope that I have gone some way to reciprocating.

Robert A. Gross provided ideas and enthusiastic encouragement from the early days of research, read the manuscript in various versions, and generously took the time to make comments. I have shared my interests with David Jaffee over many years; he too read the manuscript and gave helpful criticism, which I hope has improved the end result. Roy Rosenzweig took a generous interest in the project, read the manuscript, and gave comments and support at a crucial moment. I am grateful, too, for the suggestions of an anonymous publisher's reader.

Many other friends and colleagues have contributed to the project in different ways, and I thank them all. Conversations or correspondence with Michael Bellesiles, John Brooke, Richard D. Brown, Jeanne Chase, Nancy Folbre, Ritchie Garrison, William J. Gilmore, Mark Kaplanoff, Barbara Karsky, Gary Kulik, Jonathan Prude, Mick Reed, Winifred Rothenberg, Barbara Clark Smith, Alan Taylor, Daniel Vickers, and Marta Wagner helped me greatly. So did the comments of participants in conferences or seminars in Atlanta, London, Los Angeles, Minneapolis, Paris, Washington, and York. Stephan Thernstrom oversaw my original research. Gregory H. Nobles welcomed me to the Connecticut Valley when I started work and has been generous in his support ever since; Stephen Nissenbaum has been a staunch friend of this project; Christopher M. Jedrey took a close interest from the start and maintained it over the years; Adrian Leftwich convinced me that the effort was worthwhile when it looked as if it wasn't and helped me see what was important and what was not. James Henretta's suggestions started the thing off; Michael Merrill provided the sparks that really got it going and has given ideas and encouragement since. John Bukowczyk and Jonathan Schneer have been invaluable comrades.

When I began research, I barely realized the potential of the many thousands of documents in local libraries and other collections. I owe a particular debt to librarians for helping me find and use them. Philip Cronenwett, then curator of special collections at the Jones Library, Amherst, let me range through the manuscripts he had recently cataloged; without his assistance the project would have been much the poorer. His successors, especially Daniel Lombardo, and other staff at the Jones Library helped me on many occasions. So did Stanley Greenberg and Blaise Bisaillon of the Forbes Library, Northampton; both in the months when I virtually lived in the place and when I made brief return visits later, they and other staff of the Forbes gave unstinting assistance; I am particularly grateful to Blaise Bisaillon for arranging the interlibrary loans that enabled me to use the *Hampshire Gazette* in England. Members and staff of many other institutions have also helped: the Northampton Historical Society; Porter-Phelps-Huntington House, Hadley; the Williamsburg Historical Society; David Proper and staff at the Pocumtuck Valley Memorial Association Library, Deerfield; the town clerks' offices of Amherst and Westhampton and the city clerk's office, Northampton; the clerks of the superior and district courts of Hampshire County and their staff; the Hampshire County registers of probate and of deeds and their staff; Joseph Banukiewicz of the Worcester County Sheriff's Dept., who most cheerfully dug out from storage at Worcester State Hospital boxes of court records for me to use; the Manuscripts and Archives Department, Baker Library, Harvard Business School; Houghton Library, Harvard University; the Boston Public Library; the Research Library, Old Sturbridge Village; the New England Historic Genealogical Society; Amherst College Archives; Susan Grigg and her staff at the Sophia Smith Collection and Smith College Archives; the Massachusetts State Library; the Massachusetts Archives; the Northampton Institution for Savings; the Library of Congress; the British Library Reference Division, Bloomsbury; the British Newspaper Library, Colindale; the British Library Document Supply Centre, Boston Spa; the Brotherton Library, University of Leeds; Cambridge University Library; and—in particular—the Inter-Library Loan Department of the J. B. Morrell Library, University of York. Robert Fletcher, of the University of York's computing service, helped me prepare the map.

Financial support of various kinds helped me bring the project to fruition. The American Antiquarian Society in Worcester awarded me a Samuel Foster Haven Fellowship for the summer of 1982, which not only permitted me to work on another topic but gave me access to a range of printed and manuscript sources that have greatly influenced the present book. I am especially grateful for the enthusiastic assistance of many of the society's staff, then and on subsequent occasions. A travel award from the Twenty-Seven Foundation enabled me to travel to the United States to conduct essential research another summer. The Master and Fellows of Selwyn College, Cambridge, in electing me to the Keasbey Research Fellowship in American Studies for a year, provided me with the time and opportunity to write a first draft. Finally, another award for a different project, a Smithsonian Postdoctoral Fellowship at the National Museum of American History, Washington D.C., gave me invaluable opportunities to discuss and rethink the work I had done.

I thank Peter Agree, Marilyn M. Sale, and the other staff of Cornell University Press, whose enthusiasm and efficiency has brought this book into the light of day, and my copyeditor Joanne S. Ainsworth, whose thoughtful and painstaking work has made the book better than it would otherwise have been.

I am grateful for hospitality from Chris and Micheline Jedrey, Bob and Ann Gross, and Warren Leon and Cindy Robinson during various research trips. I wish to give special thanks to my friends Carol MacColl and Don Michak of Northampton, who have been generous on so many occasions, and to Annie S. Lamb of Lebanon and Willimantic, Connecticut, who has helped often and in many ways.

CHRISTOPHER CLARK

York, England

Abbreviations

AAS	American Antiquarian Society, Worcester, Mass.
ACA	Amherst College Archives, Amherst, Mass.
BCJL	Boltwood Collection, Special Collections Room, Jones Library, Amherst, Mass.
CVHM	Connecticut Valley Historical Museum, Springfield, Mass.
FL	Forbes Library, Northampton, Mass.
HBS	Manuscripts and Archives Department, Baker Library, Harvard University Graduate School of Business Administration, Boston, Mass.
HCL	Houghton Library, Harvard University, Cambridge, Mass.
JL	Jones Library, Amherst, Mass.
LC	Library of Congress, Washington, D.C.
MCFL	Manuscripts Collection, Trustees' Room, Forbes Library, Northampton, Mass.
NEHGS	New England Historic Genealogical Society, Boston, Mass.
NHS	Northampton Historical Society, Northampton, Mass.
OSV	Research Library, Old Sturbridge Village, Sturbridge, Mass.
PPHH	Porter-Phelps-Huntington House, Hadley, Mass.
PVMA	Pocumtuck Valley Memorial Association Library, Deerfield, Mass.
SPJM	*Selected Papers from the Sylvester Judd Manuscript*, comp. Gregory H. Nobles and Herbert L. Zarov (Northampton, 1976).
SSC	Sophia Smith Collection, Smith College, Northampton, Mass.
WHS	Williamsburg Historical Society, Williamsburg, Mass.

PART I

INTRODUCTION

Chapter 1

Interpreting
Rural Economic Change

When Sylvester Judd died in Northampton in 1860, aged almost seventy-one, his chief legacy was a vast collection of notes on the history of the Connecticut Valley towns in Massachusetts, together with the nearly completed manuscript of a *History of Hadley*, which would be published three years later. Judd's principal concern was to chronicle the early chapters of white settlement in western Massachusetts from the town records and genealogical data he had transcribed into his notes. But his emphasis on the colonial period derived from a strong sense of the changes that had taken place during his lifetime. In his own career and the careers of his neighbors and acquaintances he measured the speed with which rural life had been transformed. Like other local historians of the mid–nineteenth century, he sought in the recovery of the "distant" colonial past a means of orienting himself and his contemporaries in the altered world in which they had arrived.[1]

1. Sylvester Judd, *History of Hadley, including the early history of Hatfield, South Hadley, Amherst, and Granby, Mass.* (Northampton, 1863). Judd's biography is in an obituary, *Hampshire Gazette* (Northampton), Apr 24, 1860, and in notes added to *History of Hadley* by his sister-in-law Arethusa Hall. Brief modern biographies are in the introduction to *SPJM*, and Altina Waller, "Sylvester Judd: Historian of the Connecticut Valley," *Historical Journal of Massachusetts* 10 (June 1982): 43–56 (and there is also useful material in the biography of his son, Sylvester Judd III, a Unitarian minister and novelist: Richard D. Hathaway, *Sylvester Judd's New England* [University Park, Pa., 1981]). For comments on Judd's interest in "the early settlers of New England," see the exchange of letters between Judd and Lucius M. Boltwood, Mar 9–11, 1848, L. M. Boltwood Papers, BCJL; D. J. Russo, "The Deerfield Massacre of 1704 and Local Historical Writing in the United States," in *The Triumph of Culture: Eighteenth-Century Perspectives*, ed. Paul Fritz and David Williams (Toronto, 1972), is useful on the genre Judd helped to pioneer, but stresses economic change less than is justified by authors' concern with it.

Judd was so impressed with Horace Bushnell's famous Litchfield Sermon of 1851, which described "the complete revolution of domestic life and manners" that had occurred since "the age of homespun," that he used parts of it in his book. In the diary he kept for the last twenty-five years of his life, he followed the state of farming, observed new factories making goods that had once been produced at home, and noted the construction of railroads. Thousands of families had migrated to the expanding West. Thousands more, Judd's own included, had moved from the land into growing towns and cities. Farmers and crafts-men who, two generations before, had dealt mainly in a world of independent producers like themselves, now faced larger, competitive markets, corporations, and other institutions, greater social distance, and impersonality.

Judd's attitude to these changes was ambivalent. His early reading and experience had made him optimistic that the American republic's independent yeomanry would enable it to avoid the evils of European societies, with their aristocracies and mass poverty. Like many others after the Revolution, he was hopeful that a widespread distribution of property would give farmers and their families the means to control their own production and labor, and so secure "independence" from the economic and political patronage of the wealthy. Yet over time his Calvinist background and critical observation of people and institutions led Judd to doubt that America and Europe were fundamentally dif-ferent. Few people, even himself, measured up to the strict moral standards he saw as the root of a good society. Interviewing some old people in the 1850s, he noted that "both reckon the past was happier and with more neighborly feeling" and was inclined to agree: "Part of this may arise from the predilections that old people have for the scenes, customs, etc., of their youth. But there is doubtless more 'strife for preeminence' more attempts to out do each other in what is showy and fashionable than formerly." Judd did not, however, glorify a "purer" past: "there was aristocracy then as now in the large towns and villages." Changes had been profound, but Judd was not certain that they had been wholly to the good or to the bad.[2]

This ambivalence grew from his own career. By the standards of his family's past, he had failed. Born in the upland town of Westhampton in 1789, he was named for his father, one of the town's early settlers, a

<hr>

2. Judd Manuscript, "Miscellaneous," 14:366, FL. The Judd Manuscript, chiefly con-taining Sylvester Judd's historical notes and transcriptions of records, consists of more than sixty bound volumes, arranged in several titled series. (It is hereafter cited as Judd MS, with the name of series and number of the volume within the series.) Extracts from the Judd MS have been collected in *SPJM*, but since copies of the latter are available in only a few libraries in the Valley and the Judd MS itself has been microfilmed, I have included references to both where applicable.

farmer, storekeeper, and justice of the peace. At fourteen, the young Sylvester Judd was clerk in the store. Later he was a clerk in Boston, before returning to Westhampton to run the store as the branch of a larger business owned by his brother and two cousins. After his marriage in 1811 to Apphia Hall of the neighboring hill town of Norwich, he sought to establish himself as a farmer. Profits from the store, together with the assistance of his father, enabled him to acquire land from an insolvent estate in 1813. Over the next three years, he improved the buildings and land, entered town politics, and seemed set to become as prominent in Westhampton as his father was. But the end of war with Britain in 1815 found him overextended in trade. The following year, having assumed responsibilities for the building of a new meeting house, he was caught out by the bankruptcy of another man and saddled with debts that he could not meet. For several years, he struggled with farming, tanning, and storekeeping to overcome his difficulties, but ended up only more heavily in debt. In 1819, overcome with self-disgust, he considered moving west and traveled to Ohio to look over the country. But he did not like what he found and returned. Only with the help of his father, who took land back from him in return for assuming his debts, did Judd manage to clear himself by 1822. Out of debt, but having failed to make a living from the land and local trade of his home town, he had to start again.[3]

Once more, his family enabled him to do so. His brother Hophni, who had died in 1817, had been part owner of the *Hampshire Gazette*, published in nearby Northampton and the voice of western Massachusetts federalism. Judd had long been attracted to literary pursuits, had written for the paper during the 1812 war, and by 1820 had accumulated a collection of about 170 books. He moved his impoverished family to Northampton and became the paper's editor. Over nearly thirteen years he became increasingly critical of the county's establishment and its "aristocratic" pretensions, expressing sympathy, but not wholehearted support, for the Anti-Masons and Workingmen whose campaigns convulsed local politics in the early 1830s. His independent line brought pressure from critics and rivals. He became disillusioned with party factionalism. His father's death in 1832 left him with enough property and income to live on modestly. In 1835, to the annoyance of his radical friends, he sold the *Gazette* to a Whig and turned for good to historical and genealogical research. For the rest of his life he and his

---

3. Judd MS, "Commonplace Book," pp. 77–79; Waller, "Sylvester Judd," passim. In his "Journal of Journey to Ohio," 1819, Judd Papers, 55M-1, Box 1, HCL, Judd wrote that his trip west was motivated in part by "curiosity," but that "the embarrassment of my affairs and the horrors of approaching bankruptcy had created in me such a disgust and wearisomeness of all things around me, that I resolved to leave."

family made do on his earnings from investments, on occasional payments for research, and on cooperation with kin to eke out their resources. He secured a livelihood not as a yeoman farmer but in the newer world of the small-town middle class.[4]

Judd's ideas were steeped in the republicanism of the revolutionary generation. He respected hard work and self-restraint as the means of getting a living and believed that these values had to be conveyed to the future generations in whose hands the republic would rest. But he was aware that in his own life ideals and realities clashed. He did maintain frugality and self-restraint, to such an extent that when his children grew up they would procure things for their mother that they knew Judd himself would never acquire for her. He remained a staunch critic of fashion and "trumpery." Visiting a Hartford family in 1842, he found the daughters "fashionably dressed, having the requisite supply of stuffing all around the body, and when they arose from a chair, the slender compressed body above, and the sweeping below, seemed to me to resemble a haystack with a pole projecting from the top." But while critical of the "rage for money-making" he found around him, which he attributed to a passion for self-gratification and display, he knew that he too, having left the land, lived by means that an older generation scarcely regarded as "work" and that forced him into financial transactions whose strict morality he doubted.[5]

Moreover, Judd faced difficulties in providing means for his own children. There is no evidence that he attempted to restrain them from the various courses they followed, but his diary reflected regret at their need to rely so extensively on their own resources. His five sons all made their careers away from Northampton, though one returned there in the 1840s. One of his two daughters worked away from home before her marriage, too. Judd gave them money when he could, and sometimes had to record that it had been lost in business. Above all, Judd regretted that the dispersal of his children was accompanied by religious fragmentation, another symbol of his loss of authority. He remained most comfortable with the orthodox Congregationalism in which he had been raised. One of his sons became a Unitarian minister, another a deist. He had sharp words for his young sister-in-law when she wrote of her intention to join the Episcopalians, whom he suspected of popery. But, as he knew from the proliferation of churches in North-

---

4. Sylvester Judd, "Notebooks," 1833–1860, FL, are a series of eight numbered volumes containing Judd's diary (hereafter cited as Judd, "Notebook," with volume number and date of entry).

5. On Judd's frugality: Apphia Judd Williams to Apphia Judd, Augusta, Me., June 2, 1842; on his attitude to fashion: Judd to Apphia Judd Williams, Hartford, Nov 28, 1842, both in Judd Papers, 55M-1, Box 2, HCL; references to money are made by Hall, "Biographical Notes," in Judd, *History of Hadley*.

ampton itself after 1820, his children were only following a general trend. He remained attached to the town's Old Church until decisions in 1856 to raise the minister's salary and install a new organ caused him to leave in disgust at its extravagance.[6]

Sylvester Judd's life and his historical research marked processes of change experienced by much of rural New England in the eight decades between the Revolution and the Civil War. Population growth, young peoples' search for occupations other than farming, the emergence of a cash economy, the cultural complexities of revivalism, and the marketplace profoundly affected New Englanders of Judd's generation, their parents, and their children. Another local historian would write a few decades later, "There are few instances in history of a transformation more complete than has been seen in Massachusetts."[7]

I came across Judd's notes and diaries at the start of an exploration of how industrial capitalism emerged from the rural societies of the American Northeast. I had chosen to study the Connecticut Valley of Massachusetts because of its varied landscapes, in which agriculture and industry grew together. This book draws on evidence from Hampshire and Franklin counties, focusing principally on Northampton, Hadley, and Hatfield, founded in the seventeenth century on the rich meadowlands ("intervales") along the Connecticut River, and on Amherst, Westhampton, and Williamsburg, which were among eight new towns carved from them as population expanded in the eighteenth century into the uplands to the east and west. (These are the "six towns" mentioned throughout the book; "bottomlands" refers to the fertile farmland near the river; "the Valley" refers to the region as a whole.) Together the six towns provide a mixture of backgrounds against which to study the process of economic change. From old settlements to new, from intervales to barren hillsides, they encompass many of the circumstances that could be found throughout the rural Northeast.

As well as providing evidence of the changes I seek to explain, Judd's story reflects the complex ways in which rural New Englanders confronted them. Above all, his writings showed that the abstract forces historians are fond of analyzing—"markets," "urbanization," "capitalism"—formed part of individuals' and families' own experiences. They suggested that the concerns and observations evident to contemporaries could be linked to the underlying structural shifts during their

---

6. On Judd's regret at his sons' difficulties: "Notebook," vol. 4, Nov 18, 1847; on religion and his break with the First Church: "Notebook," vol. 7, Oct 9, 1856.

7. The quotation is from Francis H. Underwood, *Quabbin: The Story of a Small Town with Outlooks on Puritan Life* (1893; reprint, Boston, 1986), p. 32. A modern account of change with a strong focus on New England is Jack Larkin, *The Reshaping of Everyday Life, 1790–1840* (New York, 1988).

lives of which they could not be fully aware. Surely, looking at the ways men and women grappled with these could throw light on the process of change.

This turned out to be so, but in unexpected ways. From my attempt to use personal documents to see how they *reflected* changes in rural society came the realization that these personal experiences formed the fabric of change itself: people did not just respond to things, they made them happen. "Experience" could not only illuminate change, but could help to explain it. Judd's confrontation with the ideals and realities of his own life was complex and ambivalent; so was the passage of rural change in general. As Judd and his contemporaries acted to try to realize their ambitions, they altered the way the rural economy was conducted. Evidence for this is buried in the multitude of letters, diaries, account books, and other documents they left behind and that recorded their activity. The book draws on this material to show how rural people transformed the world they lived in.

Between the 1780s and the 1860s the New England countryside underwent a profound social and economic transformation. From an economy dominated by independent farmers, it became part of a broader national market and an outpost of industrial capitalism. The population of the six towns grew from just over 6,000 in 1790 to over 16,000 by 1860. Whereas at the end of the eighteenth century the great majority of people worked on the land, by 1860 this was not true in many places; in Northampton, less than one-third of the workforce owned farms or labored in agriculture. Farming remained the predominant activity in the poorer hill towns and on the rich lands along the Connecticut River, but in both places, and in differing ways, the development of markets and commercial agriculture had transformed it.

Everywhere, trade and manufacturing grew in significance. Both farming and industry served to stimulate population growth even in the face of substantial outmigration to the West and to urban centers elsewhere in the Northeast. In the late colonial period, southern New England, with much of its land divided up into farms and its economy based on family labor, had attracted few immigrants; most went to other settled regions of the colonies or to the frontier. Bernard Bailyn's recent study of migration from the British Isles to America on the eve of the Revolution shows that an extremely small proportion of migrants set out for New England. By the mid-1850s, however, New England had become a major center of immigrant settlement. Even in a rural area like the Connecticut Valley, between one-tenth and one-quarter of the population in the more prosperous towns were foreign-born.[8] While

8. Bernard Bailyn, *Voyagers to the West: A Passage in the Peopling of America on the Eve of the Revolution*, with the assistance of Barbara DeWolfe (New York, 1986), p. 209, shows that of 9,364 people listed in the register of emigrants from Britain between Dec 1773 and

the outlines of such changes in the countryside are clear, however, the reasons for them have been the subject of protracted historical debate.

For a long time, historians of industrial capitalism paid little attention to older rural regions such as those in New England. The transformation of America's economy and society seemed best symbolized by the building of large factories, by the creation of new industrial towns like Lowell, Massachusetts, and by the rapid expansion of older cities like Boston, New York, and Philadelphia into teeming metropolises. Contrasted with these dramas, rural society appeared passive and backward. The countryside interested some scholars as a source of urban population and industrial labor, but such interest merely reflected its relative decline; in the nineteenth century, rural life was something people started to avoid.[9] This emphasis on towns and cities dominated the "new social history" of America up to the late 1970s and beyond.

The main reason for historians' lack of interest in rural society was that changes in it between the Revolution and the Civil War seemed to present no serious problems of interpretation. Most scholars held that Americans had been "capitalists" since the first colonial settlements— none more so than New England farmers, proprietors of their own soil and subject to no feudal or neofeudal exactions. True, colonial historians had begun to write of Puritan communalism and collective values in the early years, but most agreed that these values had succumbed to individualism and grasping ambition by the mid-eighteenth century. "Yankees" had, after all, long been proverbial for their acuteness in spotting a bargain, selling to the highest bidder, and seizing the main chance.[10] Farmers were true to type but were often hampered by poor

---

Mar 1776, only 77 (0.8%) had New England as their immediate destination. By contrast 36 percent were bound for New York and Pennsylvania and 33 percent for Maryland and Virginia. The Massachusetts census of 1855 found that 13.3 percent of Hampshire County's population was born outside the United States; in Northampton the proportion was almost 24 percent.

9. Mary P. Ryan, *Cradle of the Middle Class: The Family in Oneida County, New York, 1790–1865* (Cambridge, Eng., 1981), traces migrants from rural Oneida County to Utica but then focuses on the city itself. Studies of urban industries and their use of rural labor include Alan Dawley, *Class and Community: The Industrial Revolution in Lynn* (Cambridge, Mass., 1976), and Thomas L. Dublin, *Women at Work: The Transformation of Work and Community in Lowell, Massachusetts, 1826–1860* (New York, 1979). Dublin, in particular, has extended his research into the rural origins of migrants and industry in the countryside itself: see Thomas L. Dublin, ed., *Farm to Factory: Women's Letters, 1830–1860* (New York, 1981); idem, "Women and Outwork in a 19th Century New England Town," in *The Countryside in the Age of Capitalist Transformation: Essays in the Social History of Rural America*, ed. Steven Hahn and Jonathan Prude (Chapel Hill, 1985); idem, "Rural-Urban Migrants in Industrial New England: The Case of Lynn, Massachusetts, in the Mid–19th Century," *Journal of American History* 73 (Dec 1986). Alexander James Field, "Sectoral Shift in Antebellum Massachusetts: A Reconsideration," *Explorations in Economic History* 15 (Apr 1978): 146–171, argues that the relative decline of mid-century New England agriculture contributed to the expansion of manufacturing in the region.

10. The classic argument that America lacked feudal institutions was made by Louis Hartz, *The Liberal Tradition in America: An Interpretation of American Political Thought since the*

soils, poor techniques, distance from markets, and poor transportation; if many of them did not in fact raise and sell cash crops for profit in the eighteenth century, it was for lack of opportunity, not of the ambition to do so. The history of their integration into national markets in the nineteenth century therefore seemed quite straightforward: new roads, canals, and railroads opened access to urban markets; new farming methods, promoted by agricultural societies and progressive periodicals, raised output; new tools and implements reduced unit labor costs. Rural change seemed more a matter of techniques than of fundamental attitudes.[11]

For more than a decade, this view of the rural North has been under growing scholarly scrutiny. Many of the facts on which the old interpretation rested have survived intact, but the process of adding to them and rethinking their significance has left the interpretation itself in shreds.[12] So far, though, no single new view has emerged to replace it. The sharpest attacks on it have come from two opposite directions, the debate between which has recently begun to dominate the field of rural history.

Revolution (New York, 1955). Early communalism and its subsequent decline was the theme of Kenneth A. Lockridge, *A New England Town, the First Hundred Years: Dedham, Massachusetts, 1636–1736* (New York, 1970). Richard L. Bushman, *From Puritan to Yankee: Character and the Social Order in Connecticut, 1690–1765* (Cambridge, Mass., 1967), also discussed the growth of individual acquisitiveness. Charles S. Grant, *Democracy in the Connecticut Frontier Town of Kent* (New York, 1961), portrayed farmers as profit-oriented entrepreneurs, a view essentially accepted by some Marxist scholars too: see Douglas F. Dowd, *The Twisted Dream: Capitalist Development in the United States since 1776* (Boston, 1974), pp. 152–153.

11. This interpretation was stated most plainly in Richard Hofstadter, *The Age of Reform, From Bryan to F.D.R.* (New York, 1955), chap. 1, esp. p. 23. D. C. North, "Location Theory and Regional Economic Growth," *Journal of Political Economy* 63 (1955): 245, attributed "subsistence" farming "solely to poor transportation." George Rogers Taylor, in *The Transportation Revolution, 1815–1860* (New York, 1951), focused particularly on the role of roads, canals, and railroads in spreading commerce.

12. From 1969 onward several works stimulated new interest in rural history for what it could tell us about broader developments. The most important was James T. Lemon, *The Best Poor Man's Country: A Geographical Study of Early Southeastern Pennsylvania* (Baltimore, 1972); others included Clarence H. Danhof, *Change in Agriculture: The Northern United States, 1820–1870* (Cambridge, Mass., 1969); Diane Lindstrom, *Economic Development in the Philadelphia Region, 1810–1850* (New York, 1978); P. G. E. Clemens, *The Atlantic Economy and Colonial Maryland's Eastern Shore* (Ithaca, N.Y., 1980); Joan M. Jensen, *Loosening the Bonds: Mid-Atlantic Farm Women, 1750–1850* (New Haven, 1986); Jeremy Atack and Fred Bateman, *To Their Own Soil: Agriculture in the Antebellum North* (Ames, Iowa, 1987). Important interpretations of early New England landscape and ecology are John R. Stilgoe, *The Common Landscape of America, 1580–1845* (New Haven, 1982), and William Cronon, *Changes in the Land: Indians, Colonists, and the Ecology of New England* (New York, 1983). Social histories of New England rural communities include Robert A. Gross, *The Minutemen and Their World* (New York, 1976), and Christopher M. Jedrey, *The World of John Cleaveland: Family and Community in Eighteenth-Century New England* (New York, 1979). For a discussion of recent literature on agriculture, see James T. Lemon, "Agriculture and Society in Early America," *Agricultural History Review* 35 (1987): 76–94.

One assault, developed by Winifred B. Rothenberg, has shattered the view that New England's agricultural history was largely a continuum and that its crucial changes were those of technology and technique. Her work demonstrates that important changes in exchange patterns were taking place in the Massachusetts countryside from about 1780 onward, and she argues that these changes resulted in the emergence of new markets for produce, capital, and labor during the late eighteenth and early nineteenth centuries. These findings are significant for two reasons. First, although the growth of such markets was always recognized in the older interpretation, Rothenberg suggests that it began *before* there were substantial improvements in transportation or farming methods. Farmers were using existing technology to do something new. Second, she shows that what they started to do at the end of the colonial period *was* something new and not just a continuation of old practices. Before this, Massachusetts farmers had not contributed significant amounts of produce to competitive commodity markets, had not generally conducted exchange with negotiable paper instruments, and had not employed labor at fluctuating and competitive wage rates. Now they were beginning to do these things. The burden of Rothenberg's argument is that an important adaptation was under way in the late-eighteenth-century countryside.[13]

Before Rothenberg began to publish her work, however, another assault on the old interpretation had been opened by Michael Merrill and James A. Henretta, who directly criticized the assumption that rural Americans had "always been capitalists." Contending that this assumption rested on the view that farmers were principally individualists, motivated by the search for profit in the marketplace, they showed that this perspective on colonial rural culture was inadequate and distorted. Merrill argued that most farmers were not market oriented; indeed, he went further, to suggest that well into the nineteenth century they remained primarily concerned with production for use. Henretta stressed that, rather than the search for profit, rural families were motivated by the desire to preserve the integrity of their households and to pass this legacy to succeeding generations. Both scholars

13. Winifred B. Rothenberg, "A Price Index for Rural Massachusetts, 1750–1855," *Journal of Economic History* 39 (1979); idem, "The Market and Massachusetts Farmers, 1750–1855," *Journal of Economic History* 41 (1981): 283–314; idem, "The Emergence of a Capital Market in Rural Massachusetts, 1730–1838," *Journal of Economic History* 45 (1985): 781–808; idem, "The Emergence of Farm Labor Markets and the Transformation of the Rural Economy," *Journal of Economic History* 48 (1988): 537–566. In "Markets and Massachusetts Farmers: A Paradigm of Economic Growth in Rural New England, 1750–1855" (Ph.D. diss., Brandeis University, 1985), Rothenberg incorporates material published in the first three articles and an early version of the fourth, now superseded by the published paper.

emphasized the centrality of households to rural economy and culture. They argued that patterns of cooperation within households, the kinship and neighborhood ties between them, and the reciprocal exchange of goods and work that characterized rural life were more significant than the individualism stressed by earlier scholars. Neither, it should be noted, denied that market exchange took place in the countryside. They argued, though, that the values of household, family, and neighborhood were much more important determinants of farming strategies than the pursuit of profit from the sale of produce. If Merrill and Henretta were right, how, then, had the economic changes of the nineteenth century come about? Building on their insights, I advanced a social explanation of the emergence of rural capitalism. My book elaborates this argument, modified since its original appearance.[14]

Merrill and Henretta touched off a debate that has proceeded on two levels. First, a tendency to misread what they had written led some scholars to claim that they had reverted to an older interpretation of northern agrarian history, associated above all with Percy Wells Bidwell, which had portrayed late-eighteenth- and early-nineteenth-century farmers as "self-sufficient." Research conducted to demonstrate what Merrill and Henretta already knew, that a good deal of exchange did occur in the countryside, has nevertheless added considerably to our understanding of the rural economy and dispelled the "self-sufficiency myth" for good.[15] On another level, however, the debate has

14. Michael Merrill, "Cash Is Good to Eat: Self-Sufficiency and Exchange in the Rural Economy of the United States," *Radical History Review* 3 (1977): 42–71; James A. Henretta, "Families and Farms: *Mentalité* in Pre-Industrial America," *William and Mary Quarterly* 35 (Jan 1978): 3–32. See also Christopher Clark, "Household Economy, Market Exchange, and the Rise of Capitalism in the Connecticut Valley, 1800–1860," *Journal of Social History* 13 (Winter 1979): 169–189, and the essays in Hahn and Prude, *The Countryside in the Age of Capitalist Transformation*.

15. On the "self-sufficient" farm economy see Percy W. Bidwell, "Rural Economy in New England at the Beginning of the 19th Century," *Transactions of the Connecticut Academy of Arts and Sciences* 20 (1916): 241–399; idem, "The Agricultural Revolution in New England," *American Historical Review* 26 (1921); Percy W. Bidwell and John I. Falconer, *History of Agriculture in the Northern United States, 1620–1860* (Washington, D.C., 1925); see also Clarence A. Day, *History of Maine Agriculture* (Orono, 1954). Refutation of this interpretation was produced by Carole Shammas, "How Self-Sufficient was Early America?" *Journal of Interdisciplinary History* 13 (1982–1983): 247–272, and Bettye Hobbs Pruitt, "Self-Sufficiency and the Agricultural Economy of Eighteenth-Century Massachusetts," *William and Mary Quarterly* 41 (July 1984): 333–364. As I argue in Chapters 2 and 3, however, the existence of exchange did not necessarily imply the existence of markets. "Market" and "self-sufficiency" are idealized extremes. As Jeanne Boydston has suggested in "Home and Work: The Industrialization of Housework in the United States from the Colonial Period to the Civil War" (Ph.D. diss., Yale University, 1984), p. 57, it is important to recognize the "distinctive culture" that lay between them. See also Maurice Aymard, "Autoconsommation et marchés: Chayanov, Labrousse ou Le Roy Ladurie?" *Annales ESC* 38 (Nov–Dec 1983): 1392–1410. An excellent analysis of exchanges in cultural context is Daniel H. Usner, Jr., "Frontier Exchange in the Lower Mississippi Valley: Race Relations and Economic Life in Colonial Louisiana, 1699–1783" (Ph.D. diss., Duke University, 1981).

been over the historic importance of rural exchange. Scholars such as Rothenberg have argued that the development of markets in produce, capital, and labor was the key to economic change in the countryside, the force that led to prosperity, capital accumulation, and new social relations. Others have questioned this assertion. Debate over these two issues, the quantity of market relations and their significance, has divided historians into what Allan Kulikoff has recently dubbed the "market" and the "social" schools. As Kulikoff also observed, however, the differences between the two groups are principally ones of emphasis; a synthesis of their views ought to be possible.[16] This book seeks to offer one.

Important as they are, Rothenberg's findings on the market involvement of eighteenth- and nineteenth-century farmers are essentially descriptive. Her explanations as to *why* change occurred come down to an argument that markets generate their own influences on behavior. This circularity ignores the opportunity a social interpretation provides to suggest how change came about, and—equally important—why it happened when it did. Merrill's and Henretta's insights into rural peoples' practices, values, and motivations, together with an analysis of rural social structure and the contexts in which strategies and choices were formed, allow us to reach a more thorough understanding of change in the countryside. The chapters that follow provide a synthesis between "market" and "social" interpretations, based on the observation that "markets" are not determinant but are created in and derived from social circumstances. They are patterns of social interaction in the transmission of goods and services whose existence and varied characteristics need to be explained.[17] Indeed, the creation of "markets" was

16. The argument about the effects of markets is made by Rothenberg, "Emergence of Farm Labor Markets," p. 561. Allan Kulikoff, "The Transition to Capitalism in Rural America," *William and Mary Quarterly* 46 (Jan 1989): 120–144, distinguishes "market" from "social" approaches and calls for a synthesis; I refer to pp. 122 and 128. He provides citations to articles in the debate too numerous to list here. Other useful reviews are James T. Lemon, "Spatial Order: Households in Local Communities and Regions," in *Colonial British America: Essays in the New History of the Early Modern Era*, ed. Jack P. Greene and J. R. Pole (Baltimore, 1984), pp. 86–122, and Gregory Nobles, "Capitalism in the Countryside: The Transformation of Rural Society in the United States," *Radical History Review* 41 (1988): 163–177. The differences between "market" and "social" interpretations of American rural history have broad similarities with the wider debate conducted by "formalist" and "substantivist" economic anthropologists, prompted in particular by Samuel L. Popkin, *The Rational Peasant: The Political Economy of Rural Society in Vietnam* (Berkeley, 1979), and James C. Scott, *The Moral Economy of the Peasant: Rebellion and Subsistence in Southeast Asia* (New Haven, 1976). As I argue below, "rationality" could take forms other than those predicted by neoclassical economic theory.

17. On the histories of markets: Fernand Braudel, *Civilisation und Capitalism, 15th–18th Centuries*, vol. 2: *The Wheels of Commerce*, trans. Sian Reynolds (London, 1982), esp. pp. 223–230; and Julian Hoppitt, *Risk and Failure in English Business, 1700–1800* (Cambridge, Eng., 1987), introduction. Braudel did, nevertheless, see common features between markets widely separated in time and place.

only one part of a wider shift in social and cultural relationships, which forms the subject of this book.

Because this book is about social structures and relationships and not purely a quantitative measurement of the growth of markets, it can suggest an explanation of the emergence of rural capitalism. The concept of "capitalism" has given rise to even more debate and confusion than the concept of "markets," so a definition of what is meant by it is essential. In this book I use it to refer to the set of social relations in which labor is commonly divorced from the ownership of the land, tools, or materials that form the means of production; as a result of this, labor power is commonly hired for wages by the proprietors of land or industrial enterprises, and there exists in society a significant number of people whose principal means of livelihood is the wage work that they can obtain. For stylistic reasons, I have used the terms *rural capitalism* and *capitalism* interchangeably in places; both refer to the set of social relationships just described. I have used the term *rural capitalism*, rather than *industrial capitalism*, to indicate a stage in the development of social relations in the countryside and as a reminder that these relationships came to exist both in manufacturing proper and in farming. I argue that rural society was not, in this sense, "capitalist" at the end of the colonial period but that it had become so by the time of the Civil War. The means by which this happened is the subject matter of this book.

The "transition to capitalism" has long been a subject for discussion; the debate on rural society has helped place it high on the agenda for American social historians. Often, however, scholars have relied on single tests of the existence of capitalism comparable to the one outlined above and have advanced the view that the "transition" was a single set of processes. In what follows I have tried to show that this was not the case. In New England, the emergence of capitalism in the countryside followed a complex and uneven path, hardly reducible to a single stage. Nor, although its achievement was marked by the creation of a permanent wage-labor force, is this the only factor that needs to be traced.

In certain respects, the grounding for rural capitalism had been laid by the early white settlements in New England. Not only had colonization been motivated in part by the desire to profit from New World production and trade, but the establishment of freehold land tenure and the absence of substantial restrictions on the freedom of labor gave New England purer legal and political frameworks for capitalist development than were available in seigneurial or slave societies. But just because there had been a "capitalist" impetus for New England's development did not mean that all settlers were motivated by it, or remained so. Nor did the existence of free land and free labor mean that people would necessarily use them to create capitalist institutions. Many farmers in the interior were more concerned, as we shall see, to establish an independent household economy in which the use of wage labor and production for distant markets were severely curtailed.

Even had market orientation been greater than it was in the late eighteenth century, however, rural New England would not necessarily have been capitalist in character. As scholars of slavery have shown, it is possible to participate in long-distance trade without altering the fundamentally noncapitalist character of a social structure.[18] Only over time, and under circumstances that need to be explored, did market involvement help bring about the creation of capitalist social relations in the New England countryside. Shifts in the exchange system, the use of credit, the emergence of cash and negotiable paper instruments, and the charging of interest on debts, which have also been taken as the marks of capitalism, all contributed to the process. Produce, capital, and labor markets also reflected, under specific social conditions, the emergence of groups of entrepreneurs capable of securing control of a proportion of the goods, credit, and labor power in the rural economy. Inequalities in the distribution of land and wealth fostered the growth of a population obliged to depend on wage labor. In short, the evolution of rural capitalism was defined, not by the adoption of any one particular set of practices, but by the accretion of a series of distinctive forms and organizations that together came to form a new economic system.

Examining a process of accretion, rather than a single "transition," requires that the book's organization be essentially chronological. The seven chapters that follow this introduction are divided into three groups. The earlier and later chapters outline two distinct phases in the transformation of the countryside, the first a period of "involution," or intensification of existing practices, from 1780 to the 1820s (Chapters 2 and 3), the second a period of capitalist "concentration" from then until the Civil War (Chapters 6, 7, and 8). Between them (in Chapters 4 and 5) comes a discussion of the processes that led to the shift from one phase to the next.

Chapter 2 outlines the central role of noncapitalist household production in the late-eighteenth-century economy and discusses the distinc-

---

18. On the noncapitalist, nonbourgeois character of a slave society committed to export and import markets, see Eugene D. Genovese, *The Political Economy of Slavery: Studies in the Economy and Society of the Slave South* (New York, 1967), esp. p. 23; and Elizabeth Fox-Genovese, *Within the Plantation Household: Black and White Women of the Old South* (Chapel Hill, 1988), pp. 53–58. While I was completing the draft of my book there became available James A. Henretta, "The War for Independence and American Economic Development," in *The Economy of Early America: The Revolutionary Period, 1763–1790,* ed. Ronald Hoffman, et al. (Charlottesville, Va., 1988), pp. 45–87, which stresses the noncapitalist development of American production between the Revolution and 1815.

tive exchange relationships that governed rural life. A combination of economic and political circumstances reinforced, rather than reduced, the power of household producers in the revolutionary period. The ideal of household "independence," widely referred to in rural discourse, was more than a rhetorical device. In the context of rural social relations, it had a substantial measure of reality. Families' desire to acquire and hold onto the means of controlling their own efforts and resources powerfully influenced rural economic life. Consequently, as shown in Chapter 3, household production and exchange made such a powerful impression on agricultural and manufacturing growth between 1790 and 1820 that the emergence of capitalist production and labor relations was restrained. Throughout this period, the crucial influences on the economy were generated from within the rural social structure itself. Change was not simply imposed on the countryside from outside but generated by the pressures and conflicts intrinsic to rural life.

Change was achieved, however, only at the cost of great strain on households, due especially to the work burdens placed on women. In Chapter 4 I discuss how, during the period roughly from 1810 to 1830, rural families adapted their economic strategies, placing greater reliance than they had before on securing necessities from distant markets and adjusting production to acquire these goods. As a consequence, the relative power of local merchants and storekeepers, previously forced to compete with local families for surpluses with which to trade, was enhanced. As shown in Chapter 5, these merchants began to involve themselves more deeply, not only in exchanging the products, but in controlling the labor of rural families. This was the basis upon which more concentrated accumulation of capital was to occur up to the middle of the century, at first still largely within the social structure of the household-based economy.

Greater control of trade and access to credit also helped merchants to alter the terms on which they conducted exchange, though, as seen in Chapter 6, the shift toward a cash economy and controlled credit they were achieving by 1860 came about only through protracted struggles against economic uncertainty. Over the antebellum period, however, entrepreneurs enhanced their control of the economy. They accumulated capital and concentrated industrial production at an unprecedented rate as the countryside recovered from the depressions of the late 1830s and early 1840s. Chapter 7 traces this emergence of industrial capital and of a permanent wage-labor force to serve it. Dislocation of older patterns of rural production, together with European immigration, created new reservoirs of relatively cheap rural labor for manufacturers, who began to sever the close ties they had once maintained with rural households. As a result, both the distribution of wealth and the social patterns of access to the instruments of capitalist economic power became increasingly unequal. All these developments arose as rural production became more tightly bound to the rhythms of a national market. Outside influences began to play a greater role than factors intrinsic to the region.

Only in farming did the essential structure of the household economy remain intact by the 1850s. Even here, however, significant shifts were occurring, discussed in Chapter 8. While rural households could maintain much of the sense of independence they had sought earlier, its terms were modified. Especially in the more fertile parts of the Connecticut Valley, farmers relied to an increasing degree on the labor of permanent wage workers, whom they employed to grow and process an unprecedented quantity of cash crops. Farmers, while still essentially household producers, themselves took on the characteristics of capitalist employers. Farm wage labor changed accordingly. Again endogamous factors for change gave ground to exogamous influences.

Superficial similarities between the rural worlds of the late eighteenth and mid-nineteenth centuries partly obscured a set of profound changes, felt and responded to by contemporaries such as Sylvester Judd. These major changes were not primarily in farming technique, household labor patterns, exchange practices, markets, or manufacturing processes, but in the combined subtle changes to all of them, which, coupled with less visible changes in social structure, added up to the creation of capitalism in the countryside.

The question remains as to whether rural New England was a special case in this respect or whether it experienced patterns of change widely replicated in other contexts. In a brief conclusion, I try to locate the Connecticut Valley's experience within the broader patterns of change in rural society in North America and elsewhere. Of course all regions display unique characteristics. Rural New England, especially in the eighteenth century, had an unusual combination of widespread freehold landownership and weak staple production, which meant that its route into the future was almost certain to be a distinctive one. Indeed the emergence of rural capitalism under these circumstances was by no means a foregone conclusion. As it did emerge, however, it brought New England closer to the opportunities and problems that such developments have also created in other parts of the world. In America as elsewhere, rural economic change was an important key to broader capitalist development.[19]

19. See E. L. Jones, *Agriculture and the Industrial Revolution* (Oxford, 1974), and T. H. Aston and C. H. E. Philpin, eds., *The Brenner Debate: Agrarian Class Structure and Economic Development in Pre-Industrial Europe* (Cambridge, Eng., 1985).

PART II

INVOLUTION:
1780 TO THE 1820s

Chapter 2

Households and Power in the Countryside in the Late Eighteenth Century

In 1859 the people of Hadley, Massachusetts, celebrated their town's bicentenary; an orator reminded them of the social structure of the colonial period: "On the one side," he said, "the town was related to the family; and on the other . . . to the Commonwealth. That is, the town was made up of households." Although by the late eighteenth century Puritan theories of the patriarchal family as the "germ of church and state" had been modified by circumstance, as a description of the rural economic structure the speaker's focus on the household was still correct. By "family" he meant the kin groups connected by marriage and descent, which owned and passed on land and other property from one generation to the next. Families also provided much of the labor involved in raising crops and livestock, producing other necessary goods, and in transporting and exchanging them. By "households" he meant the central institutions of rural society: the whole group of people—family, kin, servants, and other dependents—who formed each productive unit, as well as the places of production—the farms, houses, barns, and workshops where people lived and worked.[1]

Family ties and household organization dominated the social structure of the late-eighteenth-century countryside and rural people's thinking about the way their world was ordered. That "family blessings" were normal and preferable was clear to the small number of single people who did not have them, such as the seamstress Rebecca

1. *Celebration of the Two Hundredth Anniversary of the Settlement of Hadley, Massachusetts, at Hadley, June 8, 1859* (Northampton, 1859), pp. 12–13. Useful theoretical discussions are in Elizabeth Fox-Genovese, "Antebellum Southern Households: A New Perspective on a Familiar Question," *Review* 7 (Fall 1983): 215–253, and Harriet Friedmann, "Household Production and the National Economy: Concepts for the Analysis of Agrarian Formations," *Journal of Peasant Studies* 7 (1979–1980): 158–184.

Dickinson of Hatfield, who kept a diary in the 1780s and 1790s. One day in 1787, when she felt "more lonesome than a cat," she reflected that "wee are made for Sosiety[;] the minds of men are to commune with each other[;] they are to talk and walk together but mine has fell by my Self." Dickinson knew, as we shall see, that families and households often brought tribulation, but this did not restrain her pleasure when she had the chance to share in one. Boarding in her sister's household the next summer, she wrote, "there is a great family but there is the hous where I can injoy myself[;] the Company is more than the Provision[;] how our comfort depends on the Company that wee keep." Nearly forty years later, a man from Amherst endorsed this when he wrote that without families, "we should be strangers and pilgrims here on the earth."[2]

In a society whose production was in the hands of households, power was diffused. This was partly because property was widely distributed, even in Connecticut Valley towns that had been founded in the seventeenth century and had been settled for several generations. In Northampton, where property was least evenly distributed, 64.4 percent of taxpayers owned some land in 1798, and 92 percent of houses were owned by their occupiers. Although the wealthiest tenth of Northampton residents held half the town's taxable wealth, access to the means of making a living was not narrowly constrained. Inequality was still related to age; many of the propertyless were young men waiting to acquire the skills or estate their families could bequeath to them. This was even more the case elsewhere. In Hatfield, Amherst, and Westhampton, the top tenth of taxpayers held only between 27 and 35 percent of the wealth, and land was widely owned. In 1800 nearly 82 percent of Amherst taxpayers were assessed on real estate. In Westhampton in 1810 the proportion was 87 percent, and virtually all taxpayers owned the houses they lived in. Recalling her family's move from Williamsburg to Northampton in the late eighteenth century, Olive Cleveland Clark later remarked that Northampton "people were . . . independent, mostly farmers. They raised all their own produce, made almost all their own cloth and did all their own work." Although it oversimplified matters, Clark's recollection serves as a guide to the ways people in the countryside and small towns thought about the way they organized their livelihoods.[3]

2. Rebecca Dickinson, Diary Extracts, Hatfield, Sept 5, 1787, June 15, 1788, PVMA (typescript); Martin Field to Mrs T. F. French, Newfane, Vt., May 16, 1825, Jones Family Papers, BCJL. I am grateful to the Jones Library, Inc., for permission to quote from manuscripts in the Boltwood Collection. Throughout this book, in quotations from manuscripts, I retain original spellings and punctuation as far as possible, consistent with clarity.

3. "Recollections of Olive Cleveland Clark," in Phyllis B. Deming, comp., *A History of Williamsburg in Massachusetts* (Northampton, 1946), p. 56. Property distribution data are

The diffused economic power of rural households and their commitment to independence posed a potential problem for ministers and political leaders seeking to impose a concept of authority in the countryside. Often they used the paternal authority of male heads of household as a metaphor for wider social order. Urging his hearers to obey their new pastor, the preacher at an ordination in Deerfield in 1787 reminded them that "Abraham commanded his children and his household after him, and they kept the way of the Lord." In 1814 a Federalist election poster praised the "wisdom and paternal care of Gov. STRONG."[4] The Hadley speaker of 1859 was recalling this extension of the household metaphor into the wider social arena. But as shown in this chapter, the locus of social power was a contested issue in the late eighteenth century. The character of household production, the social web of rural exchange, and the diffusion of the economic structure all placed limits on the ability even of the wealthy to gain social control and, moreover, shaped the terms on which they had to bargain for the authority they were accorded. Political and economic circumstances combined to create and maintain a rural world in which household "independence" was a feasible concept.

Independence and Interdependence

When Olive Cleveland Clark wrote that most households were "independent," she meant, not that they were literally "self-sufficient," but that they could use their property and family labor to produce enough to conduct affairs "on their own account," avoiding a "dependence" on other households or the town that could rob them of their standing and self-respect. The notion of independence, rooted in the possession of freehold property, had a long history in New England. It had led to the expansion of the colonies to provide land for a growing population throughout the seventeenth and eighteenth centuries. It had shaped the political consciousness of generations of families determined to avoid the "reduction to lordships" they had feared from the policies of James II in the 1680s, of New York Colony in its claims to the Green Mountains in the 1760s and 1770s, and of British administrations in the

from Amherst, Tax Valuation List, 1800, Amherst Town Hall; Bernard R. Kubiak, "Social Changes in a New England Agricultural Community: Hatfield, Massachusetts, 1800–1850" (University of Massachusetts, Amherst, 1972); Northampton, Tax Assessment List, 1798, Town Papers Collection, 5.7, FL; Westhampton, Tax Assessment List, 1810, Westhampton Town Hall.

4. Noah Atwater, *A Sermon, Delivered at the Ordination of the Reverend John Taylor, to the Pastoral Care of the Church in Deerfield, February 14th, 1787* (Northampton, 1787), p. 25; Circular, Worcester, Mass., Mar 8, 1814, Broadside Collection, AAS.

same period.[5] It had also brought about distinctive ways of conducting economic life. "Independent" households sought to control the means both to make a living and to pass the resources for independence on to their offspring. The methods they adopted were not individualistic but rested on cooperation and a division of labor. "Independence" required "interdependence" within households and between them.[6]

Farm and artisan households divided men's tasks from women's tasks. Although these divisions were not absolute and were constantly being adjusted to circumstances, men usually worked in the fields or workshop, women in the house. Barn and garden tasks might fall to either, while some jobs to do with producing textiles, soap, or candles might rely on men's and women's cooperation. "Men's" tasks—raising crops and livestock or making manufactured goods—and "women's" tasks—storing and preparing food, making and mending clothing, giving birth to and rearing children—were all essential to maintaining the household.[7]

Children also played an important role. Often set to work when young at indoor tasks such as helping card wool for spinning or winding yarn onto spools, children were, as they grew older, given jobs associated with their gender. "I am surprised & astonished as well as pleased to think you have been so industrious & ingenious as to twist out *ten run* with those little fingers of yours," wrote William Huntington to his little sister in Hadley. Girls were taught housework, spinning, and butter making; boys were sent to attend and feed livestock, lead plow teams, collect and cart manure, and assist in gathering and storing crops. Boys' and girls' work was usually essential, too. George Sheldon,

5. Richard L. Bushman, "Massachusetts Farmers and the Revolution," in *Society, Freedom, and Conscience: The Coming of the Revolution in Virginia, Massachusetts, and New York*, ed. Richard L. Jellison (New York, 1976), p. 90, notes farmers' fear of the effects of British policy on land tenure and of "reducing the country to lordships." Barbara Karsky, "Le paysan américain et la terre a la fin du XVIIIᵉ siècle," *Annales ESC* 38 (1983): 1369–1391, similarly stresses farmers' attachment to freehold land even in the face of economic difficulties and land shortage after the Revolution.

6. James A. Henretta, "Families and Farms: *Mentalité* in Pre-Industrial America," *William and Mary Quarterly* 35 (Jan 1978): 3–32; Robert A. Gross, "Culture and Cultivation: Agriculture and Society in Thoreau's Concord," *Journal of American History* 69 (1982–1983); Daniel Vickers, " 'Cherries . . . Are Ready Cash': A Case Study in Early American Economic Values" (Memorial University of Newfoundland, 1987).

7. Laurel Thatcher Ulrich, *Good Wives: Image and Reality in the Lives of Women in Northern New England* (New York, 1982), chaps. 1 and 2, discusses the sexual division of labor and its variants; see also idem, "Martha Ballard and Her Girls: Women's Work in 18th Century Maine," in *Work and Labor in Early America*, ed. Stephen Innes (Chapel Hill, 1988), pp. 70–105. A graphic description of women's work in the Valley at the turn of the century is in Elizabeth Alden Green, *Mary Lyon and Mount Holyoke: Opening the Gates* (Hanover, N.H., 1983). An important discussion is found in Jeanne Boydston, "Home and Work: The Industrialization of Housework in the Northeastern United States from the Colonial Period to the Civil War" (Ph.D. diss., Yale University, 1984), chap. 2.

recalling that many boys in Deerfield were set each spring to chopping up felled lumber for firewood, wrote of "one case when the boy was not big enough for the axe an axe was made to match the boy."[8]

Although the work of men, women, and children was all essential to the household's functions, its patterns reflected the fact that families and households were not egalitarian. Men's legal and formal authority over women, children, and other dependents, such as servants, was imprinted in the type and the rhythms of their respective tasks. Men's farm tasks were highly seasonal. The Connecticut Valley's climate dictated a growing season that usually started in April each year. In the eighteenth century, the hard work in April and May of plowing and sowing crops was often followed by a lull in which there was relatively little work to be done. Most farmers raised a variety of crops in small field lots. While the tasks of mowing, raking, and drying hay, reaping small-grain crops, and hoeing and cutting corn occupied much time from June until November, the work was varied and spread out. "Harvest," rather than being a brief period of intensive work demanding large amounts of labor, was distributed over several months so that the work required at any one time did not far exceed the capacity of the average farm family to provide labor. As crops were brought in, the "fall tasks" of threshing and storing grain, husking corn, pressing cider apples, and seeing to livestock for the winter occupied the time until heavy snow restricted activities. In the winter lull from December to March, well-organized farmers cut firewood, marketed surplus produce, or manufactured goods in their houses or workshops. The insistent urging of almanac writers from the late eighteenth century onward that farmers use their wintertimes more effectively suggests that these were often months of comparative ease for men. Whether they worked hard or not, however, men's diaries reflect a work pattern that at any time of year was well paced. If they worked on other farms, exchanging work or as hired hands, they commanded wages according to the skill involved in the tasks they were doing and retained a substantial degree of control over their work.[9]

Women's and children's work reflected their subordinate status in the patriarchal household. When they worked for wages or exchanged goods or labor with other households their contributions were valued at one-third to one-half of those of men. Married women's names rarely

8. William Huntington to Mary Huntington, Cambridge, Mass., May 4, 1826, PPHH; George Sheldon, "'Tis Sixty Years Since: The Passing of the Stall-Fed Ox and the Farm Boy," *History and Proceedings of the Pocumtuck Valley Memorial Association* 3 (1890–1898): 487.

9. Susan Geib, "'Changing Works': Agriculture and Society in Brookfield, Massachusetts, 1785–1820" (Ph.D. diss., Boston University, 1981).

appeared in accounts; their goods or labor were traded in their husbands' names. Among the wide range of tasks women performed, many demanded considerable skill, and women exercised discretion over the manner in which they worked. But the pattern of women's tasks suggests a degree of intensity usually absent from the paced, seasonally variable character of men's work. They often faced pressing, complex burdens. Cooking, taking care of clothes, and other housework were a continuous process, not seasonal. Childbearing and looking after children were other constant struggles. About 1800, rural women bore, on average, seven or eight children each between their twenty-fourth and thirty-eighth years, at intervals of two years or less. In addition to all this, many women undertook seasonal manufacturing tasks. Although untypical, in that her husband owned one of the largest farms in the Valley and she usually had one or more servants to help her, Elizabeth Phelps of Hadley did or supervised a great variety of jobs during her forty-two years of marriage. Her diaries reflect the constant pressure of housework, spinning yarn, making and maintaining clothes, dairying, and making soap and candles, which occupied the time of farm women. Those from more modest families often undertook the same range of work with less help than Phelps obtained. Furthermore, the boundaries between "men's" and "women's" work, while never rigid, appear to have been more permeable in permitting women to enter the men's sphere than the other way round. Women found themselves called to do barn, garden, or field chores usually done by men if circumstances required. Instances of men doing household tasks, on the other hand, were rarely recorded.[10]

However unequally apportioned, cooperative work by their own members was the chief source of support of families and formed the most important part of the interdependence on which the independence of households rested. It also contributed to the acquisition and maintenance of resources through which families sought to provide livelihoods for their offspring. A decade ago, James A. Henretta stressed the importance in rural culture of the ideal of the "lineal family," by which property and resources were passed from parents to children down the generations. Although there have been critics of Henretta's argument, none has rebutted his central observation that concern for the future of offspring provided an important motivation for households' economic strategies. This concern suffused the range of their activities.[11]

10. Elizabeth Porter Phelps, Diaries, Hadley, 1763–1812, PPHH. Mary Beth Norton, *Liberty's Daughters: The Revolutionary Experience of American Women, 1750–1800* (Boston, 1980), discusses the burdens of women's work.

11. Henretta, "Families and Farms," pp. 21–32; James T. Lemon, "Agriculture and Society in Early America," *Agricultural History Review* 35 (1987): 83 n., argues that Henret-

Securing the future of children and the means of support for parents in their old age occupied a significant part of households' calculations in producing goods, organizing work, and accumulating land and other property. Such interests were central to the patterns of gifts, deeds, and bequests parents used to transfer property to their children. Though suggesting that "lineal values" were of diminishing importance as scarcity of resources increased at the end of the eighteenth century, Toby L. Ditz has shown that a determination to set up children in viable households of their own continued to govern parents' use of the inheritance system. This often involved placing on siblings obligations to provide support and assistance to each other and their parents in order to eke out scarce resources. So as well as cooperating in the work required for immediate needs, families imposed on their members the demand that they cooperate in providing support for the future. Biblical authority fostered the ethic of household independence in its concern to provide "for their children and their children's children."[12]

Cooperation within families and households was complemented by interchange between them. As noted earlier, "independence" did not imply "self-sufficiency." Farmers would have been puzzled by the notion that they might stand alone, by their own resources; frequent exchanges of goods and work with neighbors, kin, and others were part of the fabric of their lives. Recent research by economic and social historians has vividly demonstrated the extent to which rural households depended on exchange for their livelihoods and has convincingly refuted the myth that farm households maintained a form of autarky. But farmers' use of "exchange" should not be regarded simply as evidence of "market-orientation." To explore the late-eighteenth-century rural economy it is helpful to distinguish between two forms of exchange: local and long distance. Each followed its own rules and usually fulfilled a distinct set of purposes. The differences were to be crucial to the pattern of change in the countryside during the decades that lay ahead.[13]

---

ta's concern with the lineal family "overstates its importance relative to economic institutions." As I hope is made clear in what follows, I would suggest that these are not separable categories and that familial concerns ("lineal" or otherwise) strongly influenced economic practices.

12. Toby L. Ditz, *Property and Kinship: Inheritance in Early Connecticut, 1750–1820* (Princeton, 1986).

13. Henretta, "Families and Farms"; Michael Merrill, "Cash Is Good to Eat: Self-Sufficiency and Exchange in the Rural Economy of the United States," *Radical History Review* 3 (1977): 42–71; Christopher Clark, "Household Economy, Market Exchange, and the Rise of Capitalism in the Connecticut Valley, 1800–1860," *Journal of Social History* 13 (Winter 1979): 169–189; John T. Schlotterbeck, "The 'Social Economy' of an Upper South Community: Orange and Greene Counties, Virginia, 1815–60," in *Class, Conflict, and Consensus: Antebellum Southern Community Studies*, ed. Orville Vernon Burton and Robert C. McMath (Westport, Conn., 1982): 3–28.

Distant Trade and Local Exchange

Since the beginnings of white settlement, trade had been conducted into and out of the Northampton region, overland to Boston or by river to Hartford and the Connecticut coast. Economic historians have estimated that in parts of the rural Northeast by 1800, households spent as much as 25 percent of their disposable incomes on goods obtained outside their localities; households in the Connecticut Valley may have spent as much. But these purchases were either of necessities unobtainable locally, or of "luxuries" and "decencies" such as liquor, tea, sugar, and dry goods, which formed a substantial proportion of imports. Even in a prosperous rural region, households satisfied three-quarters of their demand, including most of their basic needs, by their own production or by local exchange. Some of these needs were foodstuffs that would largely have been unobtainable from stores or traders and available only from other households. Because the Connecticut Valley lacked a staple export crop in the late eighteenth century, the sale of produce from the region to purchase imported goods took second place to the provision of basic needs at home. The economy was primarily a "subsistence-surplus" one; that is, most of the products exported beyond the Valley were necessities extra to the requirements of local households or by-products of their production.[14]

Trade on the Connecticut River reflected this economic pattern. The accounts of a shipper who carried goods in the 1750s from Middletown, Hartford, and other Connecticut points to customers in Springfield, Northampton, Hatfield, and Deerfield, show that upstream traffic was in goods unavailable locally, while return cargoes consisted of the kinds of goods also used by the households producing them. In 1754 he brought up grindstones, tools and implements, pots and pans, nails, glass, turpentine, codfish, sugar, molasses, rum, and large amounts of salt. He returned with peas, flaxseed, and wooden products such as laths and boards, none of which was produced solely for market sale.

14. Carole Shammas, "How Self-Sufficient Was Early America?" *Journal of Interdisciplinary History* 13 (1982–1983): 247–272; Bettye Hobbs Pruitt, "Self-Sufficiency and the Agricultural Economy of Eighteenth-Century Massachusetts," *William and Mary Quarterly* 41 (July 1984): 333–364; Sarah F. McMahon, "A Comfortable Subsistence: The Changing Composition of Diet in Rural New England, 1620–1840," *William and Mary Quarterly* 42 (Jan 1985): 26–65. On subsistence-surplus economies, see Henretta, "Families and Farms," p. 20, and Steven Hahn, *The Roots of Southern Populism: Yeoman Farmers and the Transformation of the Georgia Upcountry, 1850–1890* (New York, 1983), pp. 29–40. For a critique, see David F. Weiman, "Farmers and the Market in Antebellum America: A View from the Georgia Upcountry," *Journal of Economic History* 47 (1987): 627–648. Gavin Wright, *The Political Economy of the Cotton South: Households, Markets, and Wealth in the Nineteenth Century* (New York, 1978), chap. 3, provides a useful discussion of the distinctions between production for use and production for market.

From year to year the pattern varied slightly. The volume of dry goods and of luxury items for the Valley's elite increased in the 1760s and 1770s. Potash and pearl ashes, produced by farmers who burned felled lumber to make "black salts" and lye for processing and shipment, were an important export item until the 1790s. But these were by-products of settlement and land clearance; in time the potash trade would decline. Trade at the century's end was essentially little different. The accounts of a Williamsburg teamster show that during the 1790s he carried pork, beef, butter, leather, and tallow out of the region and returned from Boston or the downriver towns with dry goods, earthenware, rum, sugar, salt, glass, paper, and gin. In 1802 a Deerfield boatman carried barrel staves down to Hartford and brought back brandy, sugar, tea, and salt. The Hadley merchant William Porter sent and received similar shipments in 1810.[15]

The lack of a staple export and the subsistence-surplus character of the economy meant that the Valley's traders had to work hard and use far-flung networks of connections to bring together consignments to pay for imported goods. The diffuse, diverse, and irregular pattern of local supplies kept the mercantile sector small and relatively centralized. The most prominent merchants were based in old towns like Northampton and Hadley, whose position on the river helped them control the flow of goods in and out. From there, they relied on contacts and partnerships scattered throughout the region. When the Northampton merchant Levi Shepard dissolved his partnership with Ebenezer Hunt in 1784, his share of the proceeds included promissory notes from 175 customers scattered between Ludlow, Massachusetts, and southern New Hampshire. Toward the end of the century some traders organized branch stores in partnership with settlers of newly expanding hill towns. But the number of traders was small. Northampton appears to have had no more than nine merchants at any one time before 1800, Hadley no more than four.[16] Their influence was spread thinly throughout the Valley.

By contrast, local exchange among neighbors and kin was frequent,

15. Evidence for the 1750s is in an anonymous Account Book, 1753–1756, BCJL; the Williamsburg teamster: Jesse Wild, Account Book, Bodman Family Papers, Box 1, SSC; Deerfield boatman: deposition in the case of Arms v. Loomis, Hampshire County Court of Common Pleas, Files, May 1802, no. 286, Massachusetts State Archives, Boston, Mass.; Porter's accounts are in William Porter Papers, Box C, folder 1810, OSV.

16. "A List of Notes and Book Accts due at this Time to the Late Compy of Shephard and Hunt and this day set of[f] to Levi Shephard," Northampton, July 12, 1784, Shepard Papers, MCFL, Box 31. (Members of the Shepard family spelled their name several different ways. Except in quotations, I have adopted one spelling throughout.) Estimates of the number of traders are based on advertisements in *Hampshire Gazette* (Northampton), 1790–1800; see also Margaret E. Martin, "Merchants and Trade of the Connecticut River Valley, 1750–1820," *Smith College Studies in History* 24 (1938–1939).

often involved essential goods, and was part of the cooperation and division of labor vital to the household economy. Relatively few families in the late eighteenth century owned all the necessary means of earning a livelihood. Reciprocal exchanges enabled them to borrow what they did not own. In Amherst in 1795, for instance, about seven out of ten landholders owned cows, but only four out of ten owned draft oxen for plowing or carting. Those who did not relied on hiring teams to get their work done, paying for this with food or other goods, or by providing labor in exchange. Local exchanges of work and goods supported the craft occupations of blacksmiths, shoemakers, house carpenters, weavers, and tailors, whose trades households could not or chose not to provide for themselves.[17]

Exchanging work also provided essential extra labor during haying or harvest, or for special tasks such as framing and raising buildings whose demands exceeded families' own supply of labor. As many account books show, members of poorer households worked more frequently for their wealthier neighbors than the other way around and often took their pay in food or other essential items. But only the largest farmers did not swap some work with their neighbors, and there was an essential assumption of reciprocity in the informal rituals and obligations that governed this exchange. It did not simply correct imbalances of resources, for example. Two Amherst farmers, Elisha Smith and James Hendrick, who both owned yokes of oxen, combined efforts in September 1788 to complete fall plowing, each putting in two days' work with his team on the other's farm.[18]

Kinship and neighborhood both created obligations to cooperate in exchanging work and goods. Not only did farm families—whether in old or in new towns—live comparatively close to one another, but they were frequently related as well. In 1798, Northampton's 400 taxpayers shared only 133 family names. The fact that 129 were placed on the (nonalphabetical) list next to another taxpayer of the same name suggests that neighbors were often kin as well. President Timothy Dwight of Yale praised the Connecticut Valley towns for their "general harmony and good neighborhood, . . . sober industry and frugality, . . . hospitality and charity," characteristics he attributed to their distance from commercial markets. Local exchange was part of a set of reciprocal practices deeply embedded in the cultural fabric of the countryside, whose significance was not just instrumental.[19]

17. Amherst, Tax Valuation List, 1795.
18. Elisha Smith, Account Book, Amherst, 1784–1822, BCJL.
19. Northampton, Tax Assessment List, 1798; proximity of kin was a notable aspect of New England society in this period: see Daniel Scott Smith, " 'All in Some Degree Related to Each Other': A Demographic and Comparative Resolution of the Anomaly of New

Long-distance "trade" and local "exchange" were distinct from one another, served different purposes, and conformed to separate patterns. Although they often involved the same goods, the significance of these goods differed. Local products traded locally were often essentials. Sold to traders, they were surplus to requirements. Superficially, local and long-distance dealings often seemed to follow similar methods and practices. But, involving trade over differing geographical distance, they operated in different social contexts and so followed contrasting, sometimes conflicting, moral standards. Indeed, it is possible to talk of an "ethic" of local exchange quite distinct from that governing long-distance trade.[20] We can see the distinction if we compare the correspondence of a prominent trading firm of the 1770s and 1780s with the account books that recorded the transactions of farmers and others exchanging goods locally.

Shepard and Hunt's Northampton firm traded not only throughout western Massachusetts but with the port towns of the lower Connecticut River, with Boston, and even with London. Their business, like that of all long-distance merchants, rested on a paradox: they had to establish bonds of trust amounting to friendship with men whom they would not normally meet. They conducted business by letter, using the accounts, receipts, notes, and bills of exchange that were the machinery of trade. They relied on recommendations and connections to assess the men they were trading with and closely observed each others' conduct of business. To reduce the risks of trading over long distances with strangers, merchants expected transactions to be conducted according to certain standards, violation of which could result in loss of reputation and credit. Above all, they required regular payment for goods consigned, within the terms set by any extension of credit. If they could have got it, merchants would always have liked immediate payment in cash. In practice, they had to grant credit and accept payment in whatever goods or paper the state of trade made available. But they charged for these deviations. Prices offered for remittances in goods were bargained over, bills were often discounted, and late payments charged interest on the grounds that they represented an opportunity cost to the creditor. Jonathan Brown, of the London firm of Thomas Corbyn and

England Kinship," *American Historical Review* 94 (Feb 1989): 44–79. Timothy Dwight, *Travels in New England and New York*, 4 vols., ed. Barbara M. Solomon (Cambridge, Mass., 1969): 1:240 and 2:230, commented on neighborliness in the older Valley towns; Barbara Karsky, "Sociability in Rural New England," *Travail et loisir dans les sociétés pre-industrielles* (Nancy, forthcoming), provides a wider view. Kinship and neighborhood did not, however, imply absence of conflict, as the following discussions make clear.

20. I owe this suggestion to discussion with Michael Merrill and to his "Gifts, Barter, and Commerce in Early America: An Ethnography of Exchange" (Paper presented to the 78th Annual Meeting of the Organization of American Historians, Minneapolis, Apr 1985).

Company, writing to Shepard and Hunt early in 1771, noted that he had not yet received a remittance for a previous consignment and would in future charge interest on balances for which cash was not received within twelve months of shipping. Six months later, Brown had still not received payment, despite several letters to Northampton warning that Corbyn's might have to withhold the next shipment of goods. Corbyn himself wrote in August that "we can't be easy to send your present order." The goods were sent, but by the next year Corbyn was advancing them only on six months' credit.[21]

Delays required explanations. Not only were Shepard and Hunt writing to London and elsewhere explaining the difficulties they faced collecting the means for repayment, but they also received excuses and pleas for understanding from their own contacts in the countryside. Two physicians in Williamstown described in 1774 how a smallpox outbreak was preventing them from sending a remittance for drugs supplied by the Northampton firm: "our Patients at Present in Inoculation are in No upwards of 20 and in a Very Scatter'd situation, and altho' upwards of 100 have safely Pass'd the Operation . . . we have not Collected more than about 30 dollers Cash." The merchants' response to this is not recorded. Three decades later a West Springfield firm asked to delay payment for goods shipped them by a Hartford merchant and got a sharp lecture in return: "such disappointments are of evil tendency in Society, but the reverse, viz, slow to promis, prompt to fulfill enables us not only to command our own [respect?] but our neighbours."[22]

Failure to repay would eventually lead to a lawsuit. The mechanisms of long-distance trade, the correspondence, circulating paper, systematic accounts, fixed-term credit, and interest charges were all calculated to permit pressure to be exerted for payment and, if necessary, to provide the sound evidence of the existence of a debt that would be essential to sustain a debt action in court. Long-distance trade had an insistent rhythm and strict expectations. Promptness and system were essential to commercial morality.

The rules of local exchange were different. Dealings were over short distances, often face-to-face, and frequently between relatives or neighbors. From 1796 onward the Westhampton farmer Solomon Bartlett kept regular accounts with sixteen other people. Seven of them were

---

21. Thomas Corbyn and Co. to Shepard and Hunt, London, Feb 28, Aug 17, 20, 1771, Shepard Papers. On the importance of short-term credit to a commercial economy, see Jeanne Chase, "Credit à court terme et croissance d'une capitale commerciale: New York, 1786–1820," *Géographie du capitale marchand aux Amériques, 1760–1860*, ed. Jeanne Chase (Paris, 1987), pp. 79–108.

22. Fay and Mack to Shepard and Hunt, Williamstown, Feb 21, 1774, Shepard Papers; Ebenezer Barnard to Hanford and Ely, Hartford, Nov 18, 1806, Barnard Family Papers, LC.

neighbors who lived within two miles of Bartlett's farm in the southern part of town. Another six were relatives—three brothers and two nephews, who were also neighbors, and his niece's husband, who lived in the adjacent town of Norwich. Only three of Bartlett's sixteen contacts are not identifiable as near neighbors or relatives. Like those of thousands of rural people his dealings centered on people he knew.[23]

Moreover, as the French traveler Brissot de Warville observed, these dealings rarely involved cash:

> Instead of money incessantly going backwards and forwards into the same hands, they supply their needs reciprocally in the countryside by direct exchanges. The tailor and the bootmaker go and do the work of their calling at the house of the farmer who requires it and who, most often, provides the raw material for it and pays for the work in goods. These sorts of exchanges cover many objects; they write down what they give and receive on both sides and at the end of the year they settle, with a very small amount of coin, a large variety of exchanges which would not be done in Europe other than with a considerable quantity of money.[24]

Cash payment connotes immediacy and a certain anonymity between dealers. Once a debt is paid off, obligation ceases. A debt paid off in cash implies abstraction—a social distance between buyer and seller—because the form of payment can be turned to any use. We shall see later that in the countryside of the late-eighteenth and early-nineteenth centuries cash did, indeed, have specific social uses and meanings distinct from other forms of payment. Noncash payment and extended indebtedness entailed a different kind of relationship. Forms of payment had always to be negotiated, with due recognition of particular households' needs and abilities. Delays to payment resulted in perpetual, complex webs of credit and debt throughout the countryside that linked households to one another. Local exchange created networks of obligation alongside those already created by kinship or neighborhood. These obligations should not be sentimentalized. Frequently enough they gave rise to conflicts. But they were real, and they embodied the distinctive moral demands made by rural people on each other when they exchanged goods, labor, and other services.[25]

23. William and Solomon Bartlett, Account Books, 2 vols., Westhampton, 1704–1857, HBS.

24. Etienne Clavière and J. P. Brissot de Warville, *De la France et des Etats-Unis, ou de l'importance de la révolution de l'Amérique pour le bonheur de la France* (London, 1787), p. 24; the authors remarked that "it is most astonishing that of all the travelers who have gone through the United States not one has given a detail of the manner of exchanging the various necessities and comforts of life."

25. This discussion accords with Bruce H. Mann, *Neighbors and Strangers: Law and Community in Early Connecticut* (Chapel Hill, 1987), although the intention of his argument may differ from mine. Mann notes the differing character and social implications of book

In practice the accounting process was less tidy and orderly than Brissot's description implied. Many farmers may not have kept written accounts at all. Those who did were often unsystematic or careless. A memorandum book presented as evidence in an 1806 court case contained "the items of said account filed, which were entered therein intermixed with various charges, notes, receipts and memorandums, related to . . . dealings with other persons, alike irregular, in whatever blank spaces [the owner] happened to find, without any regard to order of dates or pages." From the 1790s onward almanac writers urged farmers to keep clear accounts and settle them regularly, but many ignored this advice. As a newspaper editor scathingly remarked in 1830, "it matters not how much business a man does if he be not regular in keeping his accounts. Mechanics and farmers are proverbial for their neglect in this particular. Many keep no account book at all; a piece of chalk and a pine board constitute their only materials of record."[26]

Credits and debits accumulated over considerable periods. Settlements were infrequent and irregular. Almanacs repeatedly suggested that accounts be settled each winter when there was little work to do. But over three-fifths of the accounts kept by the Amherst farmer William Boltwood between 1800 and 1805 show no sign of having been finally closed, while repayment times on outstanding debts to him ranged from four months to thirteen and a half years.[27] Boltwood's accounts were kept in a well-ordered and systematic manner; the delays reflected, not carelessness, but the distinctive rhythms and demands of local exchange.

Some local dealings were literally barters, direct swaps of work or goods considered to be of equivalent value. Their extent is hard to measure, because many probably went unrecorded. Book accounts occasionally contained adjustments for uneven trades, such as the charge of two shillings and sixpence set down by Solomon Bartlett

accounts and written instruments (p. 39) and the different treatment accorded neighbors and strangers (p. 19), though he stresses (pp. 19, 66) the potential for conflict among neighbors.

26. The case was Cogswell, exx. v. Dolliver, 2 Mass. Reports (1 Tyng) 217–218. Robert B. Thomas, *The Farmer's Almanack for the Year 1798* (Boston, [1797]); *Hampshire Sentinel* (Belchertown), Nov 24, 1830. Useful unpublished work on local exchange, in addition to that already referred to, includes Michael Bellesiles, "The World of the Account Book: The Frontier Economy of the Upper Connecticut River Valley, 1760–1800" (Paper presented to the 79th Annual Meeting of the Organization of American Historians, Apr 1986), and Mick Reed, "Neighbourhood Exchange in Nineteenth-Century Rural England" (Paper presented to History Workshop 22, Brighton, Nov 1988). I am grateful to both authors for sharing their findings with me. Jack Larkin's "Accounting for Change: Exchange and Debt in the New England Rural Economy" (Paper presented to the 10th Annual Meeting of the Society for Historians of the Early American Republic, July 1988) is an excellent discussion of the subject.

27. William Boltwood, Account Book, Amherst, 1789–1830, BCJL.

against his neighbor Chester Strong "in swoping sise for $\frac{1}{2}$ bu[shel] of be[a]ns." But most recorded transactions were running tallies of credits and debts incurred in a continuous process of bargaining and exchange. Goods, labor, or services were given out in the expectation that a return for them would be made in due course. Farmers provided food to poorer neighbors on the promise of future work in their fields. Men worked for others on the expectation of repayment in kind at a future date. Even the language of local exchange differed from that of long-distance trade. People did not speak of "buying" or "selling" things. They "took" or "gave" them.[28]

The spirit of "give and take" helps explain the complex tangle of unsettled debts that crisscrossed the countryside. Many accounts were closed only when administrators sorted out the estates of the dead, if then. People "gave" when they had the means to. After balancing accounts with a servant in 1790, Joseph Clarke of Northampton noted that "there is now due to her seven dollars which I am to pay her as soon as I conveniently can." In this instance, and in many others, the poorer woman had to wait upon the convenience of the richer man for her pay. But it worked both ways. Whereas in long-distance trade creditors assumed the right to press for repayment and sue when debts were not settled, the local exchange ethic emphasized restraint, caution, and consideration of debtors' means to pay.[29]

Securing repayment required tact and subtlety. The means existed, of course—they were the same as in long-distance trade—but they had to be used carefully. Interest was rarely charged on book accounts. Indeed, even to calculate it required drawing a balance and that was often difficult enough to arrange. Robert B. Thomas's almanac reminded farmers that in order "to preserve a good understanding and continue in friendship with friends and neighbors," they should each December "call upon all those you have had any dealing with the preceding year, and make a complete settlement."[30] But pressing for settlement could cause offense by implying lack of trust, or could be seen as an attempt to take advantage.

Especially when resources were scarce, the ideal time to settle accounts was when they were close to balancing, so that little payment

28. Solomon Bartlett, Account Book, vol. 2, entry for 1819.
29. Joseph Clarke, Account Book, Northampton, 1786–1794, NHS, A.A. 17.5. The *Anti-Monarchist* (Northampton), Jan 17, 1810, condemned the well-off who neglected to pay poorer creditors but noted, nevertheless, that "there is but one valid apology for not paying money when it is due, and that is, not having it to pay."
30. Thomas, *Farmer's Almanack for 1798*. William J. Gilmore, "Elementary Literacy on the Eve of the Industrial Revolution: Trends in Rural New England, 1760–1830," *Proceedings of the American Antiquarian Society* 92 (Apr 1982): 150, notes that the ritual of signing accounts formed part of a network of community trust.

would have to change hands. But in the uneven tempo of rural life and work, these occasions did not occur regularly. Although some farmers, including William Boltwood, kept ledger accounts of both credits and debits—what was "given" to him and what he "gave" to others—the majority whose books have survived kept complete records only of debits—goods they had given or work they had done. An English description of rural accounting suggested that neighbors resented men who kept both credit and debit accounts because it enabled them to calculate balances and call for settlement when these were in their favor. Possibly many New England farmers also regarded keeping both sides of the ledger an affront to neighborhood and were content to see the whole picture only when they met with other men and their books to make a reckoning.[31]

"Reckonings" could involve bargaining over the goods and work to be counted and the values to be assigned them. Disagreement was quite possible. "Noah Thompson [was] here," wrote Rev. Justus Forward of Belchertown in his diary in 1786; "we did agree to settle Accounts by his letting me have a calfskin on his Account which I had of Capt Watson last fall." But Thompson was still dissatisfied: "he did not chuse to sign my Book, pretended he had paid me a Dollar the forepart of August '83." The minister evidently felt that *he* was being taken advantage of. Even the agreement that he almost came to had not involved any repayment, merely an adjustment involving a transaction that had already occurred between Forward and a third man. Although this would have brought Forward's account with Thompson into alignment, both Forward and Thompson would have needed to square things with Watson as well. The debt was thus transferred, not expunged. Bargaining such as this enabled householders to eke out their resources to the utmost and helped create the complex tangle of rural debts and credits.[32]

Striking a balance often led only to the continuation of a debt. Even

31. Walter Rose, *Good Neighbours: Some Recollections of an English Village and Its People* (Cambridge, Eng., 1942); the description appears in a chapter called "Gnawing It Out." I am grateful to Mick Reed for this reference. Of a sample of sixteen from among the Connecticut Valley ledgers I examined, only two contained complete entries on both the debit and credit sides. The remainder had room for debit and credit entries on facing pages but were incomplete on the credit side. Harris Beckwith (Northampton) gave the goods and services he provided on the debit pages of his ledger, but often recorded credits only *after* settlements, with entries such as "by his account," or "by his account and note to balance" (Harris Beckwith, Account Book, 1803–1807, MCFL). In other words, he did not record payments as they were made to him. A small proportion of surviving ledgers contain debit pages only.

32. Justus Forward, Diary, Aug 26, 1786, MS Collection, AAS.

Robert B. Thomas, advocate of the regular settlement, saw that payment would not necessarily follow. "Pay them off," he advised, "if the balance be in their favour," and "if convenient." If the balance is "in yours and they find it not convenient to pay, put it to the new account and pass receipts."[33] Account books reveal that this often happened. Balances were simply carried forward into another period of "give" and "take." Thomas's advice assumed that "convenience" rested on having means available at that moment to pay off the outstanding balance. The frequency with which this was avoided, or efforts made to square accounts somehow, suggests that this view of "convenience" was widely accepted. Two comments from as late as 1830 throw light on common attitudes. An editor criticized those "too indolent to dun others" and the "false delicacy which prevents them," urging that "fear of giving offence by asking payment of honest dues, should never be indulged." But an almanac writer was more acerbic: "If you wish to make friends, trust and never demand your pay; if enemies, demand it."[34] At this point the contrast between the ethics of local exchange and long-distance trade was at its clearest.

"Putting a balance to the new account" usually meant that no interest would be charged on the debt. Neighbors rarely charged interest on small amounts. Where larger sums were involved, however, or if the creditor did not know or distrusted the debtor, he might demand security in the form of a note, sometimes with the endorsement of a third party. Usually payable on demand, in theory permitting peremptory calling-in, these notes were often used in the countryside to avoid specifying a particular date for payment. Merchants, preferring specified payment dates, sometimes accepted them reluctantly, as one put it, to "benefit . . . country People."[35] Interest was payable if it was specified, usually after at least one year had elapsed. It was also due on mortgages and other loans to acquire land, houses, or livestock, where wealthier men were usually granting credit to their poorer neighbors. The instruments of negotiable paper and of debt enforcement were therefore part of local exchange in circumstances of inequality, where the reciprocal assumptions of "give" and "take" did not apply. However, to go to law to seek repayment of these debts was still regarded as a violation of "neighborhood" well into the nineteenth century. In

33. Thomas, *Farmer's Almanack for 1798*.
34. *Hampshire Sentinel*, Nov 24, 1830; Nathan Wild, *The Farmer's, Mechanic's, and Gentleman's Almanack for 1831* (Amherst, 1830).
35. The quotation is from Jno. Brown to Shepard and Hunt, London, Feb 28, 1771, Shepard Papers; Brown noted that he was "troubled by taking notes on demand," but felt obliged to do so.

many towns lawsuits for debt were brought by one townsman against another only infrequently. Most debt actions were between strangers who lived at a distance from one another.[36]

Rural households' sense of "independence" therefore rested on circumstances that held them distinct from, but interdependent with, their neighbors and held their neighborhoods at arm's length from the pressures of the commercial world beyond their part of the Valley. Cooperation and division of labor within households was based on the unequal assumptions and realities of patriarchal authority. The desire to secure livelihoods for the present was complicated by the need to make provisions for the future of parents and children. The aspiration for household "independence" relied on the necessity of exchanging goods and labor with neighbors and kin. The assumptions of reciprocity and equality in local exchange were, on the one hand, undermined by the realities of bargaining and negotiation between individuals who were not always equal, and, on the other, sustained by the restraints of "neighborhood." Both the household itself and the wider terrain of rural society were arenas of conflict and negotiation. No one knew this better than the ministers, merchants, and larger landowners who formed the Valley's social and political elite, for whom the ideal of the patriarchal household remained the model for wider social authority. In the last quarter of the eighteenth century their assumptions of power were widely challenged by household producers for whom the model of the local exchange system, with its notions of reciprocity, had much appeal.

Households and Elites

Family labor and household production had evolved in seventeenth-century New England as assumptions brought by English settlers were adapted to conditions of widespread landownership and relative equality. Daniel Vickers has pointed out that, as in some other freehold farming regions, use of family labor was rural New England's response to the labor shortages faced by all early American colonies. Whereas the staple-crop regions of the South came to rely on slaves, and indentured servants filled many households' demands for labor in the middle colonies, most New England households relied on their own family members to work for them. Rural slavery was rare; taxes on "servants

36. This conclusion is based on an analysis of debt suits in Hampshire County Court of Common Pleas, Records, vols. 7–8 (1804–1809), Hampshire County Courthouse, Northampton. Similar findings have been made for southern Vermont: see Bellesiles, "The World of the Account Book."

for life" were levied on only 4 taxpayers out of 132 in Hadley and 2 out of 134 in Amherst in 1771, for example. Servants were more common, but only wealthy families constantly employed them; Timothy Dwight noted that there were fewer servants in the New England interior than in commercial towns on the coast. Many were, as one woman put it, young men and women "lent" by their families to neighbors and relatives.[37] But the household system we have observed at the end of the eighteenth century was not simply "traditional." It had come about in the context of important changes in rural society, despite the fact that much of the original labor shortage came to an end.

The household system had dissolved other types of social organization in the countryside by the early 1700s. Springfield, for example, the first white settlement in the Valley in Massachusetts, had been strongly controlled by its proprietors, the Pyncheons, during the seventeenth century; many inhabitants had been obliged to rent land or provide labor for them in order to make a living.[38] But after 1700 the Pyncheons' authority broke down; Springfield became like other Valley towns, where property had from the start been more widely distributed and where wealthier families could exert less of the same influence over their independent neighbors. The defeat of Indian resistance to white settlement during the first half of the eighteenth century made possible an expansion into the hills surrounding the Valley proper. Especially after 1720, migrants to the region joined the offspring of local families to carve out new farms and townships.

Beyond the bounds of the original town grants, migrants purchased land individually or in groups from proprietors and speculators who had held large acreages in the hope that settlement would expand. In the 1740s, for instance, a group of Scotch-Irish Presbyterians purchased what would become the town of Pelham, in the hills to the east of the Valley. In the center of the Valley, though, the outlying lands of older towns were divided off from them, to create new towns or districts often settled by children of the old towns' residents. Hadley's Third Division became a separate parish in 1739 and the district of Amherst in 1759. In 1771 Hatfield contributed its northern section to the formation of Whately, and its hilly northwestern extremities to the new district of Williamsburg. Northampton split four ways. Early settlement in the

37. Tax data are from Bettye Hobbs Pruitt, ed., *The Massachusetts Tax Valuations of 1771* (Boston, 1978); Dwight, *Travels*, 2:184, referred to servants; on "lending" kin and neighbors: [Arethusa Hall], "Sathurea: The Story of a Life," 1864, Judd Papers, 55M-1, Box 2, HCL, p. 37; on the blurred line between living with kin and hiring out as "help," see Faye E. Dudden, *Serving Women: Household Service in 19th Century America* (Middletown, Conn., 1983), p. 20.

38. Stephen Innes, *Labor in a New Land: Economy and Society in Seventeenth-Century Springfield* (Princeton, 1983).

broad valley west of Mount Tom led to the incorporation of Southampton in 1753 and later the district of Easthampton in 1785, while movement into the hills west of the original town gave rise to Westhampton, set off in 1778. The availability of land at the edges of the Valley ensured that labor remained scarce during the first half of the eighteenth century. Wages for farm labor doubled between the 1680s and about 1750. Farm families used their own labor as much as they could and bargained with their neighbors for what they could not provide themselves.[39]

But as towns were settled and population grew, the labor shortage began to end. Wage rates flattened out, remaining approximately even for the rest of the century. Between 1720 and the 1760s most of the newly available land was purchased and divided up. From 1763 to 1774 alone seventeen new towns were established in Hampshire County. Population growth, fed by high fertility rates, low mortality, and inmigration, was rapid. Between 1765 and 1790, population in what later became "new" Hampshire County rose by an average of 7.7 percent a year; from then to 1810 it continued to grow at an average rate of 1.5 percent. The area had 6,500 inhabitants in 1765. By 1810 there were 24,553. Population density trebled, and was especially high around the better farmland, in towns such as Amherst and in valleys and meadowlands in the hill towns. The conditions that had given rise to the household system had largely ceased to exist.[40]

Yet the system essentially survived. There was no return to the kinds of social and economic control exercised by the Pyncheons in seventeenth-century Springfield. Neither did the systematic use of wage labor supplant family-based labor in this period. The number of poor, transient people had increased by the 1760s, and there was more hiring and servanthood than there had been before.[41] But as we shall see in Chapter 3, these increases took place largely within the framework of the household system and according to its terms. They did not threaten the independence of most rural households. Why was this so?

Foremost among the reasons was the absence of a rural elite powerful

39. The daily wage rate for general farm labor, quoted at two shillings in Springfield in the 1680s (Innes, *Labor in a New Land*, p. 170), was usually four shillings in mid-eighteenth-century account books.

40. Land settlement and division in the mid–eighteenth century is discussed in Gregory H. Nobles, *Divisions throughout the Whole: Politics and Society in Hampshire County, Massachusetts, 1740–1775* (Cambridge, Eng., 1983). On population growth, see Jesse Chickering, *A Statistical View of the Population of Massachusetts, 1765–1840* (Boston, 1846).

41. Douglas Lamar Jones, "The Strolling Poor: Transiency in 18th Century Massachusetts," *Journal of Social History* (Spring 1975). Daniel Vickers, "Working the Fields in a Developing Economy: Essex County, Massachusetts, 1630–1675," in Innes, *Work and Labor in Early America*, esp. pp. 55–56, documents the low rates of servanthood in earlier New England agricultural communities.

enough to create and control a dependent labor system. The wealthy families that did live in the Valley faced problems of their own after the 1750s. Their situation was such that they could negotiate to secure various kinds of peripheral influence over middling and poorer households in some towns, but not so strong that they could alter these households' essentially independent status by controlling their labor.

Rapid population growth not only enhanced Hampshire County's overall political significance in Massachusetts but brought a number of families in the older towns to social preeminence. At the apex of these families was the small group, including Stoddards, Williamses, Worthingtons, and Hawleys, who came to be referred to as the "River Gods." As well as having significant landholdings and positions in trade or as lenders of credit, these families had by the middle of the century succeeded in dominating county institutions—the courts, the militia, and the ministerial association at the core of ecclesiastical politics. Most judges, senior officers, and pastors were members of the leading families or had met their approval. Less wealthy families with local influence, such as the Strongs and Lymans of Northampton and the Porters of Hadley, had business or kinship ties with them. Israel Williams of Hatfield maintained such influence in the 1750s and 1760s, including connections with the colonial government in Boston, that he became known as the "monarch of Hampshire." Williams and the others distinguished themselves from the majority of their neighbors by assuming the characteristics of a rural gentry. Their houses were larger, and sometimes more elaborately and finely finished. They purchased imported wines and household goods and wore distinctive styles of dress. They were also more substantial employers of labor. They hired craftsmen to make, furnish, and decorate their houses; retained house and field servants, including some slaves; and hired extra hands at busy times of year. Charles Phelps, who married into the Porter family in 1770 and, with 600 acres, became Hadley's largest landowner, "kept," according to his grandson, "quite a retinue of laborers and at times . . . made considerable levies on the working force" of the village. After the Revolution he employed a former soldier who was reputed to be the only gardener in the Valley.[42]

But these families never came close to matching the power and posi-

---

42. Kevin M. Sweeney, "River Gods in the Making: The Williamses of Western Massachusetts," in *The Bay and the River, 1600–1900*, ed. Peter Benes (Boston, 1982), pp. 101–116; see also Kevin M. Sweeney, "From Wilderness to Arcadian Vale: Material Life in the Connecticut River Valley, 1635–1760," in *The Great River: Art and Society of the Connecticut Valley, 1635 1820* (Hartford, 1985). Phelps is mentioned in T. G. Huntington, "Sketches by Theodore G. Huntington of the family and life in Hadley, written in letters to H. F. Quincy," n.d., PPHH (typescript).

tion, say, of the Virginia gentry in the same period. Indeed their weakness became increasingly evident after mid-century, and explains why their modes of living and organizing work did not become more common as labor supply increased. Large landowners were weakened economically by the decline of the one local crop—wheat—which had historically been a staple export and which had formed the basis of the Pyncheons' earlier prominence in Springfield. Just when world demand for wheat was increasing, stimulating increased production in the middle colonies and the upper South, New England's wheat crops were stricken by soil exhaustion and disease. "Rust," "blast," and the so-called Hessian fly discouraged wheat production and it declined rapidly, especially in older towns. Even in newer areas such as Amherst, where fresher soil encouraged one farmer in ten to raise wheat at the end of the century, it was grown only in small quantities. By 1801, wheat accounted for only 3.4 percent of Hampshire County's grain output, and almanacs were suggesting that it be sowed along with rye "to have it free from smut." The lack of a marketable staple crop made elite control of land and labor difficult, indeed pointless, even though the labor now potentially existed to be hired. The effect was to restrain the elite's accumulation of wealth. Some of the large houses built in the middle of the century were never finished to the intended standard. A few were merely imposing facades, masking commonplace household interiors.[43]

The elite's political prominence turned out to be something of a facade too. Counties, the level of government that the elite controlled, were not as powerful or important in New England as they had become farther south. Relatively autonomous towns counterweighed the influence of county officers. Elite influence was greatest in old towns and in those, such as Westhampton, which had been settled by the descendants of old Valley families, but inevitably its sway was reduced as settlement spread and new towns were created on the edges of the Valley. In any case, it faced popular opposition. Numerous disputes during the middle of the century, especially over religion and the splitting off of new towns and parishes, revealed the fragility of the gentry's position in a rapidly expanding region.[44]

---

43. On the decline of wheat: Dwight, *Travels* 1:31; Sylvester Judd, *History of Hadley, including the early history of Hatfield, South Hadley, Amherst, and Granby, Mass.* (Northampton, 1863), pp. 362–363; Percy W. Bidwell and John I. Falconer, *History of Agriculture in the Northern United States, 1620–1860* (Washington, D.C., 1925), p. 90; on the elite and their houses: Kevin M. Sweeney, "Mansion People: Kinship, Class, and Architecture in Western Massachusetts in the Mid–Eighteenth Century," *Winterthur Portfolio* 19 (Winter 1984): 231–255.

44. Political conflict is discussed in Nobles, *Divisions throughout the Whole*, chap. 6; the weakness and eventual decline of the regional elite, in Robert Blair St. George, "Artifacts

In 1774 this opposition surfaced decisively in resistance to British rule. Whereas the Stamp Act crisis and other disputes in the 1760s had produced only muted protest from the Valley, this time the organizing work of the Boston Committee of Correspondence after 1772 and widespread outrage at the Coercive Acts' assaults on local Massachusetts institutions ensured that things would be different. Determined, as the people of Williamsburg expressed it, "to Resist Great briton in their unconstitutional measures," committees visited the prominent men appointed as mandamus councillors or judges under the Massachusetts Government Act, and urged them to resign their royal commissions. Armed crowds confronted those suspected of refusing, surrounded courthouses, and extracted resignations. Clergymen sympathetic to the Crown were also subjected to "regulation." Within a few months in 1774 and 1775, many members of the Valley elite found their power broken. Israel Williams and his son, confined to a smokehouse in Hadley one night by a crowd, returned home, left office for good, and remained suspected of pro-British activities. Others, like the Stoddards of Northampton, also left public life for a period. Tories faced being disarmed and removed from office. Men like the Southampton merchant Jonathan Judd, Jr. expressed concern about "mob rule" in private but were careful not to question the authority of revolutionary committees too openly. His colleague Samuel Colton of Longmeadow, accused of profiteering, had goods seized from his store by a town committee. Refusing the payment he was offered for them at the legal price, he ended his life in a bitter and fruitless quest for compensation. Even Joseph Hawley of Northampton, the most prominent River God to support the patriot cause, withdrew from politics into insanity during the Revolution.[45]

The decline of wheat and the absence of a staple export crop encouraged many of the wealthier men in the Valley to enter trade or the land market, rather than to attempt to hire labor directly for production. The political reverses the elite suffered in the Revolution led them to negotiate for influence over their neighbors rather than assume it, and no new leaders attained the county-wide prominence that the River Gods had held. Economically and politically, therefore, conditions favored

---

of Regional Consciousness in the Connecticut River Valley, 1700–1780," in *The Great River*, pp. 29–40.

45. Robert J. Taylor's *Western Massachusetts in the Revolution* (Providence, 1955), chap. 4, is the standard account. Nobles, *Divisions throughout the Whole*, chap. 7, details several episodes in the unseating of Hampshire County leaders, and quotes the Williamsburg letter on p. 163. Jonathan Judd, Jr., Diary, Aug 31, Sept 3, 7, 13, 20, 1774; Feb 18, 19, Apr 1, 12, 22, 1776, FL. Barbara Clark Smith, *After the Revolution: The Smithsonian History of Everyday Life in the Eighteenth Century* (Washington, D.C., 1986), pp. 3–7, 30–42, recounts Colton's fate.

the preeminence of the household system. There was no power base within Hampshire County with the means or the wish to challenge it.

Shays's Rebellion

When crisis arose in the 1780s, it centered not on rural households' control of labor, which remained untouched, but on their participation in exchange and the terms on which farmers handled their connections with long-distance trade. Shays's Rebellion, rural Massachusetts' most serious political crisis, touched on a complex series of issues whose implications continue to be explored by historians.[46] Important among these issues, and the two most pertinent to this discussion, were a clash between the ethics of local exchange and long-distance trade, and the ability of the elite in some Valley towns to establish their claim to political authority on certain terms.

Shays's Rebellion was the ultimate result of mounting rural indebtedness and pressure to pay it off, which brought the relaxed, informal practices of local exchange and the insistence of long-distance trade into sharp conflict. Debts of three kinds combined to create a formidable debt crisis throughout much of the Massachusetts interior by the mid-1780s. Many households had suffered material or financial losses during the revolutionary war and sought to recover their depleted resources. The state government, meanwhile, strongly influenced by coastal mercantile interests in the General Court, tried to reduce its own public debt by raising taxes, doing so by laying particular emphasis on poll taxes, which fell disproportionately on rural households and their labor. In addition, peace with Britain in 1783 unleashed both a flood of new imported goods, payment for which became pressing in 1784 and 1785, and the revival of lawsuits by British creditors for debts incurred before the war. The combination of depleted resources, tax demands, and new debts placed heavy burdens on country people. They, in turn, found their attempts to negotiate repayment of debts hampered by the General Court's refusal to grant debtor relief and its insistence on the use of specie or other limited items of tender for the repayment of public

---

46. Taylor, *Western Massachusetts in the Revolution*; Barbara Karsky, "Agrarian Radicalism in the Late Revolutionary Period, 1780–1795," in *New Wine in Old Skins: A Comparative View of the American Revolution,* ed. Erich Angermann, Marie-Luise Frings, and Hermann Wellenreuther (Stuttgart, 1976); David Szatmary, *Shays' Rebellion: The Making of an Agrarian Insurrection* (Amherst, 1980); I have also benefited from reading the essays in *In Debt to Shays: The Bicentennial of an Agrarian Insurrection,* ed. Robert A. Gross (Charlottesville, Va., 1990), and am grateful to Robert Gross for the opportunity to see these papers before publication.

debts. The trade depression of 1784–1785 also reflected the difficulty of procuring goods from the interior for settlement of trade debts.[47]

The existence of these burdens, added to the already complex patterns of local indebtedness which, as we saw, were a normal part of rural life, prompted widespread attempts by creditors to secure repayment. In Hampshire County alone, just under 3,000 debt suits were brought before the court of common pleas between August 1784 and August 1786. Household goods, land, and other property put up for sale at sheriffs' auctions were often knocked down at ruinous prices to satisfy executions for debt. The jails began to fill with able-bodied men who had no property to be attached. Petitions to the General Court for relief, such as that drawn up by a convention at Paxton in Worcester County in September 1786, emphasized that rural resources were being overwhelmed by the speed with which repayment of debts was sought:

> The produce of the present year and the remainder of our cattle even were we to sell the whole, are totally inadequate to the present demands for money—such has been our situation for a long time past—an amazing flood of law suits have taken place—many industrious members of [the] community have been confined in gaol —and many more are liable to the same calamity—in a word, without relief we have nothing before us but distress and ruin.[48]

Rural people who normally frowned upon insistent dunning of debtors, and who believed that when pressure was exerted it should take regard of debtors' means, were overwhelmed by an avalanche of lawsuits demanding repayment at an impossible rate.

Pressure to settle debts came from three directions. Importers and other coastal creditors with remittances to pay overseas pressed for payment from their own inland customers. Where these inland traders had good connections, payment was often forthcoming, but Boston and Connecticut merchants complained of the great difficulty they faced collecting debts during what one called "the Troubles in Hampshire."[49] Local traders sought, in turn, to collect remittances from their own debtors. Finally, the general pressure of debt, including demands from

---

47. See George R. Minot, *The History of the Insurrections in Massachusetts, in the Year MDCCLXXXVI, and the Rebellion Consequent Thereon* (Worcester, 1788); Robert A. Gross, *The Minutemen and Their World* (New York, 1976), pp. 178–179, traces the effects of British debt collection on one family in Concord, Mass.

48. Petition, Sep 28, 1786, Shays's Rebellion Collection, folder 1, AAS. Szatmary, *Shays' Rebellion*, p. 29, calculates that the 2,977 debt cases brought before the Hampshire County Court of Common Pleas between Aug 1784 and Aug 1786 involved 31.4 percent of all males in the county aged sixteen or over.

49. Matthew Talcott to Jonathan Amory, Middletown, Conn., Mar 27, 1787, Amory Papers, Box 3, LC.

traders and other local creditors, caused people who had not necessarily been involved in trade to seek repayments either to cover the demands being made on them or to secure themselves in the general collapse of credit. "I need the Ballance of your Note," wrote Abraham Burbank of West Springfield to Capt. Lemuel Pomeroy of Northampton in April 1785: "I wish you may be disposed to pay it without a Suit." No single cause could therefore be ascribed for the crisis. The pattern of debt suits did not reveal a single line of pressure from coast to interior, for example. As the historian George R. Minot wrote in his account of Shays's Rebellion in 1788, crisis had been precipitated by "a relaxation of manners, and a free use of foreign luxuries; a decay of trade and manufactures, with a prevailing scarcity of money; and, above all, individuals involved in debt to each other." The pressures of debt were so widespread, a local newspaper had commented during the crisis, that "the most prudent people were deeply embarrassed."[50]

These circumstances led individuals to collect debts owed them by people relatively nearby, including their own neighbors. Of fifty-three debt actions brought by or against residents of Pelham between 1783 and 1786, over a quarter involved plaintiffs and defendants who both lived in the town; in 1784 the figure reached 36 percent. Violation of the usual standards of neighborhood dealing caused much of the resentment that led to Shays's Rebellion. The sense of disgust created is illustrated by evidence that among the Pelham men who joined the insurrection were former plaintiffs, as well as defendants, in these suits. Legislation of 1786 compelling courts to proceed with suits and to execute judgments further inflamed opinion against laws that systematically conflicted with rural economic morality.[51]

Rural outrage had accumulated over several years. Sporadic riots in early 1782 to break up sheriffs' sales of the property of poor families coalesced with Samuel Ely's armed march to close the Northampton courts in April that year. By 1783 demands for modifying the debt process were being voiced more widely. A county convention held in Hadley called for court fees to be reduced and for the upper value of cases that could be heard in local justices' courts to be raised from forty shillings to twenty pounds. When this plea failed, some petitioners sought the division of the county itself, so that the courts would be more localized.[52] By 1785 and 1786 condemnations of the debt process were

50. Abraham Burbank to Lemuel Pomeroy, West Springfield, Apr 18, 1785, Pomeroy Family Papers, MCFL, Box 30; Minot, *History of the Insurrections*, pp. 28–29; *Hampshire Herald*, Sept 7, 1784, quoted in Taylor, *Western Massachusetts*, p. 125.

51. Daniel Shelton, "'Elementary Feelings': Pelham, Massachusetts, in Rebellion" (Honors thesis, Amherst College, 1981), table following p. 119.

52. John L. Brooke, "Towns, Courts, Conventions, and Regulators: Revolutionary Settlements and the Crisis of the Economy in Massachusetts, 1786–1787," in Gross, *In Debt to Shays*.

numerous, and many towns based petitions for relief on principles central to the local exchange ethic: that debts would be paid as means were available and that legal action circumvented the normal processes of negotiation and accommodation that should occur between creditor and debtor.

Many of these pleas made it clear that it was not the debts themselves that were seen as unjust, but the peremptory demands for their repayment. "We are sencable . . . that a great debt is justly brought upon us by the war," declared the town of Greenwich in January 1786, "and are as willing to pay our shares towards itt as we are to injoy our shars in independancy and constatutional priviledges in the Commonwealth." If only "prudent mesuers were taken and a moderate quantety of medium to circulate so that our property might sel for the real value," the petition concluded, "we mite in proper time pay said debt." Armed men gathered and marched to close courthouses, not to avoid paying debts in the long run, but to suspend a collection process that seemed unjustly swift and indiscriminate. As conflict between rebels and state militia lay immediately in prospect in January 1787, John Billings, chairman of a county convention held at Hatfield, called for restraint. "Our matters may all be compromised," he argued, urging "that we may be in a way to convince each other of our error, and cultivate that unity which is necessary in a community."[53] His language—"compromise," "unity," "community"—was that of local assumptions about how to settle debts.

The affront to rural economic morality did not send all the men sued for debt to take up arms. In Pelham, although some plaintiffs and defendants in debt cases joined the insurrection, they were more likely to have supported petitions for relief. Young, poor, or transient men for whom the crisis had spelled poor employment and dismal future prospects made up more of the rebels' armed support from the town.[54] Action was taken by such people who lived in the towns most pressed by the crisis. As John Brooke has found, these were often places where elite authority was weak. Many insurrectionists, for example, were Congregationalists from towns or parishes without settled ministers.[55]

53. Town of Greenwich, Petition, Jan 16, 1786, Shays's Rebellion Collection, folder 1, AAS; "An Address from the Convention at Hatfield," *Massachusetts Centinel*, Jan 17, 1787 (copy provided me by Robert Gross).

54. Shelton, "'Elementary Feelings,'" pp. 114–122. Alan Taylor has suggested to me that some young men joined the insurrection because their families assigned them the task of taking up arms for them, as in previous wars; this would imply that participants' motives must be sought in social values and neighborhood rifts and alliances, as well as in the grievances of individuals. See Gregory H. Nobles, "Shays's Neighbors: The Context of Rebellion in Pelham, Massachusetts," in Gross, *In Debt to Shays*.

55. John L. Brooke, "A Deacon's Orthodoxy: The Religious Context of Shays's Rebellion" (Paper presented to a conference at the Colonial Society of Massachusetts, Boston, Oct 1986).

Conversely, where the elite was strongest, support for the insurrection was weak. Daniel Shays exaggerated when he claimed that the rebellion was supported by all Hampshire, except for fifty or so men in North-ampton and Hadley.[56] But he correctly identified the centers of support for the government. Had he literally been correct, he and his fellow rebels might have won their argument. But the Valley elite, centered in those two towns, had resources of their own to call on.

Not only were Northampton, Hadley, and Hatfield prosperous com-pared with the hill towns that supported the rebellion, but they had strong ties with the towns around them, especially with families de-scended from former residents who had settled in Westhampton, Wil-liamsburg, Amherst, and elsewhere. Prosperity and kinship provided important channels of influence for the river towns' leading families. Northampton merchants and landowners helped found the weekly *Hampshire Gazette* in September 1786 as an organ of support for the government. Ministers with whom they were connected, such as Joseph Lyman of Hatfield and Enoch Hale of Westhampton, preached against the rebels.

Above all, it was easier in towns where wealthy men lived or had connections for the debt burden to be eased by informal means. Court cases were still brought, but neighborly assistance or indulgence was more likely to be forthcoming than in poorer towns. Elite patronage also played a role. Probate records of the unpaid debts of men who died in the 1780s suggest that obligations to prominent supporters of the gov-ernment were quite common. Twenty years later, John Miller, a small farmer in Northampton, related how after being "reduced to misfor-tune" and owing more than he was worth, he had applied to Caleb Strong for assistance and been given it on several occasions. Though Miller owed Strong "a considerable sum, and more than I owed every body else, he never asked me for the money, but told me to pay him as fast as I could conveniently, and no faster."[57] But such assistance was overwhelmingly confined to the oldest Valley towns and those adjacent to them. Of twenty-one such debts that can be traced in the probate records, only two were owed by men in the hill towns. Obligations of kinship and neighborhood helped inflame passions against the govern-ment in outlying towns; similar obligations helped maintain support for government where the elite had connections or where means of relief were available. In Amherst, for example, support for the rebellion was stronger in the town's east parish than in the older west parish, where descendants of older county families and the county sheriff, Ebenezer

56. Quoted in a purported interview, *Massachusetts Centinel*, Jan 20, 1787.
57. Miller's story was printed in the *Hampshire Gazette*, Mar 26, 1806.

Mattoon, lived. In Westhampton, opponents of the Shaysites included not only Rev. Hale but many of the town's farmers, who had close kinship ties with old Northampton families.[58]

Yet the government's defeat of the Shays rebels did little to alter the real balance of rural economic power. This still rested firmly with household producers and with the local exchange ethic they subscribed to. Merchants trying to collect rural debts during and after the insurrection found attitudes unchanged. The Granby physician Daniel Coit ordered a new supply of drugs from Levi Shepard in Northampton early in January 1787, while making it clear that he could not yet pay for the last consignment. "Well may you think I mean to take advantage of the *Times*," he wrote, but "Disappointments are the sertain Concomitents of human nature therefore he who expects to pass the sceans of life without them, will shurely meet with the greatest." If Shepard had not already grasped what was coming, Coit quickly reached the point: "I cannot possibly get the grain for you at present which I thought I was as sertain of as tho' I had it by me." He offered some fox and sable skins instead, which he thought he would be able to obtain if Shepard offered a good price.[59] In May 1787, when the Boston merchant Jonathan Amory sought to collect debts in Hampshire and Worcester counties, his agent reported a familiar litany of responses. One man "would do nothing concerning the debt"; another "refused to give any further security . . . he says that by the Fall he can pay you if you incline . . . in neat stock." A woman "cant pay you at present she will send you something in one or two months." One man explained that, although "it would give him pleasure to discharge the debt," he would have to treat Amory "as the Laws enable others to treat him."[60] Merchants must have been frustrated by the sense of self-righteousness these letters conveyed, but they would have been wrong to regard it as humbug. From the local perspective, refusal to pay a debt could be justified if means were unavailable or if other obligations had to be met. These people were not avoiding payment but proposing ways to make it in the future.

Although the military defeat of the rebels led to the reopening of county courts and the resumption of the debt process, widespread sympathy was evident for the Shaysites and the economic morality they had defended. The spring elections of 1787, Minot wrote, "seemed to indicate a revolution in the publick mind." Having proposed amnesty for the rebels, John Hancock defeated the incumbent governor James

---

58. Data drawn from inventories and administrators' accounts, Hampshire County, Probate Records, vol. 15 (1784–1789) CVHM (microfilm).
59. Daniel Coit to Levi Shepard, Granby, Jan 2, 1787, Shepard Papers, MCFL, Box 31.
60. "R.G." to Jonathan Amory, Springfield, May 31, 1787, Amory Papers, Box 3.

Bowdoin by a three-to-one margin. Three quarters of the representatives and two-thirds of the senators in the General Court were replaced. The new representative from the town of Chesterfield was instructed "that the whole weight of your influence may be for the encouragement of the labouring part of the community," and, specifically, that he vote to reduce taxes on polls and estates and increase those on luxuries.[61] The General Court did reduce taxes. It also passed exemption laws, permitting delays to debt suits, and reduced the scale of court fees. Jonathan Judd remained anxious during the summer of 1787 that military success would turn to political defeat. Writing to his brother about selling cattle, he noted, "I am much at a loss what to do but think it better to wait . . . until I know whether the General Court are so infatuated as to make Paper Money."[62]

The legislature did not make paper money. Demand for paper ebbed as the crisis eased and debtors found other ways of settling or compromising with creditors. But the issue of the timing and pressure of calls to settle debts did not go away. In the longer term, according to the historian Peter J. Coleman, Massachusetts governments learned lessons from Shays's Rebellion and began to build into the law some of the lenience that petitioners had sought and that was embedded in the ethics of local exchange. A 1794 statute exempted certain household goods and other property from attachment and permitted the taking of a poor debtor's oath to obtain discharge from obligations. Legal changes well into the nineteenth century continued this move toward leniency.[63]

Tensions between local exchange and long-distance trade remained after the rebellion as before. Traders often had to take what households were prepared to grant them, on terms dictated by local needs and concerns. For several decades to come, the ethics of local, rather than long-distance exchange, would dominate rural economic life. And although they were never again so serious, the kinds of conflicts over debt that had been behind Shays's Rebellion remained endemic.

A Marginal Elite

The defeat of Shays helped restore the political morale of the Valley elite. Order and deference had been restored. Rev. Joseph Lyman of

---

61. Minot, *History of the Insurrections*, pp. 175–177; the Chesterfield instructions were printed in the *Hampshire Gazette*, Oct 24, 1787.

62. Jonathan Judd to Sylvester Judd, Sr., Southampton, June 2, 1787, Judd Papers, MCFL, Oversize Files.

63. Peter J. Coleman, *Debtors and Creditors in America: Insolvency, Imprisonment for Debt, and Bankruptcy, 1607–1900* (Madison, Wisc., 1974), pp. 34–52.

Hatfield remarked in an election sermon in 1787 that "communities constitute certain of their brethren to rule over them: and, thus constituted, they are the *ordinance* of the Supreme Ruler."[64] The dangers of Shays's Rebellion and its example of disorder were frequently reiterated by the builders of western Massachusetts federalism, as they obtained formidable political support in Northampton and environs during the 1790s, using the *Hampshire Gazette* as a mouthpiece. By 1800, with Caleb Strong's election as governor, they had created the semblance of a unified, deferential politics. In several towns between 1800 and 1803, Strong consistently received 75 percent or more of the votes cast in elections, and support for him remained high after that.[65] Consistency and deference often marked town politics as well. Amherst selectmen chosen between 1800 and 1810 served an average of 3.5 years. Hatfield selectmen averaged 4.5 years, and all were from among the top 40 percent of the town's taxpayers.[66] Serious religious divisions were rare. Orthodox Congregationalism was stable and dominant. Most towns had only one organized church. Ministers served long careers, in several cases up to fifty years or more, in the same town.[67] Although tensions lay beneath the surface, political and religious leaders could claim some of the authority once associated with the River Gods. Merchants such as Jonathan Judd in Southampton and his brother Sylvester Judd, Sr., in Westhampton, with close ties to church and bench, retained preeminence in local affairs, including some power over appointments. "Tell Ensn. King," wrote Jonathan to Sylvester, after they had organized a shipment of military supplies, "by his loading the Teams he will be fit for a Deacon by and by." When another man sought appointment as justice of the peace in Westhampton, nineteen neighbors supported Sylvester Judd, Sr.'s petition opposing it.[68]

Deference relied partly on the use of patriarchal rhetoric. Town lead-

64. Joseph Lyman, *A Sermon Preached before His Excellency James Bowdoin, esq., Governour . . . of the Commonwealth of Massachusetts, May 30, 1787, being the Day of General Election* (Boston, [1787]), p. 13.

65. Election returns reported in the *Hampshire Gazette*, Apr 9, 1800; Apr 8, 1801; Apr 7, 1802; Apr 6, 1803; Apr 4, 1804; Apr 3, 1805; Apr 9, 1806; Apr 8, 1807. The number of votes cast in Northampton in the gubernatorial election of 1800, for example, was 108 percent higher than in the election of 1790, though the town's population had grown by only 35 percent: *Hampshire Gazette*, Apr 7, 1790; Apr 9, 1800.

66. Town Meeting Records for Amherst reprinted in Edward W. Carpenter and Charles F. Morehouse, *The History of the Town of Amherst, Massachusetts* (Amherst, 1896); Kubiak, "Social Changes," p. 24, tab. 8.

67. Lists of ministers in *Creed, Covenant and Rules, and List of Members of the First Congregational Church in Amherst, Mass.* (Amherst, 1859); Daniel W. Wells and Reuben F. Wells, *History of Hatfield, Mass., 1660–1910* (Springfield, 1910), p. 343; Northampton First Church, *Meetinghouses and Ministers from 1653 to 1878* (Northampton, [1878]).

68. Jonathan Judd to Sylvester Judd, Sr., Boston, Nov 6, 1780, MCFL, Box 18; the petition against Joseph Kingsley is in Judd Papers, MCFL, Oversize Files.

ers and ministers claimed the authority that fathers claimed in their own households. Like those of fathers, who were having increasing difficulty maintaining their control of families, these claims were sometimes resisted, but the use of familial metaphor to bolster political authority seems to have succeeded in the Valley, at least for a time. Federalist rhetoric emphasized respect for age. When young men gathered to vote for the first time in Northampton in 1811, reported the *Hampshire Gazette*, they were led to the polls by one of the town's oldest citizens and all cast their votes for the Federalist candidate. Patronage, the ability of men with means to provide the kind of indulgence and flexibility that the local exchange ethic stressed, reinforced this order. The Northampton farmer John Miller explained in 1806 what the assistance of Caleb Strong had meant for him. Without it, he declared, "I should probably now have been poor and destitute." He continued: "I am lame and have seldom gone to town for five or six years, except on the first Monday of April, when I have attended, every year, to give my vote for Mr. Strong as Governor. Though I don't pretend to meddle in politics; yet as long as I can ride five miles, and he is a candidate, I will attend to vote for him. I don't know as he desires to be chosen, but I wish to shew that there is one man who is not ungrateful." The historian James M. Banner located rural support for federalism among farmers concerned to maintain a distance from the market. But these men were also drawn to a vision of patriarchal order that conformed with their hopes for their own households and their position in local exchange.[69]

While they sought to construct political order in the context of a powerful household system, members of the Valley elite knew that their economic power was relatively slight. They could not directly control land or labor for production. There were limits to the amount of land that could effectively be worked as one unit and no staple crop that could be raised for export on the large farms that did exist. The absence of a staple, and the diffusion, irregularity, and variety of produce available for shipment out of the region made trade uneven and perplexing. Consequently, men with wealth to invest were impelled to support risky schemes, seemingly marginal to the economy's operation. Family labor and household production pushed capital to the edge of the rural economy.

Several Northampton men, with associates in other towns, turned in the 1780s and 1790s to speculating in "western" land and sponsoring internal improvements. They included members of old elite families, like the Stoddards; substantial local merchants, like Levi Shepard and

---

69. James M. Banner, *To the Hartford Convention: The Federalists and the Origins of Party Politics in Massachusetts, 1789–1815* (New York, 1969); Miller's story: *Hampshire Gazette,* Mar 26, 1806; the account of polling day: *Hampshire Gazette,* Apr 10, 1811.

Ebenezer Hunt; and smaller traders, like Benjamin Tappan. Through both types of venture they sought to profit indirectly from a rural economic structure direct control of which was closed to them. Buying land in regions beyond the margins of settlement, they hoped to profit from rising prices, as land-pressed New England farmers or their children migrated north or west. In the 1790s they were particularly interested in western New York State and the Connecticut Reserve lands in Ohio, but Valley speculators had dealings elsewhere too. Closer to home, they hoped that by building river improvements to circumvent obstacles to navigation on the Connecticut and by establishing bridges and turnpike roads, they could stimulate trade and then charge carriers for the use of their facilities. River improvements in particular would benefit from increasing traffic from the upper Connecticut Valley as settlement proceeded in New Hampshire and Vermont. Receipts from land sales and tolls from road, bridge, and canal traffic were the lowest common denominators for seekers of profit from an economy that gave little scope for other kinds of investment.

A close-knit group of local merchants and lawyers dominated most public improvement schemes chartered in the Northampton region between 1791 and 1806. Eleven Northampton men led the founding of nine canal, bridge, turnpike, banking, and insurance companies. Several of them, including Levi Shepard and Ebenezer Hunt, were involved in four or more projects each, using their connections to draw in outside capital, including some from Europe. Most of these schemes shared common local sponsors with others. The principal exception, the Hatfield Bridge Company, which completed the first bridge across the Connecticut River in 1807, was also the shortest-lived. The better-backed Northampton Bridge opened at a more convenient site the following year. The Hatfield bridge gradually fell into disuse before it finally collapsed about 1820.[70]

But few of the schemes were wholly successful or fulfilled the early hopes of their founders. With the high costs of upkeep, and tolls that could be evaded, turnpike companies made profits slowly. The Third Massachusetts Turnpike, from Northampton to Pittsfield, averaged a net return of only $600 a year between 1801 and 1814 and had barely repaid the capital invested in it when it was made a free road in 1829. Canal companies also faced difficulties. The South Hadley Canal pro-

70. On bridges, see Samuel Willard, *A Sermon Preached at Northampton, October 27, 1808, at the Opening of Northampton Bridge* (Northampton, 1808); Wells, *History of Hatfield*, pp. 214–216. On canals, see *Private and Special Statutes of the Commonwealth of Massachusetts*, 7 vols. (Boston, 1805–1837), 1:329. On turnpikes, see *Private and Special Statutes* 2:78–81, 130–134, 140–144, 295–299, 327–331. See also Martin, "Merchants and Trade," pp. 200–202.

voked vigorous criticism from farmers and fishing interests upstream and, after 1800, accusations that by swamping lands and restricting drainage its dam was causing disease in Northampton and elsewhere. The company finally agreed in 1805 to rebuild its works and pay compensation for damages. Timothy Dwight, though noting that traffic on the river increased, summed up the early canal ventures as "a serious misfortune to the proprietors, and a source of not a little regret to the community." River traffic was, in any case, restrained by the continued need to transship goods at the falls in Enfield, Connecticut, which were not bypassed by locks until 1829.[71]

Land speculation also brought misfortunes. Some local figures, such as Jonathan H. Lyman of Northampton and Oliver Smith of Hatfield, were eventually to make money successfully from land in New York, Pennsylvania, and Ohio. The Northampton merchant Benjamin Tappan also had holdings in and around Cleveland that promised substantial profits by the early nineteenth century. But others were unlucky. John Stoddard of Northampton wrote to John Worthington in Springfield in 1798, lamenting the latter's loss of $400 in a purchase Stoddard had advised him to make. With a gambler's optimism, he urged Worthington to part with more cash to "make good that loss [and make?] something handsome to yourself." William Edwards, who had been Worthington's partner in the venture, later claimed to have lost several thousand dollars by it. Even Benjamin Tappan's good fortune only became apparent over time. For many years, his son Lewis was later to write, his speculation in Western Reserve lands "was a subject of anxiety and embarrassment to him," from which he was only relieved by the assistance of one or more of his sons.[72]

Internal improvements and investments in land were, at best, long-term solutions to the weak position of merchants and other investors in a household-centered economy. We shall see in Chapters 5 and 7 how over several decades such ventures provided part of the basis for more concentrated and successful capital investment. But for the most part, the late-eighteenth- and early-nineteenth-century rural economy kept power diffused, in the hands of the farmers, craftsmen, and other household producers who dominated the social structure. These men and women, despite the upheavals of the revolutionary period and its

71. Harry A. Wright, *The Story of Western Massachusetts*, 4 vols. (New York, 1949), 2:485–486; Dwight, *Travels*, 1:236; W. DeLoss Love, "The Navigation of the Connecticut River," *Proceedings of the American Antiquarian Society*, n.s. 15 (Apr 1903): 385–441.

72. John Stoddard to John Worthington, Northampton, Mar 1, 1798, NHS, A.S.L. 17.2; William Edwards, *Memoirs of Col. William Edwards* (Washington, D.C., 1897); on the Tappans' holdings, see the *Republican Spy* (Northampton), July [?], 1806, and Lewis Tappan, "Autobiographical Sketch," Lewis Tappan Papers, Container 14, LC (microfilm, reel 7). See also Martin, "Merchants and Trade," pp. 176–183.

aftermath, had succeeded in retaining effective control of rural production and the patterns of exchange.

Households and Conflict

Most rural households were able to maintain the independence that they valued well into the nineteenth century. By then, commentators were extolling the virtues of family life, giving the image of the rural household a roseate tinge that has surrounded it ever since. In 1834, for example, Rev. James Flint wrote an article, "Picture of a New England Family," nauseating in its sentimentality. "Ambition has infused no storm into their tranquil bosoms," he wrote of an imaginary husband, wife, and children seated round the fireplace. "Behold the scene! It is the sole-surviving trace of paradise on earth, unspoiled by the perverted tastes and distempered cravings of artificial life, or the costly inventions of pride and luxury."[73] Late-eighteenth-century people would have found this description ludicrous. The world of households they inhabited was often hard, cramped, and fraught with conflict.

Farmers' and artisans' houses were crowded, busy places. Few could advertise, as did Noah Webster when he prepared to leave Amherst in 1822, a house with "eight large rooms, exclusive of the kitchen, which contains two rooms." Evidence on house sizes, collected for the federal direct tax of 1798, has not survived for any of the six towns, but returns for the surrounding area suggest the probable pattern. Large two-story houses were most common in old settlements near the river. Toward the hills and in newer towns, smaller dwellings predominated. Everywhere, though, in poorer households and in many young ones where children were being brought up, space was at a premium. In 1805 a young Hadley farmer, Jonathan Warner, was given an old schoolhouse to live in, which probably contained only one or two rooms.[74] Working, eating, and sleeping places became more crowded during the winter, when rooms were closed off and fires kept in kitchens for warmth. Except in some new settlements, such as Westhampton, a number of dwellings housed more than one family, usually parents together with a married child and the child's spouse and own children. Between 1790

73. James Flint, "Picture of a New England Family," *Hampshire Gazette*, Feb 26, 1834.
74. Webster advertisement, *Hampshire Gazette*, Apr 10, 1822. There was a higher proportion of small houses in upland towns than in the bottomlands; in 1798, 70 percent of houses in Pelham and 54 percent in Belchertown had only one story, compared with 35 percent in Westfield and 21 percent in Easthampton (Massachusetts, Direct Tax Censuses, 1798, 17:78–83 and 19:789–802, 816–820, NEHGS [microfilm]). None of the relevant schedules for the six towns has survived. Warner is mentioned in Elizabeth Phelps, Diary, Nov 3, 1805.

and 1830 roughly 11 percent of Amherst and Hadley families shared houses in this way. As Mary Graham of Buckland learned when her widowed mother was courting a second husband, privacy was hard to find in a small house. "It reminds me of a few years ago when you got out of the window so many times," she wrote to her sister; "I have not exactly done that but sat on the stairs till I was tired." Going into the room once in time to hear "the old man" say "he could not tell until he tried it," she "did not dare stay longer, did not know what would come next."[75] Family life may have been warm, but it was not easy.

Sharing out work, reconciling the uneven burdens of men's and women's tasks, providing for daily needs and for the future livelihoods of children were constant sources of friction. To the catalog of difficulties caused by illness, death, separation and migration may be added those resulting from the need to operate in a constrained economic environment. Rebecca Dickinson of Hatfield, though saddened at being single, consoled herself in 1787 that "family blessings" were double-edged: "the gifts of time alwais bring sorrow along with them[;] a numerous family and a great Estate bring a great concern upon the minds of the owners more than a ballance for all the comfort that they bring."[76]

The pursuit of independence by families hedged in by material constraints did engender local cooperation of the kind we examined earlier, but it also led to attempts to exclude from consideration people unable to provide reciprocal goods or work, and those otherwise regarded as "outsiders" or subordinates. John Miller explained that he had originally applied to Caleb Strong for assistance with his debts when his neighbors had ceased to help him; "although I believe [they] all thought me honest, they were not generally fond of trusting a man who had no estate."[77] As Douglas L. Jones has shown, one of the consequences of eighteenth-century population growth was an increase in the numbers of poor, landless, often transient people forced to live at the margins of rural society. To avoid supporting outsiders who became destitute, older towns continued to "warn out" newcomers until new laws of the 1790s provided for state assistance to paupers without legal residence. In 1791, for example, 119 families or individuals totaling well over 200 people were formally "warned out" of Northampton; Hadley dealt similarly with another 29. This happened again, on a smaller scale, in

75. Mary Graham to Lewis Edwards, Buckland, Aug 5, 1842, Edwards Family Correspondence, MCFL.
76. Rebecca Dickinson, Diary, Aug 2, 1787. Jan Lewis, *The Pursuit of Happiness: Family and Values in Jefferson's Virginia* (Cambridge, Eng., 1983), discusses the difficulties of family life.
77. *Hampshire Gazette*, Mar 26, 1806.

1794 and 1796. Some of the people named remained in town and set-
tled. Nathan Storrs, one of Northampton's jewelers in the early nine-
teenth century, had been named in the warning-out warrant of 1791.
But others were less fortunate. Caesar Prutt, a black man warned out of
Hadley in 1796, was being supported as a pauper in Amherst in 1800.[78]
Many others just moved on.

After 1800 perhaps several hundred people a year were passing
through the Valley, sick or seeking employment: here a man who
"supported himself by day labor"; there an Irish-born journeyman
hatter who "has of late years been to[o] feeble to labor and has led a
wandering life"; here a woman unable to find work, and "such have
been her habits of life, that she has never earned any property."[79] Even
after the law provided support for "state paupers," endless wrangles
over residency occurred, as towns tried to pass costs back to places
paupers had previously lived in. Independent farmers, gathered in
town meetings each spring, watched the poor rolls closely and bargained hard to reduce the cost of relief as much as possible. In 1801 the
Amherst town meeting voted that Caesar Prutt "be Set up at vendue, to
the Lowest bidder For Victualling and Beding," and he was then
"Struck of[f]" to a farmer for a dollar a week. The next year the town got
the weekly price down to eighty-five cents. What sparked the town's
indignation was a successful attempt in 1803 by Daniel Kellogg, one of
Amherst's most prosperous farmers, to have his insane brother supported by the town. While the town meeting, on legal advice, reluctantly voted to provide the money, it had a strong condemnation of
Kellogg placed on its records, "as a rare instance of the want of broth-
erly affection." "Devoid of all the natural and social feelings of human-
ity; wrapt up in the barbrous garb of self-interest," Kellogg stood as "a
deplorable monument of human depravity."[80]

Kellogg's public rebuke by his neighbors reflected the fine tensions
inherent in farm families' intent, on the one hand, to "keep a good
neighborhood" and, on the other, to provide for their own and their
children's livelihoods. "Neighborhood" implied a recognition of needs
and abilities that, although it obliged the town to support Kellogg's

78. Jones, "The Strolling Poor," passim; Warning-Out Warrant, Northampton, Nov
24, 1791, BCJL; Hadley warrants copied in Judd MS, "Hadley," 3:355, 361; Storrs is
mentioned in Philip Zea, "Clockmaking and Society at the River and the Bay: Jedidiah and
Jabez Baldwin, 1790–1820," in Benes, *The Bay and the River*, p. 44; for Prutt, see Amherst,
Town Meeting Records, reprinted in Carpenter and Morehouse, *History of the Town of
Amherst*, pp. 187, 189.

79. Northampton, Overseers of the Poor, Case Histories, Town Papers Collection,
5.14, FL.

80. The town's proceedings in the Kellogg case are reprinted in Carpenter and Morehouse, *History of the Town of Amherst*, pp. 192–193.

"wretched and distressed" brother, more strongly implied that Kellogg himself could afford to do this better than his neighbors. "Livelihood" impelled someone in Kellogg's position to put his own interests first, but it also provoked the resentment of neighbors forced to assume the burdens he had avoided. This tension, together with the other conflicts in the household system drove the rural economy into the nineteenth century. The ways in which rural households acted in their diffuse social structure, pursuing independence but demanding interdependence, powerfully influenced the shape the economy would take.

Chapter 3

Households, Farming, and Manufacturing

Historians broadly agree that important changes were taking place in the New England countryside by about 1790. Robert Gross showed how the Revolution subtly altered patterns of life in Concord. Not only the stringent demands of war, with its disruptions, inflation, and indebtedness, but also new awareness of the world beyond the village, created an irreversible thrust for change. The historical geographer J. S. Wood, too, has drawn attention to increasing levels of production, exchange, and other activity in rural areas and has suggested that the period around 1790 was "crucial" in the transformation of rural life. Winifred B. Rothenberg has documented shifts in several vital indexes of rural economic activity. Farmers traveled more to exchange produce than they had in the colonial period. Prices assigned to major items of farm produce, even in local exchanges, increasingly converged with each other and with those in distant urban markets, suggesting greater "market" influence in the countryside and the emergence of commodity markets. Land changed hands more often. Dealings in produce and land called forth greater quantities of negotiable paper, which circulated more rapidly to create, in Rothenberg's view, a new rural capital market. And, finally, she has also found evidence of an increasing use of wage labor in the countryside, suggesting the creation of a labor market.[1]

1. Robert A. Gross, *The Minutemen and Their World* (New York, 1976); J. S. Wood, "Elaboration of a Settlement System: The New England Village in the Federal Period," *Journal of Historical Geography* 10 (1984): 331–356; Winifred B. Rothenberg, "The Market and Massachusetts Farmers, 1750–1855," *Journal of Economic History* 41 (1981): 283–314; Rothenberg, "The Emergence of a Capital Market in Rural Massachusetts, 1730–1838," *Journal of Economic History* 45 (1985): 781–808; Rothenberg, "The Emergence of Farm Labor Markets and the Transformation of the Rural Economy," *Journal of Economic History* 48 (1988): 537–566. The importance of the 1780s and 1790s for parallel readjustments in family law and ideology is discussed by Michael Grossberg, *Governing the Hearth: Law and the Family in Nineteenth-Century America* (Chapel Hill, 1985), chap. 1.

This evidence is often taken to suggest that the postrevolutionary period was the point at which rural people abandoned their former isolation from the rest of the country and became "market oriented" in a radically new way. However, this conclusion cannot be drawn without examining the reasons why the changes just described took place. While dramatic changes in rural production and exchange undoubtedly occurred in the half-century after the Revolution, they did so substantially within the household-based economic structure that had become so powerful. Rather than being the "crucial" point in the transformation of the countryside, this period saw a sustained attempt by household producers to maintain control of their ways of doing things. Increased levels of production, exchange, and wage labor took place more as incidental results of this effort than as conscious attempts to change the economy's direction. More important, in the short run they left the structure of rural production essentially unchanged. The ambitions and needs of household producers left a firm imprint on the economy, restraining the creation of new institutions and practices. Although the countryside took on a new dynamism, its precapitalist structure remained recognizable, even in the 1820s.

Population Growth and Inequality

Late-eighteenth-century circumstances, especially the indebtedness that led to Shays's Rebellion, encouraged rural families to use the forms of production and exchange that they had already evolved in an intensification of their efforts to supply their needs and to fulfill the desire to provide for their children. Two related problems dominated rural households' calculations and underlay their experience of the debt crisis.

One problem was relative land shortage. As settlement in the Valley and its surrounds began to be completed, most usable land came to be appropriated and divided between landowners. Because of continued population growth, access to land became more difficult than it had been in the middle of the eighteenth century. Lower population densities in hill towns compared with the older Valley settlements were counterbalanced by the poorer land available there. Although in Westhampton before 1800 it was still regarded as the custom "in many cases for the father to build a house for his son when the young man was ready to marry and locate," it was much less so in older towns. Everywhere, the opportunities to settle children on land became fewer or more expensive. Amherst, approaching its third generation of settlement, saw land prices rise more steeply after 1790 than they had before.

While taxable real estate values rose by an average of 2.6 percent each year between 1771 and 1790, the rate increased to 4.8 percent between 1790 and 1795 and 6.0 percent up to 1800.[2]

The second problem, coupled with the first, was that land was unequally distributed. In older towns, especially Northampton, landlessness was increasingly common. By 1798, 30.5 percent of Northampton's taxpayers were assessed on no real property at all. Another 5 percent were taxed only on buildings they lived or worked in, suggesting that they did not own the land the buildings stood on. Many who did own land had little beside their homelots than holdings of woodland, rough pasture or other unimproved acreage. The wealthiest tenth of Northampton's families owned half of its taxable property. Although about 55 percent of the town's population lived in families that owned improved land other than their homelots, only 45 percent of taxpayers had the elements of a complete farm: a homelot with buildings, improved land for cultivation, pasture, and woodland.[3]

Even among farmers, however, land was unequally distributed, especially in the older Valley towns. Table 1 sets out the distribution of all acreage held by owners of improved land in Northampton and Hatfield.[4] Given the fact that Hatfield farmers' homelots are not counted in these figures, it appears that similar proportions of farmers in both towns held small or middling amounts of land. Only one in five Northampton farmers had more than one hundred acres, while in Hatfield the proportion was about one in four. Although a small number of farmers in the older towns had holdings of two hundred acres or more, men like Charles Phelps, with his six hundred acres in Hadley, were notable for being so rare. Even in Amherst and Westhampton, where more recent settlement made inequality less pronounced, the poorest 40 percent of the population owned only one-tenth of the taxable wealth.[5]

2. The problem of land scarcity was explored by Kenneth L. Lockridge, "Land, Population, and the Evolution of New England Society, 1630–1790," *Past and Present* 39 (Apr 1968), reprinted with "Afterthought, 1970" in *Colonial America: Essays in Politics and Social Development*, ed. Stanley N. Katz (Boston, 1971), pp. 466–491. The Westhampton quote is from Samuel L. Wright, "Westhampton Local History," 3 vols., compiled 1892–1905, 2:36, FL (typescript); Amherst land values are based on Bettye Hobbs Pruitt, *The Massachusetts Tax Valuation of 1771* (Boston, 1978), and Amherst, Tax Valuation Lists, 1790–1800, Amherst Town Hall. A useful discussion of inheritance practices is Carole Shammas, Marylynn Salmon, and Michael Dahlin, *Inheritance in America: From Colonial Times to the Present* (New Brunswick, N.J., 1987), chap. 3.

3. Northampton, Tax Assessment List, 1798, Town Papers Collection, 5.7, FL.

4. Northampton, Tax Assessment List, 1798; Bernard R. Kubiak, "Social Changes in a New England Agricultural Community: Hatfield, Massachusetts, 1800–1850" (University of Massachusetts, Amherst, 1972).

5. Amherst, Tax Valuation List, 1800, Amherst Town Hall; Westhampton, Tax Valuation List, 1810, Westhampton Town Hall.

Table 1. Distribution of farms by size, Northampton, 1798, and Hatfield, 1800

No. of acres	Farms in Northampton, 1798[a] (%)	Farms in Hatfield, 1800[b] (%)
1–25	26.4	33.3
26–50	29.3	19.7
51–100	24.7	23.1
101–150	11.5	7.7
151–200	2.9	8.5
200+	5.2	7.7
Total	100.0	100.0

[a]Including homelots; $N = 174$.
[b]Excluding homelots; $N = 117$.
Sources: Northampton, Tax Assessment List, 1798, Town Papers Collection, 5.7, FL; Bernard R. Kubiak, "Social Changes in a New England Agricultural Community: Hatfield, Massachusetts, 1800–1850" (University of Massachusetts, Amherst, 1972), p. 11, tab. 1.

Scarce and unequally distributed land meant that families faced difficulties settling children by dividing up farms, as early settlers had been able to do. By the end of the eighteenth century perhaps as few as one in five Northampton farmers had enough land to consider dividing it between sons. This option was not open to everyone in newer towns either. An agricultural journal claimed in 1819 that opinion as to what constituted a reasonable sized farm had been revised downward over the years. At the start of settlement 200–400 acres had been regarded as necessary. By the early nineteenth century this amount had been reduced to between 80 and 150 acres.[6] But these were the standards of a gentleman farmer. Even in Amherst, average landholdings were only just above 50 acres. Larger amounts of land were beyond most farmers' reach.

Some families, even in older towns, were of course able to settle more than one son on land they owned. Northampton families had maintained a long tradition of settling sons in neighboring towns. As late as 1801 Bela Strong bequeathed land in Westhampton for his elder son to farm on, reserving his own Northampton farm for his younger son. But it was now rare for families to have so much land to bequeath.[7] In Westhampton itself, though, more families had plenty of land to divide up. William Bartlett, one of the town's largest landowners at the end of

6. "Remarks on the Agriculture of Massachusetts," *Massachusetts Agricultural Journal* 5 (1819): 320–322.
7. Bela Strong, Will, Hampshire County, Probate Records, 22:284, Hampshire County Hall of Records, Northampton (microfilm).

the eighteenth century, was able to divide his land between four sons, each of whom settled on a farm within a short distance of their father's house. The Fisher family, also early settlers in Westhampton, had 320 acres to divide between three sons, at least two of whom were able to carve out new farms for their own sons a generation later.[8] But the majority of families had to find livings for their offspring without such resources so readily to hand. It was their activities in pursuit of alternative means that helped bring change to the countryside.

Migration to land in new regions had been the traditional New England solution to land shortage and inequality, a solution of which successive Connecticut Valley settlements had themselves been results. Migration from southern New England to New Hampshire, Vermont, and Maine, and then to upstate New York, Ohio, and elsewhere, which was in full flood by 1800, continued the tradition. Many people left the Valley. Ephraim Wright, a Westhampton tavernkeeper, had seven sons. Three moved to Vermont in the 1790s and settled near one another. One went to Southampton and a fifth son to the West Farms district of Northampton. By about 1810 only two remained in Westhampton. Many other families had similar experiences.[9]

In few cases, though, did families remove from their homes entirely. Both in the Valley proper and in hill towns, "those who stayed behind" outnumbered those who migrated.[10] These people had to find ways to make a living within the existing rural economy. The rest of this chapter traces how they did so. Their decisions to stay led to important changes.

Two basic strategies were available to those who sought livelihoods and provision for their families in the face of scarcer resources. One was to acquire and make more intensive use of land. Pressure to seek out property and constantly to trim landholdings to families' needs and strategies helped generate a new land market. Various strategies for purchasing, exchanging, and renting land were the inevitable consequence of scarcity, but land acquired in the land market was put, not to new uses, but to the kinds of purposes it had long been used for by farm households. At the same time, landholders were devoting more effort to clearing and improving what they already owned, so that over several decades the agricultural output of the Valley significantly increased. The desire to provide livelihoods for family members played an

8. Wright, "Westhampton Local History," 1:172.
9. Ibid., 1:30–34.
10. Of 227 men and women born in the years 1780–89, traced in Lucius M. Boltwood, *Genealogies of Hadley Families: Embracing the Early Settlers of the Towns of Hatfield, South Hadley, Amherst, and Granby* (1905; reprint, Baltimore, 1979), at least 123 (54.2%) and probably as many as 162 (71.4%) stayed in the six towns or in an adjacent town. If the "uncertains" are removed, of the total 188 known, about 65.4 percent stayed and 34.6 percent moved elsewhere.

important role in determining what improvements were made, when, and by whom.

The second set of strategies was to acquire new skills with which to earn a living separately from or in conjunction with farming. As a result, a variety of new manufacturing activities grew up in the Valley in the generation following the Revolution. It has long been commonplace to view these early manufactures as forerunners of the capitalist industrial revolution that was to follow later in the nineteenth century. Undeniably, there were important connections to it. But early nineteenth-century rural industry differed considerably, both from what had come before and from what was to succeed and largely supersede it. It was a vibrant manufacturing sector, organized largely on family or household lines. Again, the essential purposes of the development of rural manufacturing, and the social structure that it arose in, made a strong imprint on it.

Changes in farming and manufacturing were at the heart of a dynamic change in the countryside that took place within the existing social framework up to the second decade of the nineteenth century. In this chapter I will examine them each in turn and then discuss the rural labor system, where household strategies and social structure were also crucial in determining who worked for whom and on what terms. If there was a rural "labor market" it was shaped by familial concerns and had not yet become dominated by the existence of a large class of workers with nothing to sell but their labor.

Before turning to those matters, however, it is worth examining the conduct of the exchange system within which these developments occurred. This was also an adaptation of existing rural exchange practices. Local exchange provided much of the mechanism by which farming and manufacturing were expanded, and labor hired and paid for. It also provided the ethical framework within which change took place and was understood by rural people. Conducting trade with distant markets continued to create tensions, as it had in the 1780s. But it did not fundamentally alter the local exchange system.

Reciprocity and Obligation

The Hampshire County probate court oversaw the administration of the estates of twenty-two men and women who had died between 1799 and 1802. Between them, these people had an average of $1,483.13 each in notes or on book accounts that they owed their creditors or their debtors owed them. These obligations, which had to be painstakingly documented and collected by their executors, represented just a part of the massive volume of debts and credits by which country people were linked to neighbors, kin, and strangers at various distances from their homes. The extent to which people were mutually entangled in credit and debt is suggested by the fact that of the ten decedents in the group who were net creditors, only one did not also have outstanding debts to other people. And of the twelve who owed others more than was owed to them, most had debts to be collected as well as to be paid.

The complexity of these networks of mutual obligation varied enormously according to individuals' circumstances. A Northampton shoemaker, Festus Morgan, who died in 1800 leaving a house, workshop, tools, and household goods, had debts of $36.67 owing to him, but obligations to pay $125.26 to sixteen creditors. Two of the creditors, however, were mercantile firms, whom he owed $73.38. The remainder of Morgan's debts, like the debts owed to him, were small accounts with individuals, averaging only $3.71 in value. Another man whose obligations were mostly small was the Amherst farmer Asahel Clark, who owned over forty acres of land and one-third of some grist and saw mills. He owed $279.17 to eighty-three different creditors, in amounts ranging from $47.80 down to $0.06 and averaging only $3.36. Clark had been close to bankruptcy; he had been obliged to sign notes even for small amounts, and the year after his death the probate judge approved the sale of $750 worth of his land to cover debts and legacies. At the other end of the scale was David Morton of Hatfield, who in addition to a good farm had personal property worth almost $6,500. He owed more than $2,560 to thirty individuals, most of them either neighbors, kin, or other creditors within the Valley. The appraisers of his estate traveled to Whately, to Hadley, twice to Amherst, once more to the "further part of Amherst," and several times to Northampton to settle books. They made sixteen journeys in all and did seven and a half days' further work clearing up Morton's affairs. There were compensations; they consumed three quarts of rum at the estate's expense, while witnesses at the probate court received dinners and mugs of flip. But they had to work hard to cut the affairs of the deceased from the complex network of personal and financial obligations in which they were entwined.[11]

The scale of these connections was largely a consequence of the practices of local exchange that governed most rural transactions. Indeed, the transactions that surface in probate court records are only the most formally conducted ones, those set down on paper in a form that administrators could find and act upon. But the evidence of account books and other, more casual, references to dealing show the pervasive-

11. Administrators' Accounts, Hampshire County, Probate Records, for: Festus Morgan, 22:24v.; Asahel Clark, 21:120 and 22:8v.; David Morton, 21:12.

ness of the methods of exchange outlined in the previous chapter. Book accounts, in which debits and credits were accumulated over time, and often left for long periods without settlement, were common enough to require special recognition at law. An opinion of the Massachusetts supreme judicial court noted that "the admission of proof by the book of the plaintiff himself appearing to be of his own handwriting, and supported by his supplementary oath, is a practice, in the extent to which it has been carried, peculiar to *New-England,*" but one "which has been long established, and seems to have arisen . . . out of the necessity of the case, and a conformity to the actual state of things." The court also ruled that the six-year statute of limitations did not apply to unsettled debts on running book accounts whose most recent transactions had occurred less than six years ago; debts could be collected even if there were long gaps between settlements.[12] These and other decisions explicitly recognized the practices that had long governed local exchange. They relaxed the tighter rules associated with long-distance exchange in order to permit the debt process to operate in the rural context.

The rules of local exchange were becoming more important. Exchanges using payment in goods and services, rather than coin or other cash representations of value, remained common. In a system in which all payments were made directly in cash we would expect exactly half the entries in ledgers recording individuals' transactions with others to be for cash, whether counting the number of transactions or their value. (This is because for every entry on one side of the ledger describing goods or services advanced, there would be a corresponding cash payment on the other side.) Early-nineteenth-century farmers' ledgers do not show such a balance. Between 1800 and 1805 William Boltwood made 212 entries in his accounts of dealings with his Amherst neighbors. Of these only 7.5 percent in number and 10.6 percent by value were for cash, and another 4.3 percent (5.7 percent by value) were in notes or other paper instruments. Altogether, aside from the 3.5 percent by value of his accounts that were never settled, Boltwood conducted 88.2 percent of his transactions (80.2 percent by value) in goods, labor, or services. He traded rye, wheat, corn, pork, veal, hay, lumber, flax, and other produce from his farm; performed day work or sent his son to do it; and lent out his plow or horse for others to use. He took labor, farm produce, and other goods in return. Other accounts show a similar pattern. Joseph Eastman of North Amherst made a total of 994 entries on both sides of his ledger between 1804 and 1825, of which 902 (90.7 percent) were for goods or services. Abner Brown, in Brimfield in

12. Prince, admx. v. Smith, 5 Mass. Reports (4 Tyng): 455–459 (1808); Cogswell, exx. v. Dolliver, 2 Mass. Reports (1 Tyng): 217–223 (1806).

the early 1820s, took or gave goods or labor in 89.5 percent of his transactions. Even in cases where settlements were made and notes given for the balance, payment in goods was often specified. After reckoning with his neighbor Eliphalet Spear in 1810 and finding that he owed Spear $3.89, Joseph Eastman noted that the amount was "Due to him in Produce."[13]

Indeed, there is evidence that cash payment became less frequent during the late eighteenth and early nineteenth centuries, at least for the normal run of rural transactions. Cash remittances to some merchants were less common around 1800 than they had been before the Revolution. In 1771, 10 percent of Northampton taxpayers were listed as having "money at interest"; by 1798, the proportion had fallen to only 5.2 percent. In Amherst, the fall was even greater, from 19.8 percent of taxpayers in 1771 to 6.3 percent by 1790. Several factors explain the reduction. War, inflation, and taxation to redeem public debts had drained much money from the countryside. Many private cash holdings were wiped out. "Cash shortage" became a perpetual complaint of the postrevolutionary period, particularly in debt crises, when urgent demands for money to repay debts drove what little cash there was into fewer hands.[14]

But the fundamental cause of "cash shortage" was the structure of rural economic activity itself. Lacking a staple crop for sale, the Valley's farmers were not in a strong position to acquire large amounts of cash. Surplus goods that they sold at long distance did bring in some, but, particularly if they traded at local stores, farmers' remittances of produce merely tended to balance the goods from outside the region that they needed to purchase. However, "cash shortage" was a problem only in certain contexts. For most of their regular transactions farmers and others in the countryside had no need of cash and could secure necessities without it. Some came to rely on it even less over time. Joseph Eastman, for example, used cash for over 11 percent of his transactions between 1804 and 1809, but for only 4 percent from 1820 to 1825.[15]

In commercial exchange promissory notes and other paper instruments effectively circulated as cash, their negotiability guaranteed by

13. William Boltwood, Account Book, Amherst, 1789–1830, BCJL; Joseph Eastman and Chester E. Marshall, Account Book, North Amherst, 1801–1835, BCJL; Abner Brown, Account Book, Brimfield, MS Collection, AAS.

14. Margaret E. Martin, "Merchants and Trade of the Connecticut River Valley, 1750–1820," *Smith College Studies in History* 24 (1938–1939): 150; Pruitt, *Massachusetts Tax Valuation*; Northampton, Tax Assessment List, 1798; Amherst, Tax Valuation List, 1790; "Recollections of Olive Cleveland Clark," in *A History of Williamsburg in Massachusetts,* comp. Phyllis B. Deming (Northampton, 1946).

15. Joseph Eastman, Account Book.

court rulings intended to ease the flow of paper. These instruments were generated in local exchange too, some against outstanding balances on book account, more in relation to land deals and other large transactions. They became more common in the late eighteenth century, but only for certain types of dealing, where pressure was greatest to ease the constraints of direct exchange of goods or work. Farmers and other employers of labor began to pay workers in orders drawn on local stores. More orders against third parties circulated as people with no immediate means to pay pressing debts transferred the burden to their own debtors. But evidence from account books suggests that payment by note or order remained rare for day-to-day dealings. Joseph Eastman used them in fewer than 2 percent of transactions before 1810, even less after that.[16]

This need not have been the case: farmers and others could have insisted on the passing of notes every time they gave out goods or did work. That they did not reflects the ethical restraints that they accepted against pressing for payment and their preference for settling debt by reciprocal exchange over the course of time. Because demanding a note or security for a debt could cause embarrassment, usually it was done only in certain instances. For large debts, it was expected and acceptable. When someone was running close to bankruptcy, or might have other difficulty making payments, it might also reasonably be demanded. This is one reason notes appear so frequently in administrators' accounts. Many people who later died had been old or sick beforehand, less able than others to make payments in the normal course of events. Giving a note to a creditor and receiving a note from a debtor was a device for having affairs straightened out after one's death, when administrators could collect debts owing and make payments out of an estate even where means had not existed while the decedent remained alive. Even so, of twenty-one decedents in the years 1799 to 1802 who owed debts to others, thirteen had not given notes for them. Even of the twelve who were net debtors, seven had not been asked to sign notes.[17]

Cash, too, served particular purposes in local exchange. It was neither a universal equivalent nor a generally convenient method of payment. Even among the well off, desire to acquire cash usually related to its specific uses. Charles Phelps's daughter Elizabeth traveled to Boston in 1800 to buy clothing and other goods before her marriage to Rev. Dan Huntington but found few merchants prepared to sell to her except for cash. She arranged some purchases on her father's credit, noted that others might as well be made for goods or credit in Northampton, and

16. Ibid.
17. Hampshire County, Probate Records, vol. 21.

suggested postponing the marriage until these arrangements could be completed.[18] Charles Phelps, it will be recalled, was one of the Valley's largest farmers. His daughter's problem was not the lack of wealth, but of immediate means. Cash was called for in particular circumstances, to acquire certain things, or from certain people, or in certain places. Its uses were socially determined.

Cash was, above all, a medium of exchange between strangers or in circumstances when other available goods and services were not needed and therefore not acceptable in payment. People could go to great lengths to avoid using cash, either because they had none or because they wanted to conserve what they did have for other purposes. After David Mack migrated from Connecticut to the new settlement of Middlefield in the 1770s and needed some goods, he found that the nearest store was twenty miles away at Westfield. Having no cash, and preferring not to ask for credit from a merchant who did not know him, Mack chose instead to ride the sixty miles back home to Hebron to get what he needed.[19] Cash was more often demanded of people coming from a distance than from locals. Members of a town committee charged with building a new bridge in Northampton in 1794 were authorized to draw money from the selectmen to purchase planks "providing they are obliged to go out of town to procure them." A Northampton storekeeper kept accounts with seventy-two customers between January and March 1804, of whom twenty-seven (37.5 percent) eventually settled in cash. Fourteen of these lived in Northampton, but they represented only 25 percent of the store's customers from the town, the rest of whom paid in produce or services. Thirteen (81.3 percent) of sixteen nonlocal customers, however, paid cash.[20]

Cash was more likely to be demanded for certain goods. The Amherst farmer Asa Dickinson ran a small store or tavern early in the nineteenth century, selling rum and sugar to several dozen customers, mostly from the neighborhood. Of payments to him over a fourteen-month period in 1804–1805, 44 percent by value was in cash, usually for imported West India rum and sugar. New England rum could be paid for by other means; Dickinson took a note in June 1806, for example, from a farmer who promised to pay "the sum of five cords of pitch pine wood cut and split d[e]l[ivere]d at his dore . . . by the first of October."[21]

Direct reciprocal exchanges were the most common form of transac-

18. Elizabeth W. Phelps to Charles Phelps, Boston, Sept 28, 1800, PPHH.

19. Joseph Clarke, *A Sermon Preached at Middlefield, at the Funeral of Hon. David Mack* (Northampton, 1845), appendix, p. 16.

20. Northampton, Town Meeting Warrant, Apr 30, 1794, BCJL; Store Ledger, Northampton, 1803–1814, NHS, A.A. 18.24.

21. Asa Dickinson, Account Books, 2 vols., Amherst, 1792–1799, 1804–1811, BCJL.

tion. Ethical standards were based on the assumption that this would be the case, and that the yardstick of economic performance was not the ability to make a profit but the ability to have the means available to make payments over time in the normal run of farming or other affairs. These standards for dealing affected not just local exchange itself, but spread into longer-distance transactions when farmers and others could make bargains that gave them the same kinds of latitude they were granted locally. They preferred, when they could, to obtain not only generous amounts of time to settle debts but the ability to pay them off in means they had at hand. They perceived transactions in concrete, not abstract, terms, focusing not on overall questions of price, profit, or loss but on immediate issues such as who needed this, who could let someone have that, or who had enough of the other to pay off an outstanding debt.

This concreteness of approach has two implications. First, it calls into question the suitability of regarding local exchange practices simply as variants of "market" behavior. Certainly many of the instruments of more abstract market exchange were present. Prices, especially for bulk farm produce, did increasingly converge with those in other regions. The account books used by some farmers were similar to those used by merchants and other long-distance dealers, and most rural people who kept them had grasped at least the rudiments of commercial accounting practice, however unsystematic they might be in applying it. But rural practice emphasized what Max Weber called "substantive" over "formal" rationality. When Richard Williams of Williamsburg copied out arithmetical instructions from a textbook in 1791, he particularly noted sections relevant to local exchange. "Equation of Payments," he wrote, "is the finding of a time to pay at once several debts due at different times so that no loss shall be sustained by either party."[22] He conceived "loss" not as an unfavorable balance between incomings and outgoings, but as any need to make an outgoing payment during the normal run of transactions.

Second, in the actual conduct of exchange the concept of "price" was itself something of an abstraction. Farmers used money prices to give book values to the goods and labor they exchanged and these moved increasingly with the rhythm of distant markets. But in a set of long-running book accounts they had less direct meaning than might appear, since their actual value was only notional. The real "prices" for goods were not in cash but in the other goods and labor that were exchanged for them. These, in turn, were constantly being bargained over. It is likely that farmers used "market prices" for farm produce as markers in a complex pattern of dealings. But when two farmers came together to

22. Richard Williams, "Arithmetical Manuscriptum," Williams Family Papers, Box 6, folder 2, PVMA.

settle accounts, they often had other goods and work to include for which "market prices" were not available. The ledger belonging to Abner Brown of Brimfield contained prices for work and services but also many entries for goods such as corn, rye, turkeys, and liquor for which no price was given. Pricing was evidently done at the time of settlement; the goods had changed hands without agreement as to the value to be attached to them.[23] Annotations in account books often indicate that particular goods were "called" a certain amount in order to help bring accounts into balance. All this suggests that prior calculations of costs may have played a lesser role in bringing transactions about than practical questions of need and availability. In a decentralized, household-based economy, individuals could use their bargaining skills to determine terms of settlement after transactions had taken place.

Local exchange also had expansionary effects. Long-running book accounts, especially those paid off irregularly or at long intervals, were effective instruments of credit. The credit advanced was informal, based on the needs and potentialities of different households. Often, between the same households, the balance of credit and debt shifted from one to the other at different times, so that credit was not simply a one-way flow from more to less powerful families but was widely diffused. If it remained simply as book debt, without being subject to interest, this credit was also inexpensive. Avoidance of cash and commercial paper instruments provided a degree of insulation to the local economy against speculative surges. Holding assets in useful goods, rather than in cash, was a hedge against price fluctuations. Direct exchanges also stimulated demand for local goods and services, because it was relatively easier to negotiate purchases from local sources than to obtain cash to buy goods from outside the region. As population grew, and pressure on land and other resources became more intense, strains developed in the system. But, compared with the more centralized commercial credit and payments systems of staple-crop regions, the diffused local exchange system may have been crucial in permitting a dynamic household economy to evolve. It evolved, moreover, largely on its own terms, without relying heavily on outside sources of credit.

Farming

Local exchange and the sale of surpluses, along with inheritance, production, and acquisition of land, formed the strategies farm families

---

23. Abner Brown, Account Book.

used to provide for their own needs and to secure means of advancement for their children. Shortage of land led to more intensive use of all of these, and so to a significant degree of agricultural change and expansion. Although, as population grew, nonagricultural pursuits increased in proportion, farming remained by far the most important occupation throughout the Valley well into the nineteenth century. Even in Northampton, the most diversified town, nearly 63 percent of household heads listed agriculture as their occupation in the 1820 census. In Amherst, the proportion was almost 73 percent. In Hadley, Hatfield, Westhampton, and Williamsburg it ranged from 80 percent to nearly 89 percent.[24] While a few farm families had, as we have seen, adequate land to provide for their present and future needs, most had to seek other ways of doing it. Some examples will illustrate how families with different levels of assets attempted to find security without sacrificing independence.

Caleb Cook of Hadley was one of the substantial minority of landowners who had inadequate land to make a living entirely out of farming and who used local exchange to compensate for this. He had received some land from his father, Aaron Cook, when the latter died in 1800, but Aaron had bequeathed his own farm and the residue of his estate to Caleb's brother Daniel. Caleb was left with thirty acres, which he owned in common with an uncle. Had he controlled this land outright, it might have been sufficient to support a family. As it was, Cook had to supplement his family's takings from the land with work as a carpenter. He or members of his family worked at weaving and shoe binding; Cook also hired himself out in a variety of farm laboring jobs, earning food and small household goods. Local exchange was for Cook an essential means to cobble together a living out of a range of skills and slender resources.[25]

For households with more property, local exchange served more as an adjunct to farming than as a vital part of earning a living. But different circumstances could lead in different directions, as the contrasting examples of Solomon Wright of Northampton and William Boltwood of Amherst suggest. Wright farmed eighteen acres of improved land in Northampton in 1798, as well as ten acres of unimproved outlands, which included a woodlot and probably some pasture. He

24. U.S. Fourth Census, 1820, Massachusetts, National Archives, Washington, D.C. (microfilm). The study of agriculture that follows has drawn on Margaret R. Pabst, "Agricultural Trends in the Connecticut Valley Region of Massachusetts, 1800–1900," *Smith College Studies in History* 26 (Oct 1940–July 1941), and John Ritchie Garrison, "Surviving Strategies: The Commercialization of Life in Rural Massachusetts, 1790–1860" (Ph.D. diss., University of Pennsylvania, 1985); see also Howard S. Russell, *A Long, Deep Furrow: Three Centuries of Farming in New England* (Hanover, N.H., 1976).

25. Caleb Cook, Account Book, 1794–1838, NHS, A.A. 17.9.

was also taxed on a horse, a cow, a few other cattle, and some hogs. Without a grown son to help him, this modest farm would have kept Wright busy, though even if his crop yields were modest too, he should have been able to raise enough to feed his family. He traded his own labor and the produce of his household systematically to obtain things the family needed. He lent his horse and farm tools to neighbors and exchanged day work with them at busy seasons. His wife's work at weaving cloth, making gowns, and mending clothes, exchanged for extra food, footwear, or household goods, also figured prominently in his accounts. Wright maintained extensive contacts with other branches of his family. He swapped work, did weaving, and exchanged produce with his brother Elijah. He had acquired some of his land from his brother-in-law Benjamin Southworth and grew corn and flax "on shares" on land rented from him. He obtained goods from a local storekeeper, Joseph Clarke, paying for them with farm produce and sledloads of wood in the wintertime. Constant trading and juggling goods for labor gave the Wrights their living. This exchange took place mainly within the confines of the town. Although wage labor and sharecropping were part of his strategy, Wright did not become dependent on them. They were supplementary to the land and household labor that were the family's main assets.[26]

But living in Northampton, where settlement was old and relatively dense and good land was hard to obtain, Wright was able to do little more than get by through these methods. Over in Amherst, William Boltwood used them to build more than just a livelihood. Born in 1766, Boltwood had been trained as a blacksmith but apparently preferred farming. He had received land from his father, and started out with resources roughly similar to Wright's. About the time of his marriage to Eunice Noble in 1789, Boltwood swapped his land with a brother's, procuring a forty-four-acre farm in Amherst's west parish. This was smaller than the average size for a farm in the town but, like Wright, he found that it was more than sufficient for a young man with little help. He raised a mixture of grain crops and reared a small number of animals, trading work with neighboring farmers when he needed assistance. By 1795 he was producing fifty bushels of grain, more than enough for his family's needs; what was left over supplemented the seven tons of hay he also raised for animal feed. By now he was growing flax, too, from which he either exchanged the fiber or, having had it spun into yarn at home, traded it to pay for weaving. In 1796 he started trading in land, carefully buying, selling, and swapping parcels with other Amherst farmers. By 1800, he already had sixteen more acres than

26. Solomon Wright, Account Book, 1787–1810, NHS, A.A. 17.6.

he had started with, and his holdings put him among the most prosperous fifth of Amherst taxpayers. As his sons became old enough to
help, Boltwood extended his improved land, from twelve acres to
twenty acres between 1795 and 1800 alone. Boltwood was using his
land, his family, and his local dealings as a basis for a steady accumulation of land; he would continue doing so until he had secured enough to
carve out a new farm for one of his sons.[27]

Taken together, the differing strategies of families like the Cooks,
Wrights, and Boltwoods brought about substantial change in agriculture without fundamentally altering the household economy itself. A
closer look at the town of Amherst allows us to trace this process. Its
position on fertile land at the eastern edge of the Valley proper gave
Amherst's farmers good conditions for growing crops. By the end of the
eighteenth century, though, the second and third generations of settlers in the town were facing constraints on access to new land, most of
which had been divided up. Comparison of the town tax assessment
lists for 1795, first with the valuation of 1771 and then with nineteenth-
century data, provides evidence about the effects of the settlement
process and subsequent scarcity of land.

Although the 1771 returns for Amherst survive only in incomplete
form, they provide data for 96 of the 117 taxpayers assessed that year.
Between them, these households produced 10,062 bushels of grain
from 1,132 acres of tillage, a mean output of 8.89 bushels per acre. This
would have been more than adequate to feed the small but growing
population of over 900.[28] According to the 1795 returns, Amherst's 170
taxpayers produced only 4,914 bushels of grain from 1,350 acres, a
mean yield of only 3.64 bushels per acre. This was almost certainly an
underestimate, although it is difficult to be certain by how much. Bettye
Hobbs Pruitt's estimates of minimum consumption requirements suggest that the grain output recorded in the assessment list would have
been about 12.5 percent less than what was needed to feed the population of about 1,290. However, although the output figures would have
to be revised upward, the 1795 assessment list implies that over the
revolutionary period Amherst's early grain surpluses were reduced.
Since there is no evidence from account books or other sources of a
substantial trade in grain or flour in or out of the town in the 1790s, the
reduction is likely to have brought grain output more nearly into balance with local demand.[29]

There were two reasons for the decline in grain output. Soil exhaustion almost certainly reduced yields on older farming land, and by the

27. William Boltwood, Account Book; Amherst, Tax Valuation Lists, 1790–1820.
28. Pruitt, *Massachusetts Tax Valuation*.
29. Amherst, Tax Valuation List, 1795.

1790s many farmers were using a portion of their tillage to raise non-grain crops, especially flax for household linen production. At least half of Amherst's farmers grew flax by 1795, despite the fact that most were cultivating less land than their predecessors. Those assessed in the 1771 valuations had an average of 11.8 acres of tillage each. By 1795 this average had fallen to just under 8 acres as a result of the subdivision of land and some redistribution of tillage to new farms. So farmers were heading closer to the margins of adequate provision for the local population. Some years these margins were slim. In Hatfield in 1789, Rebecca Dickinson wrote of the difficulties arising from "the want of bread and the want of money to gain that same article," and noted that harvests were expected to be poor: "there is no hope of the grain." A baker in Northampton faced one or two years in the first decade of the nineteenth century when he was forced to import flour. One of them was 1809, when local storekeepers took the unusual step of advertising flour for sale and a man from Goshen was moved to write, "Last year we complained because we had more than enough of the good things of this life, and this year the Lord has cut short our crops, so that we have not the wherewithal to subsist upon."[30]

Margins, though sometimes reached, were not seriously breached. Overall, late-eighteenth-century farmers succeeded in diversifying production while maintaining adequate provision. Three things helped prevent a slide into famine during lean years. One was mixed cropping. Another was local exchange. The third was the increasingly important role accorded livestock as guarantors and regulators of the food supply.

Most farmers grew a variety of crops. Of the food crops and feedstuffs counted in the 1795 tax-assessors' returns—wheat, rye, corn, barley, oats, pulses, and hay—three-fifths of Amherst farmers produced at least four each and 94 percent produced at least three. Rye was raised by 70 percent, corn by 95 percent, and hay by virtually all. The few farmers who produced fewer than three crops each were those with the smallest amounts of land. Invariably the larger the farm, the larger the range of crops it produced; size was associated with diversity, not specialization. Of the two rationales behind this mixed-crop regime, one was the desire to spread the labor burden as much as possible, so as to optimize the use of family, rather than hired labor. The other was to protect against shortfalls. While in poor years one or two crops might fail or produce low yields, this was unlikely to happen to three or four. The strategy's worth was illustrated in 1816, "the year without a summer," when

---

30. Rebecca Dickinson, Diary Extracts, Hatfield, Spring 1789, PVMA (transcript); letter from "A Christian," *Anti-Monarchist* (Northampton), Oct 18, 1809. William Porter, the Hadley merchant, advertised wheat for sale when grain was scarce in 1806: see *Hampshire Gazette* (Northampton), Apr 9, 1806.

exceptionally cold and dry weather produced frosts each month and severely jeopardized crops. Whereas most were poor, rye harvests in the Valley and elsewhere were good.[31]

Averting famine depended on redistribution of scarce food. Account books provide abundant evidence that, in good or poor years, food-stuffs were exchanged between households, usually in small quantities, in return for labor or other services. A sample of one in five of Amherst farmers on the 1795 tax list reveals the inequalities in production that underlay this need for local exchange. Farmers in the sample produced a mean of 40.29 bushels of grain each per year. This average was well above the minimum of 25 to 30 bushels which most families would have required for their own consumption, but overall it would have provided no more than what Sarah F. McMahon has called "a comfortable subsis-tence" for each household. The distribution of output was not even, however. Of thirty-four farms in the sample, sixteen, or 47 percent, produced less than 30 bushels each. On the other hand seven, or 20.6 percent, produced more than double that amount. As suggested in Table 2, farms fell into three categories. Almost half had grain supplies below the 30-bushel "subsistence" level for the average family, al-though, allowing for some undercounting in the returns, it is likely that fewer than one-third were seriously below it. Another third produced enough to provide a comfortable grain supply. Only the top fifth of farms produced enough to have substantial amounts available for feed-ing livestock or trading. Exchange of grain and labor between the larger and the smaller producers helped correct the imbalance between them. This accords with Bettye Hobbs Pruitt's finding that exchange in many parts of New England derived not from the existence of substantial surpluses for sale but from deficits on many farms that needed to be made up.[32]

While exchange redistributed uneven supplies of grain and other produce between households, livestock provided the single most im-portant guarantee of adequate food supplies overall. Livestock raising also fitted well into farm households' strategies for using land and

31. Wright, "Westhampton Local History," 1:309.
32. Thirty bushels of grain was established by Bettye Hobbs Pruitt, "Self-Sufficiency and the Agricultural Economy of Eighteenth-Century Massachusetts," *William and Mary Quarterly* 41 (July 1984): 333–364, as the average family minimum annual requirement, a significant downward estimate from those of most earlier studies; see also Sarah F. McMahon, "A Comfortable Subsistence: The Changing Composition of Diet in Rural New England, 1620–1840," *William and Mary Quarterly* 42 (Jan 1985): 26–65. Surpluses and deficits were calculated from crop figures in Amherst, Tax Valuation List, 1795, converted to corn equivalents according to the following ratios: 1 bushel of Wheat equal to 1.104 bushels of corn; Rye, 1.050; Corn, 1.000; Barley, 0.866; Oats, 0.433; Potatoes, 0.220; (Roger L. Ransom and Richard Sutch, *One Kind of Freedom: The Economic Consequences of Emancipa-tion* [Cambridge, Eng., 1977], p. 247, tab. E-2).

Table 2. Distribution of annual grain output, Amherst farms, 1795

Total grain output (bushels)	Percentage of farms[a]
Under 15	17.6
15–22	14.7
23–30	14.7
31–38	8.8
39–45	11.8
46–60	11.8
61 or over	20.6

[a]$N = 34$, a 20 percent sample of Amherst farms in 1795.
Source: Amherst, Tax Valuation List, 1795, Amherst Town Hall.

labor. In the six towns in 1791 there were altogether more than 2,300 beef and dairy cattle older than three years, as well as nearly 2,200 swine. This represented an average of 2 pigs and more than 2 cattle for each family in the region. Swine and cows were owned by many non-farm families as well as farmers. Cattle were particularly important. More than nine out of ten Amherst farmers kept milk cows in 1795 and most kept beef cattle too, while only just over half kept swine.[33] Meat was an important part of most families' diet, and milk, though occasionally drunk fresh, went to make cheese or butter. Hides and skins, tallow for candles, bristles, and other animal by-products found extensive use in households and appeared in local exchange.

Livestock also served another role, as a kind of "regulator," balancing the economy's need for sufficiency and the problems of producing too much. In good years, when grain and hay were plentiful, surpluses could be directed to fattening cattle and hogs for slaughter, or for exports to Boston and other markets on the hoof. Butter and cheese production would also rise, for sale as well as for family consumption. In poorer crop years, however, with feedstuffs rarer, cattle and swine could be slaughtered in greater numbers for household and local consumption, or for export as dried meat. Winifred Rothenberg's research has suggested a link between slaughter rates and urban grain and hog prices by the early nineteenth century, and it is possible that larger farmers were beginning to gear their decisions about livestock to the

33. Mass., General Court (Committees), Aggregates of Valuations, 1791, Mass. State Library, Boston (microfilm).

"market" conditions indicated by price movements.[34] But it is likely that many farmers responded less to prices than to their households' needs and local crop conditions. David Hoyt, an elderly Deerfield farmer, kept notes in his diary in 1804 about his son's cattle and the decisions that would have to be taken about them as winter approached. When there was already enough snow on the ground in mid-November "that the cattle cannot get anything to Eat abroad," he expected that they "therefore must be put to Dry meat if the weather continues." The weather moderated, however, and the cattle remained in pasture for another month. When they were eventually brought into the barn in mid-December, Hoyt expected that they would now be able to last the winter on the available feed. In especially poor years, meat provided an essential supplement to the diets of families short of grain. At the end of 1816, for example, the West Farms school district of Northampton contemplated having no school for the winter. Grain was so scarce that no family was willing to board a schoolteacher. When a farmer offered a heifer, for which he had no feed, the problem was solved. The heifer was slaughtered, there was now sufficient food to board a teacher, and "school was kept."[35] There was no neater illustration of the regulating function of livestock.

Livestock suited household production strategies because their direct labor requirements for a given output were relatively small. They therefore represented a good return to labor, over which households attempted to keep most stringent control. Dairy cows needed the most constant work and attention, and although most households kept at least one, few kept more than two. Milking and barn chores were among the tasks handled either by men or by women as household conditions dictated, although butter and cheese making was mostly done by women. Pigs, fed on household scraps and other surplus items, also placed few demands on family labor time. Beef cattle, which required hay and feedstuffs for part of the year, were nevertheless handled in such a way as to minimize their use of labor at busy seasons. They were often left to forage for themselves in backlots or woodland. Children too young for other tasks were assigned to drive cattle to and from pastures.[36]

Moreover, livestock permitted families to expand somewhat beyond

34. Rothenberg, "Markets and Massachusetts Farmers: A Paradigm of Economic Growth in Rural New England, 1750–1855" (Ph.D. diss., Brandeis University, 1985), pp. 66–72.

35. David Hoyt, Diary, Nov 16, 18–19, 20, Dec 3, 1804, MS Collection, AAS. Wright, "Westhampton Local History," 1:309.

36. George Sheldon, "'Tis Sixty Years Since: The Passing of the Stall-Fed Ox and the Farm Boy," *History and Proceedings of the Pocumtuck Valley Memorial Association* 3 (1890–1898): 472–490.

their limited land resources. Cattle and hogs were not restricted to the property of their owners but under certain circumstances could browse freely on unenclosed land. This helped poor families as well as wealthy ones keep stock fed. Some towns, including Northampton and Hatfield, permitted cattle to run at large and browse on highways during the summer. In older towns, such as Hadley, Hatfield, Northampton, Westfield, and Deerfield, they were also permitted to graze in meadows and common fields after the end of the growing season. Toward the edges of the Valley, unimproved uplands served the same purpose. In other words, livestock were not reliant purely on cultivated feedstuffs. The use of such land for grazing livestock, however, could lead to friction. Seventeen farmers in Northampton's South Farms district petitioned the selectmen in 1800 against the tendency of others "to turn their sheep and cattle upon our farms" near Mount Tom. But livestock remained at large well into the nineteenth century, as voters at town meetings resisted attempts to end the practice or voted to maintain common-field fences.[37]

Animals and their products appeared in local exchange and long-distance trade in multifarious ways. Not only was meat commonly exchanged between households, but it came to be traded over middling distances within the Valley. At least two farmers from Williamsburg started in the 1780s to carry meat to customers in Northampton. One of the two, Orange Wright, set up a permanent butchering business, with customers among Northampton's nonfarming population, and for a time at the beginning of the nineteenth century employed another man to walk around the town selling meat from a basket.[38] But this business remained small-scale. Larger overall, but more intermittent in character, were long-distance sales of livestock, meat, dairy produce, and other animal products, which became Valley farmers' principal source of outside income. But the levels of exports varied with conditions in the local household economy. If grain was short, households slaughtered cattle and swine for dried meat. Supplies of live animals for market fell. The mechanism for handling livestock supplies therefore remained informal and flexible. Country storekeepers, such as Sylvester Judd, Sr., of Westhampton, served as collecting agents for cattle from a wide area around, sending droves on to market after farmers had individually consigned the animals in small numbers. Alternatively, drovers started traveling through the countryside collecting cattle for sale, often having to cover long distances putting droves together. Farmers en-

37. *Hampshire Gazette*, Mar 17, 1800; Hatfield, Town Meeting Records, 2:25, Apr 1815, FL (microfilm).

38. Judd MS, "Northampton with Westfield," 2:194, FL; Judd MS, "Hadley," 3:37, reprinted in *SPJM*, pp. 388–389.

sured that their own needs were going to be met before sending animals off to market.[39]

Livestock, though, provided the best means for farmers to adapt their strategies to meet the challenge presented by population growth, land scarcity, and inequalities. Until about 1800 they had relied on "extensive" rearing practices, using unimproved land and browsing rights as major sources of food for their animals. Now more and more farmers sought to increase output, to secure their immediate and future needs within the constraints of the household system.

They approached this goal in two ways. They added unsettled or unimproved areas to pastures, clearing new land in order to modify their existing extensive methods. And they began to make more systematic use of livestock as part of a process of extending and improving tillage and meadowlands, gradually shifting to more intensive methods. Over time, more and more animals were grazed on properly cleared pastures, rather than in woods and wastes, while their manure was also applied more widely to cultivated land.

In Hadley, Hatfield, and Northampton in 1791, tillage accounted for between 20 percent and 25 percent of land recorded in the tax assessments, but in newer towns like Williamsburg, it represented as little as 5 percent. All towns finished the eighteenth century with large amounts of land divided up between owners but uncultivated. Over the following decades, up to 1831, perhaps as much as 30,000 acres of unimproved land were brought into productive use of some kind. Much of this land had been held in reserve by households seeking to use it to help provide livings for their offspring. As population grew and land became harder to acquire, they sought to make better use of what they already had. In Amherst, for example, the average farmer's total landholding in the 1790s was about 56 acres, but only about one-sixth of that was tilled and another sixth used for mowing and pasture. By about 1830, though average holdings had fallen to around 50 acres, more than 75 percent was in use. Tax lists of 1802 and 1822 permit us to see this land improvement in more detail. Of thirty farmers who appeared in both lists, and who had unimproved land in 1802, only four had not increased their improved acreage by clearing or acquiring land twenty years later. Sons inheriting parts of their fathers' farms worked to clear unimproved land to give themselves more room to farm in, or to make small improved acreages into viable farms. Asiel Blodgett, for instance, owned 104 acres in 1818, only 30 of which were taxed as "improved" land. Five years later, he owned the same total acreage, but had 22 more acres of im-

39. Sylvester Judd, Sr., Receipt, Oct 5, 1789, loose papers with Account Books, Westhampton, 1752–1832, MCFL.

proved land. Overall, as many as 7,000 acres of land in Amherst were brought into farming use between 1791 and 1831, at an average rate of just under 1 acre per household per year. Similar improvements were taking place throughout the Valley, both in older and newer towns.[40]

How was this newly cleared land used? Pasture was the single most important addition to farms. In Amherst, the reported increase in pasturage, at nearly 7,000 acres, was almost equivalent to the reduction in unimproved land. In Westhampton and Williamsburg pasturage expanded by more than 4,000 acres each. Undercounting of land in the 1791 valuations may exaggerate these increases, but there is no doubt that pasture expanded rapidly in this period, especially at the edges of the Valley. Of total farm acreage in the six towns in 1791, it accounted for about one-eighth. By 1831 pasture accounted for one-third. Not surprisingly, there was a substantial increase in livestock raising. The expansion of both dairy and beef production meant that the number of cattle more than doubled, from 2,300 in 1791 to more than 5,400 in 1831. But sheep raising expanded even more rapidly. From a few small flocks at the end of the eighteenth century, the number grew until there were 12,000 sheep in 1831, concentrated in the upland towns, where they were raised partly for meat, mainly for wool.[41]

As well as clearing land for pasture, many farmers also expanded their tillage and mowing lands, adding a total of as much as 7,000 acres throughout the six towns. In Hadley and Hatfield, where the largest changes occurred, tillage and mowing acreage almost doubled. Some of this increase was brought about by improvement to previously unused or unusable land, but given that in Hatfield, for example, the decline in acreage recorded as "pasture" was equivalent to 80 percent of the increase in tillage and mowing, it is likely that the conversion of pasture provided much of the new cultivation. Farmers not only cultivated more land, however, but did so more intensively. The increase in livestock provided manure, which farmers applied more systematically to their land. Sylvester Judd, Jr., while farming in Westhampton between 1817 and 1820, calculated that he increased his hay yields from five or five and one half tons per acre to eleven or twelve tons within three years "from the effects of manure and attention." Improvements such as more careful seed drilling and new strains of grasses helped raise the total output of field crops, as did the gradual spread of grain cradles, which reaped more efficiently than sickles. In Northampton,

40. Mass., General Court, Aggregates of Valuations, 1791, 1831; Amherst, Tax Valuation Lists, 1802, 1822.

41. Mass., General Court, Aggregates of Valuations, 1791, 1831; these may have undercounted beef cattle, in particular, since valuation lists were frequently drawn up after stock was moved to market or to pasture each spring.

total grain production recorded in tax assessments quadrupled in the half-century between 1771 and 1821. In Amherst, Hadley, Hatfield, and Northampton together, the four towns with the most extensive grain crops, grain output tripled between 1791 and 1831. Given that tilled acreage in these towns rose by only 56 percent in the period, it is likely that more than two-thirds of the increased output was due to higher yields. In Northampton alone, grain output rose by 29 percent between 1821 and 1831, and yields per acre by over 30 percent.[42]

Increased crop and livestock production were linked. As grain supplies began to overtake local population increases, more corn in particular became available for animal feed. Together with hay, this provided sufficient feedstuffs for farmers in the older Valley towns to undertake winter cattle fattening on a regular basis, without such concern as they had once had for fluctuations in output near the margins of subsistence. Winter fattening for market became an established practice on more farms. Cattle drives grew in size and regularity. The Judds of Westhampton provide an example of the contrast. In 1789 Sylvester Judd, Sr., collected fat cattle from his and other towns "to drive to Boston market." This was in October, so these were animals that were not to be fed for the winter. The consignment included nineteen cattle belonging to six different farmers. One of these men shipped nine animals, but the remainder sent only one, two, or three each. By 1818, when Sylvester Judd, Jr., sent cattle to Boston, he did so in April after fattening them for the winter, and the twenty-four animals were all his own. Local credit and noncash exchange helped some farmers expand their herds.[43]

As the livestock trade increased, a shift in farming strategies began to take place. Whereas in the late eighteenth century both Valley and hill towns had practiced mixed cropping with a view to undertaking all the functions of farming for themselves, by 1820 elements of specialization were emerging. In Hatfield, pastureland was diminishing, while in neighboring Williamsburg it was increasing. This was an example of a wider process. Valley farmers converted pastures to tillage and sought out new pastures for their cattle in the hills. Animals were driven from the Valley into the hills for the summer and returned each fall for winter feeding and fattening on the grain and hay grown in the Valley meadows. Before the spring drives back to the hills or to market in Boston,

42. Sylvester Judd made notes on his crops in Judd MS, "Book of Fragments," Apr 1818, May 1, 1819; general data is from Mass., General Court, Aggregates of Valuations, 1791, 1821, 1831.

43. Quotation from Judd, Sr., Receipt, Oct 5, 1789, Account Books; Judd MS, "Book of Fragments," Apr 1818. The *Republican Spy* (Northampton), Apr 1, 1806, referred to farmers who had obtained cows with credit advanced by Caleb Strong, against notes payable in produce.

farmers had collected manure in their barns to be spread on the fields prior to planting. Meanwhile, hill farmers supplemented their incomes by renting out pasture or by taking cattle onto their land at an agreed price per head for the summer. The manure that resulted would assist their own crops the following year. Both in Valley and hill towns the increase in cattle permitted greater production of cheese and butter. Indeed, one means of paying rent for pasturing cattle was to permit the owner of the pasture to take all or part of the cheese produced from any cows milked during their stay.[44]

Improving land and establishing this cattle-crop cycle were the most important parts of the new strategies, but farmers also found other ways of increasing output. Especially in upland areas favorable to orchards, cider making became an important side activity. Several farms in the southern part of Westhampton, for example, had cider presses and stills in the early nineteenth century; cider brandy became a common feature of local exchange. As grain surpluses increased, so did distilling, although it was usually done on a larger scale by a few manufacturers. By the mid-1820s there were at least two distilleries in the southern part of Amherst or adjacent Hadley. An article in the *New England Farmer* noted that throughout the Valley in Massachusetts "rye is extensively cultivated, and after supplying the inhabitants, a large surplus is left for the distilleries or exportation." It estimated that as much as 100,000 bushels were consumed by distilleries in Granby, South Hadley, Westfield, and other towns.[45]

On the fertile lands of the river meadows, meanwhile, especially in Hadley, an increasing number of farmers were growing small plots of broomcorn, to supply farmers and workshop producers who manufactured brooms during the slack winter months. This was a gradual adaptation by white farmers of techniques originally used by nonwhites. Corn brooms had originally been made by native Americans, some of whom remained to peddle them around the Valley at the end of the eighteenth century. There is evidence that in the late 1790s small patches of broomcorn were raised by two black farmers in Hadley, but credit for the adoption and expansion of broomcorn raising and cornbroom making was left to a white man, Levi Dickinson, who with his son gradually built a regular export trade in brooms during the first decade of the nineteenth century. Other farmers started to follow suit, producing broomcorn either to manufacture into brooms themselves or to sell to established makers, such as the Dickinsons.[46]

44. E.g., agreements between Dan Huntington, Hadley, and upland farmers, loose papers in PPHH.
45. *New England Farmer*, Dec 8, 1826.
46. Judd MS, "Hadley," 3:13, reprinted in *SPJM*, pp. 390–391.

Farmers and Markets

Together, the improvements in farm output increased the volume of goods traded out of the region between the 1790s and the 1820s, giving many households contacts in distant markets they had not had before. As Winifred Rothenberg has shown, journeys to carry goods and make exchanges became more frequent and, as information spread more rapidly through the countryside, prices for staple goods converged. Farmers' incomes from the sales of goods became more important for settling debts or acquiring new property. They complained of "hard times" when prices fell.[47] But this engagement with wider markets did not itself make rural producers "market oriented": the engagement took place on terms largely set by rural people themselves, within the household economic structure. When farmers traded more of their produce outside the region, their chief purpose was not to engage in the market economy but to satisfy the demands placed on them by the household economy. Stronger markets indeed resulted from their actions, but they were the unintentional result, not the cause, of farmers' economic decisions. What arose in this period was not a rural "market" economy but an extension of subsistence-surplus production.

All the new strategies that I have described took place with reference to local conditions or involved products that had local, as well as distant, uses. Certainly, some large farmers sought new crops that they could produce for cash sale. A few experimented with hemp during the 1812 war period. Some tried to raise teasels for sale to wool carders. But none of these schemes was widely successful.[48] The Valley remained what it had been in the late eighteenth century—a region without a staple export crop. This had disadvantages, to be sure. Farmers who wanted to escape from the burdens and obligations of local credit networks and noncash payment found few ready sources of cash to enable them to do so. But it also helped sustain the region's independence and enabled the local economy to become denser and more diversified.

Farmers continued to raise all the essential items they could. Hannah Dickinson wrote in 1813 that "Amherst produces almost all the necessary articles of food." People satisfied their own needs before sending goods off to sell. Eli Cooley, a prosperous Deerfield farmer, who received a Massachusetts Agricultural Society prize, or "premium," for hogs he shipped to market in 1815, had raised eight animals—an un-

---

47. Rothenberg, "The Market and Massachusetts Farmers" passim; in "Markets and Massachusetts Farmers" (1985), pp. 60, 64, however, Rothenberg notes that the process of price convergence occurred later in western Massachusetts than in the eastern part of the state.

48. See, e.g., Joseph Williams, Account Books, WHS.

usually large number—and kept two back for his own family before sending the other six to Boston.[49] Before the 1820s the region did not depend to any significant extent on imports of produce that could be raised locally. Farmers' and merchants' accounts confirm this. Amasa Wells's accounts with the Hatfield traders Fields and Dickinson show that he often purchased groceries such as spices, sugar, tea, coffee, rum, raisins, and codfish from the store, but only rarely items like butter, corn, or cheese. These, indeed, would have been local produce that the storekeepers had accepted in exchange for other goods. Expecting a prosperous year at his Westhampton store in 1815, Sylvester Judd, Jr., stocked it with 146 types of goods, not one of which was a basic food item or of a type that was also locally produced.[50] The goods most rural households purchased from stores continued to be either essentials not produced in the region or "luxury" items. They did not depend on the "market" for their livelihoods. Purchase of sugar, tea, and other imports depended on families' means. A prosperous farmer like William Boltwood made quite frequent purchases of this sort, but those in tighter circumstances could not. The credit columns of Solomon Wright's ledger, for example, mainly feature necessities obtained from neighbors. He did not have the surpluses to trade for imported goods.[51]

Moreover, farmers usually raised products with several potential uses. Foodstuffs could be eaten at home, exchanged in the neighborhood, sold at the store, or shipped to market. Grain could be directed to human or animal consumption. By-products such as tallow had household uses, while hides could go for shoes, harnesses, or a variety of other leather goods. Much of the expansion of agricultural production that occurred up to 1820 was in crops that had long been grown in the region. The two chief innovations, sheep and broomcorn, succeeded because they met the test of multiple function. Sheep could supply wool or meat. Broomcorn, though principally intended for its brush, could be allowed to run to seed and the seed used for cattle feed. Farmers remained wary of producing things that committed them in advance to a particular course of action. The Valley's mixed agriculture contrasted with staple crop regions, where production was geared to distant sale.

Goods that did go to market were of a type that had more than one role in the local economy too. Rye was used at home, swapped with neighbors, and sold at a distance, but it also went to supply local distilleries. Indeed, the *New England Farmer* suggested in 1826 that it

---

49. Hannah Dickinson, "Geography of the Town of Amherst," (Westfield Academy, 1813), BCJL; Cooley's premium was reported in *Massachusetts Agricultural Repository* 3 (1815). 377–378, and *Hampshire Gazette*, Jul 12, 1815.
50. Judd MS, "Book of Fragments," entry for Apr 1815.
51. William Boltwood, Account Book; Solomon Wright, Account Book.

was the distilleries, rather than distant urban markets, that had the most powerful influence on the price of rye in the Valley.[52] Fattened cattle had often circulated to hill and valley farms, contributed their manure to barnyards and grasslands, and played a role in households' summer and winter work before they were driven off to market elsewhere. Broomcorn went through the hands of local broom makers before leaving the region. In other words, unlike many traditional staple crops, these products made several contributions to the local economy and helped reinforce it.

The strategy of seeing to family and local needs first before shipping off surpluses had several consequences. It helps explain the increase in Massachusetts farm prices that took place between 1795 and 1815. Urban populations grew more rapidly than rural producers were prepared to supply them with food. Even though rural production was expanding in the same period, rural households' concentration on their own needs left them unwilling or unable to match supply to demand. The creation of national markets for foodstuffs shipped between eastern port cities in this period was partially a result of these constraints on supply.[53]

When farmers did ship goods, though, they often prompted complaints about the low quality, poor packing, and uneven quantities of the produce they supplied. This, too, reflected the low priority many households accorded the task. Quite apart from the temptation to cut corners or give short measure on goods that would end up in the hands of strangers, the goods households sent to market were often literally "surplus," things for which they had no other use. In 1826 the *New England Farmer* urged farmers to regard it as an axiom that they send their best grain to market, not their poorest, because "it is only in dear and scarce seasons that there is a demand for grain of an inferior quality." Two years before this a Greenfield newspaper had criticized the poor standard of butter shipments from Valley farms, suggesting improvements that precisely reflected the problems of shipping "surpluses." The paper claimed that too much butter had inadequate salt in it to prevent spoilage and ended up being sold for soap grease at minimal prices. Butter was rarely packed properly. To sell in the best market, it should be in kegs, the paper advised, not in "tubs, barrels, boxes, &c" or, worse still, sold in "lumps" to traders. The writer regarded these practices as the result of carelessness, but they were probably more than that. Although he warned that buyers "will not eat our rancid Butter," many families with small surpluses to trade proba-

---

52. *New England Farmer*, Dec 8, 1826.
53. For price movements, see Winifred B. Rothenberg, "A Price Index for Rural Massachusetts," *Journal of Economic History* 39 (1979): 975–1001.

bly had no choice but to consign it in small quantities and odd sizes, or to send larger amounts packed in layers over a period of time, so that the quality was uneven.[54]

Household Strategies and Productivity

Closer examination of farmers' reasons for increasing production reveals the importance of household concerns and strategies in creating surpluses. New farming strategies developed firmly within the context of the household system. Households retained control of production and tried to make it serve their needs. Preserving independence and providing for offspring were the motives that impelled many of them. Other facets of the system, including local exchange and the rituals of "neighborhood," also continued to play an important role.

Cooperation and "swapping" goods and labor continued. Some farmers took their teams and plows onto each other's land to help out with "spring and fall work." In Hadley, according to Sylvester Judd's later interviews with elderly residents, it was common for two or three families to join together and take turns to make cheese. When William Bliss, a carpenter of Northampton, failed in business and went insane in 1816, a cousin saw to the cultivation of the land left in his wife's hands: "He did the sowing and planting," Bliss's son remembered, "without any charge, except a return for this service in the help given on his own farm by [my brother] and myself."[55] Women organized sewing and quilting bees. Slacker seasons were punctuated by corn huskings, cider making, maple-sugaring parties, and other functions that combined production with neighborly sociability. Days were appointed for the collection and presentation of the minister's wood, for which the minister would provide flip or other drinks in return. Barn or house raisings, or the framing and raising of public buildings such as meetinghouses, were similarly occasions for public drinking at the owner's expense. Sylvester Judd, Jr., reckoned that "Rum Brandy and Sugar" for the raising of his barn in June 1814 cost him thirteen dollars, while the wood house and shed he had raised the following month cost him only two dollars in grog.[56]

54. *New England Farmer*, Sept 1, 1826; *Greenfield Herald and Public Advertiser*, May 25, 1824.

55. Judd MS, "Hadley," 3:15; Theodore Bliss, *Theodore Bliss, Publisher and Bookseller: A Study of Character and Life in the Middle Period of the Nineteenth Century*, ed. Arthur A. Bliss (Northampton, 1941), pp. 6–7.

56. Sylvester Judd, *History of Hadley, including the Early History of Hatfield, South Hadley, Amherst, and Granby, Mass.* (Northampton, 1863), p. 339; Judd MS, "Book of Fragments," June and July 1814.

Even as livestock production increased, neighborly or cooperative practices continued to be associated with it. As noted earlier, towns permitted animals to browse in highways and common fields well beyond this period. At least until 1827, the Hatfield town meeting voted every year to "provide Bulls for the use of the Town." Animals and their meat were a focus for the kind of friendly rivalry the economic historian William N. Parker called "individualistic-neighborliness." Sylvester Judd recalled that "when a man killed an animal, he sold some, and he lent some to his neighbors, who made a return when they killed." Theodore Bliss wrote of the "ardor and zeal" with which Northampton people vied with each other "in having the fattest pigs in the neighborhood," but that when the animals were finally slaughtered the meat was shared out. Even buying cattle for the fattening stall provided occasions for neighbors to restrain someone quietly trying to get ahead: "it was considered a fair game and a good joke for one to cut in and buy upon the sly a pair of oxen which a slower neighbor had spotted and was leisurely trying to get at a bargain."[57]

But competition between neighbors was real enough. Family concerns, not cooperative ones, primarily determined households' strategies and led in the early nineteenth century to increased farm output. Inevitably, pursuit of these concerns caused strains between families and neighbors. Hannah Dickinson wrote of her Amherst townsfolk in 1813 that they "are generally avaricious; they want to get as much property as they can; they are generally honest, but tight in their dealings."[58] When households sought to increase their output, it was often to fulfill their immediate needs or to assist in providing for their children. In the context of population growth and scarce, unequally distributed land, new strategies caused friction not only between families but within them as well.

The need to provide for their children's future strongly influenced farmers' decisions about production. When Simeon Cowles began farming in the 1790s he had enough land to put him in the top quintile of Amherst's taxpayers. But as his nine children were born, he felt the need to extend and improve his land in order to provide for them as best he could. Using surpluses from his annual production to obtain materials or credit from neighbors, he bought extra land and devoted time and labor to clearing and fencing what he owned. In fifteen years, from 1798 to 1813, he later claimed, he raised the value of his holdings from $1,300 to over $6,000. By the mid-1820s, having passed one-sixth of his property to his eldest son, he was still seeking to obtain land in the hope

57. Hatfield, Town Meeting Records, 1:453, 2:150; Bliss, *Theodore Bliss*, p. 12; Sheldon, "Stall-Fed Ox," p. 481; William N. Parker, "From Northwest to Midwest: Social Bases of a Regional History," in *Essays in Nineteenth-Century Economic History: The Old Northwest*, ed. David C. Klingaman and Richard K. Vedder (Athens, Ohio, 1975), p. 16.
58. Dickinson, "Geography of the Town of Amherst."

of settling the rest of his children before he died. One of his sources of income was the proceeds of the timber he stripped from the land he was clearing.[59]

Family life cycles and concern to accumulate means for children made an even clearer impression on the activities of Cowles's fellow townsman William Boltwood. Having established himself on the land acquired from his brother seven years before, Boltwood initiated in 1796 a twenty-year process of accumulating property. He traded produce with his neighbors to obtain labor and other services to help him work it and sold surpluses to raise the means to buy more land. Having started in 1789 with forty-four acres, of which fourteen were improved, he had acquired another sixteen acres by 1800 and expanded his improved holdings to twenty-two acres. By this time he and his wife had five children, and he was seeking ways to provide for them. He did not use his extra land to grow more grain but kept his output at fifty bushels a year. Instead, as we have seen, he grew flax for household use or local exchange. He added to his cattle, possibly supplementing their feed with surplus flaxseed, and traded meat with local families for work, with storekeepers for imported goods, and with two local physicians for cash. Between 1800 and 1810 he continued to trade in land, so that by the latter year he owned ninety-three acres, seventy-two of which were unimproved.

As his children grew up, Boltwood's strategies shifted and he stopped acquiring land. From 1809 on he turned his attention to providing for them from the resources he had accumulated. He gave a dowry to a daughter who married that year, sent his son Lucius to Dartmouth College in 1810, and when a second daughter married in 1813, gave her furniture and household goods worth $180. Boltwood appears to have paid for these partly from small sales of land, but also from farm income and extra work he did on other farms, at carting, at providing draft animals, lumber, and other construction materials. After this another task arose. His son William, Jr., born in 1802, was reaching the age when he could work, and Boltwood intended to provide him with his own farm in due course. Accordingly, he again changed direction and, using his own, his son's, and hired labor, cleared some of the unimproved land he had bought before 1810. By 1820, Boltwood was taxed on twenty-five more improved acres than he had been before. By 1830, William Boltwood, Jr., now married and with two daughters, was settled on a small farm near his father's.[60]

59. Simeon Cowles to Moses Eli Cowles, Amherst, Feb 2, 1826, NHS, A.L. 18.90.
60. William Boltwood, Account Book; Amherst, Tax Valuation Lists, 1790–1820. William Boltwood, Jr., is listed in U.S. Fifth Census, 1830, Population Schedules for Hampshire County, MCFL. David F. Weiman discusses life-cycle effects in "Families, Farms, and Rural Society in Pre-Industrial America," *Research in Economic History* 10 (1988), supplement.

The Boltwoods' activities had varied according to their family life cycle. The different stages, of acquiring, clearing, and disbursing property, made different contributions to the wider economy. As Boltwood purchased and swapped land between 1796 and 1810, he helped generate a local land market, but after that he withdrew from it. Providing for dowries and his son's education led him to increase his production for local and distant sale. Clearing land for his younger son increased his demand for local labor and absorbed farm produce to pay for it. Similar patterns of accumulation and production can be traced in other families. In 1794 and 1798 the farmer Nathaniel Goodale acquired two parcels of land in Belchertown, totaling 75 acres, for between eight and ten dollars per acre. In 1799 he gave half of this land to his son Moses for use as a farm. When Moses in his turn had sons to provide for, he also sought more land. But the market for it had become tighter in the course of a generation and Moses' means were not as great as his father's. Even though he acquired marginal land, for as little as four dollars an acre, it took him the fourteen years from 1815 to 1829 to accumulate 22.8 acres, some of which he passed to his son Asahel in the early 1830s.[61]

Misfortune could thwart such attempts to acquire or work land. Asa Dickinson, the son of one of Amherst's early settlers, possessed ninety acres of land, including fourteen improved, by the time of his father's death in 1796. Six years later, however, he was apparently heavily in debt and lost most of his property. In 1802 he borrowed from a more prosperous neighbor, Jonathan Dickinson (a distant relative), and had to sign an agreement that permitted him to stay on his own farm for one year, but no longer, required him to board his creditor's laborers if necessary, and obliged him to feed his cow and horse on Jonathan Dickinson's hay—in other words to buy hay only from him. From these humiliating terms, Asa Dickinson slowly recovered by renting small plots of land and running a store or tavern, until he had once again accumulated land to pass to his own son. But he never obtained as much land as he had lost. At their peak, his holdings reached fifty acres.[62]

Farming had helped get Asa Dickinson in debt, and he turned to other activities to help get out of it. Sylvester Judd in Westhampton was doing the reverse. His attempts to succeed as a farmer between 1817 and 1820 were part of his effort to pay off the debts he had incurred in storekeeping as a result of the slump of 1815, debts that had been compounded in the disastrous summer of 1816 by financial difficulties

---

61. Deeds in M. W. Goodell Collection, BCJL.
62. Asa Dickinson, Account Books; Amherst, Tax Valuation Lists, 1800–1820; John Dickinson to Asa Dickinson, Purchase Agreement, Apr 6, 1802, BCJL.

in building a new Westhampton meetinghouse for which Judd had responsibility as a town officer. Judd read the agricultural press and set out to be a model farmer, determining to plant seven crops, to drill seeds, and to introduce new grasses. In 1818 he wrote that he intended to raise no fewer than twenty-eight different species of grass, herb, vegetable, and grain crop. He also listed eighteen different materials that could be used as manure, including old hair, old potash, mud, and leather. But it was the proper application of animal dung that led him to claim a doubling of his hay output within three years. Still, Judd could not pay his debts off and he passed the farm back to his father. But the purpose behind his efforts had been clear. Like many other farmers he attempted to produce more to clear himself from debt. This may have made him more conscious than most farmers of the need to reckon costs. He calculated that the twenty-four cattle he sent to market in 1818 earned him $311. But figuring that they had cost him "say $400" he decided to cut back. The next year he raised only four or five animals, but still calculated that he had lost $17.85 on them after they had gone to market. This reckoning, in turn, helped him decide to give up farming and seek another livelihood.[63]

Inheritance also played a part in determining patterns of accumulation and production. As land became scarce and resources dwindled, families were faced with the complex decision whether to persist with the patterns of partible inheritance that had been traditional in New England, or to adopt some form of impartibility that would preserve farms and maintain at least one child at a standard comparable with that of the parents. Few seem to have been willing to take the latter course. Of twenty-nine wills probated in the six towns between 1800 and 1803, only six devised land to one son when there was another son surviving. More than two-thirds of the wills provided for a division of land between two or more heirs.[64] As Toby Ditz has suggested in a recent study of inheritance in Connecticut, concern to create new household units for children dominated many families' calculations. Even when parents used what Ditz calls "preferential partibility"—dividing estates unequally so that a substantial share passed to one heir—they often imposed heavy obligations on the favored child to assist parents and siblings. Favored heirs used mortgages to provide payments to siblings not granted land, or were required to give support to their parents and their minor or unmarried brothers and sisters. Others might receive property that they had to hold in common with relatives.[65]

63. Judd MS, "Book of Fragments," 1818–1819.
64. Hampshire County, Probate Records, vols. 21–23.
65. Toby L. Ditz, *Property and Kinship: Inheritance in Early Connecticut, 1750–1820* (Princeton, 1986), esp. pp. 158–160.

Inevitably, this affected the terms on which they could run their farms. When Benjamin Wait, a Northampton farmer, died in 1800 he was not a poor man, having twenty-three acres of land in a town where one-third of the men had none, but he only owned a quarter share of a house and one-fifth of a barn. His patrimony had been one acre of land and the share in the barn. He had accumulated the rest himself. But he was insolvent when he died, and part of his property had to be sold to pay his debts, so his own offspring were in as tight a position as he had been.[66] Even prosperous families found that the process of dividing estates to provide for children eroded their position in the long run. William Bartlett was one of Westhampton's wealthiest farmers after he settled there in the 1760s. His sons, who shared his property between them, ranked in the bottom of the first quartile of property owners by 1810. Their sons in turn, though mostly able to retain their relative position, were from the 1820s onward obliged to do more work for other people than their grandfather had done.[67]

Scholars have accorded differing weights to the tendencies in the early-nineteenth-century farm economy discussed here. Winifred Rothenberg has emphasized the creation of markets and the expansion of trade in produce for sale. Toby Ditz has stressed the use of inheritance practices to maintain the viability of households. In addition, Nancy Folbre has called attention to the conflicts within households that occurred as fathers attempted to maintain their patriarchal authority. Using their power to confer land, many fathers sought to influence the terms on which their sons would set out to make livings. Often, particularly when they had relatively little property to hand out, they failed, and their sons took their own courses of action.[68] But these aspects of rural life all related to a single point—families' attempt to maintain the household system of production in a period of dwindling land resources and greater inequality.

Fathers such as William Boltwood and Nathaniel Goodale entered the land market in order to make up for their own shortages of land, as part of a strategy to maintain control over their children. In these cases, the strategy worked, but when Moses Goodale attempted to use it for his own sons, it was less successful. Simeon Cowles was to find, with more bitterness, that enlisting his children's help to provide means for one another would not prevent some of them distancing themselves from his control when they had received their own shares. But into the 1820s

66. Benjamin Wait, Will, Hampshire County, Probate Records, 21:75v.
67. William and Solomon Bartlett, Account Books, 2 vols., Westhampton, 1704–1857, HBS, Westhampton, Tax Valuation Lists, 1810, 1855.
68. Rothenberg, "Emergence of Farm Labor Markets," p. 561; Ditz, *Property and Kinship*, p. 83; Nancy R. Folbre, "The Wealth of Patriarchs: Deerfield, Massachusetts, 1760–1840," *Journal of Interdisciplinary History* 16 (Autumn 1985): 199–220.

at least, the attempt to maintain the household system was the dominant factor in the patterns of farm production. Contact with the world beyond the Valley was made for purposes and on terms dictated from within it.

The tendency of farmers to give family needs priority over production for market infuriated some gentlemen farmers whose larger resources permitted them ambitions greater than most. One suggested in 1816 that this was why Massachusetts farming practices compared unfavorably with those in Great Britain. Rejecting the common argument that British agriculture was more efficient because labor was cheaper than in New England, he concluded that the difference lay in "the greater capital employed by the British farmer, a superior spirit of enterprize, and the convenience of more ready markets." The fault for this, he asserted, lay with "our farmers": "How can they ever accumulate capital, if they limit their labour to the raising barely enough to keep their cattle through the year, and to the disposal of a surplus barely sufficient to pay their taxes, and supply them with a few foreign commodities?" Although farmers were in fact clearing land, adding to their acreages and increasing output, this writer did not regard the purposes for which they did it as significant.[69] Two years later, however, the founders of the Hampshire, Franklin, and Hampden Agricultural Society expressed those purposes succinctly: "While our citizens are mutually dependent upon each other, they may be wholly independent of every other portion of the country, in respect of the produce of the soil and the great articles of family consumption." In their view "the encouragement and improvement of Agriculture and Manufactures" was congruent with household production and local exchange.[70]

Rural Manufactures

As farm output increased between 1790 and 1820, so did manufactures. In the late colonial period manufacturing in rural Massachusetts had been largely confined to household production, to essential craft occupations, such as blacksmithing and shoemaking, and to the skilled crafts conducted in the larger village centers, largely for members of the elite, by carpenters, joiners, and a handful of silver makers and pewterers. By the early nineteenth century, though, manufactures had become more common, more varied, and more widely diffused geographically.

69. "Analysis or Examination of the Present State of Agriculture in Massachusetts," *Massachusetts Agricultural Repository* 4 (1816): 284.
70. Hampshire, Franklin, and Hampden Agricultural Society, Circular, Jan 2, 1818, Broadside Collection, FL.

In 1810, farmhouses, country workshops, artisans' shops in the towns, tanneries, and small mills were producing an impressive flow of goods. Hampshire County was producing yarn and cloth of several kinds, including 60,000 yards of linen and over one million yards of other cloth, as well as silk, fur hats, bar iron, nails, clocks, gold and silver work, tinplate goods, tanned hides, sole leather, boots, shoes, saddles and harnesses, sweet and distilled cider, gin, furniture, paper, rope, brooms, combs, straw bonnets, gunpowder, potash, whips, carriages, wagons, and woodenware.[71] By 1820 just over 30 percent of Northampton's household heads described themselves to the census takers as primarily engaged in manufacturing. The proportions in other towns were not as high, but they were significant—nearly 26 percent in Amherst, 17 percent in Hadley, and 15.3 percent and 12.3 percent, respectively, in Williamsburg and Westhampton. Even Hatfield, always the most "agricultural" of towns, counted over 8 percent of its householders as manufacturers.[72] So while Northampton retained its local preeminence, manufacturing spread widely in the countryside too, for reasons similar to those for the expansion in farming. Manufacturing was largely an outgrowth of the household system.

Since most families had insufficient land to settle more than one or two of their sons in farming, many young men and women faced the prospect of finding alternative occupations. Some migrated, but as we have seen, they were a minority. Young men from families with sufficient means, such as Lucius M. Boltwood, secured a college education. Others sought clerkships in stores or training from lawyers or physicians. Samuel Shaw of Plainfield, who in 1807 suffered typhoid fever attributed to "overwork on the farm," determined to seek a professional career, worked for two summers as clerk in a store, served as a teacher in several towns for a period, and then apprenticed himself to the Cummington physician Peter Bryant.[73]

However, for people staying in the Valley who could not depend on farming, manufacture of some kind was the most common occupation. Boys and girls were apprenticed to craft trades, or adopted manufactures later as part of their own household strategies. It was another channel for energies constricted by the scarcity of land. Joseph Kingsley

71. U.S. Treasury Department, *A Statement of the Arts and Manufactures of the United States of America for the Year 1810* (Philadelphia, 1813). The discussion of manufacturing that follows accords with James A. Henretta, "The War for Independence and American Economic Development," in *The Economy of Early America: The Revolutionary Period, 1763–1790*, ed. Ronald Hoffman, et al. (Charlottesville, Va., 1988), p. 45–87, which became available after this chapter was written.

72. U.S. Fourth Census, 1820, Massachusetts.

73. Clara E. Hudson, *Plain Tales from Plainfield, or the Way Things Used to Be* (Northampton, 1962), p. 49.

of Westhampton had ten children in the 1770s and 1780s. By 1809 he had decided to pass his farm to his fourth surviving son, now twenty-four, who stayed at home to look after his aging father. Even though some of his brothers received land of their own, they undertook small amounts of manufacturing in addition to farming.[74]

In March 1788 the *Hampshire Gazette* printed an extract from the famous description of pin making in Adam Smith's *The Wealth of Nations*, which the editor commended to readers as a clear exposition of "the Advantages of the Division of Labour." But in the very next column there also appeared, as part of the paper's campaign for ratification of the Federal constitution, the verses of "The Raising: A New Song for Federal Mechanics":

> Come muster, my lads, your mechanical tools,
> Your saws and your axes, your hammers and rules;
> Bring your mallets and planes, your level and line,
> And plenty of pins of American pine;
> *For our roof we will raise, and our song still shall be—*
> *A government firm, and our citizens free.*[75]

The metaphor of the "raising" had strong meaning in a culture that stressed neighborly cooperation. Its juxtaposition with Smith's description of an opposite concept pointed to a tension between the possible ways of organizing production that was to underlie the development of rural manufacture over the next few decades. But the primary assumption was that the household system would form the basis of it. Households' preoccupations and priorities shaped manufacture as they did farming, and were to restrain the growth of large, subdivided manufacturing processes before the 1820s.

Patterns of Household Production

Until the 1820s most rural manufacture was in the direct control of households. Four different patterns of organization were discernible: independent household manufacturing proper; itinerant production; exchange production; and craft manufacture. These distinctions are conceptual as much as real, because the four overlapped with each other and were often mutually interdependent. A fifth form of production, in custom mills of various kinds, usually involved more invest-

74. Wright, "Westhampton Local History," 1:97–98.
75. *Hampshire Gazette,* Mar 5, 1788, reprinted from *Pennsylvania Gazette,* Feb 6, 1788: see Philip S. Foner, *American Labor Songs of the Nineteenth Century* (Urbana, Ill., 1975), p. 5.

ment than a single household could muster. But the work of these mills in the early nineteenth century was very closely linked to the activities of household producers.

Independent production proper, conducted within households with family labor, "on their own account" was roughly divisible into men's and women's occupations. Household textile and clothes making, by far the most important activity, represented a seasonal burden of work on top of women's regular household tasks. Hannah Dickinson wrote of Amherst in 1813 that "almost every family . . . manufactures clothing for its own use, and some of them manufacture for other people." While cloth imported into the region was growing in importance at the end of the eighteenth century, many farm families continued to make their own or acquire it locally. Arethusa Hall, describing a hill town girlhood in the 1810s, recalled that "all the clothing of the family was home-made, in the strictest sense, the wool and flax being raised up on the farm, and the carding, spinning, dyeing and weaving all being done by the household."[76] Inventories taken between 1800 and 1803 show that a considerable proportion of households, regardless of wealth, possessed some tools for textile manufacture. Of twenty-nine inventories, thirteen (44.8 percent) listed at least one spinning wheel, eight (27.6 percent) listed wheels and looms, one (3.4 percent) listed a loom only, and only seven (24.1 percent) contained no reference to either. So nearly three-quarters of these families could have made yarn, and one-third their own cloth as well.[77] As trade was disrupted by the embargo and War of 1812, household textile production probably increased. Hampshire County's annual production of linens, wool, and other cloths was valued at an average of $7.87 per capita in 1810. This was the highest of any Massachusetts county and the eleventh highest of the fifty counties in New England. Most of this output was produced at home.[78]

Premiums offered by the Hampshire, Franklin, and Hampden Agricultural Society for the best "household manufactures" show that output was varied, even in the early 1820s. The categories for 1821 included "blue woven cloth," cassimere, flannel for fulling, dressed flannel, "wove carpeting," stair carpeting, hearth rug, cotton counterpane, stockings, mittens and gloves, linen sheeting, shirting and diaper, cassimere shawl, and blankets.[79] Virtually all spinning and a good deal of

76. Dickinson, "Geography of the Town of Amherst"; [Arethusa Hall], "Sathurea: The Story of a Life," p. 9, Judd Papers, 55M-1, Box 2, HCL.

77. Hampshire County, Probate Records, vol. 22.

78. Rolla Milton Tryon, *Household Manufactures in the United States, 1640–1860* (Chicago, 1917), p. 170, tab. 12.

79. Handbill, Northampton Cattle Show, 1821, NHS; Hampshire, Franklin, and Hampden Agricultural Society, Certificates of Premium, 1821, 1824, MCFL, Oversize Files.

household weaving was carried out by women, who would do the work in "stints" along with other tasks or set daughters old enough for it to work for longer periods. The Amherst farmer Henry J. Franklin provided in his will in 1800 that his two daughters should receive fifteen pounds of wool and "40 weight" of flax each year until they married.[80] Processing home-produced flax and wool or imported cotton involved considerable work. A Hadley woman recalled that spinning flax often began on the Monday after Thanksgiving and could last until May; many families, she said, "cooked so much for Thanksgiving that they might have the winter to work in." Wool, on the other hand, was spun in the summer, after sheep were sheared each June. Olive Cleveland Clark later claimed that "when she was young every girl in Northampton used to spin," then qualified this, recalling that there were exceptions among the town's "ladies." Farm women were contemptuous of others who had not been trained to "work." In Williamsburg it was said that Rev. Joseph Strong had taught his own daughters to spin because "his wife was brought up a lady and did not know how to."[81]

Men often used independent manufacture to even out the seasonal irregularities of farming. Winter employment producing brooms, tools, and other woodenware, or boots and shoes for home use or exchange, became increasingly common. Thomas Cole of Northampton spent part of his time making tools or pump handles after 1800. Caleb Cook of Hadley worked two days in a neighbor's plane shop one winter but mostly worked for himself, making furniture, kitchen utensils, a clock case, parts for sleighs and wagons, broom scrapers and broom racks, seed harrows, and hayracks. This was custom work, done intermittently when required. But some farmers extended such activities into full-time craft production. After 1810, Eli Dickinson began making wooden faucets in a shop on his South Amherst farm, assisted by three young sons, who worked when they were not attending school.[82]

Itinerant workers frequently assisted with household work, or completed it. While William Boltwood's children were young he hired two local women to come to his house to spin and weave cloth for the family, only ceasing this around 1803 when his elder daughter became old enough to do some of this work herself.[83] Weavers and shoemakers traveled from house to house doing custom work, "whipping the cat" as it was known. Tailors, seamstresses, and dressmakers, such as Re-

80. Henry J. Franklin, Will, Hampshire County, Probate Records, 21:157.
81. Judd MS, "Miscellaneous," 19:344; Judd MS, "Northampton," 1:326; "Recollections of Olive Cleveland Clark," p. 57.
82. Caleb Cook, Account Book; on Dickinson, see Edward W. Carpenter and Charles F. Morehouse, *The History of the Town of Amherst, Massachusetts* (Amherst, 1896), p. 303.
83. William Boltwood, Account Book.

becca Dickinson of Hatfield in the 1780s and Rhoda Clark of North-
ampton in the early 1820s, also "boarded around," working for families.
For men and women who were often poor and single, it was an ill-paid
and precarious living. "My daily bread depends on my labour," wrote
Dickinson in 1787. "God has in great mercy this summer back given me
work[;] he heard my poor request and has sent imploy for my hands."
But two months after this she wrote, "This day I am out of employ. . . .
How hurried I was formerly at this season of the year." In 1822 Rhoda
Clark earned only two meals and 25 cents a day making men's and boys'
clothing in Northampton households.[84]

Because they were usually from property-owning households, manufacturers working on an exchange basis—swapping work or goods in
the neighborhood—were more secure than this. They fell into two
groups. The less prosperous were men like the Westhampton farmer-
shoemaker Elijah Norton, whose small property placed him ninety-fifth
out of 144 Westhampton taxpayers in 1810 and who "carried on his
farm, in part at least, by making shoes for his neighbors in return for
which they would work on his farm."[85] In Amherst, Chester Lamb did
the same thing, interspersing his shoemaking with day work on other
farms too. The Hadley woodworker Joseph Marsh did day work on
farms in exchange for assistance in his shop. Women's work also entered these exchange relationships. Among the men Marsh swapped
work with was the carpenter Caleb Cook, who, in addition to trading
his own custom work in the neighborhood, entered in his accounts
large amounts of weaving done by his wife or another member of his
family. Asa Dickinson too, struggling out of debt in Amherst after 1802,
entered weaving in his book, but the fact that it began to appear only
after his marriage suggests that it was his wife's work. Occasionally, a
woman such as Submit Williams, married to a Williamsburg farmer,
would sign her own name to work she had exchanged, in her case
making clothes for various neighbors and their servants.[86]

Larger farmers also used their property and credit to build up manufactures for local exchange. Joseph Kingsley, ranked eleventh in the
Westhampton tax list of 1810, established himself as a tanner and shoemaker, taking small batches of hides from surrounding farms. Two of
Kingsley's sons were among the Westhampton farmers who set up
cider mills to process their own and neighbors' fruit for local consump-

84. Rebecca Dickinson, Diary Extracts, Sept 5, Nov 23, 1787; Judd MS, "Miscellaneous," 14:246. Hiring labor for production is discussed in Faye E. Dudden, *Serving
Women: Household Service in Nineteenth-Century America* (Middletown, Conn., 1983), pp.
12–14.
85. Wright, "Westhampton Local History," 1:68.
86. Caleb Cook, Account Book; Asa Dickinson, Account Book; Joseph Williams, Account Book, Williamsburg, c. 1802–1841, WHS.

tion. Such activities were often seasonal. They accompanied and depended on farming and its products but provided a means of enhancing
these particular farmers' positions in local exchange. Having cider to
exchange was literally a potent means of securing day labor.[87] The
extension of manufacturing by farmers and the expansion of livestock
raising in this period complemented one another. Newly cleared land
and larger numbers of livestock provided raw materials, in particular,
wood, wool, hides, and tallow. The lower labor demands of pastoral
farming, especially in the uplands where so many animals were pas-
tured, left more time for manufacturing activities in a family's schedule
of work.

Out of such exchange manufacturing grew craft production proper,
skilled work conducted full time in shops that might also employ journeymen and apprentices. Low levels of local demand and the intermittent pace of work made property ownership an advantage for craft
producers. About 85 percent of the craftsmen identifiable in the Northampton tax list of 1798 owned some land. One-quarter of these men
held twenty or more improved acres, which could have made adequate
farms for them. The majority, however, had been drawn to craft work
by their shortage of property. Just over half the Northampton craftsmen
owned ten acres or less.[88] With their propertyless neighbors, they were
encouraged to establish full-time manufacture. Families whose children
had no prospect of land for a patrimony sought out apprenticeships
with these craftsmen as the surest means left of securing a livelihood in
the Valley. Chairmaking in Northampton, metal tool making in Williamsburg, shoemakers, hatters, and wood turners in various towns
grew in number as the number of people obliged to leave the land
increased. Groups of artisans in neighborhoods began to provide work
for each other, applying a simple division of labor between shops and
supplying parts to other makers for final assembly into goods. At first
such work was done on a custom basis, but the scale of production
outran intermittent local demand. Increasingly, while seeking agreements with local producers to supply parts, craftsmen contracted with
Valley merchants or entrepreneurs in larger manufacturing towns to
take shipments of completed locally made goods for distant sale.

The unequal distribution of property pushed more and more artisans
into making a permanent living from their work. This expanded supplies of goods, but it also placed nominally independent craftsmen in
dependence on others. Working arrangements varied. Harris Beckwith,
a Northampton chairmaker, appears to have made occasional ex-

87. Wright, "Westhampton Local History," 1:147.
88. Northampton, Tax Assessment List, 1798.

changes with other craftsmen to carry on his business. From 1803 to 1806 he made a rocking chair and a little chair for Thomas Pomeroy, provided sashwork and other materials for Pomeroy's shop, and worked in it for half a day. Beckwith entered these items in his ledger and, when the two men settled accounts in 1806, took Pomeroy's note for the outstanding balance due him.[89] A lawsuit between two North-ampton cabinetmakers in 1803 reveals a more dependent relationship. Lewis Beals had contracted to complete furniture for David Judd. Judd advanced $116 worth of materials and also provided store credit on account while Beals was working for him. When Beals failed to fulfill the contract, Judd had his personal property attached. This included not only the materials for two sideboards, six tables, and a cherry stand, but Beals's tools, apron, and greatcoat.[90]

These four types of organization—independent, itinerant, exchange, and craft workshop—formed the basis on which much of the increase in rural manufacturing took place during the first quarter of the nineteenth century. Some trades, such as the broom making that grew up, mainly in Hadley, after 1800, straddled all four forms at once by the 1820s. Levi Dickinson and his son had begun production in a small shop built near their farmhouse. Many brooms continued to be made each winter by independent farmers who had grown their own broomcorn the previous season. Occasional itinerant workers may have assisted in their yard or attic workshops, but family labor would have been called upon too. Some farmers secured materials and tools for broom making by exchanging labor with neighbors, and a few larger producers began running workshops that employed several broom workers. Among these was John Shipman, a son-in-law of Levi Dickinson, whose broom workshops were to grow into the largest in Hadley in the 1830s and 1840s.[91]

The Local Bases of Manufacturing

While the social relations of manufactures varied and began to shift, these trades nonetheless shared common features. The bulk of the products listed in the 1810 census were made from local raw materials. Metalworking and some tanning were the chief trades based on imported materials, but they were less significant than the textiles and wooden products that made up most of the output. Local supplies, local

89. Harris Beckwith, Account Book, MCFL.
90. Judd v. Beals, Hampshire County Court of Common Pleas, Files, Aug 1803, no. 147, Massachusetts State Archives, Boston, Mass.
91. Judd MS, "Hadley," 3:186–187.

exchange networks, and the structure of the household-based economy helped determine the shape of this manufacturing system and made the costs of entry to it relatively low. Raw materials could be swapped for farm produce or family labor or could be secured on credit in the knowledge that, as with Harris Beckwith's accounts, local exchange practices would not necessarily demand rapid settlement and repayment.

Young men also took up manufacturing to augment income or occupy themselves while waiting for land. Ira Chaffee Goodale, son of the Belchertown farmer Moses Goodale, described how he used family resources, local contacts, and credit in 1824 to go temporarily into making one-horse wagons, so as to finance time to study in preparation for college. Working on his father's farm in exchange for board, he received shop space and the use of tools from a local toolmaker in return for working in the tool shop. On credit, he bought enough wood for four wagons and, working part time between May and November, made and assembled these wooden parts. After resuming his studies over the winter, Goodale again arranged to work on the farm during the 1825 season, borrowed money to pay for more materials, bargained locally to get the necessary blacksmiths' work and painting done on the four wagons, and expanded production to six wagons. His methods reveal both a close connection between family work, local exchange, and manufacturing and his use of wagonmaking to further his own career.[92]

The initial aim of most manufacturers was to supply customers in the neighborhood or surrounding region. From Hadley, Levi Dickinson, having made 100 brooms in 1798, "took them in a horsecart with some reeds and sold them in Williamsburg, Ashfield, Conway, etc." The Williamsburg blacksmiths who took up ax and edge-tool making about the same time also dealt at first on a relatively small scale within the region. Wagonmaking, which started in Amherst about 1805, was taken up by one or two makers each in Hadley, North Hadley, Hatfield, and Belchertown by about 1809.[93] Always the initial impulse seems to have been toward variety, to secure local patronage, rather than concentration or specialization. Both in the countryside and in village centers, this perception of manufacturing as a locally based activity was reflected in advertisements. A Northampton cabinetmaker, James Dunham, thanked customers for their assistance to him in overcoming debts in 1806. A decade later, the widow Olive Wright sought for her blue-dyeing business "the patronage of friends of the widow and the father-

92. Ira C. Goodale to Lafayette W. Goodale, New York, June 30, 1874, M. W. Goodell Collection, BCJL.
93. On wagonmaking, see Judd MS, "Hadley," 3:9.

less."[94] Advertisements for property in outlying towns stressed that manufacturers would be serving neighborhood needs. The *Hampshire Gazette* printed a notice in 1787 for "a very convenient and well-adapted piece of ground for pot-ash and tan-works, both of which are much wanted in this quarter," while a house for sale in Worthington in 1794 was described as "where the Clothier's business has been carried on for some years, and it is where one is much wanted." Two advertisements in 1816 used the same language. In Westhampton, one announced, "a Hatter or Edge-tool workman would find great encouragement," while in Hatfield, the other stated, "a good Clothier would have a large run of custom, and be punctually paid by his employers."[95]

Two reasons, though, led some manufacturers to attempt to make more distant sales. Selling goods at a distance could bring in cash or exchange goods not available locally, and so provide means to pay off debts. When Seth Nims set off from his parents' home in Conway to travel to Georgia in the winter of 1822–23, they gave him cloth to sell in the hope that they could settle some pressing obligations. In May 1823, Nims's father wrote to ask about it: "we sent a pice of Cloth by you and we expected to receivd the mony for it this Spring for we are in great want of it if you have sold the cloth and got the money for it if you have any chance to convey the money with safty I should be very glad, if you could send forty or fifty dollers more you would ablige me very much and I would endever to make it out to you when you come home." His mother added a warning not to "let money carry your mind from things of more importance," but could not conceal her anxiety about their debts: "if you have an opportunity to send us the money for we are drove."[96]

Second, local demand, particularly for durable goods, quickly became saturated so that outlets had to be found elsewhere. Levi Dickinson rapidly found the saturation point with his Hadley broom business and started annual trips with his products to New London, Connecticut, and subsequently to Boston and Albany too. Eli Dickinson made similar journeys each year from Amherst to Baltimore, with faucets and pumps to sell.[97] Such manufacturers had to learn how to bargain in distant places, without the safeguards of local exchange, and to face the problems of dealing in a growing but fickle nationally based economy. These ventures had a speculative character at odds with the more cautious spirit of most household strategies.

Yet they were also rooted in these strategies. Broom and woodenware

94. *Hampshire Gazette*, Apr 12, 1815.
95. *Hampshire Gazette*, Aug 8, 1787; Mar 26, 1794; Mar 27 and May 1, 1816.
96. Israel Nims to Seth Nims, Conway, Mass., May 3, 1823, BCJL.
97. Carpenter and Morehouse, *History of Amherst*, p. 303.

makers not only continued to function on farms and to use local raw materials but depended on the household-based social structure for labor and for the opportunity to seek out distant buyers for their output. Journeys to sell brooms and pumps, such as those made by the Dickinsons in the 1800s and 1810s, represented an extraordinary investment of time and effort in relation to the value of the products they were carrying, and hence a low valuation on the time they took to sell goods. Men's absence from farms or workshops for weeks at a time was possible only because they traveled in slack seasons, or had other family members and neighbors available to do necessary tasks at home; this work back home by other members of their households effectively reduced the risks of such marketing journeys. These manufacturers did not commit their families' fortunes fully to the market, but made a calculated partial engagement with distant buyers.

While small producers were seeking distant buyers for their goods, larger ventures in local manufacturing were based on the provision of services to rural households. The water-powered gristmills and sawmills that had dotted the Connecticut River's tributaries since the colonial period had been the principal exceptions to the rule that manufacturing was located in households. Representing larger investments of capital than other activities, they were usually owned not by individual families but by partnerships. Many had been granted water privileges on condition that they would provide custom services to the locality. Although some operated on a "merchant" basis by the late eighteenth century, buying grain and wood for processing and sale on their own account, they continued to work as custom mills as well, charging a toll for processing materials brought them by local households. From the 1790s onward, new or existing proprietors installed carding and fulling machines at many sites to process wool and cloth for local spinners and weavers. While this represented a change in function, it did not initially change the organization or local relationships of milling, which continued to serve rather than supplant household production.[98]

By the time of the 1810 census, there were fifty-seven carding machines and sixty-seven fulling mills scattered throughout Hampshire County, almost one-third of the total number in Massachusetts. Most were owned by partnerships; all but one of the mills in Northampton in 1798 were held in one-third, one-quarter, one-fifth, or one-sixth shares by families who also owned farmland. Their operations were deeply embedded in local exchange practices. When Roger Wing set up a carding mill in Williamsburg in 1803, on land owned by the Bodman family, he agreed to pay his annual rent in carded wool. Most mills

98. On earlier mills, see Judd MS, "Northampton with Westfield," 2:60.

operated on a custom basis and relied on local demand for their services. A new carding mill in North Amherst drew customers from Hadley and elsewhere in 1804 and 1805, but when a mill opened in Hadley about 1806, families such as the Phelpses carried their wool to be carded there instead. By 1815 there were as many as four carding mills in Northampton, two in Williamsburg, one in Hadley, and one in Amherst. In addition, there were two fulling mills each in Northampton and Amherst and at least one each in Hadley, Hatfield, Westhampton, and Williamsburg.[99] Several of these millsites served different functions from season to season. Carding mills ran in the summer, after sheep shearing. The gristmill season peaked in the autumn and early winter, after harvest. Sawmills worked from early spring, after farmers had cleared land and brought lumber in for cutting while snow was on the ground. Fulling also took place in spring and early summer, as households sent in cloth that they had made during the winter to be dressed. Virtually all mills advertised their services in exchange for farm produce, as well as cash payment. The accounts of the farmer Joseph Williams, who owned a share of a mill in Williamsburg between 1808 and 1818, show that in addition to custom work the mill sold cloth on its own account to purchasers in Williamsburg, Hatfield, and Northampton, both for cash and for payment by goods in exchange.[100]

Together, the handicraft and custom-milling sectors deepened the exchange networks on which the household system rested. Much of the work of constructing and equipping manufacturers, from the simple workshops and tools required by hand producers to the more sophisticated installations at mills, was carried out from within the region. A new gristmill built at North Amherst in 1804 was framed by a man from Leverett, raised with help from the neighbors, equipped by a Leverett millwright with stones brought from Pelham, had its wheel pit built by a man from Shutesbury and ironwork forged in Montague. Only some castings made in Springfield did not come from the surrounding area.[101] From the 1780s, when a Hadley craftsman offered his Windsor chairs in exchange for "a few thousand white pine SHINGLES," to the 1820s, when Caleb Cook received fulled cloth in return for painting some wagon wheels and making "axtrees and gearing" for a wagon, direct exchange of goods frequently provided raw materials and parts.

99. Agnes Hannay, "A Chronicle of Industry on the Mill River," *Smith College Studies in History* 21 (1935–1936): 18; advertisement for Amherst carding mill in *Republican Spy*, Dec 24, 1806; account of Hadley mills in Judd MS, "Hadley," 3:15; Williamsburg carding mill advertised, *Hampshire Gazette*, July 17, 1805; Northampton mill, *Republican Spy*, May 19, 1807. See also Elizabeth Porter Phelps, Diary, Hadley, Nov 4, 1804, noting journeys to an Amherst carding mill, and Aug 6, 1809, noting use of the newer mill in Hadley, PPHH.
100. Joseph Williams, Account Book.
101. Paper in Marquis F. Dickinson, Account Book, BCJL.

Sylvester Judd traded rags to the Northampton papermaker and printer William Butler between 1814 and 1821, receiving mainly books and paper in return.[102] These exchanges effectively lowered purchase and credit costs by eliminating some of the risks from shifting prices that would have resulted from exchanging rural produce for these goods in distant markets. A local "import-substitution" effect helped broaden the base of rural manufacturing, so that by 1820 it was employing up to one-fifth of the labor force.[103]

Rural manufacturing was both a result of the household-based structure of the economy and an instrument in reinforcing it. Although manufacturing centers such as Northampton continued to grow during the early nineteenth century, the diffusion of activity throughout country districts was more rapid and more striking. With the exception of water-powered mills, which were also diffused along streams throughout the region, there were few technological constraints on the location of manufactures. Accordingly, they appeared where family circumstances or local demand dictated. Access to navigable rivers or good roads played a much less important role in locating production than access to local raw materials and local credit within a reciprocal exchange network. Thus the sights, sounds, and smells of workshops, tanneries, and mills could be found throughout the countryside, from the meadows of Hadley to the hills of Cummington. But the location of particular activities was influenced most of all by the availability of labor. Here the imprint of the household system and its demands were felt in all areas of rural production.[104]

Labor in the Household Economy

Throughout this expansion of production the household system restrained the development of a permanent wage-labor force in the countryside, despite the fact that hired labor played an important role, both in farming and in manufacturing. The expansion of wage work helped absorb a growing population into the rural social structure. Large numbers of men, and many women too, exchanged their labor or products with other rural households. Account books show that men commonly exchanged work with neighbors or hired themselves out for payment in goods. Servants were also more common than they had probably been

102. William Shipman, advertisement in *Hampshire Gazette*, May 7, 1788; Caleb Cook, Account Book; Judd MS, "Book of Fragments."

103. U.S. Fourth Census, 1820, Massachusetts.

104. Cf. Henretta, "War for Independence," p. 87, which stresses the precapitalist character of postrevolutionary manufacturing.

in the colonial period. Daniel Vickers calculated that in mid-seventeenth-century Essex County, Massachusetts, male farm servants comprised no more than 5 percent of the population. Data from a sample of Hadley and Amherst families in 1820 suggest that live-in servants of either sex accounted for just over 15 percent of the population and that almost 54 percent of households had at least one live-in servant.[105]

But these figures, while they provide a rough index of the growth of hiring up to the early nineteenth century, tell us very little about the social context or significance of rural labor. By themselves they both overstate the permanent character of waged employment and understate the extent to which people were involved in it. While production was centered on households, wage labor could expand without creating a substantial permanent rural proletariat. Wage work was intermittent. Families used their own labor whenever they could. While many men hired out their labor from time to time, in a society in which perhaps nine-tenths of the adult male population had either property or a skill, they were not fully dependent on doing so. So both the supply and demand for labor fluctuated greatly according to families' individual circumstances.

This situation had several consequences, and various groups of people often paid a price for it. The one-tenth or so of men who had no property or trade of their own were obliged to live with an uncertain supply of the work they depended on. Moreover, as Nancy Folbre has emphasized, the absence of a large permanent wage-earning class in the countryside was possible because women and children in rural households were subject to male authority over their labor. Finally, as we shall see, the intermittent character of wage work in the household economy served to restrain some investors' attempts to accumulate capital and apply it to large-scale production.[106]

The Peculiarities of Supply and Demand

As late as 1830, an almanac summed up the attitude of most rural families in the saying "Don't hire, when you can do the work your-

---

105. Daniel Vickers, "Working the Fields in a Developing Economy: Essex County, Massachusetts, 1630–1675," in *Work and Labor in Early America*, ed. Stephen Innes (Chapel Hill, 1988), p. 55. Taking genealogical data from Lucius M. Boltwood, *Genealogies of Hadley Families: Embracing the Early Settlers of the Towns of Hatfield, South Hadley, Amherst, and Granby* (1905; reprint, Baltimore, 1979), I constructed age profiles for forty-one families as they would have been in 1820 and compared them with the age profiles given in U.S. Fourth Census, 1820, Massachusetts. "Extra" males or females in each age group up to thirty-four were assumed to be servants. The imprecisions in this method are outweighed by the absence of other evidence and are likely, on balance, to be biased toward overestimating the number of servants.

106. Nancy Folbre, "Patriarchy in Colonial New England," *Review of Radical Political Economics* 12 (Summer 1980): 5.

self."[107] Repeatedly we find evidence that households placed first reliance on their own family labor and "hired work done" only when they had to. Ira Chaffee Goodale expressed this impulse to avoid outside help when he proposed to work on his father's Belchertown farm one summer, arguing that it "would save hiring a man through haying." However, when Josiah Quincy addressed the Massachusetts Agricultural Society in 1819, he criticized the maxim "labour runs away with all profits in farming," which led farmers "to do with as little labour as possible."[108]

When they did hire servants or exchange work, families did not regard it as a permanent condition or a permanent necessity. They sought labor for particular purposes, to assist at busy times on the farm or to help with the production of cloth or butter. Abraham Ball, needing boards from the Amherst farmer Chester Marshall, arranged to reap one and one-half acres of rye for him. On another occasion Marshall hired a man to reap two acres of rye in exchange for two bushels of the crop. One of the reasons that local book accounts often ran for considerable periods was that households avoided hiring people at slack times of the year but were prepared to furnish food or other goods on credit in order to secure labor later.[109] Special contingencies often forced families to hire help reluctantly. A Buckland woman wrote that her husband and children had been ill and that "I have stood it very well so far but was obliged to have a girl a few days." When Arethusa Hall went away for a while from her sister's family in Westhampton where she lived, another girl was immediately found to live in and help. The sister wrote her that "she is a very good girl for one of her age. . . . [I] will keep her until you return." A young Amherst woman was sent to help relatives who had recently settled in Vermont. When they installed an aqueduct to carry water to their house they did not need her any more and sent her back.[110] But the most important general influence, apart from the seasons, on households' demand for labor was the family life cycle. Of the households that had live-in servants in 1820, 86 percent were either headed by a man over sixty or included children under ten, or both. Families with young children faced heavier demands and had less labor

107. Nathan Wild, *The Farmer's, Mechanic's, and Gentleman's Almanack for 1831* (Amherst, 1830), p. 5.

108. Ira C. Goodale to Lafayette W. Goodale, New York, June 30, 1874; Josiah Quincy, *An Address Delivered before the Massachusetts Agricultural Society at the Brighton Cattle Show, Oct. 12th, 1819* (n.p., n.d.), p. 13.

109. Chester E. Marshall, Account Book. Important discussions of wage labor on farms are to be found in Rothenberg, "Emergence of Farm Labor Markets," and in Paul G. E. Clemens and Lucy Simler, "Rural Labor and the Farm Household in Chester County, Pennsylvania, 1750–1820," in Innes, *Work and Labor in Early America*, pp. 106–143.

110. Apphia Judd to Arethusa Hall, Westhampton, Dec 17, 1821, Judd Papers, 55M-1, Box 2, HCL. Dudden, *Serving Women*, p. 16, cites the distinction made by a woman in New York State between "hiring to spin" and being "obliged to hire help" with housework.

than others. Elderly people were also likely to require extra help. The presence of servants in their households reflected their particular needs for hired labor. Conversely, 84 percent of households without servants either had no children in them or had children over ten to assume part of the work. Only families with large properties or incomes hired servants and other assistance as a matter of course, and these accounted for a small proportion of the total.[111]

Patterns of hired labor on most farms reflected the attitude that families did their own work when they could. Demand was irregular and generally in short spells. During the 1790s some farmers in Amherst and Hadley hired labor in return for orders redeemable in goods at William Porter's Hadley store. Most of the orders that Porter received were for small sums, reflecting the fact that they represented work for short periods. Of forty orders issued between 1796 and 1800, nineteen were for one or two days' wages, sixteen were for three to five days', and only five were for periods of between ten days and one month. The distribution of orders Porter took between 1819 and 1821 was even more skewed toward short periods.[112] The accounts of a Northampton farmer who hired sufficient help in 1809 that he kept a separate "labor book" to keep track of it, strikingly reflect a similar pattern. Most of his work was done between May 4 and November 14 that year, during which time there were 198 possible workdays. He hired men on only 72 of them and obtained in all 150 man-days of work from them. In other words, he did not have enough work for a full-time laborer. But he employed no fewer than thirty-four different men at various times, who worked for an average of just under $4\frac{1}{2}$ days each. One man worked for 33 full days and 4 half days, another for 22 full days and 3 halves, but there were only three others who worked more than 6 days each. Twenty-nine men worked for a week or less: thirteen did between $1\frac{1}{4}$ and 6 days' work, the remaining sixteen only 1 day or less.[113]

As in this instance, some farmers did hire laborers for long periods. The man who worked 35 days may have been contracted to work for one month. Monthly, six-monthly, or annual contracts for hire became more common in the 1790s than they had been before. In a region whose population was growing and where land was scarce and unequally distributed, this is not surprising. But these term contracts did not account for the bulk of the work that was done, nor were they used by most families. Nor did the farmers who hired labor this way necessarily rely on it permanently. Joseph Eastman of Amherst, for example, obtained labor by different means from year to year. Sometimes he

111. Data from Boltwood, *Genealogies.*
112. William Porter Papers, Box A, folder 1796–99, and Box E, folders 1819, 1821, OSV.
113. Labor Book, Northampton, 1809–1814, NHS, A.A. 18.3.

contracted with a man or a boy who would work for six or seven months, but in other years he relied on hiring by the day.[114] Population growth may have had the effect of increasing the availability of day laborers in some neighborhoods, so restraining the development of a permanent work force. Wage rates altered little during the early part of the century.

However, men like Eastman also varied their hiring patterns because, paradoxically, men or boys were not always available to be hired on contracts. Why, given a rising population, land shortage, and inequalities, did farmers often complain of being unable to find people to work for them when they wanted? Rev. Justus Forward of Belchertown had trouble getting his hay mowed in 1786 because men he had engaged to do it "disapointed me, did not come to mow."[115] Larger farmers often faced difficulty finding enough men and women to do the farm and housework they wanted. Charles Phelps of Hadley complained in 1802 that "we are not more than half Mand, in or out of doors." His son-in-law Dan Huntington faced the same problem. "We have had a *sweat of it*, since you left us," he wrote to one of his sons in 1825. "I never knew it so difficult to get help." On one occasion, when "it was necessary to have a man," Huntington hired "for the first time & I believe the last, . . . a Bartlett," which proved less than satisfactory: "It was one day work, very moderately however, & the next a fox-hunt. Within a week, we were through with the contract & a new man to be found."[116] Population increase, labor shortages, and stagnant wage rates could exist simultaneously.

The reason for this apparent incongruity was that just as the household system made demand for labor intermittent, it helped keep the supply irregular too. While considerable numbers of people did some hired work, relatively few needed to do it full time or permanently. Most of the live-in servants identifiable in 1820 were young. Four out of every five were under twenty-seven years of age.[117] Few expected that they would remain servants. For men in particular, wage work was often part of a strategy of putting together a livelihood from various tasks and occupations. Thomas Cole of Northampton followed a different pattern of work each summer from 1800 to 1804. In 1800 he combined day work on several farms with shaving bark for a local tanner, for which he was paid by the cord. In 1801 he hired himself out to a farmer for six months. From 1802 onward he obtained day work in

114. Joseph Eastman, Account Book.
115. Justus Forward, Diary, Belchertown, July 10, 1786, MS Collection, AAS.
116. Dan Huntington to Edward Huntington, Hadley, Jan 14, 1825, PPHH.
117. Servants' ages were determined from the comparison of genealogical and census data discussed in note 105, above.

various places but during 1804 began weaving as well. In Hadley, Caleb Cook did short stretches of day work for farmers, usually in the winter or at harvest time. At other times of year he did house carpentry, repair work, coffin making, toolmaking, and other jobs. Both men owned small amounts of land, but not enough to farm.[118]

The broad but unequal distribution of property and skills caused this situation, in which wage workers were becoming more common but at the same time hard to find. Men and women who from time to time hired themselves out also had other tasks to attend to, or demands on their time from their families. Solomon Wright did considerable amounts of day work for his Northampton neighbors but fitted his work for others around the needs of his own eighteen-acre farm. In 1805, Orange Wright agreed to work for Joseph Eastman during the summer, but only on alternate weeks, so that he could attend to tasks elsewhere.[119]

The growth of by-employments merely exacerbated the situation. Ethan Marshall ran a small farm in Northampton, did hired labor for the judge Samuel Hinckley and was also one of six partners in a company that organized the spring shad fishery in the Connecticut River. By "putting together" various tasks to make a living, people could find themselves proprietors one day and workers the next. This also reflected the seasonal character of farming and rural manufacturing. Moses Woods wrote to his brother in June 1816, "I reside in Hadley with your old friends the Mr Lamsons where I am engaged in the carding business with them. . . . I expect to continue in their employ till August next when I shall return to my own shop in South Hadley, where I carry on the Cloth Dressing business."[120]

The convenience of the households supplying the labor often determined its availability. Families might make their children available as farmhands or servants; Joseph Eastman hired at least eleven of his neighbors' sons at different times between 1803 and 1816. When Arethusa Hall wrote, "If the members of one household were not able, from want of health or from scarcity of members, to do their own work, members of more numerous families were 'lent' as it were, to supply the deficiency," she was emphasizing the role of family strategies in making both the demand for and the supply of rural labor uneven.[121] Families also attempted to control the terms on which their younger

118. Thomas Cole, Daybook, Northampton, c. 1797–c. 1825, MCFL; Caleb Cook, Account Book.

119. Solomon Wright, Account Book; Joseph Eastman, Account Book.

120. Moses Woods to Aaron Woods, Jr., Hadley, June 20, 1816, Woods Family Papers, MCFL.

121. [Hall], "Sathurea," p. 37.

members worked for others. Searching for labor in 1802, Charles Phelps hired a boy from Pelham as a live-in farm servant. In due course, he was visited by the boy's father, who demanded "more liberty" for his son. "I asked him what liberty," wrote Phelps. "Liberty of the house," replied the father. Phelps "told him he would not have more liberty than he had and if he could not put up with such fare as he had, he was welcome to seek other quarters." It was agreed that the boy would "quit after he had tarryed his month out." Phelps preferred to let him go, despite being "only half Mand," so as to maintain control of his own household. To avoid such interference, when Northampton straw-hat makers advertised for "8 young Ladies as Apprentices" in 1822, they specified that "those from a distance would be preferred."[122]

Labor and the Limits to Capital

The influence of households on the supply of and demand for rural labor was sufficiently powerful to restrain the creation of large units of production in the countryside and to affect the terms on which the few factories that were built in this period operated. Particularly during the expansion of domestic industry that occurred as a result of the embargo of 1807, various local merchants and manufacturers attempted to expand production at existing rural millsites, to add spinning and weaving to carding or fulling operations, and to move from custom work into direct production. A classic example of this vertical integration was to be found in Williamsburg, where A. H. Bodman and Company adapted its fulling mill, so that by 1814 it included carding and dyeing equipment and its own looms. Yarn was apparently given out to be spun in local families, probably from a general store in which the Bodmans had an interest. The mill work force remained small.[123]

The Bodman mill survived the depression at the end of the 1812 war, but many similar operations did not. Particularly vulnerable were the manufacturers who had attempted to expand mill production to employ a larger work force. In North Amherst in 1809, Ebenezer Dickinson set up the Amherst Cotton Factory in a three-story wooden mill to do spinning by machine. The instability of credit, the presence of household spinners in the neighborhood, and the difficulty of recruiting a labor force probably all contributed to the collapse of this firm in 1812,

122. Charles Phelps to Elizabeth Phelps, Hadley, Apr 30, 1802, PPHH; *Hampshire Gazette*, Apr 10, 1822. Advertisements in the *Hampshire Gazette*, May 4 and Oct 12, 1831, for boys to work as laborers or apprentices each specified that "one from out of town would be preferred."
123. Hannay, "Chronicle of Industry," pp. 18, 31.

well before the downturn in trade and the influx of British textiles, which caught out so many other firms at the end of the war. Faced with overwhelming debts, Dickinson fled to the West. A group of his local creditors tried to refloat the business in the hope of recouping their losses, but the end of the war ended their attempts too.[124] The manufactures that survived the postwar depression were either highly capitalized firms backed by substantial funds in trade or small, household-based producers who could trim their sails to the wind by turning to other activities. The Valley had many of the latter, but few of the former. Households remained at the center of the region's manufacturing as a result.

The exception that proved the rule that large businesses would fail in this period was the Northampton Cotton and Woolen Manufacturing Company, established by three sons and a nephew of the merchant Levi Shepard in 1809. With capital of $100,000 and as many as fifty employees, this was for a while one of the largest woolen mills in America. Three factors helped this firm overcome the difficulties faced by others over the next decade. One was the capital and credit from trade that the Shepards assumed from their father and uncle at his death in 1805. The others derived from the firm's accommodation to the rural labor supply. The Shepards had long manufactured linen, employing outwork labor in local households; although they frequently had to struggle to maintain numbers, they continued to use outworkers to prepare materials for use in the mill. And while evidence about their mill labor force is scanty, it appears that they were able to draw upon the groups whose position in the household economy was most marginal: the poor and the young. One of the Shepards' women operatives, Phila Richardson, came from a Stafford, Connecticut, family so poor that when, in 1811, "she became deranged in her mind," and was returned to her home by the Overseers of the Poor, they "could obtain no remuneration" from her father. As the firm was building up its work force in 1810, it advertised for boys aged seven to sixteen to serve as apprentice carders, spinners, and weavers. Five years later, it sought young men aged eighteen to twenty-five. An apprentice spinner who ran away from the mill in 1815 was aged eighteen. A weaver who was charged with assault the same year was sixteen.[125]

124. Carpenter and Morehouse, *History of Amherst*, pp. 288–291; *Private and Special Statutes of the Commonwealth of Massachusetts*, 7 vols. (Boston, 1805–1837), 5:22.

125. Hannay, "Chronicle of Industry," p. 32; Phila Richardson: Northampton, Overseers of the Poor, Case Histories, group 2, Town Papers Collection, 5.14, FL; advertisements: *Anti-Monarchist*, Oct 17, 1810, *Hampshire Gazette*, Oct 15, 1815; runaway advertisement: *Hampshire Gazette*, Sept 13, 1815; weaver: Joseph Cook, "A List of Prisoners Committed to Gaol on Criminal Actions," in Hampshire County, Jailer's Book of Record, Feb 7, 1815, MCFL.

The Shepards had the connections and resources to bypass some of the constraints that the household system placed on concentrating labor and capital. Another Northampton entrepreneur, who attempted to invest heavily in labor-saving devices to avoid relying on a large labor force, was less successful. The tanner William Edwards, a grandson of Northampton's most famous minister, moved to the town in 1790, having been brought up in Stockbridge and apprenticed to a tanner in New Jersey. With funds of his own and from his father to use as working capital, and with strong connections to Northampton's leading families, Edwards borrowed heavily for land and equipment from local merchants and lawyers. By 1794 he was shipping tanned leather to Boston, and he expanded his works until a fire destroyed it in 1799. With funds subscribed by local friends to rebuild it, Edwards went further into debt to build equipment specifically designed to save labor in handling and processing. By 1809, he claimed, he had reduced the price of tanning sole leather from twelve cents a pound to four. By then his works included three tanneries with 672 vats, three bark mills, and rolling machines for softening hides, all run by only twenty-five workers. But to do this, Edwards was forced into partnership with Boston creditors who, as his burdens mounted, forced him out of business in 1815. It was twenty years before his local creditors were invited to apply for part payment from a $20,000 trust fund. If the household system made systematic hiring of labor difficult, the rural economy was also a difficult context in which to borrow and invest large amounts of capital to avoid having to do so.[126]

Careers and the Limits to Families

The concern for "careers" and the various methods of putting together livelihoods for children was not confined to economic effects nor to the family activities of organizing work, dowries, and inheritances. It sent a strand deep into early-nineteenth-century culture and public rhetoric. The assumption remained strong that young men would move up from poverty to "competence" as they acquired property or skills from their elders and that young women would obtain the benefits of these through marriage. But the increasing uncertainty of these prospects as population grew led to action designed to maintain provision that had once seemed guaranteed.

126. William Edwards, *Memoirs of Col. William Edwards* (Washington, D.C., 1897); see also Edwards to Postmaster of Northampton, Nov 29, 1809, in [Albert Gallatin], *Report from the Secretary of the Treasury on the Subject of American Manufactures* (Boston, 1810), pp. 30–32; notice to creditors, *Northampton Courier*, May 24, 1837.

While apprenticeships were declining in urban industrial areas during the early nineteenth century, rural families continued to make use of the device to obtain labor for themselves and training in other households for their children. The form apprenticeships took was designed to reinforce patriarchal authority and keep young people under the control of families. Families' role in finding positions for their offspring reflected this intention. The children of William Bliss, the Northampton carpenter who went insane in 1816, were left under the control of their mother and male relatives, who placed them in apprenticeships with kin or contacts in Northampton, Pittsfield, and elsewhere. The youngest child, Theodore, later wrote that by the time he was ready to be placed, the matter was in the hands of his eldest brother, who "without any consultation with me," put him under the charge of his own employer, a Northampton bookbinder.[127]

The supreme judicial court underlined the familial, rather than purely economic, character of apprenticeship when it ruled that it was a "personal trust" and illegal, for instance, for masters to assign apprentices to other employers. In political thinking and public discourse households were widely regarded as the central social institution. After the Revolution, rhetoric about bringing up children assigned women the vital role in educating their offspring and inculcating them with the values that would fit them for citizenship in a republic; this set of ideas, which the historian Linda K. Kerber has called the concept of "republican motherhood," stressed the moral superiority of the domestic environment. Discussions of manufacturing, especially among Jeffersonian republicans, shared this emphasis and urged avoidance of the factory system. Benjamin Austin, writing in 1815 to ask Thomas Jefferson to clarify his views on manufactures, argued that "*Domestic* manufactures is the object contemplated; instead of establishments under the sole controul of capitalists, our children may be educated under the inspection of their parents, while the habits of industry may be duly inculcated."[128]

Yet formal education outside the home also became more important. For those with the means, it was straightforward to arrange. In the will he drew up before his death in 1801 the Northampton merchant Joseph Hunt Breck specified that his real estate should remain in his wife's

127. Bliss, *Theodore Bliss*, pp. 6–7, 10, 18–25. Ditz, *Property and Kinship*, p. 162, notes that the division of labor and the spread of farm-family members into other occupations contributed more to household security in this period than did agricultural specialization and "enterprise management."

128. The court decision was in Hall v. Gardner, 1 Mass. Reports 172 (1804); Linda Kerber, *Women of the Republic: Intellect and Ideology in Revolutionary America* (Chapel Hill, 1980). A discussion of the Jeffersonian emphasis on household manufactures is in Drew R. McCoy, *The Elusive Republic: Political Economy in Jeffersonian America* (Chapel Hill, 1980), pp. 223–233.

hands until his children came of age or married, and that she should apply the income from it to their schooling. Less prosperous families had to find other ways. "Most of the farmers fat cattle," wrote Hannah Dickinson of Amherst in 1813, "and send them to Boston or some other market, which helps to supply them with money to educate their children."[129] Some families, including Dan Huntington's in Hadley, used various exchange arrangements to help provide or prepare for education. He sent a daughter to Emma Willard's school in Troy, New York, during the 1820s, taking Willard's son in exchange as a boarder in his own house. Two of Huntington's sons worked summers on the family farm to pay for winters of studying to prepare for college. Ira Chaffee Goodale intended his complicated arrangements for wagonmaking and working on his father's land to pay for board "while fitting for college," an attempt that in his case was to be thwarted by economic misfortune.[130]

Public action reflected these concerns. Throughout the Northeast the desire of many families to obtain more than a primary education for their children led in the 1790s to the establishment of private academies, many of them in rural districts. Amherst Academy was chartered by prominent townsmen in 1814, relatively late in the day. But it signaled an outburst of activity over education in the Valley towns that dominated the next decade or so: well-publicized but unsuccessful attempts to relocate Williams College in Northampton; sponsorship of Amherst College in 1821 and a four-year struggle in the General Court to obtain a state charter for it; and the foundation of voluntary organizations to provide charitable support for college education. These organizations included not only the Hampshire Education Society of 1814, formed by worthies from several of the larger towns in the Valley, but local groups such as the Female Education Society of Amherst, set up in 1817 "to aid indigent young men of piety and talents, in obtaining an education, with a view to the gospel ministry," whose constitution was signed by no fewer than seventy-six women and eighteen girls.[131]

College education provided one means for young men to avoid the constraints of the household system. David Allmendinger's research on New England colleges before 1850 suggests that, early on at least, education societies and other charities had considerable success in mak-

129. Hannah Dickinson, "The Farmer's Annual Employment," (Westfield Academy, 1813), BCJL.
130. T. G. Huntington, "Sketches by Theodore G. Huntington of the family and life in Hadley, written in letters to H. F. Quincy," n.d., p. 43, PPHH (typescript); Ira C. Goodale to Lafayette W. Goodale, New York, June 30, 1874.
131. For Amherst Academy, see *Private and Special Statutes*, 5:111. See also Hampshire Education Society Papers, MCFL, Box 1a; Female Education Society of Amherst, Constitution, Sept 9, 1817, BCJL.

ing college available to some children of poorer households. Provision was made in the context of households' needs, often through local exchange. Families had to deploy resources to support one of their number in college. Young men had to work for their own or other households to prepare for periods of study and often had to interrupt their studying to renew their means of support. More than half of Amherst College's graduates up to 1842 were over twenty-three years old when they left the college. Education societies solicited local donations in cash and in goods.[132] For the first few decades of the nineteenth century, provision for school and college education closely followed patterns imposed on it by the household system. The spread of effective school reform from the 1830s onward and the increasing closure of colleges to the offspring of poorer families reflected in part the system's progressive decline.[133]

While productive activity remained largely under household control into the 1820s, the need for households to overcome the system's constraints, to create channels and institutions to help them do so, set off subtle changes in rural society that were to lead to a shift in the balance of power during the following decades. In particular, the burdens faced by households themselves led them to seek new connections with merchants, which would profoundly affect the rural economy, while merchants, in turn, began to act on Josiah Quincy's dictum that "labour [is] the root and spring of all profit."[134]

The shift of power away from the household system accompanied wider cultural changes in the countryside, which signaled the breakup of the social and political order that had fostered it. The long period of Federalist hegemony came to an end, to be replaced by the early 1830s with a period of sharp political conflict out of which arose a new two-party system. At the same time, the longer ecclesiastical hegemony of orthodox Calvinism also collapsed into fragmentation and conflict. The six towns had long been noted for religious stability before 1820; only in Amherst was the town's population divided into two parishes, after a split had occurred in the early 1780s. Now a torrent of issues, some of them tangentially related to the question of rural "careers," burst forth with new energy. Disputes over Unitarianism split the church in Northampton and provoked secessions in Hadley and Hatfield. Population growth and the demand for new churches split Amherst further, so that

132. David F. Allmendinger, Jr., *Paupers and Scholars: The Transformation of Student Life in Nineteenth-Century New England* (New York, 1975), p. 136, tab. 13. In *Hampshire Gazette*, Jan 7, 1818, the Hampshire Education Society solicited donations "either in monies, in classical books, in cloth, in clothing or in bedding and furniture."
133. See Michael B. Katz, *The Irony of Early School Reform: Educational Innovation in Mid-19th Century Massachusetts* (Cambridge, Mass., 1968); Carl F. Kaestle, *Pillars of the Republic: Common Schools and American Society, 1780–1860* (New York, 1983).
134. Quincy, *Address, 1819*, p. 13.

by 1826 it had four parishes. Revivalism and the growth of new sects produced new congregations—temporary or permanent—in Northampton and Westhampton. Long-serving ministers died or were dismissed, to be replaced by men whose local standing and length of tenure were considerably diminished from their predecessors'.[135]

Behind the rapid development of a revivalist culture in the Valley during the 1820s, when these upheavals were occurring, were the emergence of a new morality of individual economic behavior, the concern for religious education expressed in the campaign to charter Amherst College, and the growth of voluntary organizations—some of them run by women—to sponsor religious causes or enforce moral propriety. Waves of revival activity swept new converts into the churches in the 1820s and 1830s. In Northampton, for example, membership in orthodox congregations alone rose from under 13 percent to over 20 percent of a growing population between 1820 and 1832.[136]

Two groups in particular became prominent supporters of the Evangelical movement. Women formed between 60 and 70 percent of church membership throughout this period, a proportion that did not significantly change during revivals.[137] Foremost among male converts was an emerging group of small storekeepers, merchants, and manufacturers. Both groups played key roles in the economic changes that dominated rural life between about 1810 and the 1840s.

135. The political upheaval of the early 1830s is discussed more fully in Chapter 6, below. Until 1820 the six towns contained only seven permanent churches. By the early 1830s there were seventeen. The origins and growth of Northampton Unitarianism may be traced in *Statement of Facts in Relation to the Call and Installation of the Rev. Mark Tucker over the Society of Northampton* (Northampton, 1824); Henry Shepard, "Some Recollections of the Second Congregational or Unitarian Society and Its Members," typescript of 1895 MS, NHS, Archive Files, and Altina Wilson, "The Beginnings of Unitarianism in Northampton" (University of Massachusetts, Amherst, 1972). Records of the short-lived Second Congregational Society of Hadley are in PPHH. Lists of ministers in *Creed, Covenant, and Rules and List of Members of the First Congregational Church in Amherst, Mass.* (Amherst, 1859); Wells, *Hatfield,* p. 343; and Northampton First Church, *Meetinghouses and Ministers from 1653 to 1878* (Northampton, [1878]), reveal the shift from long to short ministerial tenures in many churches. Revivalism reached Westhampton in the late 1820s in a short-lived Union Church opposed to the long-established town minister Enoch Hale. Critical references to this church and its minister may be found in Hale Family Papers, Box 6, folder 209, SSC, and Judd Papers, 55M-1, Box 2, HCL. The more amicable permanent division-into-two of the Northampton First Church after the revival of 1831 is reflected in a circular, "To the Members of the First Church in Northampton" (n.d.), Trumbull Collection, MCFL.

136. Information on church membership is drawn from *Creed, Covenant, and Rules;* First Church in Northampton, *Confession of Faith and Catalogue of Members, Jan 1, 1832* (Northampton, 1832); *The Church Book of the First Church of Christ in Northampton, 1860* (Northampton, 1860); *Catalogue of Members of the Edwards Church in Northampton: to which are prefixed the Confession of Faith, Covenant and Articles of Practice of the Church, May 1857* (Northampton, 1857).

137. Nancy F. Cott, *The Bonds of Womanhood: "Woman's Sphere" in New England, 1780–1835* (New Haven, 1977), p. 143, suggests that 60 percent of New England converts between 1798 and 1826 were women; some local church membership lists give a higher proportion.

PART III

THE BOUNDS OF
INDEPENDENCE

Chapter 4

Family Burdens and
Household Strategies

Giving an address in 1821, Rev. Henry Colman praised the farmers of New England's interior who, living far from urban markets, had "acquired not only a competency but an independency." Colman saw the best chance to preserve this in "frugality in living" and avoidance of the "foreign luxuries" that "constitute a very considerable item of expenditure." "It would seem a most important rule," he concluded, "for every farmer to live as far as possible within his own resources; to depend upon his farm for the subsistence of his family, as far as it can be applied to this purpose."[1] Over the next two decades, however, many farm households in the Valley were to modify their subsistence-surplus strategies and come to depend more heavily than before on distant markets. Not only would they sell more of their produce to earn income, but they would start purchasing some of the necessities they had once provided for themselves or obtained locally. How did this happen? The growing importance of rural merchants played a key role in this shift in households' strategies. But before examining that, we must explore the conditions within households themselves that brought the shift about.

New Englanders were already conscious of a crisis in the rural economy. The same year Colman spoke, Epaphras Hoyt of Deerfield warned the Hampshire, Franklin, and Hampden Agricultural Society of the need for improvements that could halt the flow of New England migrants to the West. Although migration was nothing new, the 1812 war period created unprecedented awareness of the opportunities and problems it presented. A man traveling across Massachusetts on his

1. Henry Colman, "An Address Delivered before the Massachusetts Agricultural Society at the Brighton Cattle Show, 17th Oct. 1821," *Massachusetts Agricultural Journal* 7 (1822): 6.

way west in 1818 wrote that people sometimes observed, "I wish I was going with you." In 1819, frustrated by debt, Sylvester Judd, Jr., left Westhampton to visit Ohio, with a view to moving there. Judd came back to stay, but thousands of other individuals and families moved. Samuel Partridge, recalling twenty families that had lived near his home in Hatfield about 1810, noted only four whose children all stayed in the town but six whose children all moved away. Migration had once seemed necessary to relieve the pressures of population growth on limited land. Now men such as Hoyt perceived it as a threat that would remove valuable people from a rural economy already afflicted by labor shortage. Opportunities for a balanced rural life, he argued, lay not in the "uncivilized" West, but at home.[2]

Underlying migration and the fear of its effects lay serious strains in the household economy, especially apparent in the succession of economic slumps and poor harvest years between 1815 and 1820. The increased output discussed in the previous chapter was achieved at a cost. The control that rural households succeeded in retaining over their economic affairs and that Colman praised in 1821 often proved fragile. Household production rested on three types of cooperation and interdependence: between households, in the local exchange system; between generations, in the provisions made by parents for the future support of their children; and between members of households themselves, in family labor and the sexual division of work. Cooperation had always been a source of tensions. As the strains mounted toward 1820, households began to revise their strategies in an attempt to relieve them.

Local Exchange and Indebtedness

Local noncash exchange would continue to be significant for some decades yet, but it was clear during the early nineteenth century that it created difficulties. By bargaining and negotiation, farmers and craftsmen tried to juggle the conflicting pressures of meeting needs, obtaining equity, and following the market prices that were increasingly influential in dealings involving bulk produce. Elisha Smith of Amherst charged Chileab Smith "for 2 sheepskins that you was to pay for in Hats at Stanley at 3/- each." Joseph Warner of Northampton gave a note to

2. Adolphus Fletcher, Diary, June 1818, quoted in Harry A. Wright, *The Story of Western Massachusetts*, 4 vols. (New York, 1949), 2:487. "Recollections of Samuel David Partridge," in Daniel W. Wells and Reuben F. Wells, *A History of Hatfield, Massachusetts, 1660–1910* (Springfield, 1910); Epaphras Hoyt, "Address delivered at Northampton before the Agricultural Society," Hoyt Family Papers, Box 2, folder 5, PVMA.

Orin Kingsley for $12.65 in produce "at market price" and received an order to pay another man "three dollars in Grain or Money" in order to pay "for some Coale that I had of him."[3] While most such arrangements facilitated the provision of households' needs, some undoubtedly added to the complexity of local exchange. After selling his orchard to a neighbor in 1804, a Monson man claimed that he was to be repaid in cider at the rate of 200 barrels a year, together with interest either in cider or in apples. He was also permitted to take apples from the orchard at a fixed sum per bushel, these amounts to be deducted from his neighbor's cider payments at the rate of nine bushels of apples per barrel. This attempt to conduct exchange without cash led only to a lawsuit. The two men had failed to agree on which of them should provide barrels for the cider and whether or not the neighbor should deliver the cider to the seller's house.[4] Contention over such issues tended to grow as output increased and the rate of local exchanges with it.

The language and practice of the debt-collection process reflected the continued power of a local exchange ethic that condemned undue pressure for settlement of debts and demanded closer attention to circumstances than to the letter of the law. Rebecca Dickinson of Hatfield wrote in 1793 that her brother-in-law had "fallen into the hands of that vile oppressor who has wrongfully taken his Property," and wrote of the creditor that "God will requite him[;] as he has meshured so may he find the meshure . . . how he has given cause of a curs to his inheritance." Images such as that presented by a republican newspaper in 1809, of a "trembling Debtor" in jail, his wife and family starving while the "vengeful creditor . . . with eyes of fire, / Sneers at her sighs, and scoffs at every moan," expressed the popular sense of justice that had sustained the local exchange ethic. Court officers expressed regret at the hardships that the law obliged them to bring to "honest" and "respectable" farmers and mechanics. "I lament that men possessed of so much goodness should be suffering under the hard hand of misfortune," wrote the county sheriff Ebenezer Mattoon to jailed debtors in Northampton in 1811; "it has been produced by circumstances not under your controul and accompanied by no dishonourable act."[5]

3. Elisha Smith, Account Book, Amherst, 1784–1822, BCJL; Sereno Clapp to Joseph Warner, Northampton, [month illegible] 13, 1819, A. S. Warner Collection, MCFL.

4. Sabin v. Truesdell, Hampshire County Court of Common Pleas, Records, 7:53–54v. (1804), Hampshire County Courthouse, Northampton.

5. Rebecca Dickinson, Diary Extracts, Hatfield, May 1793, PVMA (transcript); the lines of poetry are from "The Debtor," printed in the *Anti-Monarchist* (Northampton), Mar 22, 1809; "Ebenezer Mattoon to Col. Benjamin Olds and others on the limits of the gaol yard in this town," Northampton, Nov 8, 1811, copy in Amherst Historical Society Collection, Hollinger Box no. 2, JL.

Suits between neighbors were still comparatively rare. Of 174 cases involving the six towns' residents between 1804 and 1809, only 36 (20.7 percent) were between plaintiffs and defendants from the same town. In Amherst, Hadley, Hatfield, and Williamsburg the proportion averaged only 15 percent, and in Westhampton there were no such cases at all. Even when debt suits were most numerous, as for example in the summer of 1804, these proportions remained similar.[6] Advertisements calling upon debtors to settle accounts were usually circumspect, taking care not to cross the boundary between legitimate demand and excessive pressure. Jonathan Richardson of Cummington, announcing in 1806 "that he is in want of MONEY, and that this season of the year renders it peculiarly necessary that his request should be complied with," hastened to add that "necessity alone compels him to request this prompt attendance to his just demands." Pressure to repay was usually justified by special circumstances, such as the creditor's need to settle his own debts before leaving town. Joseph Utley, a Northampton Democratic-Republican, made as much political capital as he could after bankruptcy in 1807 forced him to call in local debts. Having been "made a wreck on these shores and his property sacrificed by the wreckers," he explained that he was compelled to collect small debts "to enable him to pay his passage to another port." He asked his debtors to comply, "lest the more fashionable practice of this place [that is, a lawsuit] should be adopted," but added, *"No Democrat need apply."* As it happened, Utley shortly died and reached another port for nothing, but his advertisement revealed the popularity of using restraint in pursuing debts.[7]

Although it eased some of the more cumbersome features of direct exchange, the use of orders, notes, and other circulating paper instruments also created difficulties. A creditor's order to a debtor to pay goods to a third party was an efficient way of "discounting" two sets of debts at once. But as the networks of local exchange became more complex and individuals' connections ramified throughout a neighborhood or region, the risk increased that such a call for payment could not be satisfied because it came at an unexpected time or from an unexpected quarter. Similarly, the use of notes could lead to sudden and awkward demands for payment. Court decisions progressively eased the circulation of private paper. At the same time, the law sought to protect creditors against debtors who transferred property out of their own names to avoid payment. These two trends conflicted in the rules of trusteeship. Men who had endorsed the notes of neighbors or otherwise assisted them with the burden of their debts might find themselves

6. Hampshire County Court of Common Pleas, Records, vols. 7–11 (1804–1809).
7. Richardson advertised in *Hampshire Gazette* (Northampton), Feb 19, 1806; Utley in *Republican Spy* (Northampton), Mar 4, 1807.

sued by the neighbors' creditors as "trustees" for their property. The ethics of protection for creditors' rights and of accommodation for debtors unable to repay debts continued to conflict as they had in the past. But as production and exchange increased, this conflict was brought closer to the heart of local exchange itself.[8]

Consequently, the pressure of debt was considerable. Although they never again reached the levels of the 1780s, debt suits remained endemic, and periodic crises provoked flurries of them. Between May and August 1804, for example, 127 cases were brought either by or against residents of the six towns, a rate that involved the equivalent of one in twelve of their adult male population. In Northampton 26 percent of debt suits between 1804 and 1809 were brought by residents against other townspeople. Every year between 1811 and 1822 there were at least 50 men from throughout the county jailed for debt in Northampton. In peak years the numbers were much higher: 135 in 1812 and 146 in 1817, in each case the equivalent of one-twelfth of Northampton's own adult male population.[9]

Rural people not only came into conflict over debts but contested the conduct of the debt process itself. The county sheriff or his deputies were regularly brought to court for wrongful attachment or seizure of goods, violence, false imprisonment, letting jailed debtors escape, or falsely accounting for fees. When the constable of Belchertown ordered a cornfield harvested and the crop removed to satisfy a debt, he was sued up to the supreme judicial court before the legality of his action was established. A New Salem man unsuccessfully brought criminal complaints against sheriffs' deputies in 1806 for assaulting his wife and "violently removing from under her the bed in which she was lying," but later won a civil suit for trespass, breaking and entering, taking property, and "assaulting, terrifying and falsely imprisoning" his wife and daughter.[10]

The extension of household production and local exchange had broadened and deepened the networks of local credit and noncash exchange. Transactions governed by the rules of local exchange now occurred over a wider geographical range, blurring the distinctions

8. An Act of 1794, chap. 65, which provided a remedy for creditors whose debtors had placed goods in the hands of others, in trust, to avoid the ordinary attachment process, was repeatedly upheld in the courts: see the judgment in Kidd v. Shepherd, 6 Mass. Reports (4 Tyng): 238–239 (1808).

9. Hampshire County Court of Common Pleas, Records, vols. 7–11 (1804–1809); Joseph Cook, "An Account of Prisoners Committed to Gaol in Civil Actions," in Hampshire County, Jailer's Book of Record, Northampton, 1811–1822, MCFL.

10. The Belchertown case was Penhallow v. Dwight, 9 Mass. Reports (7 Tyng): 34–35 (1810); the New Salem cases were Commonwealth v. Sexton, Hampshire County Court of Common Pleas, Records, 8:232 (1806) and Heminway v. Sexton et al., 5 Mass. Reports (3 Tyng): 222–223 (1807).

between local and long-distance exchange. As exchange relationships developed like a matrix over the countryside, tensions inevitably grew between needs and opportunities that were locally perceptible and demands from a greater distance. As the evidence presented in Table 3 suggests, most debt suits in the Valley in the early nineteenth century were between debtors and creditors more than a half day's convenient ride apart from one another, but not at a great distance. While relatively few creditors brought suit against their own townsfolk, or residents of adjacent towns, they brought a considerable number in towns beyond that or in the adjacent counties. The majority of suits arose between individuals who did not have the opportunity to settle their disputes face-to-face; these accounted for well over half of the total. Taking legal action against neighbors, on the other hand, was relatively frowned-upon.[11]

Yet the presence of local suits at all in towns such as Amherst, Northampton, and Williamsburg reflects the strains placed on local exchange by the expansion of production. No fewer than sixteen Northampton craftsmen appeared in court between 1804 and 1809, four as plaintiffs and twelve as defendants in debt suits. A disproportionate number of these cases were between townsmen, either as craftsmen sued each other for fulfillment of contracts or as merchants sought repayment for supplies they had advanced.[12] Although local exchange practices did much to promote new output by effectively reducing credit costs, it also made the success of production heavily dependent on personal relationships. Especially in times of crisis, these relationships could become very fragile. The diary of Hezekiah Wright Strong, an Amherst storekeeper who was himself to go bankrupt in the 1820s, was dotted with anxious references to economic difficulties in the post-1815 period. Some related to the wider problems of the economy: he noted at the end of 1818 that banks had ceased discounting bills and that there was "great demand for dollars." Others referred to their local effects. Earlier that year a drover from the neighboring town of Pelham had taken fat oxen on consignment from several Amherst farmers, sold them in Boston, and absconded with the money. In June, the Amherst lawyer Noah D. Mattoon, son of the former county sheriff, "fail[ed] for a large amount and elope[d] in the night to avoid his creditors." The "Berkshire Road," leading westward from Northampton toward Pittsfield and the New York line, became popularly known as the "Shirkshire Road," a favorite escape route for debtors overburdened with obligations.[13]

11. Hampshire County Court of Common Pleas, Records, vol. 7 (May–Aug 1804).
12. Ibid., vols. 7–11 (1804–1809).
13. Hezekiah Wright Strong, Diary, Amherst, Mar, June, Dec 1818, PVMA (typescript).

Table 3. Geographical relationships between opponents in lawsuits for debt involving residents of the six towns, May–August 1804

Residence of plaintiff or defendant	Residence of opponent in lawsuit			
	Same town	Adjacent town*a*	Other in same or adjacent county	Beyond adjacent county
Amherst	2	5	2	0
Hadley	2	7	22	2
Hatfield	0	4	6	1
Northampton	17	11	37	2
Westhampton	0	1	1	0
Williamsburg	5	8	2	2
Total	26 (20%)	24 (19%)*a*	70 (55%)	7 (6%)

*a*There were twelve lawsuits whose plaintiffs and defendants lived in adjacent towns among the six towns. These suits are counted only once in the bottom row, so the figure in the "Adjacent town" column adds up to twelve fewer than the sum of the figures above it.

Source: Hampshire County Court of Common Pleas, Records, vol. 7, Hampshire County Courthouse, Northampton.

Ira Chaffee Goodale's excursion into wagonmaking in 1824–1825 illustrates the destructive effect these fragile connections could have on output. As we saw, he used several local contacts to enable him to become a small manufacturer. But the outcome of his efforts was determined by the effect of seemingly trivial events, which turned his network of connections into a house of cards. As Goodale's credit collapsed, the local exchange ethic would keep him out of debtor's prison, but it could not keep him in business as a wagonmaker.[14]

By the spring of 1825 Goodale had partly completed four wagons and had acquired materials for two more. He hoped that the eventual sale of these wagons would earn him between $150 and $180. But he also had outstanding debts, amounting to $97.50, for materials and labor on the wagons and for board and other costs during the winter. In order to pay for wood purchased the previous year, Goodale turned to his friend and neighbor Chester Bliss, who loaned him $25 in cash. Goodale then quickly completed two wagons, selling them for the good price of $30 each and paying off $60 of the older debts that he owed. However, before he could complete the other four wagons he ran afoul of his most prominent creditor, the merchant James Kellogg, whom he owed $32.50 for board. Coming out of meeting one Sunday, Kellogg had overheard someone remark that Goodale would not be able to repay further debts.

14. The next two paragraphs are based on Ira C. Goodale to Lafayette W. Goodale, New York, June 30, 1874, M. W. Goodell Collection, BCJL.

He promptly sought security from Goodale, obtaining a guarantee of payment from his father. This action caused Bliss to panic.

Fearing that Goodale would be unable to repay his loan and hoping to get ahead of other creditors, Bliss sued for repayment. He brought his action, not in Hampshire County, but in the Franklin County court at Greenfield, and Goodale later accused Bliss of doing this in order to increase the traveling expenses that the court might award him. Given Bliss's anxiety not to lose his cash, this seems plausible. At any event, when Goodale did not appear to contest the action, Bliss obtained a judgment against him. He then accompanied the Belchertown constable, the latter armed with a rifle, to the Goodale farm to see it executed and hovered in the background while the officer searched Goodale's belongings and warned that he would have to take Ira to jail if there were no means of payment. Bliss's presence provoked Goodale's mother, who had been watching from the porch of the house, to attack him bitterly: "Oh . . . what a scathing, and what a blistering denunciation did she pour out upon Chet Bliss, my *warmest friend*—as well as a friend of *my father's whole family*. Yes my mother's tongue was all on elocutionary fire, in portraying the *duplicity*, the *treachery*, the most diabolical *perfidy* and *blackheartedness* even beneath and beyond the devil himself." Chet Bliss, wrote Goodale, "never forgot that awful scarification that my mother gave to his dying day." This, and "the second lashing from my *father*," made Bliss "so *cowed* and *ashamed* and humiliated" that he "agreed to have the business settled amicably." He backed off from a course that he was legally entitled to take but that was, in his neighbors' eyes, wrong. Goodale did not go to jail but was forced into an immediate compromise with his remaining creditors, losing the four uncompleted wagons in the process. He never went into manufacturing again.

Goodale's misfortune supports the observation of the economic historian Maxine Berg that early industry depended less on access to technology or transport than on more contingent issues such as credit, debt, bankruptcy, and the availability of labor.[15] This applied to farming as well. Households maintained control of rural production, but in the context of land shortage and population growth, and with an increasing number of distant exchange connections, even local dealings such as Goodale's were brought under strain. Nevertheless, difficulties of this kind were only part of the dilemma that household producers faced about 1820. They also had to confront two sets of tensions within their own families and households. One was intergenerational. The other was over the division between men's and women's work.

15. Maxine Berg, *The Age of Manufactures: Industry, Innovation, and Work in Britain, 1700–1820* (London, 1985), esp. pp. 118–122.

Inheritance and Its Tensions

The central position of the household system was maintained in the early nineteenth century only at the expense of severely modifying the ambitions of parents to provide livings for their offspring. The old assumption that families would themselves be able to pass land, skills, or dowries to their children, had in many cases been wrecked by the shortage of resources. The best most families could hope to do under the circumstances was to reserve substantial property for one or two sons and make arrangements to give other children a start in the world through gifts, apprenticeships, or education. While this contributed to the broadening of the rural economy and did not in itself undermine the household system of production, it altered the character of relations within families. Above all, as Philip Greven and, more recently, Nancy Folbre have argued, over a long period from the late eighteenth to the early nineteenth centuries, it undermined patriarchal authority. Fathers no longer able to make full provision for their sons could exercise less control than they had once assumed. Sons facing the prospect of receiving limited resources from their families were more inclined to seek their "independence" away from home, taking to the road or to new occupations. For them, Folbre has written, "the road to prosperity diverged from the road to maturity."[16]

The break was gradual. As Folbre's data shows, sons in prosperous households were more likely to remain at home to a late age than those of poorer ones, suggesting that they would still choose to take familial resources when these existed. Moreover, as we have seen, the work of Toby Ditz has drawn attention to the modification of families' inheritance patterns to deal with scarce resources. Though no longer straightforwardly "lineal," in the sense that fathers provided for sons and sons depended on their fathers for provision, bequests continued to reflect the desire to maintain family influence by arranging for collateral provision. Sons receiving substantial parts of their fathers' estates frequently assumed also the obligation to make some provisions for their siblings, so that brothers and sisters in turn had to depend as much on each other as they had once done on their parents.[17] This familial, but less lineal pattern maintained the tradition of family provision in a new context.

It led to two sets of problems. First, it increased parents' anxiety about relying on their children in old age. Men with resources could continue to provide for their widows by assigning a life interest in all or part of

16. Nancy R. Folbre, "The Wealth of Patriarchs: Deerfield, Massachusetts, 1760–1840," *Journal of Interdisciplinary History* 16 (Autumn 1985): 220.

17. Toby L. Ditz, *Property and Kinship: Inheritance in Early Connecticut, 1750–1820* (Princeton, 1986), esp. pp. 30, 57, 83.

their estates; Ebenezer Pomeroy of Hadley did this in 1800, giving his wife the use of half his land, buildings, and furniture for life. But as children became independent of their parents for livelihoods, or as their resources dwindled, some men sought to achieve the same end by making conditional grants of property to one son. Joseph Kingsley of Westhampton passed land to one of his sons about 1800, with the proviso that the son maintain his parents, while Ebenezer Cowles of Hatfield willed land to two grandsons on the partial condition that they take care of their mother should she be widowed.[18]

Disputes over the fulfillment of such conditions dominated some families' correspondence. The mere fear of noncompliance called forth strong language. In 1827, while in her eighty-fourth year, Eunice Pettengill of Belchertown received a letter from her brother to ask how her son was looking after her: "I hope he is very kind to you in your old age[;] if he is so God will reward him sevenfold in this world & peace will rest in his bosom. if he is not good & kind to you God will regard his deeds by blasting his substance and Conscience will as it were Harrow his flesh from his bones when you are under the Cold Clods of the valley." Pettengill's family had indeed been disputing over the son's treatment of her for at least two years. "We are sorry that Paul and his family are so cruel to Mother," wrote one of her daughters, "but we do not know what to do."[19]

In this case the child-parent dispute was connected with the question of the distribution of property between siblings, which formed a second set of problems families had to face. As a ballad put it before 1800,

> From father to mother, from sister to brother,
> From couzin to couzin, they'll bite one another,
> Since biting has got to be so much in fashion,
> I'm afraid it will spread quite over the nation.[20]

In 1821 one of Paul Pettengill's brothers commented after a stormy visit that he had expected "those things I . . . saw woud come to pass" from a "person that will start so low as flattery and deceit to gain property" and

---

18. Ebenezer Pomeroy, Will, Hampshire County, Probate Records, 20:179–180, Hampshire County Hall of Records, Northampton; Ebenezer Cowles, Will, ibid., vol. 21:161.

19. In his will, dated 1816, now in Goodell Collection, BCJL, Nathaniel Pettengill had bequeathed the residue of his estate, including Eunice Pettengill's life interest in his real property, to Paul, making the mother dependent on her son. The hope that Paul "is very kind" was expressed in Simeon Tyler to Eunice Pettengill, Camden, Aug 20, 1827. References to strife between mother and son had appeared in Jonathan and Lydia Leach to Moses and Susanna Goodale, Harrison, July 28, 1826. Both letters are in Goodell Collection, BCJL.

20. "Broadside Ballads from the Collection of Isaiah Thomas," 1:51, Broadside Collection, AAS (hereafter cited as Thomas, "Ballads").

warned his mother and father to "look out for tiranny and oppression."[21] Parents' efforts to maintain familial cohesion by imposing obligations on particular children to provide means of support to brothers or sisters could have the opposite effect from what was intended, sowing discord between them instead.

Child-parent conflicts and disputes between siblings arose not only out of provisions in wills but also in cases where fathers tried to maintain their authority while alive by dictating terms of cooperation to their children. Sometimes this strategy succeeded. Dan Huntington, heir to half of Charles Phelps's substantial Hadley farm, sought over three decades not only to provide for his five sons but to enlist their assistance for each other when education or other provision needed to be paid for.[22] But in the case of Simeon Cowles, a prosperous Amherst farmer, it misfired, resulting in a withering correspondence between him and various sons and in-laws, conducted on and off between 1807 and 1827.

Cowles had decided to split his property between several sons, and to choose when and how much to give each of them. He had to defend himself against his eldest son's claim that he had been given less than a fair share: "I sopose a parent is the most Capebel of doing justis among children knowing all the privileg[e]s and propity that you have had of me." He also criticized this son's reluctance to help his brothers, even though they had, he said, helped him set up on his own: "I am doubtful whether Moses Eli will Ever be abel to put all the famoly under so good a [situation?] as you are in now for a living." And when another brother fell on hard times, Cowles sought assistance for him: "I hope you will consider your brother Aron['s] sittuashon and put a helping hand rathr than to se him sofer as we have done . . . he has not a house or a foot of land in the wold to corl his [own]." Simeon Cowles's concern to achieve equity between his sons accompanied anxiety about his own support in old age. Accusing his sons of ingratitude for the efforts that had been made for them and for threatening their parents' support by claiming too much property, he declared that they "would strip father and mother when sick and not abel to help themselves with money or strength of body to get a living."[23]

Tension between parental authority and children's concern to set up their own independent households had been part of the spur to increased rural output between 1790 and 1820. If, as most historians have

21. Nathaniel Pettengill to Moses and Susanna Goodale, Middleton, Nov 4, 1821, Goodell Collection, BCJL.

22. T. G. Huntington, "Sketches by Theodore G. Huntington of the Family and Life in Hadley, written in letters to H. F. Quincy," n.d. (typescript), PPHH.

23. Simeon Cowles to Simeon Cowles, Jr., Amherst, n.d., and Feb 26, 1827, NHS, A.l.18.88 and A.l.18.91.

agreed, the power of fathers was shorn by the reduced availability of land for them to disburse, some men tried to retain it by increasing the value or product of the property that they had. Simeon Cowles complained to one of his sons, "I have worked my self almost to death for to git property for to make you all comfitabel," and claimed to another that between 1797 and 1813 he had "added to property at le[a]st 300 Dolars a year . . . with out any rise of lands."[24] For smaller farmers in particular, such increases in output had to be obtained not only on the land itself but in household production and by-employments. The maintenance of household control of production was also, in part, the maintenance of patriarchal control of family labor, a rearguard action in many families short of the real estate that had once been more readily available.

The Burden of Work

While most of the effort to achieve increased output was made by household labor—by men, women, children, servants, and hired hands working under family control—its burdens were not equally distributed. As we saw, the substantial division of work according to gender gave men's work a seasonal character, while tasks were frequently added to the continuous burden of household chores that fell to women. Woodcutting, land clearance, farm-based manufacturing, and other "new" tasks were, for men, timed to occupy periods when the demands of field work were not pressing. Stall-feeding of beef cattle, concentrated in the winter months, was also arranged to fit into the slack season. Farm women of the early nineteenth century, by contrast, were taking on new amounts of home textile or dairy production in addition to regular tasks. At the same time many of them were bearing an increasing number of children.

Popular songs and ballads began to express the frustrations perceived by both men and women at the burdens of increased household production. In the song "A Pound of Tow" a young man complains of his wife's shortcomings as a provider, compared with the capabilities she had demonstrated while still living with her parents:

> Before my dame was married, she was a thrifty dame,
> She'd do all sorts of kitching work, make pudding,
>   cheese and cream,
> She'd weed potatoes, flax and corn, and milk the cow
>   and yoe;
> And rock the cradle with her foot, and spin a pound
>   of tow.

24. Ibid., n.d., NHS, A.l.18.88; Simeon Cowles to Moses Eli Cowles, Amherst, Feb 2, 1826, NHS, A.l.18.90.

But, once married to him, this paragon did not live up to his expectations:

> But now my dame is married, she does not thrifty prove,
> A scolding and a brawling is all that she does love;
> And if her wants are ne'er supply'ed, then out of doors
>   must go,
> With the reel and ladle, and distaffstick, she over my
>   head will throw.[25]

Battered by the common tools of women's household production, the young man laments his inability to control that production for himself. Two songs published as a pair in 1807 pointed up the contrast between men's and women's perspectives on household work. While "The Happy Man" celebrated the benefit he obtained from his wife's labors, "The Happy Woman" recommended avoiding household work and expressed a woman's resentment at the pressure her husband put on her to produce:

> How happy is the maid
> Whose fortune it has been
> To keep a proper distance from
> That paltry creature man: . . .
> Whose parsimonious soul
> Craves profit from the needle
> And gives the wheel's detested din
> The preference to the fiddle.[26]

Ironically, the spinning wheel and other household objects had a prominent place in male political rhetoric as symbols of household "independence." But it was an independence based on increasingly burdensome amounts of family labor. Women writing letters and diaries often reflected on the heavy and conflicting burdens that they had to undertake, whether or not they had servants to assist them. Breaking off to write to her sister in 1821, Apphia Judd remarked, "I have turned my back on mittens susspenders and as many more things that needs to be done as you can guess." Mary Bullard Graham of Buckland gave a sense of the pressure she was under when she hastily signed off a letter, "my slapjacks are all burning and I must stop," while a sister once wrote of her that "Mary is almost worn out she looks like a June shad."[27] A

25. Thomas, "Ballads," 2:55.

26. Robert B. Thomas, *Farmer's Almanack for the Year of Our Lord 1808* (Boston, 1807), [p. 43].

27. Apphia Judd to Arethusa Hall, Westhampton, Dec 17, 1821, Judd Papers, 55M-1, Box 2, HCL; Sophronia Bullard to Lewis Edwards, Buckland, Aug 9, 1831, and Mary Bullard Graham to Ann Edwards, Buckland, Dec 23, 1834, Edwards Family Correspondence, MCFL.

version of the popular song "The Cambric Shirt," from the Connecticut Valley, reflected the impossible demands placed on many women. A young woman promises her sweetheart:

> If you will find me ten acres of land
> Between the salt water and the sea sand
> And plow it all up with an old ram's horn
> And seed it all down with one kernel of corn
> Then come unto me and you shall have your shirt
> And then you can be a true love of mine.[28]

The pressure on household women during the early nineteenth century came from both of their principal economic roles, as producers of goods and household "services" and as reproducers—bearers of children. About 1810, women began to adapt their strategies so as to modify household demands on their time. Rather than simply reducing the burdens of their work, women made a shift in work patterns so as to avoid some of the most difficult conflicts between the different demands made of them. There were two strands to this shift: a gradual reduction in fertility rates and a reorganization of women's household production. We shall look at each in turn.

Fertility

Historians have long emphasized the importance of the "fertility transition," in which the high birthrates and large families of the colonial period gave way to smaller families among much of the New England–born population by the middle of the nineteenth century. In rural areas this transition took place largely between the 1780s and the 1840s.[29] Debate has focused on the reasons for this shift in reproductive behavior. Richard Easterlin and some other economic historians emphasized the role of land shortage. As families perceived greater difficulty in settling their children on the land, they began to restrict family size.[30] Other scholars, including Nancy Folbre in her studies of the Connecticut Valley, have placed greater emphasis on factors internal to

28. Helen H. Hartness, comp., *Ancient Ballads Traditionally Sung in New England*, 4 vols. (Philadelphia, 1960–1965): 1:77. The song was recorded in Miller's Falls, c. 1825.

29. Changes in fertility rates are discussed in Maris A. Vinovskis, *Fertility in Massachusetts from the Revolution to the Civil War* (New York, 1981).

30. Richard A. Easterlin, "Population Change and Farm Settlement in the Northern United States," *Journal of Economic History* 36 (1976): 45–83; Don R. Leet, "Human Fertility and Agricultural Opportunities in Ohio Counties: From Frontier to Maturity, 1810–1860," in *Essays in Nineteenth-Century Economic History: The Old Northwest*, ed. David C. Klingaman and Richard K. Vedder (Athens, Ohio, 1975), pp. 138–158.

Table 4. Mean age at recorded first marriage, Amherst and Hadley families, 1770–1809

Decade of marriage	Women		Men	
	N	Mean age	N	Mean age
1770–1779	49	23.40	54	26.12
1780–1789	71	23.91	59	26.18
1790–1799	66	25.17	58	27.09
1800–1809	53	25.36	49	25.73

Source: Birth and marriage dates in Lucius M. Boltwood, *Genealogies of Hadley Families: Embracing the Early Settlers of the Towns of Hatfield, South Hadley, Amherst, and Granby* (1905; reprint, Baltimore, 1979).

households. Fertility rates were determined less by the availability of resources than by men's perceptions of their ability to control family labor. As long as patriarchal power over women and children remained high, children remained valuable to men and fertility rates were high. As this control slipped, the value of having children fell as well. In particular, the ability of young men to find a measure of independence in work outside the household, and the inability of fathers to keep them under their control, were potent factors in bringing about the "fertility transition."[31]

Data from the towns in the middle of the Connecticut Valley, and especially from families in Hadley and Amherst, suggest that fertility rates declined as a result of the combination of these reasons with the organization of women's work and the pattern of labor available in the household economy. Like that for Sturbridge, discussed by Nancy Osterud and John Fulton, and for Deerfield, discussed by H. Temkin-Greener and A. C. Swedund, the evidence for our region points to a reduction in fertility during the late eighteenth century as land became scarce and families faced poorer future prospects than they had done during the expansion of settlement there.[32] Genealogical data on Amherst and Hadley families suggest that women's age at first marriage rose on average by almost two years between the 1770s and the 1800s (Table 4). Moreover, this rise in age was accompanied until the end of the eighteenth century by a rise of almost one year in the average age of first marriage for men. Coinciding with the completion of settlement in the Valley, these rising marriage ages appear to reflect a classic response

31. Folbre, "The Wealth of Patriarchs," p. 220.
32. H. Temkin-Greener and A. C. Swedlund, "Fertility Transition in the Connecticut Valley, 1740–1850," *Population Studies* 32 (1978): 27–41; Nancy Osterud and John Fulton, "Family Limitation and Age at Marriage: Fertility Decline in Sturbridge, Massachusetts, 1730–1850," *Population Studies* 30 (1976): 481–493.

to restricted opportunities. They were followed, moreover, by the fall in family size that could be expected. Women first married between 1780 and 1789 had on average 7.22 recorded live births, while those married during the following decade had only 6.52. Land shortage may therefore have explained a small falling off in family size and marital fertility before 1800.[33]

But this fall was not permanent. Aggregate population figures and genealogical data both point to a renewed increase in fertility early in the nineteenth century and suggest that there was a two-stage cycle to the "fertility transition" in parts of the Valley. Gross fertility ratios (the number of children under ten divided by the number of women of childbearing age) in four of our six towns rose temporarily after 1800 (Table 5).[34] In Amherst and Hadley, the downturn in gross fertility rates did not occur until after 1810 and in Westhampton not until after 1820. Hatfield experienced this second stage in the cycle even later; its ratio fell between 1800 and 1810 but then rose for two more decades before falling off again. The temporary revival of higher fertility rates is reflected in the family data from Amherst and Hadley, where women who were first married between 1800 and 1809 had a mean of 7.12 recorded live births, almost as many as those married two decades before. This increase was in spite of the fact that they were nearly eighteen months older than their predecessors when they married, 25.36 years on the average, compared with 23.91 years in the 1780s.[35]

The explanation for this higher fertility rate lies in the expansion of output that the household economy was achieving in this period. Despite the continuing pressure of population on land, the mean age at which Amherst and Hadley men first married was lower between 1800 and 1820 than it had been in the last three decades of the eighteenth century. Indeed, between 1800 and 1809 it was only three months higher than the mean age for women. As the opportunity increased to transfer land, raise more produce, manufacture goods, or find various combinations of independent and hired labor with which to make a living, more men were able to marry earlier. The same circumstances also enabled them and their wives to have more children. Mean household size in Amherst rose from 6.7 persons in 1800 to nearly 8 persons in

33. There are no published vital records for any of the six towns. Data are drawn from Lucius M. Boltwood, *Genealogies of Hadley Families: Embracing the Early Settlers of the Towns of Hatfield, South Hadley, Amherst, and Granby* (1905; reprint, Baltimore, 1979).
34. These ratios are calculated from data in U.S. population censuses, 1800–1840.
35. These data, and those in the three following paragraphs, are based on Boltwood, *Genealogies*. On the mid-nineteenth century, see also Mary Jane Richards Pi-Sunyer, "Households in a 19th Century Town: A Historical Demography Study of Household and Family Size and Composition in Amherst, Mass., 1850–1880" (Ph.D. diss., University of Massachusetts, Amherst, 1973).

Table 5. Gross fertility ratios in the six towns, 1800–1840

	1800	1810	1820	1830	1840
Amherst	1.48	1.67	1.33	1.01	0.91
Hadley	1.62	1.68	1.48	1.49	1.22
Hatfield	1.64	1.14	1.22	1.23	1.05
Northampton	1.47	1.39	1.29	1.03	0.92
Westhampton	1.36	1.42	1.50	1.45	1.27
Williamsburg	2.14	1.66	1.38	1.31	0.93

Note: The ratios are based on the number of children under ten years of age per woman aged sixteen to forty-four.

Sources: U.S. Census Office, *Return of the Whole Number of Persons within the Several Districts of the United States* (Washington, D.C., 1801); *Aggregate Amount of Persons within the United States for the Year 1810* (Washington, D.C., 1811); *Census for 1820* (Washington, D.C., 1821); *Fifth Census; or, Enumeration of the Inhabitants of the United States, 1830* (Washington, D.C., 1832); *Sixth Census or Enumeration of the Inhabitants of the United States . . . in 1840* (Washington, D.C., 1841).

1820, and there were comparable rises in Hadley and Northampton. This rise occurred partly because women extended their reproductive lives. Women bearing their last children in the 1820s were, on average, older than at any other time between 1780 and 1860. But it also resulted from reduced birth intervals between children. Women who married between 1800 and 1809 gave birth on average every year and ten months, compared with an average interval of more than two years for women married the previous decade. As they increased their commitment to household production, rural women were also increasing their rate of reproduction, having more children and more often than their immediate predecessors.

It was only after 1810 that the signs of a second, permanent reduction in fertility started to be apparent. Gross fertility rates in Amherst and Hadley began to fall. The marriage age of women rose toward a peak in the 1830s (Table 6). Many women had fewer children. Those who married between 1810 and 1819 had a mean of 7.03 each—slightly fewer than in the previous decade—but in the 1820s this number fell to 6.22 and a decade later to 4.47 (Table 7). By mid-century, New England–born women were bearing almost 3 fewer children on average than they had been before 1820. Average household size fell back to between 4 and 5 people. In Amherst in 1850, it was 4.65.

The rise in women's age at marriage now provided only part of the explanation for the fertility decline. Women married only six months later on average in the 1820s than they had done in the 1810s, and after reaching a peak in the 1830s the average marriage age fell. Of growing

Table 6. Mean age at recorded first marriage, Amherst and Hadley families, 1800–1849

Decade of marriage	Women		Men	
	N	Mean age	N	Mean age
1800–1809	53	25.36	49	25.73
1810–1819	45	25.11	57	26.04
1820–1829	29	25.63	32	28.13
1830–1839	30	27.54	30	25.90
1840–1849	38	25.04	25	27.21

Source: Lucius M. Boltwood, *Genealogies of Hadley Families: Embracing the Early Settlers of the Towns of Hatfield, South Hadley, Amherst, and Granby* (1905; reprint, Baltimore, 1979).

Table 7. Mean number of recorded live births, Amherst and Hadley families, 1780–1849

Decade of marriage	N	Births
1780–1789	49	7.22
1790–1799	48	6.52
1800–1809	25	7.12
1810–1819	30	7.03
1820–1829	18	6.22
1830–1839	19	4.47
1840–1849	15	4.40

Source: Lucius M. Boltwood, *Genealogies of Hadley Families: Embracing the Early Settlers of the Towns of Hatfield, South Hadley, Amherst, and Granby* (1905; reprint, Baltimore, 1979).

importance was the fact that many women curtailed their period of child rearing. The average age at which women last conceived fell by more than fifteen months after the 1820s (Table 8). This lower age of last conception suggests that circumstances within households themselves had an important role to play in the fertility transition. For an increasing number of households family labor was becoming less important than it had been before 1820. That the number of children became a matter of individual family circumstances, such as wealth, rather than broad external factors, is suggested by the variance between women's ages of last conception, which grew as the mean was reduced. Whereas two out of three women who conceived their last children in the 1810s did so within two years of the mean age, by the 1830s fewer than one-third were doing so that close to it. Early-nineteenth-century families shared fairly homogeneous notions about the numbers and value of the chil-

Table 8. Mean age at last conception, Amherst and Hadley women, 1800–1849

	Age	Percentage within two years above or below mean
1800–1809	38.64	45.5
1810–1819	38.42	66.7
1820–1829	39.00	35.0
1830–1849	37.16	31.6

Source: Lucius M. Boltwood, *Genealogies of Hadley Families: Embracing the Early Settlers of the Towns of Hatfield, South Hadley, Amherst, and Granby* (1905; reprint, Baltimore, 1979).

dren they brought up, but by 1840 attitudes varied more greatly. Prosperous families could attempt to curb the number of children they raised in order to rationalize the distribution of means to them. Poorer households were still in need of children's labor to help them make ends meet. Having little property to distribute anyway, control of the process was less important to them than maximizing the capacity to earn.

So the fertility transition was less a "Malthusian" response to the availability of resources than a reflection of the social structure through which these resources were distributed. While household production dominated the economy, fertility rates remained high. Tax data for the town of Amherst between 1790 and 1820 suggest that the burden of maintaining the household system fell disproportionately on women. Throughout this period, between 68 and 70 percent of households were taxed on one poll each, showing that there was only one male of sixteen years or over living at home. As household sizes rose between 1800 and 1820, the proportion of women among them rose also. The proportion of households taxed on two or three polls fell slightly, and the number of female-headed households increased.[36]

Household Production

The decline in fertility after 1810 accompanied several significant shifts in the production and consumption strategies of households, which would alter the terms of their independence. Like the reduction in childbearing itself, these changes modified the character of women's

36. Amherst, Tax Valuation Lists, 1800, 1820, Amherst Town Hall.

work, removing some of the most difficult conflicts they faced in demands on their time. When Rev. Amariah Chandler gave a sermon in Greenfield in 1858 to mark his half-century in the ministry, he recollected the period in which he first entered the pulpit and drew a connection between the decline in fertility and shifts in household work patterns. "Fifty years ago, children were numerous, much more numerous in proportion than now." He continued: "Farmers' houses might often remind us of a hive; not only from the perpetual hum of the spinning wheel and other implements of household industry, but from the numbers which morning by morning during the school term, swarmed forth from the door."[37]

As we have already seen, household spinning and weaving could involve long, heavy periods of work. Early in the century, there had already been a substantial shift away from linens into cotton and wool production because of the heavy demands of flax processing. After harvest, flax had to be soaked, or "retted," the seed removed, and the remainder dried and threshed. Men later "dressed" the flax, separating the woody part from the softer fibers with a flax brake, then removing the fibers with a swingling knife. They then handed the work over to women, who combed or "hatchelled" the fibers to separate the short ones (tow) from the long. Both sets of fiber were then spun into yarn, bleached, woven into cloth, and bleached again. The time involved in these processes was often prodigious. Families therefore had sought to reduce their output of linen by shifting to wool and by purchasing cotton yarn for some types of work. By 1810, according to the census for that year, linen accounted for less than 6 percent of Hampshire County's cloth production. Although the production of woolens was also demanding, wool required less processing than flax. Carding machines, which spread through the countryside in the 1800s, allowed home spinners to increase their productivity by an estimated 50 percent.[38]

37. Quoted in Francis M. Thompson, "Amariah Chandler and His Times," *History and Proceedings of the Pocumtuck Valley Memorial Association* 5 (1905–1911): 411.

38. Flax processing is described in Sylvester Judd, *History of Hadley, including the early history of Hatfield, South Hadley, Amherst and Granby, Mass.* (Northampton, 1863), p. 367. Textile output is enumerated in U.S. Treasury Department, *A Statement of the Arts and Manufactures of the United States of America for the Year 1810* (Philadelphia, 1813); Arthur H. Cole, *The American Wool Manufacture*, 2 vols. (Cambridge, Mass., 1926), drew attention to the high proportion of household manufactures among the products listed in this report. The spread of carding machines is traced in Chapter 3, above. The productivity gain from using machine-carded wool is given by David J. Jeremy, *Transatlantic Industrial Revolution: The Diffusion of Textile Technologies between Britain and America, 1790–1830s* (Oxford, 1981), p. 126. An important discussion of household production and gender roles is Jeanne Boydston, "The Industrialization of Housework in the Northeastern United States from the Colonial Period to the Civil War" (Ph.D. diss., Yale University, 1984), pp. 85–123, to which I referred in preparing the remainder of this chapter.

Several reasons lay behind these attempts to reduce heavy bouts of labor. Increases in the general level of household output, particularly of dairy produce, placed competing demands on women's time. Combined with the diffused structure of the household economy, these increases may have made exchanging or hiring outside labor to help with heavy work more difficult or uncertain. But it is likely that these savings in time were insufficient in many households. Those who started families in the 1800s and 1810s raised more children than their immediate predecessors, but there was a relative shortage of available help from the smaller cohort of children born to couples married in the 1790s. Although the demand for household textile production peaked about 1810, families' capacity to fulfill it was taxed to the limit.

Consequently, between 1815 and 1830 most households abandoned textile production. In 1815 some women in Middlefield called on their minister's wife and presented her with money and goods worth $20, including "116 runs of cotton and linen yarn, . . . cloth, flax, etc.," "an instance," according to the *Hampshire Gazette*, "of liberality, and respect for the Christian Ministry, deserving of notice." Five years later, the minister of Northampton and his wife publicly thanked "the ladies of the town" for presenting them with "near 80 runs of yarn and other articles."[39] But notices of this kind became increasingly rare as household textile production declined. Gifts, if they were made at all, took other forms.

In 1824 Elizabeth Huntington received as part of her marriage portion "the promise of all the flax and wool . . . that she could spin, to be made into fabrics." About 1830 her younger sisters still "had their regular morning tasks in spinning wool yarn," but routine of this kind was now unusual.[40] Caleb Cook of Hadley ceased making account-book entries for weaving about 1819. Sylvester Smith's family stopped making woolen cloth in 1822. In Amherst, Asa and Noble Dickinson's account-book entries for weaving ceased after 1822, and no mention of cloth appears after 1827. Chester Marshall's accounts ceased to mention spinning and cloth in 1834.[41] Although as late as 1845 a Northampton storekeeper could find it worthwhile to offer dry goods in exchange for "Domestic Flannel, Woolen Socks, White and Mixed Yarn," most independent textile production had long since retreated to the edges of the

39. *Hampshire Gazette*, May 17, 1815; Apr 17, 1820.
40. T. G. Huntington, "Sketches," pp. 45–46, 50.
41. Caleb Cook, Account Book, Hadley, 1794–1838, NHS, A.A.17.9; Sylvester Smith's recollection of the end of textile production in his family was recorded in Judd MS, "Hadley," 3:15; Asa and Noble Dickinson, Account Book, Amherst, 1817–1857, BCJL; Joseph Eastman and Chester E. Marshall, Account Book, North Amherst, 1801–1835, BCJL.

Valley. References to it appear in Westhampton in 1829, in Whately and Conway about 1830, in Williamsburg in 1839 and in Buckland and other Franklin County towns in the 1840s, but these references are scattered and largely relate to spinning. Already in the late 1820s, much of the plain cloth (as opposed to other articles) submitted for display at the annual Northampton cattle show was produced in local mills, rather than in households. By 1831, the show's report on domestic manufactures was complaining at the small number of articles submitted, which its author attributed in part to the "diversion of female industry . . . from household manufacturing."[42]

In place of their own products, or the work they hired done in the neighborhood, rural households now purchased foreign or American factory-made cloth at local stores. Store-bought cloth had played a role in the rural economy for a long time. Since the eighteenth century purchases of dry goods imported to the region had increased. But for long they had consisted mainly of high-quality materials used in wealthier households or of cheap goods intended for laborers, servants, and apprentices. After 1815, though, with the resumption of imports from Britain and the renewed expansion of American factory textile production, a wider range of cloths for rural markets became available at prices lower than before. The most straightforward explanation for households' substitution of factory-made for homemade textiles would be simply that they sought to take advantage of these cheap goods, whose prices now fell below a level that had once restrained them from buying.

Although there is truth in this explanation, it only partially accounts for a more complex series of changes. Both the presence of large quantities of store goods and the decisions of families to buy them were the results of processes involving more than simple calculations of price. The decision to buy rather than to make cloth was not straightforward. It depended above all on having means to exchange for it. This in turn depended on the organization of both women's and men's labor. Between about 1815 and 1830, the increases in household output which had begun in the late eighteenth century were turned more and more toward providing the means to substitute store-bought for home-produced textiles.

New Strategies: Women

Abandoning household textile production permitted some women to reduce their work burdens. Apphia Judd, after she moved from West-

---

42. References include M. Colton to Ann Bullard, Conway, Mass., Nov 11, 1826, and C. B. Bullard to Ann Bullard, Conway, Mass., n.d. [late 1820s], both in Edwards Family

hampton to Northampton in 1822, found time from her household tasks to dress and receive company during the afternoons. When her sister Arethusa Hall returned to live with the Judds for a time in 1825, she was told that "you might employ about half your time in studies and anything else you choose," the rest helping with sewing, washing, and housework: "you could be a *lady* part of the time, but not all."[43] This, though, was in a town household supported by a salary. Most rural women found that, if anything, their abandonment of textiles left them with an even more diverse range of tasks than before. But the nature of these tasks was such that it is likely that they were better able to tailor household work to the labor they had available. By removing a single heavy demand on their time, they left themselves a multitude of jobs that could be accomplished in smaller bouts. The reallocation of work took several forms. There were new activities for the household itself, the continuation of some forms of independent manufacture, and increased processing of farm produce in preparation for exchange. In addition, as we shall see in the next chapter, was the release of women's labor to work for entrepreneurs.

Richard and Claudia Bushman have noted the new attention to cleanliness and household amenities that affected various types of household work from the late eighteenth century on.[44] "We have gone thro' with a great white washing," wrote Charlotte Porter from Hadley in 1813, "& it has caused a pleasing change in the looks of the house." A variety of objects and activities facilitated cleaning. In Hadley, women could buy sand for scouring from peddlers who brought it from Pelham in carts. Hatfield's town meeting preserved the public's right to dig from a bank of suitable sand. Families made soap. Brooms and brushes were an expanding local industry in Hadley and other towns.[45] One sign of the increasing concern for cleanliness was men's uneasy ridicule of it, as in this song of 1817:

> Mops, pails and brushes, dusters, mats and soap,
> Are sceptres of control—her joy, her hope.
> Each day we scrub and scour house, yard and limb,
> And on Saturday, ye maids; we swim—

Correspondence, MCFL; Polly Cathcart Tilton, Diary, Williamsburg, Feb 12, Oct 24, 1839, PVMA. C. P. Huntington's report on household manufactures exhibited at the Northampton Cattle Show is in *Hampshire Gazette*, Nov 9, 1831.

43. Sylvester Judd to Arethusa Hall, Northampton, May 19, 1825, Judd Papers, 55M-1, Box 2, HCL.

44. Richard L. Bushman and Claudia Bushman, "The Early History of Cleanliness in America," *Journal of American History* 74 (Mar 1988): 1213–1238.

45. Charlotte Porter to Caroline Porter, Hadley, Apr 29, 1813, Williams Family Papers, Box 7, folder 11, no. 2, PVMA; on soapmaking see Judd MS, "Miscellaneous," 15:273; broom making is discussed in Gregory H. Nobles, "Commerce and Community: A Case Study of the Rural Broommaking Business in Antebellum Massachusetts," *Journal of the Early Republic* 4, no. 3 (1984): 287–308.

or an Amherst man's description of a visit to his aunt a decade or so later:

> She rises about daylight, and *trots* incessantly till ten or twelve at night, and every moment is spent in *cleaning up*. She began at the bottom of the cellar and has gone over the whole house, at least three times, during the past week, to the top of the garret. . . . As nigh as I can calculate the granite hearthstone in the kitchen and dining room lost each about one inch . . . ; and this she did by main strength, and under the greatest disadvantage, having nothing to work with, but an old broom, mop, soap and sand.

In addition to cleaning and other housework, women were also making an increasing range of items to enhance the comfort and decoration of their houses. A cattle-show report from the 1830s noted the award of premiums for "pieces of flannel and . . . dressed cloth blankets, quilts and counterpanes, carpeting, hearth rugs, hosiery, and a great variety of fabrics of a useful as well as an ornamental character."[46]

But before they had time for these things, most women still had to make and keep in repair the bulk of their households' clothing. Substitution of store-bought for home-produced cloth did not end independent household manufacture but merely pushed the most important part of it one stage along in the production process. Where spinning and, to a lesser degree, weaving had once occupied women's time, sewing became a constant activity for mothers, daughters, and, where they were present, servants and visitors as well. When Irene Hall of Norwich prepared to leave to teach in Virginia in 1829, her sister wrote that "we found many who interested themselves in her welfare and have assisted . . . without reward" in making clothes for her. In 1830, the first "Ladies' Fair" held in Northampton displayed the products of domestic sewing.[47]

While much of this work was for families' own consumption, women who needed income continued to manufacture various items for exchange as well. In Hawley in 1830, Esther Grout, living at home with her mother and "finding my health insufficient to do anything which required much strength" determined "to earn something with my needle," and started to learn millinery. Over the next year she worked at bonnet making for local customers, naming each one in her account book, interspersed with short spells of work in other households for pay in cloth, materials, and cash. "I already began to realise some

46. Verses: *Hampshire Gazette*, Feb 5, 1817; description: Martin Field to Esther S. Field, Fayetteville, Vt., Nov 9, 1828, Jones Family Papers, BCJL; report: *New England Farmer*, Oct 24, 1838.

47. Apphia Judd to Arethusa Hall, Northampton, Dec 27, 1829, Judd Papers, 55M-1, Box 2, HCL; *Hampshire Sentinel* (Belchertown), Nov 3, 1830.

profits," she wrote, "and perhaps flattered myself too much with the idea of being able to bear my own expenses," when she suffered a bout of fever that left her health worsened. A number of Hadley women wove carpets during the 1830s, while the South Amherst widow Judith Nutting wove rag carpets for local customers throughout the 1840s.[48] Up and down the Valley women found substitute work as they and their households sought to earn extra income from independent production.

Above all, women's work helped to raise the income with which farm families obtained store-bought cloth in the first place. Reduction of flax cultivation had helped farmers shift toward the increased livestock production that we noted earlier. This increase included larger numbers of dairy cattle. By 1831, there were nearly 2,900 cows listed in the valuations from the six towns, an increase of 135 percent or more over the previous four decades; in Northampton alone the number had increased by about 50 percent since 1821. Women were largely responsible for processing the products of these animals into cheese and, increasingly, butter, which became significant exchange items with local stores. At Sylvester Judd's Westhampton store in the early 1820s, not only did dairy produce form a considerable part of his business, but it was the principal item brought in by all the women who traded in their own names. The historian Joan Jensen has estimated that by 1840 between 14 and 23 percent of New England farm incomes were earned from dairying. In the Connecticut Valley, Amherst in particular became an important center of butter making, producing at one point the fourth largest quantity of any Massachusetts town.[49]

Women's redeployment of their time into dairying and the processing of other farm goods involved coordination with men's shifting farm strategies and an unprecedented engagement in exchange with local stores to satisfy part of their households' essential needs. The shift out of textile production therefore had profound consequences for the whole position of farm households in the economy. It represented much more than an adjustment to changing price levels, although lower cloth prices were necessary for the shift to occur at all. It was part of a

48. Esther T. W. Grout, Diary, Hawley, Feb 13, 1831, Grout Papers, no. 57, PVMA; Judd MS, "Hadley," 3:18; Mary Nutting to Eli Nutting, Amherst, Aug 26 and Oct 20, 1842, Harriet Nutting to Eli Nutting, Amherst, July 3, 1847, and Apr 6, 1848, Nutting Family Correspondence, BCJL.

49. Mass., General Court (Committees), Aggregates of Valuations, 1821, 1831, Mass. State Library, Boston (microfilm); Sylvester Judd, Jr., Account Books, 2 vols., Westhampton, 1813–1822, MCFL; Joan M. Jensen emphasized that the purpose of such output was usually "to make ends meet rather than to consciously make profits" ("Cloth, Butter, and Boarders: Women's Household Production for the Market," *Review of Radical Political Economics* 12 [Summer 1980]: 21). In *Loosening the Bonds: Mid-Atlantic Farm Women* (New Haven, 1986), chaps. 5 and 6, Jensen analyzes household dairying in detail.

drawn-out readjustment of household orientation, which placed farmers in closer dependence on distant markets than they had been before.

Moreover, because patterns of household work were now more flexible than they had been during the height of independent textile production, demand for women's labor fluctuated more. Because of this fluctuation, young women in particular had more time to work outside the home, in education or in factories, or to do outwork at home for local merchants. At least two of Moses and Susanna Goodale's daughters, for instance, worked in Chicopee and Springfield mills in the late 1820s and 1830s. Some women traveled as far as Lowell and other towns in eastern Massachusetts to work. But only small numbers of women from the Valley proper can be traced in the employment records of large textile manufacturers. In areas such as this, where farming remained prosperous, they were more likely to find livelihoods in or near their homes than were women from the poorer hill towns. As Jensen noted, dairy production gave rural women contact with wider markets without altering their ties to households or to the male-dominated property relations on which they were dependent.[50]

New Strategies: Farm Production

The shift in household production and the need to rely more than beforehand on income to purchase goods accompanied a shift in farming strategies. The increased output and more intensive cultivation that farmers had achieved in the opening decades of the century allowed many of them to increase their sales of produce after about 1820. For farmers with enough land to support their families, however, family provision remained the first priority.

The Valley continued to produce most basic foodstuffs. In 1822 a list of the produce raised in Northampton included beef, pork, fowls, eggs, cheese, butter, corn, rye, wheat, oats, potatoes, and cider, together with wood, lime, and flaxseed. In Westhampton the previous year, Sylvester Judd, Jr., had noted the products of his father's farm, which included butter, beef, apples, cider, quinces, potatoes, fowls, eggs, and

50. Elizabeth Goodale to Susanna Goodale, Springfield, Aug 25, 1827; Susanna Goodale to Moses and Susanna Goodale, Cabotville [Chicopee], Apr 8, 1837, and Feb 7, 1838, Goodell Collection, BCJL. A check of the Registers of the Hamilton Manufacturing Co., Lowell, revealed only small numbers of workers, male or female, from the Connecticut Valley towns (vols. 481 [Jul–Dec 1830] and 485 [Oct 1839–Apr 1841], Hamilton Mfg. Co. Collection, D-11–12, HBS. For a general discussion of migration to factories, see Thomas L. Dublin, *Women at Work: The Transformation of Work and Community in Lowell, Massachusetts, 1826–1860* (New York, 1979), and Dublin, ed., *Farm to Factory: Letters from New England Women* (New York, 1981).

wool, aside from grain and hay crops. At the end of the 1820s, Charles P. Phelps of Hadley was calculating that the annual value of the produce of his farm devoted to family use was over $260. Again, this included rye, corn, potatoes, cider, pork, butter, poultry, wood, and garden vegetables.[51] Although few farmers depended on them to a great extent, the gradual introduction of potatoes during the early nineteenth century somewhat lowered the amount of land needed to feed a family.

So farmers continued to raise a variety of crops, and families expected that homegrown or locally grown produce would be the mainstay of their diets. When a widow from Conway married a Whately farmer in 1842, her daughter, reporting that she would "gett a good husband and a good home," noted that her new stepfather and his family had "a good farm, fruit of all kinds, raise pretty much all that they want to live on, thirty bushels of wheat this year besides all the rest of the good things and Maple sugar in the bargain." Three years later, a young Amherst woman, trying to persuade her brother to visit for Thanksgiving, described the produce that would await him: "We have got some rye, and buckwheat and corn & potatoes. . . . Only think of buckwheat cakes for breakfast pudding and milk for dinner and jonny-cake for supper, and perhaps an apple or a walnut in the evening[;] now don't your eyes water to taste of some of the good things[?]"[52] Mixed-crop production and subsistence-surplus strategies remained a framework within which farmers continued to work.

Onto this framework, though, they grafted an increasing involvement with distant markets, which intensified as the demand for household income increased. The continued expansion of livestock production, for meat, dairy produce, and wool, strengthened the connections between Valley and hill towns, as Valley farmers sought summer hill pastures for their cattle or purchased cattle for winter stall feeding each autumn from drovers and dealers who moved them from the hills. Having provided for family needs, larger farmers in particular concentrated extra effort on the crop/livestock cycle, raising field crops for animal feed, rather than just for sale. Northampton farmers, for instance, raised their total grain output from 31,497 bushels in 1821 to 41,473 bushels in 1831, an increase of nearly 32 percent. Of this, the proportion of corn rose from 63 percent in 1821 to 73 percent in 1831. They also raised 38 percent more hay over the decade.[53] A substantial

51. Northampton produce was listed in *Hampshire Gazette*, Nov 20, 1822; Sylvester Judd, Jr., Account Book, 2:38; Charles P. Phelps, Account Books, 5 vols., Hadley, 1805–1858, HBS, esp. vol. 2, entries for Dec 1829 and Dec 1830.

52. Hannah Nutting to Eli Nutting, Amherst, Nov 11, 1845, Nutting Correspondence.

53. Mass., General Court, Aggregates of Valuations, 1821, 1831.

farmer such as Charles P. Phelps might raise over 90 percent of his household's food on the premises, but by the 1840s he was also feeding nearly nine-tenths of his grain and hay crops to livestock. Some methods intentionally favored livestock feeding over other uses. The *New England Farmer* noted in 1838 that "many farmers on Connecticut river" had adopted the practice of storing hay when it was still comparatively green, rather than drying it in the fields. This made the hay unmarketable, but suitable for stall feeding. "They say much labor is saved and the hay spends better for their cattle."[54]

While Northampton farmers focused their attention on beef cattle, Amherst increased dairy output, and the hill towns increased the size of their sheep flocks, farmers in the most fertile sections of the Hadley and Hatfield meadows turned increasing attention to raising broomcorn as a supplement to their existing crops and sources of income. The introduction and spread of broomcorn in Hadley at the end of the eighteenth century and its role in supporting wintertime broom making by local farmers were noted earlier. After 1815, however, the crop became increasingly important. In 1816 it was introduced in Hatfield. As market demand rose, cultivation of broomcorn and manufacture of brooms spread more rapidly. More farmers became involved. Some, like the Shipmans of Hadley, built larger broom workshops and began to seek the benefits of more concentrated production. Purchasers of broomcorn from outside the region also began to appear.[55] By 1823, Dan Huntington could write that "The Sun in the pride of his strength sends forth his rays, in all directions. *Old Hadley*, in the pride of its commerce, sends forth its broom carts to all the winds of heaven." Writing to his daughter, Huntington pondered whether this was a good thing. Drawing a moral from it, he concluded that it was: "*Broom corn*, in fact is not an evil in our land. It contributes to the making of neat housewives, when otherwise, perhaps, we should look for them in vain." "Besides," he added, "I sold to a shaking quaker the other day, without the trouble of manufacturing it, nearly sixty dollars worth."[56] By 1826, the *New England Farmer* reported, more than 1,400 acres of land in Hadley and Hatfield were under broomcorn. This was over one-quarter of the towns' total tillage, and the crop of broom brush and broomcorn seed raised that year was expected to total over $40,000 in value. Had this been shared among every farm in the two towns it would have represented more than $150 each. Earnings like this from a single crop were a new phenomenon.[57]

54. *New England Farmer*, Aug 8, 1838.
55. Early developments in broom production are noted in Judd MS, "Hadley," 3:13, and summarized in Judd, *History of Hadley*, pp. 368–369.
56. Dan Huntington to Bethia Huntington, Hadley, Jan 3, 1823, PPHH.
57. *New England Farmer*, Dec 29, 1826. This was roughly corroborated by a report in the *Franklin Herald* (Greenfield), Jan 2, 1827, which estimated broomcorn acreage in Hadley

As broomcorn became established, its cultivation and handling progressively acquired "market" characteristics and practices. The crop spread to Northampton, at first not because local farmers were planting it, but because Hadley and Hatfield farmers rented land there to grow it on.[58] However, the burgeoning demand for broomcorn had its limits. The boom up to 1826 led to a rapid depression of prices. As the *New England Farmer* felt it necessary to point out, "when the cultivation of any article has reached the amount of consumption, an increase of the crop will lower the price."[59] As prices fell in the late 1820s, farmers cut back production, so that by 1831, Hadley and Hatfield output was only two-thirds of what it had been five years before. This in turn helped raise prices, and output increased again in the early 1830s. But there were also considerable seasonal price fluctuations. A sudden early frost in 1830 apparently damaged at least one-quarter of the broomcorn crop in the fields and prices rose sharply, by as much as 25 percent in a few days.[60] As farmers attempted to adjust to these rises and falls, some earned unexpected windfalls and others learned hard lessons. The 1830 frost sent speculators into the fields to buy up crops rapidly. While one dealer was reported to have netted $600 from a quick purchase and resale of fifteen acres of the crop as prices rose, the story was also told of a farmer who had contracted that spring to sell his crop at a price that was now half the going rate. Similarly, an unexpected price rise in 1834 left some farmers "uninformed," according to a report, and selling their crops to dealers at the previous year's prices.[61]

Not surprisingly, larger landowners stood to benefit more from broomcorn production than small farmers. They could afford to devote a portion of their tillage land to the crop without disrupting their normal mixed-crop strategies, whereas small farmers were faced with the choice of depending on broomcorn or continuing to raise their food crops. Some small farmers attempted to resolve the dilemma by renting land on which to grow broomcorn, but even so, their advantages were not great. Rent alone varied between one-third and one-half of the expected value of the crop at the beginning of the season, depending on how much preparation had been done to the land. In 1830 Thaddeus Smith rented five acres of land from Charles P. Phelps "for the purpose

and Hatfield at 1,500 (quoted in Charles Jones, "The Broom Corn Industry in the Counties of Franklin and Hampshire, and in the Town of Deerfield in Particular," *History and Proceedings of the Pocumtuck Valley Memorial Association* 4 [1899–1904]: 105). This and other reports claimed yields of 600–1,000 lbs. of brush per acre, and prices between $0.035 and $0.06 per lb. According to these figures the crop's total value would have been between $31,500 and $90,000. Since published reports usually gave optimistic accounts of yields and returns, the lower figure is likely to have been nearer to the real value of the crop.

58. *Hampshire Gazette*, Mar 30, 1831.
59. *New England Farmer*, Dec 29, 1826.
60. *Hampshire Sentinel* (Belchertown), Sept 22, 1830.
61. *Hampshire Gazette*, Sept 17, 1834.

of raising broom corn the present season." For the use of the land and for thirty "common loads of manure" Smith was to pay $90 that December. At the low prices prevailing when he made the agreement, Smith could have expected a return of little more than $50 for the crop after paying rent and before paying for labor or other expenses. This, of course, was a smaller return than Phelps was earning from the rent. Smith's fortunes that year are unknown. If his crop escaped frost damage and he was able to sell it at the high prices that prevailed at the end of the season, then he could have made as much as $190 before expenses. Owning or renting land made the difference between earning enough to cover debts and earning sufficient to accumulate more property. As a landowner Phelps was able to take the middle route, of securing a certain return for his land without having to worry about fluctuations in the price of the crop. Northampton farmers rented land for others to grow broomcorn for up to a decade before they started raising the crop themselves.[62]

Broomcorn became the Valley's closest thing to a staple crop since the decline of wheat. But it accompanied, rather than displaced, farmers' subsistence-surplus strategies. It made heavier demands for labor than Indian corn. Only farmers who habitually hired summer workers tended to grow it in large amounts. Large landowners who could not find sufficient labor rented to farmers who had the means to organize the family or exchange labor required. Pressure to use family labor was such that women and children frequently went into the fields at harvest time to begin processing the broomcorn after it had been cut. Moreover, broomcorn fitted in with other farm production. Mixed with corn, broomcorn seed could be fed to cattle. Some farmers regarded broomcorn and cattle fattening as necessary complements to one another because of the cycle of feedstuffs, manure, and crops they permitted. Broom brush was of course destined for local broom shops. In other words, while the crop represented a new source of cash income and gave rise to procedures that had up to now been unusual in the countryside, it represented only a partial and hesitant step away from older patterns.[63]

Food Consumption

Nevertheless, the rapid growth of the Valley's nonfarm population, especially in Northampton, meant that by the 1830s the region was far

62. Charles P. Phelps, Account Books, vol. 2, Mar 1830.
63. Jones, "Broom Corn Industry," pp. 105–107, provides a detailed account of the production of the crop and the use of seed for feed. Henry Colman, *Fourth Report on the Agriculture of Massachusetts: Franklin County* (Boston, 1841), pp. 30–34, discussed broomcorn and its connection with cattle raising.

from able to supply all of its own food requirements. While an enquiry into the Valley's trade in the late 1820s found that "the surplus products of some towns are almost all disposed of in the vicinity," demand was beginning to outrun supply.[64] Farmers might feed their own families and their hired hands, but they could no longer maintain regional self-sufficiency. The intermittent grain shipments that had occurred up to the early nineteenth century gradually became a regular flow, especially after the opening of the Erie Canal. By 1827, according to the trade survey, between 20,000 and 30,000 bushels of wheat each year were being brought from the canal via New York to Northampton "for the supply of a flour-mill in the town." If these figures were accurate, there would have been more than enough grain to supply the basic needs of the town's whole population. Rochester flour appeared in stores in outlying towns as well.[65]

The expansion of trade prompted new proposals for transport improvements for the first time in two decades. In the late 1820s, as rival groups promoted river improvements and a canal scheme to link Northampton to New Haven, there were early stirrings of an East-West railroad or canal project too. The completion of locks at Enfield, Connecticut, in 1829 at last provided direct access from the lower to the upper sections of the Connecticut River, although only small craft could reach upstream. By the time the New Haven–Northampton canal was fully opened in 1837, boats carrying flour and other cargoes were arriving in Northampton several times a week. Estimating total New England flour imports at 389,000 barrels in 1838, a Massachusetts legislative report noted in addition "an almost perpetual transportation by means of wagons, from Troy, Albany and Hudson, into the county of Berkshire, for the supply not only of the inhabitants of that county, but for consumption by the people of many towns in the counties of Franklin, Hampshire and Hampden."[66]

Under these circumstances farm families as well as others were likely to increase their dependence on imported foodstuffs as well as other goods. This was particularly so in fertile sections where broomcorn and cattle raising enhanced farm incomes. The trade survey of the late 1820s suggested that the shipment of goods in and out of a Valley town such as Westfield was ten times as much as shipments in and out of an

64. *Hampshire Gazette*, Feb 13, 1828.

65. Returns from the survey were published in *Report of the Board of Commissioners for the Survey of One or More Routes for a Railway from Boston to Albany*, Mass. Senate Doc. no. 5 (Boston, 1828), pp. 49–52; the quotation is on p. 52. The *Boston Patriot and Mercantile Advertizer*, Feb 9, 1828, also printed data from the survey. Flour advertisements appeared, e.g., in the *New England Inquirer* (Amherst), Apr 3, 1828.

66. Grain and flour shipments were noted on the canal by the *Northampton Courier*, July 5, 1837, and on the river by Sylvester Judd, "Notebook," vol. 1, July 12, 1837. The legislative report is quoted in Percy W. Bidwell and John I. Falconer, *History of Agriculture in the Northern United States, 1620–1860* (Washington, D.C., 1925), p. 238.

upland place like Belchertown.[67] Even in the Valley, though, household strategies varied. Charles P. Phelps continued to supply most of his household food in the 1840s, and the pattern of mixed-crop production meant that it was unlikely that many farmers came to rely extensively on imports. But after the poor harvests of 1837, Sylvester Judd noted that "very many people, farmers as well as others, have to buy bread-stuffs raised in other states." According to Rev. Henry Colman, Hatfield cattle fatteners by the end of the 1830s were purchasing, rather than growing, rye to feed to their stock, even though it cost one third more than the corn that they continued to grow in their fields. Like the Concord farmers Thoreau was later to criticize, these men fed grain to their cattle to sell in order to purchase flour for themselves at the store.[68]

The Implications of New Strategies

The altered household consumption patterns that saw many rural families purchasing essentials that even two decades before they would have acquired locally enhanced the local importance of merchants, storekeepers, and other traders whose position had previously remained somewhat marginal. As we shall see shortly, this helped change the balance of power in rural society and brought households increasingly to the point where their "independence" was compromised, not in this case by the need for interdependence with other rural households, but by essential connections with entrepreneurs.

Nevertheless, even as it grew, households' dependence on distant markets became a matter for protracted debate. By the late 1820s and early 1830s a number of consequences were becoming clear. Price fluctuations could send a season's plans awry. Cattle fatteners frequently found themselves caught out by short-term changes in the prices of cattle, beef, grain, and hay. In 1836 sudden rises in feed prices due to shortages caused "distress among the farmers, or among their stock in some places."[69] In 1830, 1834, and 1838 the decline of beef prices on spring markets made it hard for farmers to recover their costs. A committee of Franklin County farmers complained in 1834 that "the cattle which many of us purchased last autumn for the stall, and in feeding

---

67. *Boston Patriot*, Feb 9, 1828. Westfield's population was only about one-fourth higher than Belchertown's.

68. Judd, "Notebook," vol. 1, June 6, 1838. Colman, *Fourth Report*, p. 27. Henry D. Thoreau, *Walden; or, Life in the Woods* (1854; reprint, New York, 1937), p. 57, criticized the farmer who feeds his own grain to cattle and "buys flour, which is at least no more wholesome, at a greater cost, at the store."

69. Judd, "Notebook," vol. 1, Mar 9, 1836.

which nearly the whole produce of our farms has been expended, are not worth to us now more than we paid for them." A Hatfield farmer put it more pithily: all he had earned from his beef cattle was "a swearing pile of manure." When, as in 1834, prices for farm produce fell generally, difficulties were widespread. The Franklin County meeting blamed President Jackson's bank policies for their trouble. Petitioning Congress for relief, they explained that "our fat cattle, our wool and our grain . . . are upon our hands, and there is no possibility of getting rid of them, except by a great sacrifice."[70]

Because the expansion in the Valley's farm output for sale accompanied an uneven fall in produce prices between the early 1820s and the mid-1840s, these conditions became endemic. Behind the decline, in turn, was the opening up of fertile western farm regions capable of shipping grain, meat, and other produce to eastern urban centers at competitive prices. As early as 1828, the *Hampshire Gazette* noted that poor road conditions in the spring would give Valley farmers a chance to get their cattle to market before drovers from Ohio and New York could reach the area. Citing competition from New York and other regions, the Hampshire, Franklin, and Hampden Agricultural Society commented in 1830 that "the produce of the farms of this country can hardly be said to be of such kind and quality as, in the present depressed state of the markets, and where the price of labor is comparatively so high, to yield a fair profit to the cultivator."[71] Fear of transportation improvements that could make this western competition easier played an important role in local politics at the end of the 1820s. The Massachusetts governor Levi Lincoln, who had enjoyed strong support in Valley elections for several years, suffered a sharp drop in votes in 1829 after a rumor spread that he favored an East-West railroad.[72]

Opinion divided as to the best response to this situation. Some writers urged acceptance of it and stated that New England farmers should rely on producing the goods that could not easily be transported from a distance.[73] Others were more cautious. Although he criticized

---

70. "Proceedings of a Meeting of Inhabitants of Franklin County, in favour of a National Bank," U.S. Congress, House Doc. no. 480 (Washington, D.C., 1834), p. 3; Judd, "Notebook," vol. 1, Apr 6, 1838, Mar 31, 1840. The Hatfield farmer's remark was quoted by George Sheldon, " 'Tis Sixty Years Since: The Passing of the Stall-Fed Ox and the Farm Boy," *History and Proceedings of the Pocumtuck Valley Memorial Association* 3 (1890–1898): 474.

71. *New England Farmer*, May 28, 1830, quoting the *Greenfield Gazette*.

72. *Hampshire Gazette*, Apr 8, 1829.

73. W. Buckminster, in the *New England Farmer* (1838), quoted in Lester E. Klimm, *The Relation between Certain Population Changes and the Physical Environment in Hampden, Hampshire, and Franklin Counties, Massachusetts, 1790–1925* (Philadelphia, 1933), p. 76.

those who "look for nothing from their farms beyond the bare support of their families," Henry Colman argued nevertheless that "agriculture can never be looked to in this part of the country, as a source of wealth. Yet it may be made to yield an ample competence." Colman and others drew attention to the danger that excessive reliance on fluctuating markets posed to farmers' independence. Among them was Rev. Samuel C. Allen, who gained considerable local support as a Workingman's candidate in gubernatorial elections in the early 1830s, warning of the dangers of the financial entanglements markets posed to farmers. As prices fell, he argued, farmers made use of tenancy or took out mortgages to an extent that appeared to threaten their households' integrity. Some evidence bears this out. Whereas in 1810–1811 mortgage deeds had accounted for 13.8 percent of land transactions in Hampshire County, by 1830–1831 the proportion had reached 27.1 percent by number and 30.3 percent by value.[74] An article published in the *New England Farmer* in 1829 warned smallholders in particular to grow their own food grains and vegetables. Having a garden would both provide work at slack times for those who needed to hire themselves out as laborers and "almost subsist your family, instead of taking part of your day's wages for marketing." "The market is a canker," the writer warned, "that will, by degrees, eat you out, while you are eating upon it."[75]

In practice, many farm households sought to take a middle course, preserving their ability to raise supplies for themselves while raising extra surpluses for sale. Rarely did farm strategies stress seeking out profit in particular markets at the expense of maintaining a balance between subsistence and surplus. A debate in the *Hampshire Gazette* in 1829 on the cost of feeding cattle focused, not on the maximization of profit, but on the minimization of loss at a time of falling and fluctuating prices. All the participants accepted that fattening cattle was necessary to a farm's overall cycle of production even if it earned no income itself.[76] Advocates of agricultural improvements urged farmers to take up profit-earning crops, such as hemp, teasels, and mulberry. But it was widely recognized that these should accompany and not replace other activities. The few farmers who grew teasels, for example, were the larger landowners in hill towns such as Williamsburg, who could supply local carding mills with a crop they grew alongside the usual

---

74. Samuel C. Allen, *Address Delivered at Northampton before the Hampshire, Franklin, and Hampden Agricultural Society, Oct 27, 1830* (Northampton, 1830), p. 27. Mortgage data were drawn from Hampshire County Registry of Deeds, Records, Hampshire County Hall of Records, Northampton.
75. *New England Farmer*, Oct 23, 1829.
76. The debate appeared in the *Hampshire Gazette*, Apr 1, 8, 1829.

range of grains and hay.[77] When Northampton promoters set to work in the early 1830s to encourage farmers to grow mulberry trees, whose leaves could be fed to silkworms, they emphasized that this would not disrupt existing strategies. Trees could be planted on spare land, they argued; looking after them and collecting leaves "requires . . . the attention of women and children only," who they evidently assumed had nothing else to do. Mulberry leaves "therefore may be produced without at all interfering with other operations upon the farm."[78]

A speaker at an agricultural show remarked in 1828 that commercial standards of profitability did not apply to farming:

> There is not a farmer . . . who, if he opened an account with his farm, and kept it after the manner of merchants and manufacturers, but, by such account, would find himself ruined every five years of his life. Let the farmer charge his farm at the reputed value, . . . charge the labor of himself, his boys, and hired labor, charge interest on his investments—then credit his farm with all the produce, at cash price, and . . . by such an account every farmer will find himself ruined, farm, stock, and all sunk.

Yet, he concluded, "our farmers obtain a comfortable living."[79] Charles P. Phelps of Hadley, the one Connecticut Valley farmer who is known to have used accounting procedures such as these in this period, appears to have been an exception to the speaker's rule. But he owned half of one of the Valley's largest farms and had had a legal and mercantile career in Boston before returning to Hadley.[80] Phelps also fed his own family from the farm. Like most of his neighbors he would have seen his activities as part of a whole strategy, not purely designed to pursue profit in the marketplace.

The 1820s and 1830s marked a crucial period in the transition to rural capitalism. Not only did households shift their production and consumption strategies but, in doing so, they created unprecedented opportunities for local merchants to expand their role and influence in the countryside. The people most carefully calculating profits were not farmers but shopkeepers and traders, who began to handle more business. They expanded their role, inserted themselves into existing exchange patterns, and extended their influence beyond trade itself into the control of household labor. It was this, in particular, that signaled the beginnings of a new rural social structure and the curbing of the autonomous household system.

77. Joseph Williams, Account Book, c. 1802–1841, WHS.
78. Quoted in the *New England Farmer*, May 28, 1830.
79. Quoted in the *Hampshire Gazette*, Mar 26, 1828.
80. Charles P. Phelps, Account Books.

Chapter 5

Merchants and Households

When farmers sought to dispose of surplus produce, they had a number of options. They could make local exchanges with people who worked for them, but often these did not bring in cash or credit with which to acquire goods from elsewhere. They could carry goods to distant markets themselves. This practice was common early in the nineteenth century, but as rural production increased and overall prices tended to fall, small producers perceived that it was more time-consuming than it was worth. There were other risks, too. As George Sheldon pointed out, farmers with cattle to sell could drive them to Boston or other markets themselves, but they faced the danger that butchers in the market would combine to "roast" them, "both for sport and profit."[1] In many instances farmers sought out friends or relatives in the cities who could provide advice or handle their goods for them. Moses Goodale of Belchertown, for example, sent a load of brooms each year in the late 1820s to a Boston merchant, Levi Bliss, a former neighbor; in addition to discussing the market for brooms, the men's correspondence passed news of the health and affairs of mutual acquaintances.[2] But over time direct sales of small quantities of produce tended to be conducted over shorter distances. It was to local merchants that much of the responsibility for handling goods into and out of the region fell. As production and trade grew, the number and relative power of these traders increased as well.

We saw in Chapter 2 that the structure of the household economy and the increasing density of local exchange networks created particular

1. George Sheldon, "'Tis Sixty Years Since: The Passing of the Stall-Fed Ox and the Farm Boy," *History and Proceedings of the Pocumtuck Valley Memorial Association* 3 (1890–1898): 481.
2. Levi Bliss to Moses Goodale, Boston, Feb 5, 1828, Sept 1829, Goodell Collection, BCJL.

Table 9. Stock-in-trade in the six towns, 1791

	Stock-in-trade ($)	Stock-in-trade per capita ($)
Amherst	1,736	1.41
Hadley	5,000	5.67
Hatfield	1,423	2.02
Northampton	18,731	11.50
Westhampton	433	0.63
Williamsburg	567	0.54

Source: Massachusetts, General Court (Committees), Aggregates of Valuations, 1791, Mass. State Library, Boston (microfilm).

problems for the region's traders in the late eighteenth century and led the more prosperous of them to support schemes for internal improvements and other means of profiting from the limited and diffuse output of the Valley.[3] Substantial traders were concentrated in a small group in Northampton and Hadley at the center of the Valley, where there were perhaps a dozen or so at any time between the 1780s and the 1800s. These firms, in addition to handling local retail trade, were wholesale suppliers to small stores scattered unevenly through the remainder of the region. In some cases, these smaller stores were effectively branches of the Northampton or Hadley ones, partly owned by the latter in conjunction with a local relative or business partner. For trading into more sparsely populated neighborhoods, merchants like William Porter of Hadley fitted out peddlers with small assortments of goods.[4] These trading connections resembled the spokes of a wheel, radiating from the two river towns.

In 1791, Northampton's stock-in-trade was valued at $18,731 and Hadley's at $5,000 (Table 9). Not only were these figures considerably higher than for any of the surrounding towns, but they also represented

3. Contemporaries used three terms employed in this chapter—"merchant," "storekeeper," and "trader"—without drawing hard and fast distinctions between them. Broadly speaking, I use "trader" to refer to anyone who made a living from handling goods carried into or out of the region, and "storekeeper" for people who kept stocks of goods to sell. I employ "merchant" as a generic term to cover both functions, but usually indicate by the context the nature and scale of a particular individual's business.

4. The standard account of trading patterns at the end of the eighteenth century is given by Margaret E. Martin, "Merchants and Trade of the Connecticut River Valley, 1750–1820," *Smith College Studies in History* 24 (1938–1939). Evidence of the widespread connections of traders in Northampton and Hadley is to be found, e.g., in Levi Shepard, "A List of Notes and Book Accts due at this Time to the Late Compy of Shephard & Hunt and this day set of[f] to Levi Shephard," Northampton, July 12, 1784, MCFL, Box 31. William Porter of Hadley supplied stores in Worthington and Conway in which he was a partner or had an interest (William Porter Papers, Box D, folder 1815, OSV) and supplied goods to be sold on commission by peddlers (Box I, misc. undated papers).

much larger amounts of goods per head of population than elsewhere.[5] Even Hadley, whose mercantile activity was less than one-third of Northampton's and, in proportion to its population, less than half as large, had trade three or four times more significant than its neighbors Amherst or Hatfield and ten times greater than the hill towns of Westhampton and Williamsburg. A comparison of individual stores underlines this contrast. The substantial Northampton merchant Levi Shepard reported that his store inventory was worth $8,000 in 1804. When Sylvester Judd, Jr., counted the stock in his Westhampton store in 1815 he found it worth only $416.51. In fact, this could understate the difference, because while Judd was taking inventory for his own purposes, Shepard was providing a figure for the Northampton tax assessors and may have underestimated the true value of his goods.[6] As they had for more than thirty years, Shepard's business contacts radiated across western Massachusetts, tying small traders and producers into a web centered on his own store.

In the rural economy of the late eighteenth century, with its small surpluses and lack of a staple crop, substantial traders could best function at points such as Northampton, where they could organize the collection and shipment of small quantities of varied and diffused products. To most rural households these traders were geographically distant. They were also at the margins of most local exchange networks. Between the 1790s and the early 1830s, however, this hub-and-spoke pattern changed substantially. As household production increased, patterns of trade became relatively diffused, so that they came to resemble a more complex matrix, with connections running in many directions. Traders increased in number, were distributed more evenly throughout the countryside, and became more closely integrated into local exchange networks. In the long run this would give some of them an increasingly powerful role in the rural economy, although not without many difficulties and uncertainties.

The Diffusion of Rural Stores

Although in absolute terms Northampton retained its mercantile preeminence in the region, Hadley did not, and trade in both towns grew slowly in comparison with that of their neighbors. Northampton's stock-in-trade per capita grew by 22 percent between 1791 and 1821,

5. Mass., General Court (Committees), Aggregates of Valuations, 1791, Mass. State Library, Boston (microfilm).
6. "Levi Shepherd and Sons List for the year 1804," MS fragment, MCFL, Box 31; Judd MS, "Book of Fragments," Apr 1815, FL.

Table 10. Stock-in-trade per capita in the six towns, 1791–1831

	Percentage increase in stock-in-trade per capita		Total stock-in-trade, 1831
	1791–1821	1791–1831	($)
Amherst	—	450	20,250
Hadley	—	11	10,600
Hatfield	—	352	8,150
Northampton	22	77	73,450
Westhampton	—	108	1,200
Williamsburg	—	1,174	8,500

Source: Massachusetts, General Court (Committees), Aggregates of Valuations, 1831, Mass. State Library, Boston (microfilm).

and by another 45 percent in the next ten years, but Hadley's rose by only 11 percent over the four decades (Table 10). Trade in all the other towns grew much more rapidly between 1791 and 1831, Amherst's and Hatfield's by over four or five times relative to population and Williamsburg's by over twelve times. Even Westhampton, always the least commercialized of Northampton's neighbors in the nineteenth century, more than doubled its stock-in-trade per capita. In other words, the towns with the lowest levels of trade at the end of the eighteenth century developed it most quickly in the early nineteenth. Amherst, whose stock-in-trade had once been only one-third of Hadley's, now had nearly double its neighbor's, while Hatfield's and Williamsburg's were each almost as valuable as Hadley's. The distribution of trade goods had become more decentralized.[7]

The comparative reduction that occurred in the importance of Northampton and Hadley was reflected in events, as well as in the figures. The mixed fortunes of the first investors in public improvements were also experienced by the early sponsors of the Northampton Bank, founded in 1803 to discount local paper. After the bank nearly failed in 1810 it had to be reorganized and refloated. Several of Northampton's most prominent trading families faded from the scene between 1800 and the 1820s. The Shepards switched into manufacturing, and James Shepard eventually went bankrupt in 1827. Levi Shepard's son Thomas also suffered financial reverses and ended up as Northampton's postmaster—a less exalted position than his father's had once been. The Brecks left town or entered other occupations. Benjamin Tappan maintained his Northampton store, but his sons found the town too small for

7. Mass., General Court, Aggregates of Valuations, 1791, 1821, 1831.

their ambitions and left to seek their fortunes in Boston and New York.[8] In Hadley, while the number of stores remained about four, only William Porter's stayed in the same hands throughout the period. Others went through various failures, reorganizations, and changes of ownership.

One reason for this reorientation of trading patterns into a more diffused matrix lay, of course, in population growth. Amherst's population more than doubled between 1790 and 1830, while other towns also grew in size, although some only slightly. As more people lived in the outlying towns of the Valley, they provided the basis to support stores. David Mack, one of the first settlers of Middlefield, emerged as the town's leading trader in the late eighteenth century, serving as a conduit for imported goods and surplus produce in and out of his neighborhood. Advertisements well into the nineteenth century reflected the view that stores, in the same way as gristmills or particular craft occupations, provided a local service for which neighborhood patronage could be expected.[9] But this is only a small part of the picture. Northampton and Hadley actually increased their share of the total population of the six towns during the period, while some of the most rapid growth in trade occurred in Williamsburg, whose population grew most slowly.[10] The factors affecting the distribution of trading activity had more to do with social structure than the size or growth of the population. Two in particular stand out, each of them closely related to the conditions of household production discussed earlier.

Careers and Family Strategies

Entering trade by setting up a store to sell goods in the locality was one of the means by which rural families enhanced their incomes or

8. On Shepard, see Martin, "Merchants and Trade," pp. 99–101. On the Tappans, see Lewis Tappan, "Autobiographical Sketch," Lewis Tappan Papers, Container 14, LC (microfilm, reel 7), and Bertram Wyatt-Brown, *Lewis Tappan and the Evangelical War against Slavery* (Cleveland, Ohio, 1969), chaps. 1, 8.

9. A notice in the *Hampshire Gazette* (Northampton), May 8, 1805, offered for sale a house and land near an intersection of roads in Plainfield "extremely well situated to accommodate a trader, there being none, at present, in the town."

10. The comparative percentage increases were as follows:

	Population (%)	Stock-in-trade per capita (%)
Hadley, 1790/91–1830/31	91	11
Northampton 1790/91–1820/21	75	22
Northampton 1790/91–1830/31	122	77
Williamsburg 1790/91–1830/31	18	1,174

provided careers for children. Three examples, two from Westhampton and one from Hadley, will illustrate the different ways that storekeeping fitted into some families' strategies for advancement. For Joseph Kingsley of Westhampton, the small variety store that he kept on his farm was just one of a range of activities that he organized after 1800, including farming, cider making and distilling, shoemaking, tanning, and butchering. None of these operations was large, but they enabled Kingsley to enhance his income and his position in the town by drawing on exchange labor from throughout his neighborhood. The store, financed by Kingsley's credit as a substantial farmer, provided more varied goods with which to attract labor than were available on the majority of farms in the town and so increased his ability to retain the help he needed to run his varied activities.[11] Informal small stores of this kind were scattered throughout the countryside, doing intermittent trade entirely according to local labor patterns. The description of Kingsley's as a "variety store" suggests that he handled dry goods, notions, hardware, and the other small items that were the staple of peddlers' packs and store "assortments." Kingsley would also have exchanged liquor from his cider press and still for labor, as did other large farmers across the region, who bought quantities of liquor to give out or operated taverns in conjunction with their farms.[12]

Joseph Kingsley parlayed his position into a measure of political power, too. After serving as a selectman in Westhampton in 1817 he was elected three times within the next decade to serve as the town's representative in the General Court. He also succeeded in obtaining a commission as a justice of the peace, despite the opposition of the Judd family, whose early prominence in Westhampton's affairs he was now beginning to rival.[13] Ironically, Kingsley was using his store as one of the instruments for his and his family's advancement at the same time and in the same way that Sylvester Judd, Jr., was using his older store and trading connections to try to save himself from debt. Beset by the depression that followed the end of the 1812 war, the effects of the poor summer of 1816, and the failure of a neighbor with whom he was engaged on town business, Judd was increasingly entangled in a pattern of debt from which his trading activities could not in the long run save him. He rejoined an earlier partnership with his brother-in-law William Hooker but suffered further reverses in 1817 when prices fell and the store's profits were wiped out. In 1818 Judd entered a tanning business, which he helped run in conjunction with his store "in one last

11. Samuel L. Wright, "Westhampton Local History," 3 vols., compiled 1892–1905, 1:146–147, FL (typescript).
12. Ibid., p. 147.
13. The petition against Kingsley's appointment is in Judd Papers, MCFL, Oversize Files.

desperate attempt to better my affairs," but the depression of 1819 ended his hopes of making profits out of that either. He ran his store until 1822, when he moved from Westhampton for good, but he had meanwhile relinquished his farm and other activities to his father. Although his store business increased in size by about one-fifth between 1815 and 1820, an inventory of between $500 and $600 was not enough in itself to support Judd and his family.[14]

More successful in using a store to further his family's provision for the future was Dan Huntington of Hadley who, although he had inherited half of Charles Phelps's large farm in 1816, also had seven sons and four daughters to set up in the world. Starting in the early 1820s, Huntington used his credit to form a succession of partnerships with the small traders who ran a store at North Hadley Village. In 1826, one of these men expressed a wish to sell out. Huntington was able to get him to agree to wait for his share of the business to be paid for from future profits, and used the opportunity to bring in his own son Edward to run the store. For the next ten years or more, the store was Edward's "career," but the family made more of it than that. Profits from it helped to finance at least two of Edward's brothers through college. When Edward left the business in the late 1830s, his father resumed partnerships with outsiders. But he did not give up his connection with the store until his youngest son completed college in 1846. As he wound it up, he found that there were debts of $275 to be paid and asked each of his sons for contributions to cover them: "if I have to tax each of my boys . . . with $50 apiece, they will have it back again by and by." For the Huntingtons, trade was a means to other family ends, relinquished when the need for it had passed.[15]

Setting up stores for such purposes did not go uncriticized. "One fruitful source of idleness, dissipation and bankruptcy," ran an article printed in the *Hampshire Gazette* in 1817, "is the multiplication of small stores in the country." The author not only mocked young men's ambitions, but accused them of laziness and their parents of poor judgment:

> A young man who has obtained some money by his industry, or obtained some from his friends soon finds labor irksome and desires to be *a mer-*

---

14. Sylvester Judd, Jr., Account Books, 2 vols., MCFL, and Judd MS, "Book of Fragments," Apr 1815, July 1820, relate to the store. The account of Judd's affairs in the 1810s is based on Judd MS, "Commonplace Book," and Arethusa Hall, ed., *Memorabilia from the Journals of Sylvester Judd of Northampton, Mass., 1809–1860* (Northampton, 1882), Apr 10, Nov 20, 1810, and Aug 21, 1821.

15. This account of the Huntington family's strategies is based on T. G. Huntington, "Sketches by Theodore G. Huntington of the Family and Life in Hadley written in letters to H. F. Quincy," n.d., pp. 57–59, PPHH (typescript); Dan Huntington to Edward P. Huntington, Hadley, Oct 21, 1826; Dan Huntington to J. W. Huntington, Hadley, Aug 31, 1829, May 12, 1830; Dan Huntington to Frederic D. Huntington, Hadley, Apr 6, 1842, all in PPHH.

chant. . . . Such men had better stick to their farms and workshops. . . . It is a great error in fathers to prefer rearing a son behind the counter, rather than in the workshop or in the field. Can it be more honourable to measure rum and molasses, tape and ribbons, than to follow the hardy pursuits of agriculture or manufactures?[16]

The image of merchants as lazy died hard. As late as 1859 a Hadley woman recalled an early-nineteenth-century trader in the town whose family "despised labour as much as any and were above work. He and some daughters have died poor."[17] There is little doubt, however, that parents with means or connections sought to obtain positions as store clerks for sons in the hope that they would use this route to earn their own livings away from the land. However, some young men apprenticed in this way did not like the work. Samuel Hall of Norwich, sent to clerk in a store at Heath in Franklin County, petitioned his family for permission to leave again: "he could not reconcile his mind to the idea of spending his days behin a counter dealin out good to A,B,C, etc, etc." Others, including Sylvester Judd III, were dismissed for incompetence by the merchants they had secured places with.[18] But the spread of stores across the countryside in the first two decades of the nineteenth century owed more than a little to the demand for "careers" outside farming from families limited by their resources, and to farmers' and others' willingness to use this labor to do the humdrum tasks of retailing.

Stores in Local Exchange

While family needs often provided the impulse to set up stores, the conditions of local exchange profoundly influenced the character of the business they could conduct. It was the local exchange system that, more than anything else, reordered the patterns of retail trade and made the connections between traders and customers more diffuse. Critics such as the author of the *Hampshire Gazette* article just quoted were right to emphasize the risks that storekeepers faced when they set up in rural trade. An almanac printed in 1820 repeated the warning that "many who have thriven as farmers and mechanics, have ruined their circumstances by forsaking these callings and going into trade."[19] Price fluctuations and trade depressions between 1815 and 1820 had exagger-

---

16. *Hampshire Gazette*, July 2, 1817.
17. Judd MS, "Hadley," 3:187.
18. Aaron Hall to Arethusa Hall, Norwich, Nov 9, 1831; Sylvester Judd III to Sylvester Judd, Jr., Hartford, Oct 14, 1830, both in Judd Papers, 55M-1, Box 2, HCL.
19. [John Howe], *The Massachusetts Agricultural Almanac, for the Year 1821* (Enfield, 1820), [pp. 5–7].

ated them, but the difficulties were more fundamental. As the larger traders of the central Valley towns had long known only too well, retailers inhabited an uncertain position on the boundaries between local exchange and long-distance trade, with their contrasting rules and expectations. While merchants had remained few in number, they were able to survive partly by maintaining a distance from their customers, hoping to fulfill demand and soak up surplus produce along a wide-spread network of connections. As the number of stores increased, they were necessarily forced into closer relationships with their local customers. In the short run they had to adapt to local exchange patterns. Over a longer term they began to transform them.

According to the *Gazette*'s critic of 1817, the problem was that a trader would open his store, "purchase . . . goods to the extent of his capital and credit; and as country people are fond of running to a *new store*, he gets rid of his goods, and gets in return a list of bad accounts."[20] Although this description oversimplified the issue, it correctly indicated the contradictions of a trader's position. On the one hand, he was obliged to buy his stock and to promise to pay for it on terms dictated by the rules of long-distance trade. These terms usually involved fixed credits of three, four, or six months, depending on the type of goods and the trader's own credit. Moreover, he was obliged to make payment either in cash or by consigning goods that his supplying merchant had agreed to accept. The store's customers, on the other hand, were used to dealing in the local exchange economy. They were accustomed to paying for goods as it was convenient, with whatever they had on hand surplus to their needs and on terms they were prepared to negotiate. Successfully matching these conflicting ethics of exchange took skill and good fortune.

Store accounts show how difficult it often was for traders to command cash payment for goods. One factor in this was the effect of competition between stores. Where farmers and mechanics had a choice of store to deal with, they could readily enforce their local customs of exchange on either storekeeper. Traders were often hesitant to demand terms less favorable than their rivals'. But competition was only a partial reason. Even stores that had local monopolies had to accept a high proportion of noncash payment because their customers frequently had no means to pay other than in goods or services. So according to Amasa Wells's accounts, when he paid for goods taken from the Hatfield store of Dwight and Partridge in the 1790s, between 65 percent and 70 percent of his payments were in produce. After 1800 he began to fall behind on his repayments and ended up giving the store

20. *Hampshire Gazette*, July 2, 1817.

a deed to twenty-two acres of mountain land, valued at $330.[21] Similarly, Sylvester Judd's receipts from his Westhampton customers between 1820 and 1822 included only 30 percent cash and the remainder in goods and services.[22] A Hadley farmer ordered goods from the store of William Porter in 1810 promising that "I will pay the same in Produce in course of the season." This pattern was reflected further up the chain of supply. Porter supplied goods to a store in the town of Worthington that he ran in partnership with a local man. Against goods worth $1,302.10 that Porter sent out in 1815, he received cash repayments amounting to only $317.99, just under one-quarter of the total.[23] Corresponding with his father about the affairs of Hooker and Judd of Northampton in 1816, Hophni Judd remarked of one account he had settled, "I thought it best to accept of *Money* from whatever quarter it might be offered."[24]

New stores commonly faced the difficulty that they had obtained goods for cash or on short credit but were unable to command prompt cash payment from their customers. As a result, many stores were short-lived. Early in 1807 a man named John Fitch advertised confidently that he had opened a new assortment of "General Goods" in a former printing office in Northampton. Three months later, he announced a second "New Store," this time in partnership with another man. Not long afterward he disappeared from the records. Two Northampton physicians opened a hardware and fancy-goods store in 1806, but although they remained in town, their store did not last. An Amherst farmer, Friend Smith, was sued as a "trader" for a debt he owed a Hadley merchant in 1802, and may have been in business for only a short time. At least until 1810 he retained his sixty-three-acre landholding, but by 1815 he had lost his property. Two years after that, working as a day laborer on the Shepard family's farm in Northampton, he fell into the Connecticut River and was drowned.[25]

The terms and conditions for repayment at country stores coincided in most respects with those of other local exchanges. In only 1 out of 150

21. Hampshire County Court of Common Pleas, Files, Mar 1818, no. 59, Massachusetts State Archives, Boston, Mass.

22. Sylvester Judd, Jr., Account Books, 2 vols., MCFL.

23. William Porter to Porter and Smith, William Porter Papers, Box D, folder 1815, OSV.

24. Hophni Judd to Sylvester Judd, Sr., Northampton, June 11, 1816, Judd Papers, MCFL, Oversize File.

25. Fitch's second advertisement appeared in the *Republican Spy* (Northampton), Jan 7, 1807. Friend Smith was a defendant in Hopkins v. Smith, Hampshire County Court of Common Pleas, Files, Nov 1802, no. 15, his dwindling property can be traced in Amherst Tax Valuation Lists, 1800–1815; his drowning at the age of fifty-two was reported in the *Hampshire Gazette*, Dec 31, 1817.

transactions he conducted in January 1822, for example, did Amherst's leading trader Hezekiah Wright Strong receive immediate cash payment. The rest were on credit. As Sylvester Judd found in Westhampton at the same time, prompt settlements of any kind—in cash or goods—were the exception rather than the rule. In sixty-one of Judd's accounts where repayment dates are indicated, only five were settled immediately or within one month, twenty-five were settled over a period from one to six months, and another thirteen between six months and one year from when they were opened. This left eighteen, or 30 percent of the total, to be settled in more than one year or not at all. While Judd sold goods worth $581.58 in 1820, he received payments of only $510.04. Over 12 percent of the goods were not paid for, in spite of the fact that Judd was winding up his business by early 1822 and making an effort to collect debts, so this figure underestimates the extent to which balances remained unsettled in the normal course of events.[26]

Not surprisingly, considering the pressures that they were under, traders were the most likely group to bring the insistence of long-distance trade into local exchange. They were not always popular. Perhaps it was after having a hard bargain driven by one of Northampton's prominent merchants that an unidentified person scribbled a note in the form of an account settlement: "Mr Benj[a]. Tappan is very hard as Witness my hand Every Body." Joseph Kingsley, with his network of local connections that probably represented a considerable degree of obligation to him by his neighbors, was remembered as "the best hated man in Westhampton."[27] Traders were the most likely group to sue for the recovery of debts. Of 173 debt suits involving the six towns between 1804 and 1809, no fewer than 76 (44 percent) were brought by plaintiffs described as "merchant" or "trader," while another 39 (23 percent) were brought by "gentlemen," some of whom at least were merchants. Not only was this far in excess of their proportionate presence in the population, but their situation was noteworthy in that they were rarely sued themselves except by other traders.[28]

However, they did not exercise their power carelessly. Like other plaintiffs, they pressed suits most commonly when money was scarce and they were themselves under pressure to make remittances. The plaintiff in several suits brought during a minor panic in 1804, for example, was David Stockbridge, a Hadley trader who by all accounts

26. Hezekiah Wright Strong, Account Book, BCJL; Judd, Account Books, vol. 2.

27. The remark about Tappan is on an anonymous fragment in Accounts Collection, MCFL, Box 1; that about Kingsley, in Wright, "Westhampton Local History," 1:149.

28. Hampshire County Court of Common Pleas, Records, vols. 7–11, (1804–1809), Hampshire County Courthouse, Northampton.

was heading into financial trouble himself. Within a year, he too had been sued and his partnership with a Sunderland man broken up. On October 7, 1805, a Hatfield farmer, having obtained a writ of execution for a debt of over $200 for which no property could be found, had Stockbridge sent to jail in Northampton, where he stayed until he escaped the following March.[29]

As merchants grew in number and rural output increased, they sought to resolve the contradiction between long-distance and local rules not by violating local exchange but by inserting themselves more closely into it. They tried to ease their position by practicing the same kinds of direct exchanges among themselves that farmers did. William Porter swapped rags for the wrapping paper he acquired from a paper mill, exchanged cattle for leather with a tanner and, when the Northampton bookseller Simeon Butler sought a consignment of brown sugar in 1814, agreed to supply it in exchange for dictionaries, other books, stationery, four dozen almanacs, and two dozen primers.[30] Stores' local business was conducted face-to-face. When Judd, Hooker and Company of Northampton submitted a $200 cash payment to their supplier in 1811, the Boston merchant returned a counterfeit two-dollar bill "supposing you may recollect of whom you received it."[31] Although the names in their daybooks and ledgers were usually those of men, they dealt with any member of a household whose head had an account with them. They conducted trade on the basis of trust engendered in personal relationships. They accepted the word of children, servants, or apprentices who came to the store that they were authorized to charge to their father's or their master's account the goods that they took. Advertisements for runaway apprentices or servants usually included the warning that "he [or she] is not to be trusted on my account." Periodic accusations of theft arose when goods were taken from stores by men or women claiming to represent a local customer.[32] Although the final settlements of accounts may have occurred irregularly and sometimes over long periods, the perpetual traffic in and out of country stores by men, women, servants, and children bringing and taking

29. Stockbridge was plaintiff in several suits, Hampshire County, Court of Common Pleas, Records, vol. 7 (1804), and was in turn sued by Joseph Smith in Aug 1805. In Stockbridge v. Mattoon, 8:230 (Nov 1805), the trader attempted to regain possession of goods attached by the county sheriff. The following year, in Smith v. Mattoon, 9:215 (May 1806), Smith in turn sued Mattoon for the debt owed him by Stockbridge after the latter had escaped.

30. William Porter Papers, Box A, folder 1.

31. Matthew M. Hunt to Judd, Hooker and Co., Boston, Sept 10, 1811, MCFL, Box 1A.

32. E. g., notice of Nathaniel Coolidge, Jr., and Co., Hadley, *Hampshire Gazette*, Aug 16, 1816, seeking information about a man and woman who had taken yarn from the store in June 1815, "directed it charged to David Thayer of Belchertown" and had not been heard from since.

goods for exchange meant that a storekeeper such as Sylvester Judd could keep his remittances to suppliers up to date by gathering small payments into larger shipments.

Early critics of the expansion of local storekeeping lamented its effect in expanding demand for "unnecessary" goods in the countryside. A writer in the *Hampshire Gazette* in 1788 urged farmers not to trade their surplus produce at local stores but to carry it directly to a market where they could receive cash. While farmers might receive some necessities from the store and some "convenient" goods (though "not such as [they] would pay cash for"), they would be forced to take the balance due to them in "superfluities," because there would be no other choice. This in turn would obstruct the settlement of other debts, because each farmer would be "obliged to take goods for all he had to sell."[33] Partly to overcome this kind of resistance to dealing with them, merchants sought ways of enhancing their role in local exchange.

Many traders did so by accepting orders from their customers to pay goods on account to third parties. William Porter of Hadley took large numbers of these orders between the early 1790s and the mid-1820s, many of them drawn by farmers in favor of men they had hired for day work. Joseph Kingsley, similarly, seems to have built his network of customers in Westhampton by accepting such orders.[34] Although they had the immediate effect of extending further the credit the trader granted against his stock, store orders had the longer-term strategic result of drawing him more closely into patterns of local exchange that might otherwise have been conducted without him. They had three sets of implications. They permitted farmers to settle debts for labor rapidly, without drawing immediately on their own resources and to use their connection with the store to settle pressing debts of any kind. Although there was no marked seasonal pattern, more orders were written between April and June than in other three-month periods, reflecting the fact that farmers needed labor but did not always have foodstuffs or other goods to pay for it.[35] By the same token, laborers received more prompt payment than they might otherwise have done, though probably at the disadvantage of having to accept the store's prices for the goods they needed. Finally, merchants themselves, by granting credit in this manner, both increased their custom and potentially solved part of their difficulty in securing goods or cash to remit for supplies. They furnished goods to laborers and other creditors who would otherwise

33. *Hampshire Gazette*, Dec 3, 1788.
34. William Porter Papers, Boxes A–F; Solomon Bartlett of Westhampton settled an account with his hired laborer John Gay in 1805 by giving him an order on Kingsley (William and Solomon Bartlett, Account Books, Westhampton, 1704–1857, vol. 2, HBS).
35. Porter Papers, Box A, folder 1796–1799, 1800; Box E, folder 1819.

have been paid directly by their debtors and, moreover, they diverted into their stores a portion of the annual product of farmers who might otherwise have sold their surplus somewhere else. Their interests dictated caution in accepting store orders too freely and they readily closed off this line of credit to men they considered overextended or otherwise liable not to pay their bills. It may have been such a rejection by William Porter that prompted this rather pathetic request from Samuel Marsh of Hadley in 1797:

> Docter Porter
> i want [to] know if you would not be willing to Let me have what i want & charg it   if i should not Live i shall Leave Enoug to pay . . .   i Beleive it Save me a great Deal of trouble if you conclude to Let me ha[ve] one pint of [West Indian] & one quart [New England rum].[36]

But the insertion of traders into local exchange dealings is evident in early-nineteenth-century accounts such as that of Amasa Wells with the Hatfield store of Dwight and Partridge. Between 1802 and 1806 Wells traded his produce, including livestock, with the store, taking in exchange, among the imported goods, various items of local production. These included small quantities of corn and wheat, a broom, shirting, and "2½ yards home made cloth." By 1818, as the nonfarm population was increasing, a Hadley store held nearly 700 bushels of wheat, rye, corn and oats in stock, in proportions similar to those raised by farmers in the town as a whole.[37] Accepting the terms of local exchange enabled traders to divert more and more of it into their own hands.

Merchants Expand Their Power

Close relationships with rural households and conformity to the standards of local exchange enabled merchants to capitalize on the shifts in household production and consumption strategies noted in the last chapter. There was a significant increase in stores' business after about 1810 and especially after 1820. In Northampton, for which the available evidence is best, the number of stores rose from nine to fifteen between 1805 and 1815 and to more than twenty during the 1820s. Total stock-in-trade nearly doubled between 1791 and 1821 and then doubled again

---

36. Samuel Marsh to William Porter, Hadley, Dec 13, 1797, Porter Papers, Box A, folder 1796–99.

37. Wells's accounts are in Hampshire County Court of Common Pleas, Files, Mar 1818, no. 59. Nathaniel Coolidge, Jr., and Co. of Hadley advertised grain on hand in the *Hampshire Gazette*, Aug 11, 1818.

within the next ten years. The town's stock-in-trade per capita, which rose at an average rate of just over 7 percent each decade up to 1821, jumped by 45 percent from then until 1831. The expansion continued in the 1830s, but at a slower rate. Nevertheless, the number of stores and shops in the town rose faster than its population, reaching more than thirty by the early 1840s. Increases in the number of stores and the value of their stock took place in other towns. In Amherst during the 1830s stock-in-trade rose by nearly two and a half times.[38]

In part, this expansion took place across the range of goods that stores had traditionally handled. Sylvester Judd in Westhampton and Hezekiah Wright Strong in Amherst both sold the salt, hardware, crockery, notions, books, sugar, molasses, rum, and spices they had stocked in the past. But the 1810s and 1820s witnessed a significant increase in the volume of cloth and other dry goods sold by stores. In 1810 dry goods formed about one-fifth of William Porter's purchases for his store. By the 1830s they represented more than half.[39] Traders' advertisements stressed the range of textiles they had available for purchase. Nathaniel Coolidge, Jr., who ran a store in Hadley in the years around 1820, announced that he carried "Bombazetts, Scotch Plaids, Broadcloths, Cassimeres, Pelisse, Flannels, Baizes, Kersey, Coating, Blankets, Shawls, Handkerchiefs, Velvets, Silk, Nankin, Canton, Crepes, Lustings, Ribbons, Trimmings, Fringes, Silk Buttons, Ginghams, Calicoes, Muslins, Cambrics, Bedticking, Satinets, Checks, Sheetings, Cotton yarn, Batting [and] Wick yarn."[40] These included not only the high-quality cloths, trimmings, and accessories that stores had sold for a long time, but cheaper, everyday materials that households had, until recently, often made or exchanged for themselves and that were now increasingly factory produced. Families came to depend on stores for their supplies of cloth. In 1830, for example, the Belchertown farmer Moses Goodale traveled to Amherst with eleven brooms and a peck of chestnuts that he took to the merchant Luke Sweetser in part exchange for three and one-half yards of sheeting, two and three-quarters yards of woolen cloth, half a yard of cambric, some buttons and twist, and an ounce of indigo. By the early 1850s, Sweetser's firm held two-thirds of its stock in dry goods and another 10 percent in men's and boys' clothing.[41]

To maintain this close connection with rural households, traders had

38. Evidence on the number of stores is drawn from advertisements in the *Hampshire Gazette*, 1790–1840.
39. Calculated from receipts in Porter Papers, Box C, folder 1810, Box H, folder 1836.
40. *Hampshire Gazette*, Oct 30, 1822.
41. Luke Sweetser, Receipt, Oct 30, 1830, BCJL; Sweetser, Cutler and Co., Account Books, 2 vols., BCJL, inventories for 1852 and 1853.

to offer their goods for sale in ways families found convenient. Well into the middle of the century most stores accepted "country produce" in exchange for goods. "When harvests are in I will accept the tender of grain and goods as may be convenient," the Conway trader John Williams told his supplier; in nearby Charlemont Lewis Bodman would, he said, "sell grave stones for almost any thing except clocks and honey."[42] An Amherst store took 51 percent by number and 42 percent by value of its payments in goods in 1827, including veal, nuts, cheese, rye, corn, and cloth in quantities never worth more than two dollars, and wood, shoes, paper, tool handles, brass, and hats in amounts whose value only occasionally exceeded twenty dollars. Cash represented only 30 percent of the value of payments. The balance was made in labor, services, notes, or orders. At the Huntingtons' North Hadley store in the 1830s, the proportion of cash payment was even smaller. In 1831 Dan Huntington remarked in a letter that the store had "traded yesterday above eighty dollars, upwards twenty cash." In the depression following the 1837 panic, cash became even more difficult to obtain. In 1839 and 1840 the store took only 18.5 percent of its payments directly in cash.[43]

Merchants sought to make profits from the resale of the farm produce and other goods they collected and on the premiums they could charge for noncash payment. When Hezekiah Wright Strong received corn in 1822 and resold it on the same day, he marked the price up about 10 percent. Premiums on noncash payment varied according to the goods involved and the form of payment agreed on for them. Differentials of about 20 percent between cash and noncash prices were probably common. The actual size of markups and premiums is often difficult to measure, however. On bulk items such as grain and other foodstuffs for which market prices were known, the opportunities for merchants to swell their profits from transactions were probably small. Strong's prices for butter, for example, almost exactly matched those quoted in Northampton newspapers. But there were no widely known "market" prices for many of the dry goods, hardware, crockery, or other household items that stores held in stock. While prices for particular items may have remained consistent in a particular store for a period of time, the quality of goods sold under the same description varied so much from time to time and from store to store that comparisons are risky. It is significant that the goods, such as textiles, whose sale to households

---

42. John Williams to James B. Porter, Conway, June 8, 1837, NHS, A.l.18.21; Lewis Bodman to Luther Bodman, Sr., Charlemont, Nov 3 [1835?], Bodman Family Papers, Box 2, SSC.

43. Store Account Book, Amherst, 1827, BCJL; Dan Huntington to J. W. Huntington, Hadley, Apr 12, 1831, and Store Ledger, North Hadley, 1839–1840, both in PPHH.

increased so rapidly in the second and third decades of the nineteenth century, should have been made available on noncash terms. Traders were prepared to do this partly in order to stimulate demand from households with little cash to spare and partly because the character of the goods allowed them to evade the imposition of market prices, thus potentially increasing their profits. Given that immediate payment for goods in cash remained comparatively rare, the concept of "price" retained a nebulous quality. Although money amounts were written down in account books and goods or other payment tendered to balance the accounts, the actual form and timing of payments varied so much that effective prices remained largely a matter for negotiation between storekeeper and customers.[44]

Merchants manipulated the terms on which they offered goods for sale in order to secure the returns that they needed. If they were seeking particular items of local produce in quantity they advertised for them, offering store goods "at cash prices" or even cash itself as an inducement to trade.[45] Often, however, they were seeking cash in order to ease the burden of making their own payments. They might insist on cash payment for certain goods, especially imported items that they had obtained on short credit or in markets for which no return in goods was possible. An Amherst store announced in 1828, for example, that it would receive "country produce" from its customers for all their stock "with the Exception of Iron, Steel and Flour."[46] Merchants sought out the patronage of prosperous families and of individuals such as physicians, who often received part of their own payments in cash. Where the economy created limited amounts of cash, traders needed to induce as much of it as possible to come in their direction. Cash was like water in a sponge. The sponge had to be squeezed to get at it.

Accordingly, trade remained unstable even as it expanded. The increase in volume of rural trade and traders' connections with households roughly coincided with a shift in its personnel. Half a century ago, Margaret E. Martin concluded her study of Connecticut Valley merchants between 1750 and 1820 with the observation that their influence, and that of merchant capital, declined after the beginning of the nineteenth century. Martin was right to note that many of the merchant families whose members had dominated the restricted world of late-eighteenth-century trade had indeed faded from the scene by the

44. Hezekiah Wright Strong, Account Book, BCJL. On the store prices of staple goods, see James D. Norris, "One-Price Policy among Antebellum Country Stores," *Business History Review* 36 (1962): 455–458.

45. E.g., Seth and Daniel Wright sought flaxseed, "for which the highest price will be given in ready pay, one half in Cash, the other in English or West-India Goods," at their Northampton store (*Hampshire Gazette*, Aug 29, 1787). In the same paper, Sept 25, 1816, another storekeeper offered to pay for butter partly in cash and partly in goods.

46. *New England Inquirer* (Amherst), Jan 24, 1828.

1820s.[47] The change was partly a generational one. As we saw, Levi Shepard had died in 1805, and Benjamin Tappan's sons had left for larger cities. Smaller traders such as Jonathan Judd of Southampton had also died. Others, like his nephew Sylvester in Westhampton, had moved on. A few, including Hezekiah Wright Strong of Amherst, went bankrupt.[48] As storekeeping and other mercantile activities became geographically diffused, they lost some of their connection with social and political preeminence. But this did not mean that retailers were economically less important than they had been. In fact, the situation was quite the reverse. The interaction of stores with households and the increased dependence of local families on imported textiles and food-stuffs provided a basis for a new generation of merchants who would come to play a dominating role in the Valley's economy.

As the older generation receded, it was replaced by new men, some of whom were to retain control of their businesses for the next genera-tion or more. Samuel Clarke, a saddler in Northampton who had started his trade there in 1796, brought three sons in as apprentices as they came of age in the 1810s. Branching out into retailing and, in one case, banking, these three set up separate businesses that were to be among Northampton's most prominent stores into the 1840s. David S. Whitney, who had become Benjamin Tappan's partner in 1809, later carried on the store under his own name. In the 1820s William H. Stoddard became a clerk and then a partner in Whitney's business, before setting up his own store, which would become the town's lead-ing dry-goods retailer. By about 1830, John P. Williston, a minister's son from Easthampton, was also established in business in the shire town, where he was to remain a prominent merchant, manufacturer, and investor for three decades or more. Similarly in Amherst, Luke Sweet-ser, clerk to Hezekiah Wright Strong in the early 1820s, escaped the wreck of his employer's business to become the town's leading trader between about 1830 and 1854.[49] Few of these merchants were at first as grand as the River Gods or had the connections of a man like Levi

47. Martin, "Merchants and Trade," p. 264.

48. Strong became insolvent in May 1827 and was subsequently in jail for debt. Testi-mony about his difficulties was given in Allen v. Clark, 34 Mass. Reports (17 Pickering): 45–57 (1835), and in a libel suit he brought against the editor of the *Northampton Courier* the same year, Strong v. Atwill, Hampshire County Court of Common Pleas, Files, Mar 1836, no. 52.

49. A memoir of the Clarkes appeared in the *Northampton Daily Herald*, Nov 23, 1915. Whitney was described in Lewis Tappan, "Autobiographical Sketch," p. 25. On Stod-dard, see Stoddard Family, "Journal of a Family Meeting Held in the Month of August 1837," NHS, A.S.M.d.18.2, esp. p. 16. On Williston, see letters in the Williston Papers, NEHGS. Brief biographies of Northampton merchants were printed in the *Northampton General Directory* (Northampton, 1860) and in Henry S. Gere, *Reminiscences of Old North-ampton: Sketches of the Town as It Appeared from 1840 to 1850* (n.p., 1902). Sketches of Sweetser and other Amherst traders appear in Edward W. Carpenter and Charles F. Morehouse, *The History of the Town of Amherst, Massachusetts* (Amherst, 1896).

Shepard. They had to adapt themselves to the more diffuse structure of trade and power that had arisen since the end of the eighteenth century.

In some cases, this adaptation had literally been a struggle. As patterns of production and exchange became more widespread over the countryside few storekeepers or others could be certain that their particular location would retain its geographical significance. Early in the century Northampton citizens campaigned vigorously to prevent the breakup of "old" Hampshire County into three. They feared that the loss of court business associated with a shire town would adversely affect its traders and manufacturers too. As their efforts failed, and Franklin and Hampden counties became separate entities in 1811 and 1812, Northampton's leaders set about improving the facilities of the town center. Between 1809 and 1820 a new church, county courthouse, town hall, and store buildings were completed, giving the place an air of consequence that it had previously lacked. Northampton's pride in its response to difficulty became legendary. According to a story printed in 1830, a stranger calling at a house in the town was told by the servant that her master was away in the country for a few days. On being asked whereabouts, she explained that he had gone to Boston. Nor was this just myth. A prominent resident solemnly remarked in a private letter that the arrangement of Northampton's new buildings was "perhaps equal to any other in the civilized world."[50]

Citizens of Amherst's small village center in its west parish had difficulty resisting pressures for decentralization. Population growth and the development of manufactures took place more rapidly in other parts of town. In particular, the growth of workshop industries in the east parish, a mile from the common, and the opening of at least one new store there, threatened to displace the West Village from its preeminence, and a strong rivalry grew up between them. In 1820, when the east parish won a vote to build a new road that would bring traffic from the north into their village without passing through the West Village, virtual warfare erupted. Residents of the west parish succeeded in rescinding the vote. East Villagers determined to build the road anyway. As they spent their days laying the road out, West Village men came down at night to dig the work up. After a confrontation, which probably amounted to no more than some pushing and shoving, a number of men ended up in court, accused of riot. The road was finally completed in 1821.[51]

50. The story was published in the *Hampshire Sentinel* (Belchertown), Sept 8, 1830. The letter was from Daniel Stebbins to Rev. Perkins, Northampton, Oct 17, 1842, Lathrop-Stebbins Collection, MCFL, Box 33.

51. The "Triangle Fight" is described in Carpenter and Morehouse, *History of Amherst*, pp. 431–433, and by Theodore Baird, "A Dry and Thirsty Land," in *Essays on Amherst's*

The new generation of merchants had to work in a structure that, compared with the older "hub-and-spoke" pattern, was diffused and had more complex connections between wholesalers and retailers. Northampton and Hadley storekeepers continued to supply goods wholesale to outlying towns; William Porter supplied the new Amherst trader James Kellogg in the late 1810s and early 1820s, for example. But their focus was increasingly on retail trade, as local storekeepers forged connections of their own for supplies from within and beyond the region. This was partly a response to market developments elsewhere. The days of the small dry-goods "assortment" from a single supplier were finishing. Even quite small stores drew their goods from a variety of specialist suppliers. By 1840–1841, for instance, the Hatfield firm of Childs and Rice was buying its goods from at least twenty-five different merchants or factories, only four of whom were based in Northampton, once an important conduit for wholesale goods.[52] The distant sources of goods also changed over time, obliging local merchants to forge new connections outside the region. William Porter's business provides an example. In 1815 he had fifty-five suppliers outside the region, of whom forty-two were in Boston, eleven in Hartford, and two in Albany. By 1836 the number of suppliers had fallen to thirty-five. Of these, eleven remained in Hartford, but only twelve were now in Boston and the other twelve were in New York City. By 1844 the shift to New York was even more pronounced. Ten out of eighteen suppliers of more than fifty dollars worth of goods to the Hadley store were New York firms.[53]

Even as retail trade expanded, however, the very dependence of households on store goods presented merchants with a problem. As the number of stores increased, they were drawn into the need to offer goods on extended credit merely to avoid succumbing to competition. However, as wealth inequalities grew and as the nonfarm population of most towns increased as well, comparatively fewer people were able to trade conventional "country produce" for their goods. If traders restricted their business to farmers and others with goods to trade they would limit the number of their customers and possibly lose out to competitors. In the period after 1815, therefore, an increasing number of stores, particularly in the countryside, began to forge a new set of connections with rural households. By putting out materials for house-

History (Amherst, 1978), p. 85. Seven Amherst "yeomen" were indicted for riot, found guilty at their trial in 1823 and fined (Hampshire County, Court of Common Pleas, Records, 2:339).

52. William Porter to James Kellogg, Hadley, May 2, 1819, William Porter Papers, Box E, folder 1819, and receipts from Kellogg in folders 1819 and 1821. Childs and Rice, Account Books, 2 vols., Hatfield, 1840–1841, PVMA.

53. Receipts, Porter Papers, Box D, folder 1815; Box H, folder 1836; Box I, folder 1844.

hold manufacture, they not only secured customers for their goods but obtained a degree of control over household labor, from whose products they could also profit. This connection complemented the one households made with stores from which they sought textiles, for outwork became an important occupation for the women and children who had once produced domestic yarn and cloth.

Country Merchants and Household Labor

Although the level never approached that of the farm produce they received, stores had taken an increasing quantity of household manufactures from their customers as population and production grew in the late eighteenth and early nineteenth centuries. In the late 1780s and 1790s Amherst and Hadley stores credited customers' accounts with homemade cloth, shirts, gloves, and other clothing. By 1810 William Porter of Hadley was handling a small portion of the town's broom output; he received at least 259 brooms that year, which he consigned to two different merchants in Boston. He also handled a consignment of forty-five pairs of shoes from a local maker. By 1827 an Amherst store was receiving hats, bonnets, chairs, shingles, shoes, paper, and woodenware along with the grain, butter, and other farm produce that its customers brought to trade.[54]

The potential to earn profits on some of these goods was considerable. When William Porter took in brooms from a Hadley customer in 1826 and forwarded them to Hartford, he received the equivalent of a 600 percent markup on them, even after deductions for freight and commission. But opportunities such as this may have been rare or limited in size. Porter's profits on this transaction were about $200, but it probably arose because he was able to negotiate a favorable arrangement with a customer who was in debt to him.[55] At these markups, makers of brooms and other articles were encouraged to look elsewhere for purchasers; as noted earlier, Moses Goodale of Belchertown sent brooms directly to Boston in this period. Stores continued to handle such articles. Porter's was still receiving combs, suspenders, whips, and brushes from customers in 1844. But their supply was too irregular, too dependent on the individual decisions of local makers, for merchants to rely on them for their business.[56]

Accordingly, merchants had from the late eighteenth century onward forged closer ties with household manufacturers by putting materials

54. Porter Papers, Box C, folder 1810. Store Account Book, Amherst, 1827, BCJL.
55. Porter Papers, Box F, folder 1826.
56. Ibid., Box I, folder 1844.

out for them to work on. William Porter was shipping occasional bags of raw cotton up to Hadley by 1790 and distributing it to customers who spun it into yarn at home in return for store goods. As textile manufacturing expanded in the next twenty years, rural putting out of this kind provided part of the new labor force for New England entrepreneurs, and it is possible that some of this yarn worked up in western Massachusetts households found its way back into the new cotton mills of eastern Massachusetts and Rhode Island. By the 1812 war period, putting out had expanded into weaving. Various country stores scattered over the Valley held stocks of yarn to be woven into cloth locally in exchange for goods, while a Pelham faucet maker was making regular journeys to Providence to sell his wares and bringing back yarn to be made into cloth for Rhode Island manufacturers. A Hadley merchant was putting out blue and white yarn "to weave into Bedticking for us" in 1815. At the same time a new store in Amherst's East Village announced that it had "COTTON YARN, of an excellent quality, constantly on hand to WEAVE."[57] Local carding and fulling mills also used outwork to expand into spinning and weaving. A Williamsburg mill partly owned by the farmer Joseph Williams in 1816 and 1818 had both wool and linen produced in local families, sometimes putting both spinning and weaving out to the same person. A Worthington wool-carding mill also put out cotton yarn for weaving.[58]

There were limitations to this early outwork, however. From households' point of view it was hard to rely on. Supplies of material and demand for the work were irregular. References to outwork in this period are scattered, but the fact that the names of widows quite frequently appear in connection with it suggests that it was often done by people whose other means of support were marginal. Returns were small. Widow Sarah Scott's weaving for Joseph Williams earned her either sixpence or sevenpence a yard, depending on the cloth. Since Williams was selling cloth at prices ranging from 5s. 8d. to 15s. a yard, this suggests that Scott received only between 4 and 9 percent of the final price.[59] Consequently merchants also found outwork hard to organize on a regular basis, and their high markups reflected the risks they felt they were taking. They relied on the labor of households, which also

57. On putting out by early textile mills, see Jonathan Prude, *The Coming of Industrial Order: A Study of Town and Factory Life in Rural Massachusetts, 1813–1860* (Cambridge, Eng., 1983), pp. 72–73. The Pelham faucet maker, Ezra Brown, is cited in Clifton Johnson, *Historic Hampshire in the Connecticut Valley* (Springfield, 1932), pp. 275–276. Nathaniel Coolidge, Jr., and Co., Hadley, notice in the *Hampshire Gazette*, Aug 16, 1816. Dyer and Goodman, Amherst, advertised in the *Hampshire Gazette*, Apr 12, 1815

58. Joseph Williams, Account Book, Williamsburg, c. 1802–1841, WHS. T. and W. Ward, Worthington, advertisement, *Hampshire Gazette*, Dec 6, 1815.

59. Williams, Account Book, account with Widow Sarah Scott, 1816–1818.

had many other things to do, including production for their own use. Moreover, because raw materials, yarn, and cloth of various kinds were ubiquitous in the countryside, particular merchants had very little control over materials once they had left their hands. Although they debited the cost of materials they gave out to the accounts of the customers who took it, merchants had no certainty that the finished goods would be returned to them. The debts might be paid off in other produce and the yarn or cloth sold elsewhere or used in the household. Indeed, as long as independent household textile production remained common, there was very little means of distinguishing between it and outwork.[60]

Evidence from as early as the 1790s points to the difficulties preventing merchants from controlling household textile production. An address by Hartford merchants, published in Massachusetts newspapers in 1790, lamented the "large quantities of woollen cloth . . . made in private families . . . a great part of which is not calculated for market." In an attempt to obtain the quality of material they wanted, the merchants issued instructions to sort wool properly, to weave cloth in greater widths to allow for shrinkage during fulling, to weave standard lengths, instead of the three- or four-yard pieces commonly offered, to make white flannel instead of checked cloth and to avoid mixing yarn when making it.[61] But in addition to lacking control of the product, merchants had difficulty organizing the labor they needed. Levi Shepard took advantage of government bounties and orders for sailcloth from 1788 onward to produce canvas duckcloth from his Northampton store. He relied on local farmers to produce flax, hired workers to process it, and outworkers to spin and weave it. He faced constant problems. He urged farmers with whom he had arranged supplies of flax to deliver it promptly "so that he may be enabled to pursue his Duck Manufacture . . . without interruption." The quality of output was poor—as one local observer put it, "no kind of linen which we have lately attempted to make, has given the least encouragement for us to continue it, any further than for our own consumption." The steady supply of family labor he needed was not always forthcoming.[62] Again, in 1810 and 1811, when the political crisis with Britain redoubled the rhetoric about the need for "independent" manufactures, the Hampshire Homespun Society was formed in Northampton to promote the making and wearing of homemade cloth. But the fact that its president was Thomas Shepard, now helping run his family's woolen mill, suggests that part of its rationale was to drum up household labor to do outwork.[63]

60. Gregory H. Nobles, "Merchant Middlemen in the Outwork Network of Rural New England," *Acadiensis* (forthcoming), discusses the emergence of outwork from independent production. See also Chapter 3, above.
61. *Hampshire Gazette*, Sept 22, 1790.
62. *Hampshire Gazette*, Nov 30, 1791.
63. *Anti-Monarchist* (Northampton), Mar 21, 1810.

The intermittent character of putting out before 1820 suggests some significant contrasts between its role in New England and the more prominent place it had taken in the early industrial expansion of much of northern and western Europe during the early modern period. Historians of "protoindustrialization," following Franklin F. Mendels, have suggested that rural outwork helped initiate the shift from "premodern" to "modern" economic structures and demographic cycles, and was often the "first phase" of industrialization. Starting in many parts of Europe in the seventeenth century, at the bottom of a population cycle, outwork grew in rural areas, where, because labor patterns varied from season to season, it could provide employment in slack parts of the year. It became a means by which demographic growth became possible in the unequal and poorly resourced rural economies of northwestern Europe and was one of the means by which an industrial proletariat was created.[64] New England in the late eighteenth and early nineteenth centuries displayed some similarities to this pattern, but they are only superficial. Outwork was often seasonal, and at this stage it accompanied a demographic expansion. But it was more the effect than the cause of this expansion. Landholding was more widely distributed than in most parts of Europe, and independent household production occupied more of peoples' time and attention. Merchants in the Valley and other regions could rarely, before 1820, organize the large, regular networks of outworkers that were common in Europe. One reason that early textile mills often had to scour the countryside over a wide radius to find families prepared to spin and weave for them was that demand for the work was intermittent.

Rural Outwork: A New Phase

Critics of the "protoindustrialization" theory, such as Patricia Hudson, have pointed out that forms of outwork continued to exist in

---

64. Franklin F. Mendels, "Proto-industrialization: The First Phase of the Industrialization Process," *Journal of Economic History* 32 (1972): 241–261, has prompted a widespread debate among European scholars. See also Gay L. Gullickson, *Spinners and Weavers of Auffray: Rural Industry and the Sexual Division of Labour in a French Village, 1750–1850* (Cambridge, Eng., 1986). For a summary of European scholars' arguments that protoindustrialization led to rural demographic growth, see Hans Medick, "Structures and Function of Population Development under the Protoindustrial System," in Peter Kriedte, Hans Medick, and Jurgen Schlumbohm, *Industrialization before Industrialization: Rural Industry in the Genesis of Capitalism*, trans. Beate Schempp (Cambridge, Eng., 1981); Myron P. Gutmann and René Leboutte, "Rethinking Protoindustrialization and the Family," *Journal of Interdisciplinary History* 14 (1983–1984): 587–607, esp. 589–590. These authors present Belgian evidence that population growth did, indeed, follow industrial developments but suggest that protoindustrialization was not the primary explanation for such growth. Other critics of the concept include Patricia Hudson, "Proto-industrial-

industries such as the Yorkshire woolen trade well after factory production had been established, and that they spread into new trades as factory production increased.[65] Rural New England provides a clear parallel with this. Not only did outwork complement early factory operations, but new forms of it developed in the countryside as factory textile production became regularized in the 1820s. For it was not in the "early" stages that outwork was most common in western and central Massachusetts and neighboring regions. Systematic, widespread outwork networks grew up only after 1820, as household textile production declined. The shift also occurred precisely as the demographic transition from high to low fertility was taking place. In other words, unlike parts of Europe where outwork served to boost population growth, in New England it was associated with the peak of a demographic cycle that was leveling off. Its causes and effects were economic rather than demographic.

For two reasons, the outwork that developed after 1820 was more widespread, systematic, and regular than before. The first lay with households. As they reduced their own textile production, families, especially women and children, had labor time available for other tasks. As noted in the last chapter, this time was deployed in a variety of ways. But since most households shifted their consumption patterns so as to increase their need for textiles and other goods purchased from stores, they had to find ways of raising the income to afford them. Larger farmers and other prosperous households could afford store goods, or had sufficient crops, livestock, or dairy produce for the purpose. But middling and poorer households did not have these resources. The labor time "freed" from independent production was now available for merchants to engage in outwork. Indeed, the process was a two-way one. As the types of outwork expanded and more merchants put goods out for processing in local families, households who had been slow to relinquish older patterns of work were encouraged to do so, as one observer put it, "because it is easier to make buttons than to weave cloth."[66]

Second, merchants gained a greater degree of control over the new

---

isation: The Case of the West Riding Wool Textile Industry in the Late 18th and Early 19th Centuries," *History Workshop* 12 (1981): 34–61; R. Houston and K. D. M. Snell, "Proto-industrialisation: Cottage Industry, Social Change, and Industrial Revolution," *Historical Journal* 27 (1984): 473–492; L. A. Clarkson, *Proto-industrialization: The First Phase of Industrialization?* (London, 1985).

65. Patricia Hudson, *The Genesis of Industrial Capital: A Study of the West Riding Wool Textile Industry, 1750–1850* (Cambridge, Eng. 1986).

66. This and the next two paragraphs are based on data in *Documents Relative to the Manufactures in the New England States*, 22d Cong., 1st sess., 1833, House Executive Doc. no. 308, 2 vols., 1:298–324 (hereafter cited as McLane Report).

outwork system because they were handling materials not otherwise widely available in the Valley. The growth of outwork after 1820 occurred particularly in two activities, button making and palm-leaf-hat production. The vegetable ivory, silk, japanned metal, and other materials given out to button makers were imported to the Valley or, later, manufactured in local shops and factories under the merchants' control. Similarly, palm leaf, put out for braiding and shaping into hats, was an imported material, which merchants alone could handle. Families wanting to earn income for working on these materials had to acquire them from stores. Unlike the locally produced flax and wool, which had accounted for a good deal of earlier outwork, they were not available anywhere else. By the same token, distribution of the finished goods was largely in merchants' hands. Hats and, particularly, buttons were items of low value that families were asked to produce in quantities far beyond their own possible demand for them. "Leakage" of the finished goods into local exchange was therefore rare. Moreover, merchants had the best connections with the distant urban buyers of these goods. So when they put out button-making material or palm leaf into rural families, they had a reasonable expectation—quite apart from the debt recorded in each customer's account—that it would be returned again.

The button and palm-leaf-hat industries in the Connecticut Valley had clear differences between them. They were based in different areas, were largely organized by different groups of merchants and followed distinct paths of development. Button making, which was centered on the western side of the Valley, started first. About 1822 a Williamsburg woman devised a technique for making cloth-covered vegetable-ivory buttons. She began manufacture at home, selling her goods through a Northampton merchant to New York buyers. Other households took up making buttons as well, including the woman's daughter, who had married the Easthampton farmer Samuel Williston in 1822 and who carried on home production with some hired help. In 1827 Williston sold his farm and used the proceeds to open a store, from which he gave out button-making materials to local households. By the early 1830s he was supplying as many as one thousand families in Easthampton, Williamsburg, and other towns within ten or twelve miles to the west of Northampton, as well as traders as far away as Buckland in Franklin County, who put out work in their own neighborhoods.

As button making replaced independent household textile production it remained firmly under entrepreneurial control. The McLane Report noted in 1832 that "materials are furnished and contracts made with some hundreds of females residing in several adjoining towns, by one person who [is] considered the capitalist. They call upon him once a week and procure molds, silk and lasting, etc., and at the same time bring the product of their labor for the previous week."[67] Payment was usually in goods. Not only did button making provide families with an inducement to trade at Williston's store, it reduced his need to rely on cash to conduct transactions and permitted him to charge the customary premium for noncash payment on the goods he sold.

Meanwhile, on the eastern side of the Valley, a comparable development was occurring in palm-leaf-hat making. Early growth of the industry in Worcester County and elsewhere encouraged Amherst traders to put palm leaf out to families on a small scale in the 1820s. In 1829 Leonard M. Hills, who a few years before had moved to the town from Connecticut, opened a small store in Amherst's East Village specifically to put out palm leaf in exchange for goods. Families split the leaf by hand, braided it, and sewed and fashioned it into hats, returning them to the store for credit or payment. Evidence as to the numbers of households involved at this early stage is hard to obtain, but like button making, the industry spread rapidly. Amherst remained its local center.[68]

Both east and west of the river, outwork became sufficiently attractive to merchants and customers that networks proliferated. In Williamsburg, the brothers Joel and Josiah Hayden opened a store for button makers in 1831. By 1834 Williston had at least one rival store in Easthampton, and three men formed a partnership to put button-making materials out from Sylvester Judd's old store in Westhampton.[69] Other Amherst stores followed Hills into the palm-leaf business. When Joseph Howard opened a new drugstore there in 1831, he was optimistic that "my orders will be considerable" and told his New York supplier that "You must put the price as low as possible—especially in such articles as dyes and hatters materials—as the profit is mean though the amo[unt] is considerable." By the following year Edward P. Huntington was handling shipments of hats from his North Hadley store, including consignments sent to him for forwarding by a North Amherst or Sunderland trader. In 1836 a store in Whately, which later went out of business, was also dealing with hat braiders.[70]

By now, however, button and hat making were following divergent courses. Williston and other button merchants began to concentrate more of their production in central shops, particularly in Williamsburg,

67. Ibid., p. 324.
68. Carpenter and Morehouse, History of Amherst, pp. 291–292.
69. Luther Clapp, Easthampton, advertisement, Hampshire Gazette, Jan 29, 1834; Sylvester Judd, "Notebook," vol. 1, Apr 18, 1834.
70. Joseph Howard to George B. Archer, Amherst, June 22, 1831, BCJL; "Account of Sales of Palm Leaf Hats by Edw. M. Greenway and Co. on a/c of E. P. Huntington and Co.," PPHH; notice of assignees' sale of the stock of Levi Bush & Co., Whately, Northampton Courier, Jan 11, 1837.

and to mechanize some stages of the process; for this purpose, Williston formed a partnership with the Hayden brothers in the mid-1830s. Part of the rationale was to cut down competition in the rapidly expanding industry by restricting effective access to it. The other factor was that button making quickly became highly varied, requiring a range of products made from different materials and in different styles. This demanded greater control over production than outwork would permit.

Palm-leaf hats, by contrast, were more uniform. Different types were introduced over time, but the basic product varied chiefly according to the size and weight of leaf that was used, something that the merchant could regulate when giving it out. Concentration in workshops did not begin until the late 1830s and 1840s. Nevertheless, the shift of button making into shops did not much reduce the outwork available. Williston and others continued to put out button molds for making up in families, and palm-leaf-hat making also spread into the western part of the Valley. By 1842, for instance, Joseph Bodman was putting out palm leaf from his Williamsburg store to forty-three families in seven towns, from nearby Goshen and Ashfield to Plainfield and Savoy in the Berkshire hills. Not long after, the Hayden brothers' store was also supplying palm-leaf braiders.[71]

By the mid-1840s there were at least eleven Amherst merchants putting out palm leaf for braiding, as well as stores in Hadley, South Hadley, Belchertown, Shutesbury, and New Salem. Leonard M. Hills, still one of the leading Amherst suppliers, provided palm leaf to merchants in other towns, including William and James Porter in Hadley.[72] The production of hats recorded for Amherst alone grew from 60,000 in 1837 to 317,000 in 1845. Although prices fell slightly, from an average of $2.40 per dozen to $2.16, the total value to its merchants of the town's output increased more than fourfold, from $12,000 to almost $56,700. Given that production in neighboring Hadley increased only slightly in the same period, it is likely that these figures reflect not the output of Amherst outworkers so much as the amount of business now controlled by Amherst merchants.[73] In 1839, for example, Huntington's North Hadley store had sixteen outworkers on its books. By 1850, Sweetser, Cutler and Company of Amherst alone had 284 people listed in its "braiding accounts," many of whom lived in the surrounding area

71. Joseph Bodman, Receipts, May 1842, Bodman Family Papers, SSC, Box 2.

72. Based on advertisements in the *Hampshire and Franklin Express* (Amherst), 1845–1848. See also bills of L. M. Hills to W. Porter, Sept 17, 1845, Nov 23, 1846, BCJL.

73. John P. Bigelow, *Statistical Tables: Exhibiting the Condition and Products of Certain Branches of Industry in Massachusetts for the Year Ending April 1, 1837* (Boston, 1838; hereafter cited as Mass. Industrial Census, 1837); John G. Palfrey, *Statistics of the Condition and Products of Certain Branches of Industry in Massachusetts for the Year Ending April 1, 1845* (Boston, 1846; hereafter cited as Mass. Industrial Census, 1845).

rather than in Amherst itself.[74] Both sets of figures, however, demonstrate the importance and widespread character of outwork hat making up to the middle of the century. What was its role and significance for rural people?

Outwork and Rural Households

In addition to the factors already mentioned, there are some indications that rural households were initially attracted to outwork because it was well paid in comparison with other available opportunities. An article in the *Hampshire Gazette* claimed in 1833 that payments in goods worth $1,500 to $2,000 a week were being made to button makers who dealt with the stores in Easthampton and Williamsburg. If the estimate is correct that one thousand families were engaged in button making by then, this suggests that earnings averaged $1.50 to $2.00 per family per week. Although not large, this amount equaled the wages that most women could earn from household or other employment and so was at least comparable with other sources of income. Moreover, because buttons were made at home, married women and other household members with commitments that kept them at home could contribute to family earnings at a rate commensurate with working elsewhere. So many women had been attracted to outwork, the paper claimed, that "housework is going out of fashion" and farmers looking for domestic help found it as hard to find as people in town.[75] Later evidence from the hat industry suggests, further, that, at least as long as production remained relatively undercapitalized, returns to labor formed a larger proportion of the end price for these products than was usual, say, in textile manufacture. Women in Belchertown making hats of the finer qualities in the late 1840s may have received as much as 40 percent of the final price charged by the merchants they dealt with, compared with the sums below 10 percent that Sarah Scott had received for weaving thirty or so years earlier.[76]

74. Store Ledger, North Hadley, 1839–1840, PPHH; Sweetser, Cutler and Co., Accounts, Amherst, BCJL, "Braiding Account" for 1850. The discussion that follows owes much to Thomas Dublin's important work on the outwork palm-leaf-hat industry in New Hampshire, "Women and Outwork in a Nineteenth-Century New England Town," in *The Countryside in the Age of Capitalist Transformation: Essays in the Social History of Rural America*, ed. Steven Hahn and Jonathan Prude (Chapel Hill, 1985), pp. 51–69. Mary H. Blewett, *Men, Women, and Work: Class, Gender, and Protest in the New England Shoe Industry, 1780–1910* (Urbana, Ill., 1988), traces the parallel emergence of outwork shoemaking in eastern Massachusetts and southern New Hampshire.

75. Quoted in *New England Farmer*, Oct 16, 1833.

76. Calculated from Belchertown North Baptist Female Benevolent Society, Records, 1848–1855, BCJL.

However, this evidence needs to be treated with caution. The *Gazette*'s figures could well have been exaggerated, or at least an estimate of what *could* be earned by full-time work, rather than what *was* earned in fact. The margins that the Belchertown women apparently earned were not matched by work on lower-quality hats. In time, as production in both button and hat making became concentrated in workshops and factories, the portion of the whole process left to outworkers was reduced. Correspondingly, prices tended to fall and outworkers' share of the returns was squeezed. It is noteworthy that the rapid growth of hat production took place during the depression that followed the panic of 1837, as farm families faced the need to make up income lost through underemployment or declining produce prices. Evidence from the hat industry in the middle of the century points to three important qualifications to the suggestion that households were attracted to outwork by the returns it gave them. On the one hand, the households that took in braiding and other outwork tended to be ones that had special need for the income. They were not attracted to it but, rather, could not do without it. Moreover, production was usually intermittent, so earnings were not equivalent to those from full-time work. Finally, production was skewed toward the lowest-paid types of work.

Who did outwork? Sixty of the 284 households Sweetser, Cutler and Company had on its books in 1850 lived in Amherst itself. The analysis that follows is largely based on these families, traced in the U.S. census for the town. The census index suggests that most of the remaining two hundred or more families lived in neighboring towns. Of fifty-six men from outside Amherst who appear in Sweetser, Cutler's accounts and who can be traced in the index, twenty-three (41 percent) lived in Hadley, seven in Leverett, six in Shutesbury, and three in Pelham. These four towns account for two-thirds of the "outsiders." Others came from Sunderland, Belchertown, Granby, South Hadley, and Northampton, and from as far as Hatfield, Whately, Deerfield, Conway, and Dana. Sweetser, Cutler and Company's network therefore covered much of the eastern part of Hampshire County and overlapped slightly with the sphere of influence of the next large palm-leaf-hat center to the east, the town of Barre in Worcester County.[77]

The Amherst families that braided leaf in 1850 fell into a number of distinct categories. The work was almost always done by women and children. There are no contemporary references to men's household work at hat braiding. Many women, especially from the locality of the

77 This and subsequent paragraphs are based on Sweetser, Cutler, "Braiding Accounts"; U.S. Seventh Census, Population Schedules, 1850, Massachusetts, National Archives, Washington, D.C. (microfilm); Ronald V. Jackson and Gary R. Teeples, comps., *Massachusetts Census Index, 1850* (Bountiful, Utah, 1979).

store, had accounts there in their own names, regardless of their marital status. Seven of the sixty households were headed by women, at least four of them widows. Of the men listed in the accounts none was single and all lived in households where there was at least one woman of working age.

Most families doing outwork were connected with old rural occupations. Exactly half of the household heads were farmers. Another sixteen (27 percent) of the total were artisans or craftsmen; they included four "mechanics," three joiners, two each of masons, shoemakers, and butchers, a painter, a broom maker, and a cooper. Only five out of the sixty household heads were engaged in commerce or the professions; there was a teacher, a clergyman, a factory agent, a manufacturer, and a stable keeper. The overwhelming preponderance of farm and craft households suggests that outwork continued to fill the gap that had been left two or three decades before by the decline of independent household textile production. Evidence from Joseph Bodman's accounts with outworkers in 1842 confirms this. In nearly 95 percent of cases the store goods he exchanged for finished hats were cloth, clothing, notions, or footwear; only a handful of his braiders purchased such groceries as tea or tobacco, and none bought basic foodstuffs. Outwork allowed rural households, especially the women in them, to organize their income-earning activity around the other demands on their time.

Commentators reflected this when they praised outwork as a means for preventing "idleness" among women and children. The McLane Report noted that women did outwork "in scant times, when there is nothing else to do." Hat making, wrote one newspaper editor, "is, with many, a work of odd moments which would otherwise be unimproved, so the frugal housewife will include in her day's work a 'stent' of so much braiding to be done." But there was a clear division between those who took up outwork and those who did not. The families who took palm leaf to braid from Sweetser, Cutler's store were not its "best" customers. None of the physicians, lawyers, professors, and other prominent Amherst citizens who frequented the store took outwork there. Most braiders were of middling or poor economic status, who did outwork because they had to, in order to help make ends meet. Susanna Goodale of Belchertown had a young woman working for her as a servant in 1845, whom she gave time off to braid palm leaf on her own account; "she was owing," Goodale wrote, "and wanted to braid the hats to pay family debts."[78]

The census recorded the real estate holdings of fifty-eight of the sixty

---

78. McLane Report, p. 324. Goodale is quoted in Stephen A. Aron, "The Minds of Hands: Working People of Amherst in the Mid-Nineteenth Century" (Senior honors thesis, Amherst College, 1982), p. 93.

Amherst braiding families. Over one-third of them had no real property. Over half of those who did own land or buildings had less than $2,000 worth. However, as might be expected, it was the farm families that had the most land. Only three of the thirty farmers reported no property, and half of the remainder had over $2,000 worth. Artisans, on the other hand, were much more likely to be propertyless. Eleven of the sixteen had none and only one of the remainder had real estate of more than $2,000.

While a relative shortage of property was likely to bring families to undertake outwork, it was not the only factor. A closer look at the women in outworking families—either those named in the accounts, or those who probably did the work when their husbands brought palm leaf home from the store—suggests that they fell into three groups, each of which took on braiding under different circumstances. Of fifty-seven women identified, thirteen were single, forty were married, and four were widows living at home with children.

Of the single women, eight were less than twenty-five years old; two others were older but apparently living with parents; three more older women were living with kin or working as servants. So nearly one-quarter of women outworkers were using it to help support themselves in the households they lived in while waiting for marriage or to supplement other small earnings. To these could be added another twelve households in which the eldest women were married and aged forty-five or over, but which included girls in their teens or early twenties who may have done much of the actual work at braiding. Charlotte Dickinson, a single woman, braided hats over a considerable period, working for one merchant in 1844 and appearing in Sweetser, Cutler's account for 1850. For her, it was a means of supplementing the board provided by her family. She exchanged finished hats for cloth, including calico and gingham, and bought other small items such as ribbons, cord, candy, salt, and a whip. Dickinson evidently worked to a seasonal pattern. In 1844 she took goods from Sweetser, Cutler and Company between May and September, returning twenty-two hats to the store between December that year and February 1845. Three years later, she had goods on credit from Peter Ingram and Company between September 1847 and March 1848 but completed thirty-three hats for them in February and March.[79]

Thirty-seven of the forty married women had children at home. Fifteen were young, in the age group twenty-five to thirty-four, and another ten were between thirty-five and forty-four. Most had young children and were at a stage of the life cycle when demands on their

---

79. Charlotte Dickinson, Account Books, Amherst, 1812–1848, BCJL.

labor were greatest and assistance with it scarce. Outwork provided them with a flexible means of raising small amounts of extra income without excessively disrupting other household tasks. But households with other income from farming or a trade may only have done it intermittently, to compensate for falling prices or loss of work. In the 1830s, Mary Bullard Graham worked in her husband's shoemaking shop when times were busy and took in outwork on button molds when trade was slack.[80]

For the widows who had older children at home, outwork also provided an essential supplementary means of raising income that could be accommodated to other requirements. Letters from the family of Judith Nutting, one of Sweetser, Cutler's customers, reveal something of the place of palm-leaf braiding in her household and amply demonstrate that braiding was not, as male commentators liked to think, a task for "idle hands." It had to be fitted into household work routines that were already crowded. One of Judith Nutting's four daughters described a typical couple of weeks in the 1840s: "Last week Mother wove . . . carpet I sewed for Doria Cook, the girls braided. this week we have took up the carpets and cleand house and made soap and cut five dresses and made two or three sun bonnets Amelia has been to the Academy one day . . . all this besides braiding [which] we wont say anything about." When their brother walked off his job with a building contractor in 1841, mother and sisters had to increase their efforts to help make ends meet. "Mother will take in all the [carpet] weaving she can get hold of," wrote one of them, while another sister worked hard at braiding, finishing six hats in one day. Two years later, when her mother and sisters were away from home, Harriet Nutting had to cover their chores: "I have to be Hannah and mother in the house and John at the barn, besides braiding double rim[m]ed hats when there is 'nothing else to do'."[81] Harriet's ironic quotation of the conventional contemporary view of the role of outwork speaks volumes for its irrelevance to the poor and middling families who usually did the work. Baptist women in Belchertown who braided hats to help support their minister in the late 1840s fitted the work in among their other tasks, sometimes sharing it between them. Thirteen women, for example, braided seven hats between mid-May and early June 1848, nine more in just two weeks in mid-June and another six by the end of the first week of July.[82] Like the Nutting family's, their work rate varied considerably. Braiding was just one of the strategies for maintaining a livelihood.

80. Mary B. Graham to Sophronia Bullard, Buckland, Apr 18, 1836, Edwards Family Correspondence, MCFL.

81. Mary Nutting to Eli Nutting, Amherst, Sept 29, 1841; Harriet Nutting to Eli Nutting, May 11, 1843, June 6, 1845, Nutting Correspondence, BCJL.

82. Calculated from Belchertown North Baptist Female Benevolent Society, Records, 1848–1855.

Some families used their women's or children's labor at outwork to raise income for special purposes. In Buckland in 1841, the shoemakers Mary and Lucius Graham were planning to move to the West. They set their children to making button molds. Mary wrote in February 1842 "our children are helping us to get ready, they have earned since the forepart of June seventy dollars."[83] But there were disadvantages to outwork, especially as prices were whittled away over time. It came to be regarded as "light work," suitable for children. There was no distinction between adults' and children's wages. Women were paid at undercut children's rates. As a newspaper editor put it, "a nimble-fingered girl of ten can earn in a day as much as an adult woman."[84] Although the Belchertown Baptist women, working intermittently for their minister, sought to maximize the return for their work by braiding fine-grade number four palm leaf, which fetched up to $0.25 a hat, the majority of braiders working for their own households opted for coarse number two leaf, which could be braided more roughly for a much lower sum. When Judith Nutting's daughter finished six hats in one day, she earned the family exactly $0.54. Two-thirds of the hats returned to Joseph Bodman's store in 1842 were number twos, paid for at $0.09 to $0.13 each; fewer than one in ten were number fours. The Grahams' four children averaged earnings of $2.50 a month each between June 1841 and February 1842, at best one-third of the winter wages of a farm laborer and half those of a woman domestic servant. Even when outworkers pressed their hardest they earned what a newspaper admitted was a "mere pittance." In 1857 two girls and a boy in Barre completed a record stint of braiding, in which they produced 800 hats in thirty-seven days. At $0.08 per hat, they earned an average of only $0.575 a day each, still well below the daily rate for a farm laborer. Above all, for much of the period, outworkers usually received payment only in store goods, rather than cash. Mary Graham commented of the $70.00 that her children had earned, "it is all store pay but it helps a great deal," implying that cash would have been better.[85] With low rates and "poor pay" it is no wonder that families usually did outwork only when circumstances required it.

Merchants and the Rural Economy

Nevertheless the growth of outwork represented a considerable extension of the influence of local merchants over rural households. Be-

83. Mary B. Graham to Lewis Edwards, Buckland, Jan 26, 1842, Edwards Family Correspondence.
84. *Amherst Record*, May 3, 1871.
85. The Barre stint was reported in *Hampshire and Franklin Express*, June 12, 1857.

fore 1820 they had been dependent on households' willingness to trade
with them and obliged to adapt their methods to seek out what business
they could get into their stores. With the shift in rural consumption
patterns merchants became surer of the demand for their goods. With
the development of outwork, they could redouble their connection with
customers and be assured that their poorer neighbors in particular
would have means to pay for the goods that they "took out of the
store." Outwork not only helped boost their sales but earned direct
profits for them from the labor embodied in the work. Although, according to one account, most merchants who "take leaf and put it out in
their neighborhood . . . are satisfied if no profit is made on the braiding,
for they pay for it from their stores, making the increase in business thus
secured afford them a fair profit," some "make a profit at both ends."[86]
Scattered evidence about the charges for work and materials in the
palm-leaf hat business suggest that merchants charged braiders for leaf
put out to them as much as 35 or 40 percent more than the wholesale
price and that markups on finished hats were in the 25 to 50 percent
range.[87]

In contrast with parts of Europe, where rural outwork often long
preceded the development of the factory system, the creation of substantial putting-out networks in New England largely coincided with
the establishment of factory textile production. The same shifts in production and consumption strategies that released families and young
women to work in the new textile mills also encouraged many rural
households, especially poorer ones, to take on hat or button making,
and merchants were quick to take advantage of the opportunities for
income this afforded them.

As they added the profits of domestic manufacture to the profits of
trade, merchants not only provided means to expand their own businesses but built a basis for exercising increasing power over the rural
economy in the middle decades of the nineteenth century. Together,
retail trade and outwork enabled successful merchants to accumulate
capital with which to further the concentration of manufacturing in the
1840s and 1850s. Yet, as they sought to achieve greater power and
influence, merchants, like other rural people, faced considerable risks
and uncertainties. In trying to overcome uncertainty, they helped alter
the rules of exchange in the local economy.

Several leading traders between 1830 and the 1850s—including J. P.
Williston, William H. Stoddard, and Luke Sweetser—were active

---

86. *Amherst Record*, May 3, 1871.
87. Calculations based on values reported in Mass. Industrial Censuses, 1837, 1845,
and store accounts of Huntington (North Hadley), Porter (Hadley), Sweetser, Cutler
(Amherst), and Joseph Bodman (Williamsburg).

churchmen during the height of the Evangelical revivals. Williston associated his early success in trade with his conversion in the revival of 1831, writing to his wife the following year that "the Lord seems at last to be smiling on us in our effort to earn an honest livelihood," and remarking that "He has wisely deferred it until we were willing to acknowledge that 'unless the Lord build the house thy labor is in vain that build it.' "[88] But, while he prudently attributed his success to divine Providence, Williston was also adopting new methods of running his business. Applying principles of system and self-discipline propagated by revivalist culture, Williston and his colleagues would help influence the course of economic change.

88. John P. Williston to Cecilia L. Williston, Philadelphia, June 17, 1832, Williston Papers, I/B/9, folder 1, NEHGS.

PART IV

CONCENTRATION:
THE 1820s TO 1860

Chapter 6

"The Advantage Their Pay Demands":
Morality and Money

Rural people were poised between the ethics of local exchange and those of long-distance trade. Greater market involvement and the influence of merchants seemed set to swing the balance firmly in the direction of the latter and, in the long run, did so. By the Civil War, cash transactions and short credit had become common, though not universal, even in local dealings. But the shift did not happen easily or directly, partly because the continuation of household production and neighborhood and kinship networks made local exchange practices convenient for certain purposes. In addition, though, new household strategies and market influences had contradictory effects on the conduct of economic life. Local exchange caused frustrations and pressures that led many people to seek to avoid it. On the other hand, market fluctuations created uncertainties that encouraged people to use local exchange as a shelter from their effects. Only as successive attempts to deal with these uncertainties created new attitudes and economic discipline were cultural conditions in the countryside ripe for the widespread adoption of a cash economy.

This long ethical shift may be seen as a chapter in the story of "moral economy" in the United States. Many scholars have argued that the revolutionary period accelerated the spread of a liberal ideology that divorced economic practices from moral restraints. But there are grounds for suggesting that this ideology took a long time to become dominant. Certainly the Revolution and its aftermath witnessed the collapse of many old corporatist aspects of economic life, including most formal price controls and customary wage levels.[1] But even after

1. Joyce Appleby, *Capitalism and a New Social Order: The Republican Vision of the 1790s* (New York, 1984), argues that liberal economic ideology emerged rapidly after the Revolution. Steven Watts, *The Republic Reborn: War and the Making of Liberal America, 1790–1820*

economic liberalism entered the rhetoric of formal thought and writing, popular attitudes continued to display the wish for control of unregulated market behavior. Ruth Bogin has recently written that, well into the nineteenth century, the language of legislative petitions was rooted in the concept of a "moral economy" as farmers, artisans, and others employed the principle of "equal rights" as part of a "struggle to maintain their independent status."[2] Likewise, the ethical considerations inherent in local exchange practices continued to serve as a counterpoint to the ethics of long-distance trade. Each was concerned with reciprocity, but in a different sense. The "local" ethic valued the longer-term reciprocity between dealers embedded in a network of social connections; morality lay in accepting obligations and discharging them over time. The "market" ethic emphasized quick payment and assumed a formal equality between individual dealers at the point of exchange; morality lay in the quick discharge of obligation.

The passage from one to another was complicated by the intrusion of further moral concerns along the way, none of them straightforwardly aligned with liberal individualism. When Rev. Joseph Field of Charlemont preached to the Hampshire Missionary Society on prosperity in 1816, he urged the elevation of social and neighborhood values above individual advancement, asserting that "Jerusalem was . . . the house of the whole kingdom, a kind of public property in which everyone had his share," and referring to "that community and general interest, which has its foundation, its support and prosperity in divine grace."[3] Critics worried that market exchange and the credit system were leading to greater inequality and the subversion of republican egalitarian principles. At least in the early 1830s, some people still saw reciprocity, rather than gain, as the purpose of local exchange. Parishioners in North Amherst brought before the church a complaint against one of their deacons, objecting to "the *acuteness* he sometimes manifested in his bargains," and asserting that "Gospel rules contemplated something more *equal* among brethren, as they count up their gains and losses in their mutual dealings."[4] The religious revivals that shook New England repeatedly from about 1810 to the 1850s also brought the

---

(Baltimore, 1987), chap. 1 and passim, suggests that it happened later and that the 1812 war provided a crucial impetus.

2. Ruth Bogin, "Petitioning and the New Moral Economy of Post-Revolutionary America," *William and Mary Quarterly* 45 (July 1988): 391–425; the quotation is from p. 397.

3. Joseph Field, *Prosperity Promised to the Lovers of Jerusalem: A Sermon, Delivered in Northampton, August 22, 1816, before the Hampshire Missionary Society at Their Annual Meeting* (Northampton, 1816), p. 3.

4. George Cooke, "Reminiscences of the North Parish, Amherst, Mass. from Oct. 1838 to March 1858," 1883, part 1, pp. 3–4, AAS (typescript). That notions of equality and reciprocity were held well into the nineteenth century is suggested by the inscription on a fraktur by Franklin Wilder, c. 1865, in the Museum of American Folk Art, New York, which includes the phrase "I-O-U and U-O-Me forms a Government in perfect Unity."

morality of individual ambition and economic behavior under scrutiny. The *Christian Almanac* for 1830, having posed the question "Have I the right to make as good a bargain as I can?" answered firmly in the negative: "No man has a right to do anything which causes needless suffering."[5] So republican ideology, local exchange practices, and revivalism all promoted a vision of economic behavior tempered by moral restraints. Only in time did a more instrumental view gain weight. It did so less on its own merits than by default, as other viewpoints collapsed through their own inconsistencies.

The Frustrations of Local Exchange

Account books, letters, and other sources reveal the persistence of local exchange practices into the middle of the nineteenth century. The Amherst farmer Chester Marshall kept thirty sets of accounts between 1825 and 1833 in which he recorded both debits and credits. Only one was paid off entirely in cash. Seventeen involved no cash at all. Although he used cash more frequently twenty years later, another Amherst farmer, Horace Belding, still relied significantly on noncash payments. Of all his payments and receipts, goods and labor accounted for 81 percent and cash for only 19 percent. Tradesmen continued to negotiate direct exchanges. Needing materials in 1845 the Northampton cabinetmaker Elihu Strong advertised for "5,000 feet [of] Hemlock Boards . . . for which I will pay in Cabinet furniture, if delivered immediately." Many stores, too, continued to offer their goods for "country produce taken in exchange."[6] Willingness to accept payment in goods was often assumed. Owing a debt to Sylvester Judd in 1836, a Westhampton hatter implied that he could pay quickly only in the products of his trade: "If you will send directions . . . for a hat or two I will bring or send them to you next week or the week after." This was comparatively prompt: when Sherman Clark bought Judd's pew in the Westhampton meetinghouse in 1838 he agreed to pay for it with fifteen cords of firewood over three years. In fact, it took him more than seven years to make the final delivery. Stores, too, still had to tolerate long and irregular repayments. An Amherst merchant advertised in 1846 that "we want all our customers to understand that 12 months is the EXTENT of credit we can give."[7]

5. *Christian Almanac for the Year 1830* (Boston, 1829), p. 28.
6. Elihu and Horace Belding, Account Book, Amherst, 1816–1864, BCJL. The quotation is from *Hampshire Herald* (Northampton), Nov 4, 1845; advertisements of store goods in exchange for produce could be found in any newspaper up to the late 1850s and, in rarer instances, later.
7. Simeon Clapp to Sylvester Judd, Jr., Worthington, Mass., Nov 21, 1836, MCFL, Box 18. Sylvester Judd, "Notebook," vol. 3, Dec 17, 1845; the quotation is from the *Hampshire and Franklin Express* (Amherst), Jan 26, 1846.

But as trade increased in the 1820s and 1830s and men and women tried to harmonize local exchange with the fluctuating rhythms of distant markets, they found cause to criticize such older practices. Thomas's *Farmer's Almanac*, for example, had long scorned the neighborly habit of borrowing and lending tools and other items. Early in the century, however, it had simply given the platitudinous (and questionable) warning that "the borrower is slave to the lender." By the 1830s its objections were on the grounds that borrowers who "through extreme parsimony, neglect to provide themselves with . . . various articles," placed themselves at a competitive advantage and "live almost entirely at the expense of their neighbors." A newspaper article of 1834 went further, criticizing the farmer with means who had loaned money out at interest but had insufficient equipment. By borrowing what tools he needed without expense, "he may annually add to the amount of interest," while unjustly obliging his neighbors to bear part of his costs. What had originally been equitable assumptions could become "gross injustice" in the context of market trade.[8]

Perhaps it was not surprising that a store owner like Dan Huntington should reveal his reluctance to accept noncash payment when he asked one of his sons to collect a debt for him in Amherst in 1837: "I want you should show him his bill, get the pay if you can, if not know what he will do about it. If he works in stone, perhaps I will give him a job, if he will call and see us soon. However I wd rather have him pay you." Some years later Huntington mused on the problems of getting paid in this system: "It is a prodigious difficult thing now a days, if money is the thing hinted at, to make folks understand what you are at. You must go round & round, about the subject, with a deal of palaver; talk big; tell how much you are worth; lie a little, perhaps; & if you do not succeed, tap them upon the shoulder; draw a little nearer; hold them by the button kick their shins; & finally tell them outright what you want—& after all get flouted by some flimsy hollow-hearted come-off."[9] But farmers, artisans, and laborers also expressed annoyance at local exchange practices that appeared to them inflexible. To many of them prompt payment in cash appeared increasingly attractive. As a millwright in Chesterfield reflected, an economy where many were in debt and others had only goods to offer in payment presented lamentable difficulties: "I did work for Pease last summer to the amount of more than $300 and have not got much of my pay yet. Barnaby has gone to jail

8. Robert B. Thomas, *Farmer's Almanack for the Year 1800* (Boston, 1799), entry for February; Thomas, *Farmer's Almanack for the Year 1835* (Boston, 1834), [pp. 39–41]; *Hampshire Gazette* (Northampton), Oct 1, 1834.

9. Dan Huntington to Frederic Dan Huntington, Hadley, Dec 7, 1837, and [Apr.?] 19, [1843?], PPHH.

and I have lost that so that it has been impossible for me to do anything but work and pay the work I have done. So goes the millwright work in this country. I have done with it unless I get hold of a job where I know cash lives."[10] Skilled workmen at a Greenfield cutlery factory went on strike briefly in 1844 to demand monthly, instead of half-yearly, settlements with their employer. They were unsuccessful and returned to work on the old terms, but their action spoke for the dissatisfaction of many poorer men and women that they had to wait for their pay and, all too often, accept it in unwanted, shoddy, or expensive goods. A newspaper article pointed out that paying for work after it was done accorded with the principles of reciprocity, but was reciprocity of a very unequal sort.[11]

However, the evolution of a system of direct cash payment was complicated by the fluctuations that resulted from the rural economy's deepening involvement in distant markets. While an increasing number of workers, especially skilled men able to bargain for favorable conditions, did secure more immediate cash wages, their success and that of others was frequently undermined. Successive slumps in the 1830s and 1840s sent what cash there was in circulation into the hands of bankers and merchants, or drove it out of the region. The same slumps exacerbated debt problems in the countryside and sent people in two conflicting directions. On the one hand, they continued to seek to escape the entanglements of personal obligations; on the other, they used local exchange practices to give them some protection from market fluctuations. Their concern at the instability of economic life led to efforts to resolve it. Over time, these efforts were to alter both morality and practices.

Debt, Bankruptcy, and Panic

One indication of greater uncertainty was that actions for debt not only increased in number but were more likely to be local. By the mid-1840s, in the aftermath of the 1837 panic and subsequent depression, 40 percent of debt suits brought in the court of common pleas were

10. Patrick Bryant to Orren Bryant, Chesterfield, May 8, 1836, Bryant Collection, MCFL, Box 6.
11. The strike at J. Russell and Company's Green River works was noted by Edward J. Carpenter, an apprentice in the town: see "The Diary of an Apprentice Cabinetmaker: Edward Jenner Carpenter's 'Journal,' 1844–1845," ed. Christopher Clark, *Proceedings of the American Antiquarian Society* 98 (1988), entry for Mar 28, 1844; the original is in the MS Collection, AAS. Criticism of delayed payment, from an article in the *Philadelphia Ledger*, was reprinted in the *Northampton Democrat*, Oct 6, 1846.

between plaintiffs and defendants from the same town, twice the proportion in the first decade of the century. Moreover, the town with the highest proportion of such suits was not Northampton, the largest center, but Amherst, still dominated by farmers and small manufacturers.[12] Between 1838 and 1842, as prices and returns from local farm produce fell, the Valley felt the social as well as the economic consequences of the depression. When the price of butter fell to ten cents a pound in 1840, an Amherst woman wrote that "every body is groaning with the hard times. Almost every one wears a sombre face in this village." At the end of the following year, with no improvement in sight, she commented that "Amherst is very quiet this winter[;] every body is more or less affected by pecuniary distresses & visiting seems suspended."[13] The use of the term *embarrassment* for financial difficulty arose out of these social effects. As pressure for prompt payment increased in a society hitherto accustomed to widespread debt, face-to-face contacts became more difficult.

Cycles of failure and bankruptcy had become endemic well before the 1837 panic. The general rise in farm-product prices between 1829 and 1837 had been punctuated by temporary reversals in 1831 and 1834, which caused hardship to farmers, craftsmen, and laborers alike. As we saw earlier, price fluctuations could catch cattle fatteners out in a number of ways at the end of the season. During the inflation of the 1830s, the relative costs of labor and goods constantly changed. Rising prices for provisions caught out hired laborers, whose wages did not keep pace. Craftsmen and other independent producers who needed to swap goods for foodstuffs were similarly disadvantaged. Conversely, some poorer families found difficulty obtaining outwork, as merchants reacted cautiously to price fluctuations that made their profits unpredictable.[14]

Of 116 Northampton firms or individuals who advertised in the *Hampshire Gazette* between 1830 and 1834, 11 percent failed, assigned their property, or died insolvent during these five years alone. In 1835 the county register of deeds slipped out of town early one morning to avoid paying $4,000 in notes sent from New York and Boston for collection and was thought to have helped at least one other man escape his creditors by accepting the assignment of his furniture. By the end of the decade a local newspaper could comment that while many young men

12. Hampshire County Court of Common Pleas, Records, 1844–1845, Hampshire County Courthouse, Northampton.

13. Harriet Fowler to Eliza Jones, Amherst, Feb 14, 1840, Dec 27, 1841, in Jay Leyda, comp., *The Years and Hours of Emily Dickinson*, 2 vols. (New Haven, 1960), 1:59, 73.

14. Mary B. Graham to Sophronia Bullard, Buckland, Apr 18, 1836, Edwards Family Correspondence, MCFL.

thought it unfortunate "not to have capital enough to establish themselves at the outset of life in a good business," in fact "it is really a blessing." Over the past two decades, so many who had started out "with abundant means" had failed, "become poor, lost their place in society, and are passed by their own boon companions with a look which painfully says I know you not."[15]

The panic of 1837 and its aftermath crystallized fears of economic instability. During the spring of that year, financial troubles in the cities were reported with awe in the countryside. On April 19 the *Northampton Courier* described a "frightful tornado" in New York, Philadelphia, and Baltimore, before which "hundreds and even thousands of men of substantial wealth have been swept down." A week later, it reported "numerous heavy and extensive failures in Boston."[16] The near collapse of the New York firm of Arthur Tappan and Company caused particular shock in the Valley, not only because the Tappans had come from Northampton, but because theirs was considered an especially sound concern; as Sylvester Judd's son Chauncey Parkman Judd remarked, it was "so systematic, so prudent, so well skilled in mercantile affairs," and, above all, "appeared to have the glory of God so much in view." "When such merchants fail," Judd wrote, "I don't know what we may not expect next."[17]

What came next was the arrival of the crisis in the Valley. In April alone 124 writs of attachment were issued in Hampshire County. By May 13, banks had suspended specie payments and businesses were failing. The Northampton attorney C. P. Huntington consulted his brother in Boston about their interests at either end of the state. He reported that he was joined with five others in a lawsuit to break the assignment of property made by one local firm so that they would have a chance of receiving debts from it before other creditors could sue. He had collected one debt but needed instructions about others: "do you want Robinson and Davis sued?" He also advised about debtors in Boston ("get your pay of Foster if you ever expect to") and reflected that "you have plenty of company in your pecuniary troubles—stick to Foster."[18] This was the language and mechanism of panic. A welter of anxious bargaining, assignments, and lawsuits sought to dislodge what could be saved from other businesses before one's own ruin loomed.

15. Statistics are calculated from advertisements in the *Hampshire Gazette*, 1830–1834. Judd, "Notebook," vol. 1, Mar 11, 18, 1834; Cecilia L. Williston to J. P. Williston, Northampton, Nov 4, 1835, Williston Papers, I/B/13–1, NEHGS; *Hampshire Republican* (Northampton), May 15, 1839.

16. *Northampton Courier*, Apr 19, 26, 1837

17. Chauncey P. Judd to Apphia Judd, Hartford, May 9, 1837, Judd Papers, 55M-1, Box 2, HCL.

18. C. P. Huntington to Edward P. Huntington, Northampton, May 17, 1837, PPHH.

Ruin faced some areas of the Valley especially, as chains of long-distance and local debts brought various firms to the brink of failure. Amherst manufacturers were hard hit. The collapse of a Boston firm triggered a succession of failures, among them a large carriage-making company, a firm of gun manufacturers, the stove dealer Oliver M. Clapp, and the merchant and palm-leaf-hat manufacturer Leonard M. Hills, who had been a large endorser of local paper. Clapp and Hills would eventually recover; others did not.[19] Chauncey Parkman Judd, watching his own brother come close to failure in Hartford, well described the tension as firms struggled to avoid being dragged down by others. When, after days of anxiously collecting funds, "JW paid up a large note at the bank [I] never saw him more pleased in his life." Announcing that "he should not fail this week," he went away "in very good spirits . . . jumped into his carriage and had a fine and easy ride I think." The passions generated by debt and potential bankruptcy in these circumstances would, as much as the economic consequences, provoke efforts to resolve financial instabilities. As Judd wrote, "the cholera never had half as many terrors. Men could run away from the cholera but they can't run away from this distress."[20]

Altogether 447 writs of attachment were issued in Hampshire County during 1837 and, although this number was not reached again, there were smaller peaks in 1839–1840 and 1842–1843. Similar increases were recorded in mortgage records, as farmers, craftsmen, and traders, strapped for means of payment, were often forced to sign away valuable property in order to raise quite small sums of cash.[21] In 1839 a short-lived rally in prices was followed by a reversal that affected more local firms. Many farmers, who had contributed to speculation in mulberry trees as they sought new sources of income after the first panic, suffered reverses when the bubble burst. This also affected other dealers, such as the family of Oliver M. Clapp, who had invested in mulberry trees in the hope of bailing out their first losses in the round of failures two years before. The Amherst merchant Luke Sweetser commented, "I am in fear from present indication that it will be a long time ere business will assume any thing like its usual character."[22]

Apprehensions affected particular ways of doing business as well as the general economic climate. Up to now many people had assumed that dealing with kin, neighbors, or others known to them would

19. On failures in Amherst, see Edward W. Carpenter and Charles F. Morehouse, *The History of the Town of Amherst, Massachusetts* (Amherst, 1896), p. 297.

20. Chauncey P. Judd to Apphia Judd, Hartford, May 9, 1837, Judd Papers.

21. Hampshire County Court of Common Pleas, Records; Amherst, Records of Personal Property Mortgages, vol. 2, 1837–1851, Amherst Town Hall; Westhampton, Records of Mortgages of Personal Property, vol. 1, 1841–1877, Westhampton Town Hall.

22. Luke Sweetser to Joseph Sweetser, Amherst, Nov 2, 1839, in Leyda, *Years and Hours of Emily Dickinson*, 1:57.

minimize risks. But in the scramble to protect positions in a crumbling market, personal contacts turned out to be no guarantee of protection. Edward P. Huntington withdrew from his family's North Hadley store business in the mid-1830s and entered a Maine and New Brunswick land concern in partnership with a cousin of his father's. Having advanced money to the firm, Huntington found that its obligations were unsecured. Called upon to meet them in 1837, he lost his investment and ended up in a Boston jail. His father, angrily calling upon the cousin to assist, pointed out that Edward had "tho't himself dealing with a man of business, a man of honour, of religious principles, a responsible man, an old acquaintance and near relation. Had he supposed himself to be dealing with any other than an upright man, he would have been on his guard." A few years later the *New England Farmer* remarked that, as a result of the crisis, "one must now witness daily, acts of meanness and deception among neighbors, formerly expected only in companies of jockies and tavern-loungers."[23]

If older practices for reducing risks were no longer certain, it was evident that wider measures would have to be taken to deal with the financial instability which the 1820s and 1830s had brought. In 1847, at the age of just seventeen, the future poet Emily Dickinson reflected with wry amusement on the social burden debt and financial obligations could entail. Writing to her brother, she told of "a dream which I dreamed last night," that "Father had failed & mother said that 'our rye field which she & I planted, was mortgaged to Seth Nims.'" The joke was that Dickinson's father, Edward, had become Amherst's leading attorney, responsible for handling the collection of hundreds of debts. He was also an emerging Whig politician, opposed to Nims, who held the town postmastership under a succession of Democratic administrations in the 1840s and 1850s. Using this imagined embarrassment to poke gentle fun at the anxieties of her family and neighbors, Emily wrote to her brother that "I hope it is not true but do write soon & tell me for you know 'I should expire with mortification' to have our rye field mortgaged, to say nothing of it's falling into the merciless hands of a Loco[foco]!!!"[24]

A Search for Stability

As the local economy was drawn closer to market fluctuations in the 1820s, there started a search for economic stability that lasted until the

---

23. Dan Huntington to F. Robinson, Hadley, Jan 3, 1838, PPHH; *New England Farmer*, Jan 11, 1843.
24. Emily Dickinson to W. Austin Dickinson, South Hadley, Oct 21, 1847, *The Letters of Emily Dickinson*, ed. Thomas H. Johnson, 3 vols. (Cambridge, Mass., 1958): 1:48.

Civil War period. Three strands in this search stand out. From the late 1820s to the mid-1830s a political campaign attempted to address the problems of the debt process and its inequities. From then until the mid-1840s efforts focused on the reform of individuals' behavior as a source of greater economic predictability. This second strand carried over, in turn, to the third phase, an attempt to reform the conduct of business transactions. The strands overlapped to some degree, sharing personnel, rhetoric, and motives. But there was a progression from one to the next, each phase tending to pick up where the last had left off and to avoid its errors and shortcomings. In the end none of these approaches achieved its purpose. Economic life remained unstable in 1860. Some efforts, such as the attempt to apply tests of character to the conduct of transactions, had effects opposite to what they had intended. But the search for stability helped alter the rules by which much of the rural economy was run and underlay many of the structural changes that were also taking place.

The Workingmen's Movement

The conduct of the economy was an important subtext to the political movements between 1828 and 1836 that accompanied the rise of the "second party system" in Massachusetts. As elsewhere the political realignments that brought about the emergence of the Whig party resulted from the popularity of new parties outside the existing political structure. In the Northampton area of the Valley, Anti-Masonry attracted support, as did, for a brief time, the Workingmen's movement, with which the former had an uneasy alliance. Both groupings, populist in character and critical of existing political institutions and assumptions, combined an attachment to notions of independence and equal rights engendered by the household economy with proposals for a reform of the debt laws that could alter the pattern of power in economic disputes. While the Anti-Masons' attack on secret societies criticized wider aspects of social and political privilege, the Workingmen's movement focused particularly on the political and administrative issues that it hoped could protect the interests of "small producers."[25]

Fear of competition from western farming states and of the improved transport that could only assist the shipment of their produce was one of the sparks that set off the political upheaval in the Valley at the end of

25. Ronald P. Formisano, *The Transformation of Political Culture: Massachusetts Parties, 1790s–1840s* (New York, 1983), pp. 201–244, provides a fuller general discussion of these movements.

the 1820s. The mere rumor that Governor Levi Lincoln favored the building of an East-West railroad caused a significant shift in votes away from him to his Democratic opponent in the 1829 elections. In the four towns of Hadley, Hatfield, Northampton, and Williamsburg, Lincoln's overall vote fell by 24 percent in spite of a 15 percent rise in voter turnout. Hatfield, whose farmers were perhaps most likely to be seriously affected by competition in the beef cattle market, reduced its vote for Lincoln by more than half.[26] But the Valley's voters, largely unsympathetic to the Democrats, were not content simply to throw votes their way. Over the next few years, they provided considerable support to candidates who adopted a broader rhetoric of opposition to the changes that had been taking place over the previous decade or more.

Railroads were looked on with suspicion not just because they would bring cheaper produce into the state but because they would likely be owned by corporations, which rural politicians criticized widely during the early 1830s. Rev. Samuel C. Allen, who was to become a popular Workingmen's gubernatorial candidate, warned in a speech of 1830 that corporations threatened the equal rights of independent producers. He cited the increase in agricultural mortgages that had occurred in the previous two decades, and the extent to which they were being assumed by corporations such as the Massachusetts Hospital Life Assurance Company; these companies which would outlive any individual, were under the control of a few men and were "bringing the yeomanry . . . into a state of dependency and peril," subjecting "the whole landed interest to the domination of a monied capital." The key to preserving a republican social fabric was not a free constitution but the "distribution of rewards to labor."[27]

Fear of "monied capital" and the power of corporations was part of a wider attack on privilege that accorded with the values of a household-based economy and its ethics of reciprocity. An address in September 1830 by the "Committee of the Working Men of Northampton" called upon "farmers and mechanics, . . . the great majority of the people" to exercise their independent votes and to obtain a role for themselves in the "administration of government." Shortly afterward, a Workingman claimed that opposition to his party had been raised by "many of those who are money-holders—money lenders—penny shavers, and to the poor, heavy grinders—men . . . selfish in the extreme in their transac-

26. *Hampshire Gazette*, Apr 9, 16, 1828; Apr 8, 1829; the paper reported that in 1829 "many voted for Mr. Morton because they believed that Gov. Lincoln was for the rail road."

27. Samuel C. Allen, *An Address Given at Northampton to the Hampshire, Franklin, and Hampden Agricultural Society* (Northampton, 1830), p. 27.

tions with those around them"—in other words those not willing to abide by the ethics of neighborhood and local exchange.[28]

Central to the Workingmen's political platform was the demand for reform of the debt laws, particularly the abolition of imprisonment for debt. A Northampton petition of 1831 condemned imprisonment for debt as contrary to reason, religion, and republican principles of equal rights; "occasioning great loss of time" it prevented the debtor from paying and depleted the creditor's funds, "thus destroying the means of payment in which both have a common interest."[29] But the thrust of the Workingmen's critique was on the intervention of the courts in the settlement of debt in the first place. Workingmen accused lawyers of encouraging the law suits that lined their own pockets and disrupted the bonds of neighborhood. Another resolution of 1830 declared that "the spirit of law litigation is contrary both to reason and religion," and called for "all disputes between man and man" to be "settled by reference to their neighbors." A call to abolish county registers of deeds and reestablish them in each town was made on the grounds of "cheapness" and so that "the history of conveyances would be more perfectly known in the neighborhood of the lands."[30] Neighborhood and the equal rights of individuals could preserve an economic independence threatened by "the most alarming symptom of the times," that "the title to real estate is passing out of the hands of those who work on it" and becoming "a bob to the kite of a ficticious credit currency." Privilege, removing economic control into the hands of "money-power," was creating economic instability for the majority of producers.[31]

Household production and local exchange already provided a model for the kind of social vision that the Workingmen espoused. But they were not just backward-looking defenders of a passing social order. They viewed the household economy as a touchstone by which to judge economic and social morality. Their attacks on speculation, paper credit, mortgages, and debt suits proceeded from the knowledge that these were not inevitable. Reforms of the debt laws and support for local arbitration were designed to protect "honest, industrious families." "Sufficient property should be left free from attachment," one circular argued, "to enable an industrious family by rigid economy to support themselves."[32] The alternatives were "distress and ruin to

28. "The Committee of the Working Men of Northampton to their Constituents and Fellow Citizens," *Hampshire Gazette*, Sept 15, 1830; "A Workingman," in *Hampshire Sentinel* (Belchertown), Dec 22, 1830.

29. Northampton, Town Meeting Resolution, Feb 9, 1831, reprinted in *Hampshire Republican*, Nov 4, 1835.

30. *Hampshire Gazette*, Sept 8, 1830.

31. *Hampshire Sentinel*, Nov 17, 1830.

32. Circular, "To the Working-men of New-England," Boston, Aug 11, 1832, Broadside Collection, AAS.

thousands of industrious families, who are compelled to take the situation of tenants, or are scattered into factories or the kitchens of the rich." The factory system, "perhaps the most alarming evil that afflicts our country," threw large numbers of people together under a few employers who would "forever crush that spirit of independence which is the only safeguard of freedom." The reciprocal interdependence of farmers and mechanics, however, would not only safeguard the republic but provide a blueprint for the future. "Your influence," concluded the Northampton Workingmen's Address of 1830, "is not to be confined to this day, to this place, but its sphere is vast as the theatre of the world, and its operations lasting as the duration of time."[33]

The political influence of these views was rather more restricted than this, but for a few years the Workingmen had moderate success in Valley politics. Although his support elsewhere was small, Samuel C. Allen won a majority of votes for governor in Westhampton in 1830, and the first Workingmen's meeting in Northampton in September that year attracted as many as five hundred people. Workingmen had sufficient influence in the town to gain approval for the 1831 petition against imprisonment for debt. Anti-Masonic or Workingmen's candidates for governor received pluralities or majorities in Hatfield and Williamsburg from 1831 to 1833, and majorities in Northampton, Hadley, and Westhampton in the November 1831 and 1832 elections. Samuel C. Allen, running as a Workingmen's candidate in 1833, only achieved pluralities in Northampton, Westhampton, and Hatfield but won majorities in ten towns altogether, six of them in the Connecticut Valley, and ran strongly in towns that had usually been reluctant supporters.[34] In towns such as Amherst, where it never gained a majority, the movement still helped increase the level of political activity. But this new interest was, ironically, the Workingmen's downfall. Other parties were revived and adopted parts of their platform. Although Allen won a majority again in Hatfield in 1834, support was drifting away to the Jacksonians or Whigs, in the former case with the active encouragement of the Northampton Workingmen's most famous advocate, George Bancroft. The last Workingmen's convention in Northampton, held that year, attracted only fifty-four delegates. Although supporters retained some influence in town politics for a year or two more, by the time the statewide party was wound up in 1837, its following in the Valley had largely melted away.[35]

The renewed vigor of two-party politics and the major parties' fusion

33. *Hampshire Gazette*, Sept 15, 1830.

34. Formisano, *Transformation of Political Culture*, pp. 238–239, and election returns reported in the *Hampshire Gazette*.

35. Election returns, Northampton, Town Meeting Records, 5:83, 167, 187, 189, 206, City Clerk's Office, Northampton City Hall.

tactics certainly helped bring about the Workingmen's political defeat, but there were other factors at work too. The party was fiercely criticized by established local leaders. When George Bancroft railed against privilege in a letter published in the *Hampshire Gazette* in October 1834, he was attacked by what Sylvester Judd called "all the purse-proud in the village and all their dependents and hangers-on, and some others who are afraid of their own shadows." Criticism of Judd for publishing the letter in his newspaper probably contributed to his decision to sell the *Gazette* three months later.[36] Judd's own sympathy for the Workingmen had been tempered by the religious radicalism of some local leaders. By the time of its decline the party was having to defend itself against accusations of "infidelity" by opponents from within the resurgent Evangelical movement.[37] Both deference and the cry of infidelity played their part. Linking these, however, and helping to undermine support for the Workingmen's approach at a more fundamental level, was a growing skepticism that the political process could provide redress for economic grievances.

The debt laws themselves provided ample evidence to support this skepticism. Bankruptcy statutes came under criticism for "marring the sanctity of obligations" and for permitting dishonest debtors to sign away their debts and continue or resume business. The ability to hide property from creditors was condemned as a major cause of dishonesty. Moreover, as the Workingmen themselves argued, the cause of "equal rights" for debtors and creditors was not served when employers took advantage of their position and the law to avoid or delay paying wages to their workers.[38] To critics of political reform, the very fact that debt laws constantly required adjustment revealed the impossibility of legislating for economic stability.

Such critics constantly reiterated the old Puritan and republican notion—now refreshed by the Evangelical revivals—that cures for economic ills lay in the hands of individuals, particularly in their moral restraint. A writer in the *Hampshire Gazette*, criticizing previous attacks on the rise in the number of mortgages, asked how such a rise had come about, how property got "out of the hands of the farmer or mechanic, into the hands of the merchant, for instance?" The answer was simple, in his view: "Evidently by the farmer's buying more than his income can

---

36. Judd, "Notebook," vol. 1, Oct 8, 1834.

37. This charge was made, for example, by Whigs in the 1834 election; Judd, "Notebook," vol. 1, Nov 9, 1834. See also George Dickinson to [?], Deerfield, Feb 22, 1835, BCJL.

38. "Address to the Workingmen of Massachusetts by the Committee Appointed for that purpose by the Northampton Convention," Boston, Oct 1834, Broadside Collection, FL. Among many contemporary discussions of the debt laws, see Theophilus Parsons, *Report of the House Committee on the Judiciary*, Mass. House Doc. no. 71 (Boston, 1835).

pay for." This in turn was the result of an absence of self-control, "the desire to keep up an equality of outward show, by running into all the expensive follies of the foolish rich."[39] By the end of the decade, in the upheavals and "hard times" of the 1837 panic and its aftermath, Sylvester Judd succinctly summed up this viewpoint, with which he had always been sympathetic. "Men always expect too much from legislation," he wrote; "men who will not reform their own habits and practices need not expect any relief from any change in public measures."[40]

Temperance

The view that economic stability could be secured by reforming the moral character of individuals had, indeed, been shared by many supporters of the Workingmen, even at the height of their political activity. The Northampton Workingmen's Address of 1830 called for "economy . . . in private expenditure" and curbs on "our own extravagance in following the fashions of the rich," while this and later circulars stressed the need for "industry," "frugality," and "sobriety." In the Northampton town meeting of March 1833, it was George Bancroft who moved a resolution that the selectmen "not approbate the sale of ardent spirits."[41] But while these concerns with moral reform were genuine on the Workingmen's part, they were merely joining in a movement that had already begun outside their sphere of supporters. The Evangelical revivals had helped crystallize a widespread concern for moral reform that to a great extent bypassed or supplanted the kind of political campaign conducted by the Workingmen and their allies.

Bancroft's resolution in 1833 was recognition of the central place of temperance in the moral reform movement. The search for economic stability also became a subtext of the temperance campaign; as political efforts subsided, temperance remained its principal focus. Although it had started in the Valley fifteen or twenty years before, the temperance movement had at first been an elite attempt to maintain social control, calling on employers and parents to set examples of sobriety for their hired laborers, servants, and children. Revivalism and—to a lesser extent—the collapse of political radicalism contributed to the spread of popular temperance in the 1820s and 1830s, with a greater emphasis on reforming individuals than on social order. Amherst, a hothouse of revivalist influence after the founding of the college in 1821, was also an

39. *Hampshire Gazette,* Sep. 14, 1831.
40. Judd, "Notebook," vol. 1, Mar 31, 1840.
41. Northampton, Town Meeting Records, 5:132.

early center of temperance activity. The West Parish Temperance Association, formed in 1828, claimed more than 450 men and women members by 1830. Within another six years, according to a recent study, as many as two-thirds of the town's adult population had signed temperance pledges.[42] Elsewhere, as the political movements collapsed in 1834 and 1835, some of their sympathizers threw their weight behind the growing temperance cause. The Northampton Temperance Association, formed in 1835, counted Sylvester Judd among its officers. A new alliance of revivalism and political radicalism formed the basis for vigorous campaigns to control liquor licensing during the remainder of the 1830s and, after 1840, for a massive upsurge in popular temperance and teetotalism.[43]

Revivalism's pervasive influence on the temperance movement was reflected in the early presence of sympathetic ministers on the boards of town and county organizations, the important organizing role of prominent church members, the use of churches for temperance lectures and meetings, and, above all, the language of individual moral reformation the campaign adopted. Over time, too, the influence of political radicalism became apparent. Between 1835 and 1838 it helped politicize the temperance movement itself, until the failure of the fifteen-gallon law reinforced the disenchantment with legislative solutions to moral problems.[44] It also helped radicalize the temperance movement, strengthening the argument for total abstinence and laying the foundations for an explosion of support for total-abstinence societies in the early 1840s. By their peak in 1843, local Washingtonian societies and associated groups claimed memberships ranging from 32 to 59 percent of the total populations of their towns.[45] As these groups became established, they

42. Fuller treatment of the local temperance movement is in Stephen A. Aron, "The Minds of Hands: Working People of Amherst in the Mid-Nineteenth Century" (Senior honors thesis, Amherst College, 1982), in which data cited here are to be found on pp. 183, 187. The discussion that follows draws on Timothy L. Smith, *Revivalism and Social Reform in Mid-19th Century America* (New York, 1957); W. J. Rorabaugh, *The Alcoholic Republic: An American Tradition* (New York, 1979); Ian R. Tyrrell, *Sobering Up: From Temperance to Prohibition in Antebellum America, 1800–1860* (Westport, Conn., 1979); and Robert L. Hampel, *Temperance and Prohibition in Massachusetts, 1813–1852* (Ann Arbor, Mich., 1982).

43. Judd gave accounts of temperance meetings in "Notebook," vol. 1, Feb 26, Mar 3, 5, 12, 1835.

44. Local political temperance efforts peaked in a hotly disputed election for county commissioners in 1838; see Hampshire County Temperance Society, Circular, Apr 28, 1838, MCFL, Box 18; Judd, "Notebook," vol. 1, Apr 6, May 7, 1838. The election of temperance commissioners was challenged in the courts with partial success; see Elisha Strong, Petitioner, 37 Mass. Reports (20 Pickering): 484–498 (1838). The fifteen-gallon law banned sales of liquor in small quantities, except for medicinal purposes.

45. Sylvester Judd noted the progress of the total-abstinence movement in "Notebook," vol. 2, July 3, 1841, Feb 22, 1842, Feb 22, 1843. Membership figures were claimed in Massachusetts Washington Total Abstinence Society, *Annual Report, 1843*, Broadside Collection, AAS.

adopted some of the rhetoric and symbolism of the producer-ideology associated with the political radicals. "Whereas the Labouring classes are the mainstay of Temperance," the constitution of the Williamsburg Temperance Reform Society announced in 1842, "it is the duty of every member of this Society to labor for the improvement of this great and glorious cause." The same year a Washingtonian parade in North-ampton, reportedly attended by as many as three thousand people from the town and its surrounding area, included a banner portraying a barrel of rum, above which was "a muscular, brawny arm uplifting a huge hammer" to split it.[46]

The timing and rhetoric of popular total abstinence both point to the importance of the search for economic stability as a motive behind it. The temperance societies achieved their peak membership during the depression of the early 1840s, amid widespread concern over the soundness of the rural economy in general and of individual families in particular. Membership fell rapidly as prosperity returned in the middle of the decade. As they emphasized the need for individual action and self-control to secure economic stability, temperance reformers adopted many of the concerns expressed by political radicals ten or more years earlier.

Reformers saw drink at the root of many economic problems. In a Calvinist view, excessive drinking and general tolerance of liquor would invite punishment from God. Chauncey Parkman Judd ex-pressed the view that economic depressions, and the panic of 1837 in particular, were judgments on the nation "for its wickedness and abom-ination." A narrower, more practical interpretation simply pointed to the economic costs of drink on consumers and their families. The Hampshire County Temperance Society urged in 1838 that abolition of liquor selling would "free ourselves from the pecuniary burdens which this nefarious traffic imposes on us."[47]

Lecturers and preachers noted the wider economic benefits that would flow from the restraint of drinking. Liquor, they argued, led to ill health, crime, and violence. Total-abstinence societies attempted to enumerate the number of sick people and convicts who owed their condition to drink. Above all, drink undermined families' ability to support themselves. It fostered irregularity and excessive expenditure, which led in turn to loss of work or income, to debt and poverty. It also broke families up. Women and children, often referred to as the inno-cent victims of men's intemperance, formed a considerable part of the

46. Williamsburg Temperance Reform Society, "Constitution and By-laws 1842–1844," WHS; *Hampshire Gazette*, Mar 1, 1842.

47. Chauncey P. Judd to Apphia Judd, Hartford, May 9, 1837, Judd Papers; Hampshire County Temperance Society, Circular, Apr 28, 1838.

membership of total-abstinence societies; in 1843, over half the members claimed by societies in Amherst, Westhampton, and Williamsburg were female, while the two Washingtonian societies in Hadley were over three-fifths female.[48]

Sober habits, reformers believed, would permit individuals to secure control of their own and their families' economic circumstances. A satirical set of "Reasons for the Repeal of the License Law" published in the *Hampshire Gazette* in 1838 emphasized the distortions that drink imposed on the economy. A fictional rum seller explained why curbs on liquor were bad. "I like to see all trades live," he argued, "and how can they have profits unless they can open accounts with customers for rum, and their hearts to a mortgage of their farms[?]" Restricting drink would waste the expense that had been laid out on prisons and asylums, cut taxation, and ruin the livings of lawyers and doctors.[49] Two of the "temperance toasts" given at the Northampton Washingtonian parade in 1842 emphasized the movement's economic benefits in language once used by the Workingmen's party. One man proposed "Teetotalism—It taps the *lawyer's barrel* at both ends," while a Southampton farmer toasted "a sober mind in a healthy body—a happy family, with peace and plenty at home, and credit and respectability abroad."[50]

Unlike the *Gazette*'s rum seller, reformers did not "like to see all trades live." From the 1830s to the 1850s the temperance movement took a position strikingly at odds with the "free-market" argument that trade should be unregulated, asserting that moral considerations should outweigh absolute liberty in the conduct of transactions. For individuals to secure self-control, it was necessary for liquor sellers to be curbed. Originally this had brought the movement into conflict with local merchants, who traditionally supported the precept that trade—at least their own—should be free of interference from legal or governmental intervention.

Liquor had always played an important role in retail trade, its place in rural consumption and sociability making it the single most lucrative item in many stores; when Jonathan Judd had run out of spirits in Southampton in 1779, he complained that "people had almost forgot the way to my Shop before I had the Rum and Brandy that I have now sold. Perhaps if there shoud be no spirits to be sold there for some Time they would have to learn the Way again." As consumption continued to rise in the first quarter of the nineteenth century, liquor remained a vital part of traders' incomes.[51] But temperance reformers challenged mer-

48. Mass. Washington Total Abstinence Society, *Annual Report, 1843.*
49. *Hampshire Gazette,* Oct 31, 1838.
50. *Hampshire Gazette,* Mar 1, 1842.
51. Jonathan Judd to Sylvester Judd, Sr., Southampton, Jan 17, 1779, Judd Papers, MCFL, Oversize Files.

chants' right to stock liquor and criticized their use of it to drum up customers. A campaign in Amherst in the early 1830s was directed particularly against general storekeepers who, it was charged, not only "kept spirits for the purpose of inducing the inhabitants to trade with them," but also gave out drinks to take advantage of customers, "for the merchant understood very well that after a man had been treated and his mind became enfoged, that he could make a bargain with him to suit himself."[52] Such attacks on liquor selling amounted to an assault on the influence and practices of retail traders in general.

Merchants overcame this challenge by becoming supporters of temperance themselves. Some, such as Edward P. Huntington in North Hadley, had long expressed discomfort at the "necessity" to sell liquor. Others, converts in the Evangelical revivals such as D. S. Whitney and J. P. Williston of Northampton and David Mack of Amherst, removed liquor from their stores and took leading roles in temperance societies that used a battery of rituals to persuade their colleagues to follow suit. Public meetings, pledge signing, "cold water" parades, and picnics were all calculated to bring merchants into the fold. When an Amherst hotelier gave up selling drinks in 1842, he received a well-publicized dinner to congratulate him.[53] Revivalism and suasion meant that merchants' accounts and store inventories from the 1840s appear strikingly different from those of two decades earlier. Liquor had largely disappeared from them. Especially from the end of that decade, temperance merchants protected their trading positions by agitating for legal curbs on liquor sales. The liquor trade became concentrated in the hands of small dealers, many of whom had to operate close to or beyond the bounds of the law. When several towns adopted bans on liquor after 1850, many of these dealers were further marginalized.[54]

Temperance became associated with well-established stores, substantial employers of labor and their business associates. Amherst's proliquor advocates focused their campaigns against townwide prohibition in the early 1850s on the lawyer and Whig politician Edward Dickinson, who had been received into the First Church during the revival of 1851. Such men sometimes literally generated heated opposition. Northampton temperance leaders became targets of repeated arson attacks on their barns, shops, and houses. J. P. Williston, compiling

---

52. "Notes on Temperance," n.d., BCJL.

53. Edward P. Huntington to J. W. Huntington, Hadley, Sept 11, 1829, PPHH; notices of committees of the Hampshire Temperance Society, *Hampshire Gazette*, Jan 2, 1833, Jan 15, 1834. On the Amherst hotelier: *Northampton Courier*, Apr 19, 1842.

54. Prosecutions for liquor offenses rapidly increased in number during the 1830s and 1840s: see Michael S. Hindus, *Prison and Plantation: Crime, Justice, and Authority in Massachusetts and South Carolina, 1767–1878* (Chapel Hill, 1980). Of forty-nine prosecutions in the Hampshire County Court of Common Pleas in June 1851, for example, ten (20.4%) were for illegal selling of liquor and another eighteen (36.7%) were for drunkenness.

a list of the victims of these attacks in the mid-1850s, could include—apart from himself — the merchant William Stoddard; the judge J. F. Lyman; the master carpenter Moses Breck, long an advocate of temperance; the former hotelier Oliver Warner; and the paper manufacturer William Clark.[55] The list was a cross section of Northampton's lawyers, merchants, and manufacturers.

The return of the temperance movement to "legislative means" of curbing alcohol after the mid-1840s reflected a decline in popular confidence that individual moral reform could accomplish economic stability. Signed pledges turned out to be insubstantial guarantees of permanent reformation. Societies advocating total abstinence declined rapidly, sometimes amid acrimonious debates over backsliding and the precise interpretation of pledges.[56] As the movement in the Valley turned toward coercion, it also adopted some of the ethnocentrism that it had already acquired in some large cities. The foreign-born population of Northampton in particular increased rapidly after the end of the depression of the early 1840s; locally born temperance advocates adopted the habit of pinning the blame for drinking on outsiders, especially on Irish immigrants.[57] Temperance was no longer the prime vehicle for concern about economic stability. But, just as it had obtained some of its impetus from the political movements that had preceded it, temperance had a legacy to pass on to its successors. It emphasized the importance of businessmen's own control of trade and it helped propagate the notion that economic security could be obtained by self-discipline.

Character and Credit

Concern with individual character was the initial basis for the third set of attempts to secure stability: direct action by merchants and other

55. Sylvester Judd noted fires attributed to antitemperance arsonists in "Notebook," vol. 7, Oct 16, 1853, Dec 22, 1855, Jan 28, Apr 28, 1856. An anonymous threatening letter to J. P. Williston is in Williston Papers, I/B/9, folder 2, NEHGS, and a list of fires, dated June 5, 1855, in I/B/2, folder 22; the *Hampshire and Franklin Express*, Oct 8, 1852, indignantly denied a report in a Boston paper that Edward Dickinson had been seen buying liquor at a druggist's.

56. The last minutes in Williamsburg Temperance Reform Society, "Constitution and By-laws," noted the setting up of a committee in Mar 1844 "for the purpose of Remonstrating with Eli Hubbard [the vice-president] as a member of this society who has broken his Pledge."

57. See, for example, Sylvester Judd, "Notebook," vol. 7, July 4, 1854: "The foreigners by some means got liquor and some were drunk. Perhaps some Yankees were, though I saw none"; and "Notebook," vol. 7, Oct 12, 1854: "The foreigners, Irish, Germans, etc., . . . for the most part, love liquors."

businessmen to alter the rules of exchange. Whether they saw the panic of 1837 and its consequences as a divine judgment or as the culmination of individual actions, many observers would have argued that the "wickedness and abomination" Chauncey Parkman Judd had criticized included lack of self-control in the conduct of business. Just as they condemned consumption of drink as a moral failing, numerous writers, preachers, and editors blamed moral shortcomings for economic reverses.

A long article in the *Northampton Courier* in May 1837 cataloged some of them. "Speculation" was the worst temptation, succumbed to by the "constitution[ally] indolent," who resort to "double dealing" and "artful management" in order "to horde up wealth with a celerity virtuous industry never authorizes." Although it was less contemptible, the other chief temptation, "overtrading," was also a prime cause of distress. Unlike speculation, it was not motivated by a desire to avoid work but rather by "an honorable, though mistaken, zeal." Damaging because it led a trader to "involve . . . himself with an oppressive weight of liabilities," it reflected an inability to maintain an even middle course through the hazards of exchange. Both evils involved misuse and overextension of credit. As the former governor of Massachusetts John Brooks remarked in a lecture in the 1830s, "If intemperance . . . has brought . . . degradation and wretchedness, the credit system can boast its equal power of propagating plagues."[58] If only credit could be directed into the right hands, to people with characters strong enough to withstand the temptations to misuse it, perhaps economic stability could be assured.

Foremost in seeking a practical application of the test of character to business was Lewis Tappan, the Northampton-born New York merchant and antislavery advocate. Having failed once in the 1820s and been closely involved in his brother Arthur's misfortunes in 1837, Tappan set about establishing a means to bring the extension of credit under more careful control. Tappan's Mercantile Agency of 1841, the first successful commercial credit-reporting company, took advantage of the growing trading links between New York City and the rest of the country. A network of rural and urban contacts would provide information about local firms and individuals, to be made available to the New York merchants who subscribed to the service. In his memoirs Tappan recalled an event from his Northampton childhood that had helped form his idea. Playing once near Pomeroy's Tavern, he overheard a stranger ask "about the standing and character of Mr. Tappan." He

58. *Northampton Courier*, May 3, 1837; John Brooks, lecture to Bernardston Lyceum, *Hampshire Gazette*, Jan 1, 1834.

listened as the druggist and physician Enos Hunt "gave the gentleman an account of my father, speaking of him in very high terms." By establishing the Mercantile Agency, Tappan hoped to provide such information about reputations in bulk and at a distance.[59]

He conceived the agency as a direct application of moral principles to business, striving to recruit local reporters who were pious, well connected, and of similar mind to his own with regard to the moral characteristics required for stability. These reporters would couch estimates of their neighbors' creditworthiness in terms that included an assessment of their character and habits. Because reports in the agency's records would presumably influence wholesalers' decisions to advance or deny credit, men of poor character would be excluded from trade. This, Tappan surmised, would make it safer and more predictable than that of the 1830s. The Mercantile Agency would serve as a kind of terrestrial judgment seat, rewarding worthiness and, while punishing unworthiness, permitting those presently unable to secure credit to learn correct habits and principles by example.

Tappan's early correspondents in the Connecticut Valley shared a language for the moral evaluation of individuals' trading capacities. They approved of men and women who had "good character and business habits," and who were, among other things, "industrious," "sober," "honest," "prudent," "safe," "economical," and "respectable." Just as important, they avoided the pitfalls of "idleness," "irresolution," "speculation," and of "extravagance" either in consumption or in the overloading of their businesses. The way of economic righteousness seemed clearly marked out. The Amherst shoe dealer Jonas Winter was "economical, industrious [and] honest" in 1851, having "good habits and character." Six years later, he was still regarded as "a fair, honest, industrious man, good for any individual engagement," and "looking well to his affairs." William C. Bliss, a farmer in Hatfield, was "considered a very safe man, prudent and prompt."[60] Local reporters took the observations and opinions of their neighbors on one another and fitted them to a remarkably uniform set of standards.

Just as good character could be judged, it seemed that men of "bad" character would be easy to detect from their behavior. A Northampton cabinetmaker who had "no regularity or steadiness of purpose" in 1847

59. Tappan's biography is Bertram Wyatt-Brown, *Lewis Tappan and the Evangelical War against Slavery* (Cleveland, Ohio, 1969); pages 226–243 deal particularly with the early years of the Mercantile Agency. See also, Wyatt-Brown, "God and Dun and Bradstreet, 1841–1851," *Business History Review* 40 (1966): 432–450. The memoir is in Tappan's "Autobiographical Sketch," p. 27, Lewis Tappan Papers, Container 14, LC (microfilm, reel 7).

60. Mercantile Agency credit reports in this and later paragraphs are cited from Massachusetts, vol. 46, p. 7 (Winter) and p. 93 (Bliss), R. G. Dun and Co. Collection, Baker Library, Harvard University Graduate School of Business Administration, Boston (hereafter cited as MA 46, followed by a page number).

"was always asking [for] credit but should never have it." The Florence storekeeper I. S. Parsons was described in 1855 as "rather a speculator, dipping into various kinds of business." A tailor in Amherst, Joseph Colton, was also "a speculating man," while the Northampton tailor Samuel Wood was, in one reporter's opinion, "a harum scarum man in whom I have no confidence." Signs of "extravagance" were noted and criticized. The Northampton dry-goods dealer Enos Parsons was said in 1851 to be "building an expensive house which he can't afford." A report on the Amherst carriage maker Emerson Russell, evidently written by a man who had a dim view of the economic value of women's contributions to a household, noted that he was "an honest industrious man with a large family of daughters, [and] can't do much more than support his family." The belief that moral worthiness and business worth went hand-in-hand was summed up in a report on two brothers who were wire makers in Amherst: "intelligent, industrious, honest . . . their character is their capital."[61]

The Limits of Moral Regulation

Tappan's agency evidently had some effect on the conduct of trade. Despite the rapid development of competing services, demand for Mercantile Agency reports rose throughout the 1840s and 1850s, and the company's records contained information about a steadily rising number of firms and individuals. Did it have any effect on economic stability? The Northampton firms we examined between 1830 and 1834 failed at the rate of nearly 45 percent in twenty years. Of credit reports made between 1842 and 1861 for 270 traders, manufacturers, artisans, and farmers in the six towns, 25 percent contain evidence of failure or "embarrassment"; on the face of the evidence, therefore, the rate of failures was reduced somewhat. But many of these records ran for only a portion of the period, so this figure underestimates the true failure rate, which was closer to double that amount. Although contemporary published claims that up to nine-tenths of traders could expect to fail within twenty years were unduly pessimistic as far as the Valley was concerned, evidence from the Mercantile Agency reports suggests that the average number of failures could have been as high as 50 percent of the number of reported businesses over the same period. In other words, there was no overall improvement in business stability.[62]

---

61. I. S. Parsons: MA 46:113; Colton: MA 46:2; E. Parsons: MA 46:110; Russell: MA 46:14; MA 46:7.

62. The annual *Massachusetts State Record and Year Book of General Information, 1848* (Boston, 1848), p. 217, claimed that a trader setting up in business with $10,000 of credit had a 97 percent chance of being in debt $10,000 beyond his means after twenty-five years.

The impression that Tappan's attempt to use character to assess credit risks had limited success is supported by other evidence in the reports. Moral criteria were not always accurate predictors of success or failure. Certainly, some individuals and businesses who went bankrupt had done so predictably. Zenas Cook of Hadley, an active but apparently not entirely honest broom dealer, was described in 1851 as "one of those doubtful char[acters] that men who have dealings with them w[oul]d do well to get other security." By the end of the following year, Cook was bankrupt.⁶³ But there were others whose collapse came without warning and contrary to the favorable portrayal of character that the reporters had conveyed. L. R. Lincoln, a Northampton merchant, was said in 1847 to have "established a good character" and maintained "excellent business habits." Two years later he failed. F. A. Pierce of Amherst was "enjoying the confidence of the community" in 1853 and settling with his creditors at fifty cents on the dollar after the panic of 1857. The previous year Harris Bartholomew, a Northampton merchant and manufacturer, had also failed after fourteen years of favorable reports, "contrary to the expectation of everybody."⁶⁴ With less annoyance to creditors, but in defiance of the belief that character would be a guide to business ability, "poor" characters occasionally made good in spite of their moral deficiencies. The agency reporter did not at all like the Northampton jeweler J. H. Fowle in 1844, finding him "bad" and "dissipated" and stating that "creditors should think him doubtful." Within a decade, though, Fowle had accumulated several thousand dollars' worth of property from a business now regarded as "sound," and his creditworthiness had become "undoubted."⁶⁵

"Worth" over "Worthiness"

Accordingly, it was information other than that about moral characteristics that users of credit reports increasingly sought out. Neither Tappan nor others, of course, had ever imagined that good character alone justified credit. Comments such as "means well" or "honest, but slow pay," were evidently poor recommendations for credit. Character had to have means to accompany it. Credit reports also set out what was known about their subjects' property holdings and other financial means, and "worth" came to count for more than "worthiness." Attention to these questions formed part of a broader tendency for merchants and others engaged in local trade to alter the terms on which they did

63. MA 46:85.
64. Lincoln: MA 46:108; Pierce: MA 46:9; Bartholomew: MA 46:56.
65. MA 46:104.

business. This, as we have just seen, did not necessarily make it more certain or predictable. But in their attempts to make it so, they brought about profound adjustments to the conduct of the rural economy.

Users of credit reports were less concerned with character than with their subjects' pecuniary means. They had two questions about their debtors: "will they pay promptly?" and "how much unencumbered property do they have to be secured or attached if they fail to pay?" "Worth" resolved into a financial measure, expressed in dollars, buildings, and acres of land. Evidence of habits and respectability might influence a decision to advance credit but would not determine it. A Northampton barber, James W. Cram, though "industrious and honest," had "no attachable property" and could not be recommended. From Amherst in 1849, on the other hand, Edward Dickinson reported that the shoe dealer Oliver Watson was a "shrewd, economical manager and makes money," and was "worth probably 8 or 10 thousand dollars." In 1856 Pliny Russell, a patent-medicine maker of Northampton, though stigmatized as a "quack doctor," had "a good business," and was "worth \$8–12,000 part in Real Estate."[66] Reporters examined tax records and land deeds, asked questions of the subjects themselves, of neighbors, partners, and bank officers, and kept their eyes and ears open. A shortage of goods on the shelves of a store, uncompleted work on a house, or the arrival of packages marked "C.O.D." were all clues that a man's credit was already suspect.[67]

Yet, though "character" played a less important role than Tappan had originally hoped, his agency's credit reports helped generate and spread a new language of economic morality based more closely on financial "soundness," and contributed to a tightening of economic discipline that merchants and others sought to accomplish in the aftermath of the 1837 crisis. It is likely that the creation of the Mercantile Agency and the knowledge that local reporters were collecting information to send to New York in itself exerted pressure for greater care and system in running businesses. Benjamin North, storekeeper at the factory village of Leeds, was subject to a succession of criticisms in reports filed between 1843 and 1846. He was first "doing a large business, it is thought a good deal too much—has too many irons in the fire." Later there were signs of improvement, although he was still regarded as something of a risk. In 1846, he was said not to "manage prudently, [is] not systematic, though he now keeps books."[68]

The courts also played a role in tightening discipline by discouraging lax practices. In 1846 the Northampton blacksmith Edwin Kingsley sued

66. Cram: MA 46:62; Russell: MA 46:109.
67. See report on H. A. Marsh, Amherst, MA 46:81.
68. MA 46:103.

the new Connecticut River Railroad Company for nonpayment of a $400 debt incurred for work at his shop. When he went to court, however, he found that it was not the railroad company that was on trial but his own accounting methods. Evidence was heard that as work was completed, one of Kingsley's employees chalked it up on a board in the shop. Every week or so, Kingsley would copy the entries into his daybook, from which accounts were later posted to a ledger. The company's attorney was able to convince the court that this practice provided insufficient proof of the existence of the debt, and Kingsley lost his suit.[69] In short, he found that the informal practices that had been common in local exchange were not going to be sufficient in the more intense world of corporations and regular long-distance trade. Court decisions such as this and the indirect influence of credit reporting helped insert the tighter rules of long-distance exchange into the local economy.

Toward a Cash Economy

Crucial to this tightening of discipline was pressure to bring to an end the old practices of bargaining over prices, accepting noncash payment and granting long credit, at least in dealings involving merchants or storekeepers. J. P. Williston was among the first to seek to abandon some of these practices, finding it necessary to advertise in 1833: "Purchasers will please remember that I do not *ask one* price, and *take another*." Since at least the early 1830s, too, debates on the credit system and the reform of the debt process had advanced the ideal of an economy of direct, immediate payments, preferably in cash, especially for retail purposes. In 1834 the *Hampshire Gazette* had published an article suggesting that the abolition of imprisonment for debt would not only remove debtors' "fear of the dungeon" but lead people to "acquire the habit of paying as they go." "This habit, and this ability," it continued, "will become more and more easy as the system of trading or laboring for prompt pay approaches to universality." Lewis Tappan himself wrote that "rigid adherence to the cash system" was essential if economic crises were to be avoided.[70] Over the next thirty years, largely at the behest of local merchants, this point came closer to being achieved.

Changes in the national economy and the Valley's developing market connections with other regions meant that it was no longer as insulated from outside influences as it had been at the end of the eighteenth

---

69. Kingsley v. Connecticut River Railroad Co., Hampshire County Court of Common Pleas, Records, 31:594–599 (Feb 1847), Hampshire County Courthouse, Northampton.

70. Williston advertised in *Hampshire Gazette*, Jan 23, 1833; "The Credit System," *Hampshire Gazette*, May 7, 1834; Wyatt-Brown, *Lewis Tappan*, p. 226.

century. Not only had trade into and out of the area grown significantly, leading its activities to move more generally in tune with the rhythms of national markets for credit and commodities, but the rapid growth in the national money supply ensured that larger quantities of circulating medium were available to enter the pockets of farmers, manufacturers, traders, and their employees. Monetary growth during the early nineteenth century had been steady but relatively modest. Although total currency in circulation in the United States in 1830 was over three times the 1800 level, it represented an annual growth rate of less than 8 percent. Between 1830 and the panic of 1837, however, the amount of cash jumped rapidly, by an average of over 20 percent a year, until the financial reverses of the end of the decade led it to shrink again, to about one and two-thirds times the 1830 level by 1843. After this, the upward trend continued, at over 11 percent a year from 1843 to 1848 and by nearly 14 percent each year until 1854. By 1857, its peak before the Civil War, currency in circulation stood at more than five times the 1830 level and over seventeen times the level at the turn of the century.[71]

The uneven growth of the national money supply was, however, reflected in the uneven rate at which Valley traders were able to insist on using cash for transactions. Some retailers had long advertised that they were running "cash stores," but few were able to maintain the practice of demanding cash payment for very long. Their success in gaining access to the rural economy had depended on their willingness to advance credit and accept many of their customers' payments in "farmer's produce" and other goods tendered at irregular intervals. At his Charlemont store in 1833, wrote Lewis Bodman, "business . . . is good, but money, which is very necessary, conducting it to advantage, is scarce in this vicinity." Some Northampton merchants may have run their stores on a cash basis in the 1830s, but the evidence from account books is sketchy on this point. Advertisements that stores were adopting cash-only policies increased somewhat in number after the 1837 panic, as retailers did their best to maintain liquidity to pay off their own debts. But this increase was temporary. Into the mid-1840s most stores continued to advertise their goods in exchange for "country produce" or specified items, and some openly offered credit of up to one year without interest.[72]

Several factors changed this position before 1860. As cash became more common, retailers began to see advantages in receiving it as prompt payment for goods and to regard this as an ideal to strive for. As

71. [U.S. Bureau of the Census], *Statistical History of the United States from Colonial Times to the Present* (1957, 1965; reprint, Stamford, Conn., n.d.), p. 647, series X-284.
72. Lewis Bodman to Luther and Clarissa Bodman, Charlemont, Nov 13, 1833, Bodman Family Papers, Box 2, SSC; *Hampshire and Franklin Express*, Jan 26, 1846.

noted earlier, it was common for stores in the 1830s to take only a quarter or a third of their receipts in cash. Now the proportion was larger. An Amherst store took 75 percent of its receipts in cash from a local farmer in 1850; a Northampton store, 69 percent of its repayments in cash from a laborer who purchased goods there.[73] Especially in Northampton, retailing became more specialized. As the number of stores increased, merchants dealt with the threat of competition by limiting the range of goods that they sold, hoping to mark off segments of the market for themselves. Distinctions appeared between dry-goods dealers and merchant tailors; grocers and flour, coal, and seed merchants; furniture stores and stove dealers. Specialized stores were often less willing than general dealers to accept goods freely in payment from customers, because they were no longer in the business of selling farm produce and local manufactures themselves. Specialization also simplified stores' own lines of credit from suppliers. Differentiations began to appear between stores willing to grant long credits and accept goods on the "old pattern" and those that operated tighter credit policies and sought cash payment. In the 1850s, and particularly after the depression of 1857, considerable numbers of merchants sought to overthrow the old practices.

Change took three forms, which merchants sometimes, but not always, adopted together. One was the refusal to extend long-term credit. F. A. Pierce of Amherst announced in 1855 that he would no longer allow long-term credit to his customers because it was "against the interest of both buyer and seller," although he retained the right to make "special arrangements" with favored customers. Early in 1857 the Willey brothers, shoe merchants in Northampton, ran a long advertisement to the same effect. Shorter credit would reduce costs and prices, they argued, and place the purchaser in the advantageous position of keeping out of debt. "Having had great experience in the credit system and having made a careful examination of all its advantages and disadvantages and summing the matter all up," they too "came to the conclusion that it is not a beneficial practice for either the buyer or the seller."[74]

Accompanying the shortening of credit was a greater insistence on cash payment. When S. C. Parsons of Northampton announced "a decided contraction in our custom of giving credit," in 1858, he declared it to be "for the greater encouragement of our CASH CUSTOMERS. . . . We cannot give our paying customers the advantage their pay demands,

73. Account of Luther Field with Lewis L. Draper, submitted in evidence for Draper v. Field, Hampshire County Court of Common Pleas, Files, Feb. 1851, no. 216; account submitted in Wright v. Burke, Hampshire County Court of Common Pleas, Files, June 1851, no. 193, Massachusetts State Archives, Boston, Mass.

74. *Hampshire and Franklin Express*, Sept 7, 1855; *Hampshire Gazette*, Jan 13, 1857.

until some new method is adopted." Abolishing payment in goods, Parsons promised to lower all his prices, "as we can well afford to do, when the loss of interest, bad debts and poor pay are entirely removed." In the spring of 1858 no Northampton stores advertised that they would accept goods or "country produce" in payment. While the reluctance to take payment in goods partly reflected the need for cash liquidity after the crisis of 1857, the rarity with which they offered to take produce in subsequent years suggests that merchants, having reached the position of demanding cash payment, tried to keep things that way.[75]

Along with cash payment and short credit came the adoption of "one-price" and fixed-price policies at an increasing number of stores, especially in the dry-goods trade. These merchants abolished the differential between cash and noncash or credit prices. Some also started to fix prices on their goods, ending the practice of haggling or negotiating with customers over price and form of payment, which had long predominated in retail stores. The leading Northampton dry-goods dealer William H. Stoddard, who had adopted a one-price policy in 1856, could claim four years later that "the system has won the confidence of a wide and increasing class of customers."[76]

The new emphasis on cash and short credit suggested the increasing power of local merchants to take a hand in dictating terms on which they would do business and marked a shift of influence away from rural households and their practices. Promptness and cash payment transformed the standards of local exchange conducted at stores, bringing it more into line with the rhythms of long-distance trade. In the Valley and throughout New England, noncash exchange and long-term credit became increasingly restricted to smaller, country stores.[77]

But the change certainly influenced the conduct of direct exchanges in the countryside. Although noncash exchange and long-term accumulations of debits and credits continued to occur, especially between neighboring farmers, there was an awareness that this was now unusual, an exception to the ordinary conduct of business, rather than the dominant

75. S. C. Parsons, "Circular to Our Friends and Customers," Northampton, Jan 1, 1858, NHS, Archive Files. A check on the files of the *Hampshire and Franklin Express* and its successor the *Hampshire Express* after 1858 reveals a slight increase in the number of stores offering goods in exchange for produce in 1859, but these stores were not in the majority, as they had been in the 1840s. During the Civil War, the practice declined. No such advertisements appeared in May or Oct 1866, for example.

76. *Northampton General Directory* (Northampton, 1860), pp. 56–57.

77. Of thirty-three centers throughout New England for which newspaper advertisements from Mar and Apr 1858 were examined, only ten included any stores that offered to accept payment in goods; invariably these were in country districts: for a list see Christopher Clark, "The Truck System in Nineteenth-Century New England: An Interpretation," *Acadiensis* (forthcoming).

pattern. When the manufacturer W. R. Clapp of Northampton supplied materials to the Amherst house builder Warren S. Howland in 1861, his interest charges and repayment terms took forms that in an earlier period would have been rare. He provided the goods in April, started charging interest at an annual rate of 26.5% after only three months, and when Howland had paid just over half the original cost in November sent a sharp note with the receipt: "if you do not wish to pay cost on the above it must be settled very soon—I am not in the practice of giving such long credits." Earlier, in 1857, the Amherst merchant and manufacturer Henry F. Hills had written of that year's crisis, "The great cause of all the present financial difficulty is the long credit given in business, and if the result shall be short credits and prompt payments, much good will have come out of a great evil."[78]

The Social Implications of Cash

Cash dealing unraveled some of the complex entanglements of credit and debt that had embroiled rural people in obligations. Historians have begun to trace a decline, from about the mid-1840s onward, in the use of the book-accounting practices associated with local exchange, attributing this decline to the spread of cash transactions and the dissolution of personal obligation that such transactions implied. Cash also reduced the need for creditors to accept payment in goods that they did not really want, just to clear debts somehow. Exchange became more formalized, conducted to a greater degree by abstract rules than by bargaining and negotiation. The legal historian Morton Horwitz has argued that this change was already being embodied in court decisions in the 1850s. Judges began to turn away from the "will theory of contract," which had held the terms of individually negotiated dealings to be sacrosanct, toward a legal formalism that examined the compliance of contracts with general principles.[79]

There is also evidence that, relative to population, the number of

78. W. S. Howland, account with W. R. Clapp, 1860–1861, BCJL; Henry F. Hills to Adelaide Spencer, Amherst, Oct 28, 1857, Hills Family Papers, Box 1, folder 2, ACA.

79. Myron Stachiw, "Tradition and Transformation: Emerson Bixby and the Social, Material, and Economic World of Barre Four Corners" (Paper presented to the 10th Annual Meeting of the Society for the History of the Early American Republic, July 1988), traces an individual's gradual abandonment of his account book in the 1840s and early 1850s. Morton S. Horwitz, *The Transformation of American Law, 1790–1860* (Cambridge, Mass., 1977); on pp. 22–26 Horwitz discusses the "will theory" of contract; on p. 266 he refers to its decline in the mid-nineteenth century and replacement by "an increasingly formal set of legal rules, which were themselves now stridently justified as having nothing to do with morality."

disagreements and lawsuits arising from exchange was lower in the 1850s than it had been previously. Despite demographic growth, the absolute number of lawsuits per town in Hampshire County was barely higher in the early 1850s than it had been at the turn of the century. Moreover, the proportion of suits between plaintiffs and defendants from the same town fell to under 30%, compared with 40% a decade before. Cash and prompt payment promised the end of an era in which anxiety about debt and the possibility of legal action to recover it had dominated the lives of rich and poor alike.[80]

All the same, they also reinforced other tendencies. One was impersonality. Shorter obligations and adherence to abstract rules made exchange easier but less sociable. Another was privacy. Concern that character, behavior, and financial means were subject to observation by credit reporters and other calculators of "pecuniary ability" helped lead to more tight-lipped dealing, a closing against the world, and a tendency to act secretively. The openness and sociability of older exchange patterns had helped early credit reporters such as Edward Dickinson obtain information about his neighbors to pass to the Mercantile Agency; this had led to Tappan's being accused of commissioning "spies" and to a new reluctance to discuss business in public. By contrast, several credit reporters in the 1850s referred to the difficulty of obtaining information about their subjects. This situation in turn created new opportunities for profit. The former merchant Enos Parsons set up as a "broker" in Northampton in 1852. In addition to receiving "consignments of Books of Accounts, Negotiable Notes, Bills for Collection [and] Mortgages for foreclosure, . . . bringing the same into cash," he offered his services "getting information in relation to property or persons, of friends, debtors or creditors."[81] Privacy was not just a "bourgeois" ideal. It could be a protection against the intrusiveness of an older pattern of sociability in a new economic environment, and a protection for the weak against the inquiring eyes of the powerful.

As cash became more readily available, many rural people accepted it with equanimity. It was, after all, convenient; cash was truly becoming the universal medium of exchange, which it had previously not been in the countryside. "Money," wrote the editor of the *Hampshire Gazette* in 1857, "is a queer institution. . . . It buys provender, satisfies justice, and heals wounded honor. Everything resolves itself into cash, from the stock-jobbing to building churches."[82] Money could, in other words, dissolve disparate economic, social, and moral issues into a single stan-

---

80. Hampshire County Court of Common Pleas, Records, 1851–1853.
81. Parsons advertised in the *Hampshire Gazette*, Nov 30, 1852; see also MA 46:110.
82. *Hampshire Gazette*, Nov 10, 1857.

dard of measurement. Its increasing use was one indication of the emergence of rural capitalism.

The drift toward short credit, cash payment, and the abandonment of older exchange practices was not just a neutral, technical process. The new rules of exchange operated in a social context whose patterns of power and division their formality often masked, and which they also helped reinforce. Cash and short credit were not equally "convenient" for everyone. Merchants made it clear in their advertisements that they would make "special arrangements" only for selected customers. Where once credit had been a universal condition, it now became an instrument of inequality. Sweetser, Cutler and Company of Amherst advanced goods on credit both to its regular customers and to the palm-leaf braiders whose families were, on the whole, poorer than average. But while the average amount of credit outstanding on the regular accounts was $23.55 in 1850, on the braiding accounts it was only $8.35.[83]

Poor customers, denied credit at many stores, were forced either to deal with specialized traders who advanced credit against goods at high prices, or to pay for goods in cash as they earned it. The accounts of the Northampton laborer John Burke with Ansel Wright and Company between 1849 and 1851 show what could happen if a family fell on hard times. Burke's grocery purchases at Wright's started in November 1849. They consisted mainly of molasses, codfish, sugar, tobacco, apples, butter, pork, and coffee, all in amounts worth less than $1.00, but Burke would occasionally purchase a barrel of flour costing $6.00 or more. Overall, he was spending between $11.00 and $12.00 a month, about two-thirds of a farm laborer's wages. For over half a year, he paid off his debt regularly every two months. But after June 1850 something happened, and Burke failed to make further payments. As Wright's began progressively to curb his credit, Burke visited the store more frequently (twice a week on average, instead of once) but bought fewer and fewer goods (worth only $3.61 a month on average) and had to take flour in small quantities. After ten more months Wright's stopped dealing with him and sued for his outstanding debt. As a newspaper commented in 1854, the need to acquire goods in small amounts doubly disadvantaged the poor. They were unable to make the economies which, for example, purchasing flour in barrels permitted. They were also more vulnerable to price fluctuations.[84]

Families sometimes resorted to desperate measures to obtain credit.

83. Debts on ledger, 1850, Sweetser, Cutler and Co., Account Books, BCJL.
84. Wright v. Burke, Hampshire County Court of Common Pleas, Files, June 1851, no. 193; the story "Spoilt by Riches," *Hampshire Gazette*, Sept 26, 1854, dealt with the inequities of a merchant's requirement that flour be paid for immediately in cash.

At the same time that John Burke was sued by Ansel Wright and Company, a "Thomas and Mary Burke" (who may or may not have been the same family) were tried for obtaining goods under false pretenses. They were accused of going to a South Hadley store, falsely stating that they were owed money by boarders and that the man "was working for wages and would continue to work," and taking sixty-five dollars worth of goods on credit over several months before absconding.[85]

In his recent book *Money and Liberty in Modern Europe*, William Reddy has argued that monetary exchange, however legally and formally "equitable," in fact proceeds from inequality, from an asymmetry in access to power and resources between participants. The Burke cases reflect both the inherent inequalities of a cash system that Reddy refers to and the broader inequalities in the social system that gave rise to it. Obliged to deal in cash when they could not obtain credit, and to repay their debts in cash rather than other valuable items of exchange, laborers were forced to obtain and spend cash quickly. Unlike goods, or the larger quantities of cash that richer people could invest for a return, cash was, for the poor, an item of "negative marginal utility."[86] In the case of rural New England, this was a particularly striking contrast to the early nineteenth century, when poorer people had been able to avoid cash dealings and trade in goods that had inherent use value.

The shift to cash exchange was only part, therefore, of a broader shift in the rural social structure. It accompanied the growth of wage labor in both industry and agriculture, and the creation of a rural capitalism based on new distributions of power, wealth, and social division. Cash dealing brought the ethics of long-distance trade into the heart of the local economy, the result of a struggle for certainty and discipline waged, above all, by the entrepreneurs who were now so influential in rural life.

85. Commonwealth v. Burke, Hampshire County, Superior Court, Criminal Files, June 1851, no. 20, Massachusetts State Archives, Boston, Mass.

86. William M. Reddy, *Money and Liberty in Modern Europe: A Critique of Historical Understanding* (Cambridge, Eng., 1987), chaps. 2 and 3, esp. pp. 51–61, the discussion of "asymmetrical exchange" on pp. 64–73, and the discussion of the marginal utility of cash on p. 108.

Chapter 7

Capital, Work, and Wealth

New sources of work and wealth were readily to be found in manufacturing. By 1820 the diffused rural pattern of manufactures, largely
under household control, already engaged the energies of one-fifth or
more of adult men in some towns, in addition to the substantial efforts
of women and children. During the 1820s the populations of the towns
most heavily committed to manufactures—Amherst, Hadley, Northampton, and Williamsburg—grew by an average of 25 percent. Production expanded, partly due to the extension of existing forms of organization, but also to an increase in the number of mills, workshops, and
factories employing significant amounts of capital and more than a
handful of workers each. After relative stagnation in the 1830s, when
the towns' population growth slowed to an average of 3 percent over
the decade, and after upheavals during the economic crises of 1837
onward, manufacturing revived strongly in the 1840s and 1850s. The
spread of household-based production before 1820 had brought the first
"industrial revolution" to the countryside. The trend toward concentration in the two antebellum decades constituted a second, distinct one.

The earlier phase had extended the assumptions of household organization and patriarchal authority to manufacturing. By the second
phase, the locus of authority was shifting to capitalist entrepreneurs,
who combined patriarchal assumptions with their access to credit and
cash in order to expand control of production. In 1832, 610 men and
women in the four towns were reported to be employed in manufacturing, in addition to those who took in outwork. By 1860 this number had
risen by 134 percent, to 1,425. Over the same period, reported capital
investment in manufactures rose by 136 percent, from $343,710 to
nearly $810,000. Although the ratio between capital and labor altered
only slightly, both became more concentrated. Average capital invest-

ment in all manufacturing establishments rose from $4,841 to $8,710, while the average work force in each establishment almost doubled.[1] This concentration of capital and labor signaled the influence of entrepreneurs in a rural economy once dominated by household producers. It was reflected in the overall distribution of wealth, which by the middle of the century, had become progressively unequal. Foremost among the complex changes that brought it about was merchants' investment in manufacturing, especially from about 1840 onward.

Broad statistics mask immense variations, both in the size and character of manufactures and in the rates at which they came under entrepreneurial control. Especially up to the mid-1840s, rural manufacturing continued to be strongly influenced by the conditions of the household-based social structure in which it was located, and which provided the bulk of its labor. Only after the influx of immigrants to the Valley in the 1840s made more labor available to industrialists were some of them able to expand their operations securely. Tracing the uneven fortunes of manufacturers and workers during the period from 1830 to 1860 sheds light on two important issues: it explains a crucial phase in the evolution of capitalism in the countryside, and it suggests some of the distinctive contributions that rural social and economic conditions made to the structure of manufacturing in the Northeast as a whole. Regional specialization increased. In particular, the growth of factory textile production in eastern and southern New England and of the boot and shoe manufactures of eastern Massachusetts led to the relative decline of these industries in Hampshire County and to hardships for some of the people who relied on them for livelihoods. At the same time, the success of Valley agriculture and the persistent ability of rural households to influence the conduct of production helped mold remaining industries and the creation of new ones.

The Diversity of Rural Industry

A controlling factor in the expansion of manufactures between the 1820s and the 1840s was the perpetual search of rural households for new "careers" for offspring they could not otherwise provide for. At the same time that the decline of household textile production was making female labor available to work in factories outside the region, or to undertake domestic outwork, male production in households and small

---

1. *Documents Relative to the Manufactures in the New England States,* 22d Cong., 1st sess., 1833, House Executive Doc. no. 308, 2 vols. (hereafter cited as McLane Report); U.S. Eighth Census, Non-Population Schedules, 1860, Massachusetts: Manufactures, National Archives, Washington, D.C. (microfilm).

workshops continued in a wide range of crafts, including shoemaking, metalworking, toolmaking, the broom industry, cabinetmaking, and the making of woodenware. Independent broom makers, for example, continued to produce their wares on a seasonal basis in workshops on their farms, as part of a strategy of putting together different types of employment to make a living.

As population rose, the proportion of household heads principally engaged in manufacturing grew from 30.5 to 46 percent in Northampton, from 15 to 41 percent in Williamsburg, and from 26 to 29 percent in Amherst between 1820 and 1840. These differential rates of increase partly reflected the different qualities and opportunities for access to agricultural land in the three towns, but they also marked the growth of permanent craft employment in artisans' shops.[2] Families seeking employment for their sons and daughters, and young men seeking alternatives to the obligations of farming life turned to craft shops to provide apprenticeships or temporary employment that could secure the prospect of a future livelihood. A newspaper praised "the most enterprising young men" who entered mechanical trades in order to earn a living "in less time and with less labor than the farmer requires." Nor was this restricted to men. A growing number of tailoring and millinery businesses in Northampton and Amherst employed young farm women in their workshops. In 1822 the sisters S. and C. Osborn, who ran a Northampton hat store, sought eight "young ladies . . . who are perfectly nice with the needle" to work for them, evidently hoping to secure the labor of girls who had been trained in sewing at home and who could quickly be taught the rudiments of millinery.[3]

Textile mills and a few paper mills already combined substantial capital investments in power-driven machinery with the employment of male and female wage earners in considerable numbers. The largest example was the successor to the Shepard family's Northampton woolen mill. By 1832, the Northampton Woolen and Satinet Manufactory, as it had been renamed, employed fifty-nine men and sixty-one women to make broadcloth and satinet on waterpowered machinery. Its capital of $120,000 was the largest in Northampton or any of the surrounding towns. It shared the waterpower of the Mill River with several other mills that had grown out of earlier custom carding and fulling establishments. For instance, upstream in Williamsburg in 1832 were the broadcloth works of Isaac and Frederick Gere, with twenty-six

2. Occupational data in U.S. Fourth Census, 1820, Massachusetts, and U.S. Sixth Census, Population Schedules, 1840, Massachusetts, both National Archives, Washington, D.C. (microfilm). On craft production, see Stephen A. Aron, "The Minds of Hands: Working People of Amherst in the Mid-Nineteenth Century" (Senior honors thesis, Amherst College, 1982).

3. *Hampshire Gazette* (Northampton), Apr 10, 1822.

male and twenty female workers, and Wells and Bodman's satinet mill, which employed only four men and three women. Downstream, nearer Northampton center, lay the broadcloth mill of J. S. Kingsley, where fifteen men and eight women were at work.[4]

A few craftsmen in the metal-goods and carriage-making trades, too, were expanding their workshops to employ men and capital in larger quantities. The outstanding example was the Amherst carriage works of Knowles and Thayer, a partnership started in the late 1820s, which in 1832 was employing thirty men at an average wage of one dollar a day. By 1837 it had grown to employ almost one hundred men, with a capital of $30,000. One of the largest works of its kind anywhere in the Northeast, it was an unusual concentration of capital and labor in a non-mechanized trade.[5]

Nevertheless, the typical manufactory in the early 1830s was a workshop owned by a master artisan, employing between two and six apprentices, journeymen, or women workers, hand-making goods in batches for local and distant consumers. Variations on this pattern were numerous. In 1832 the McLane Report listed fifteen shoemakers in Northampton and another nine in Hadley and Amherst who made boots and shoes primarily for local consumption. Though all were reported as independent craftsmen, without employees, it is likely that some would either have had assistance from members of their families or would have had work done for them on contract by other part-time makers. A list of the boots and shoes taken on an attachment for debt from an Amherst workshop in the mid-1820s gave the names of other men who had presumably produced them in batches of from one to three pairs each.[6]

These craft workshops and mills were as widely diffused across the countryside in the late 1830s as their smaller predecessors had been two decades before. Although some were concentrated in village centers, such as Northampton and Amherst, many were distributed in small groups along tributary streams of the Connecticut River in mill villages and manufacturing hamlets often named after a leading craftsman or entrepreneur. Tiny settlements such as Loudville, on the Northampton-Westhampton line, and Kelloggville and Nuttingville, both in the

4. McLane Report, pp. 298–299, 310–311.

5. Ibid.; John P. Bigelow, *Statistical Tables: Exhibiting the Condition and Products of Certain Branches of Industry in Massachusetts for the Year Ending April 1, 1837* (Boston, 1838; hereafter cited as Mass. Industrial Census, 1837); descriptions of Knowles and Thayer's works were printed in the *Hampshire Gazette*, June 10, 1835; see also Edward W. Carpenter and Charles F. Morehouse, *The History of the Town of Amherst, Massachusetts* (Amherst, 1896), pp. 298–299.

6. McLane Report, 1:298–299, 310–311; undated list of goods taken on attachment from Joshua Fox, in Elisha Smith, Account Book, Amherst, 1784–1822, BCJL.

southern part of Amherst, grew up around groups of workshops mostly employing small numbers of people, often contracting with each other to provide part or all of the work and materials for a particular batch of products. At the same time, in Hadley and Hatfield, the broom industry grew up in dozens of workshops scattered among the farms and hamlets of the river meadows that grew broomcorn, providing seasonal employment for farmers and young landless men.[7]

Just as in textiles, the size and organization of these workshops varied considerably, even within the same trades. Among carriage makers, for instance, the closest rival in size to Knowles and Thayer in 1832 was a Northampton manufacturer who employed up to thirty-two hands (eight of whom were young apprentices), but with only one-tenth of the capital. The three other Amherst makers listed in the McLane Report had only $2,500 in capital between them and worked largely for themselves. Toolmakers, similarly, varied in size from individual producers to workshops like that owned by James Kellogg in Amherst, who employed ten workmen in 1837. Alongside the forty or so farmer–broom makers in Hadley, too, were a few larger workshops, such as that of John Shipman who, as early as 1830, had eighteen men between twenty and thirty years of age listed in his household by the census taker.[8]

Explaining the Industrial Structure

A mixture of small-scale and larger concerns was typical of many European and American regions that experienced rapid industrial change in this period. As the economic historian Jeremy Atack has pointed out, throughout the nineteenth century small firms continued to exist even in industries that came to be dominated by large units of production. Why did such variety exist? Atack suggests that the answer lies in one or both of two factors. The need for transportation facilities and access to raw materials permitted a widespread geographical distribution of firms, which favored the survival of small producers in areas remote from large factories. Second, manufacturers catered to segmented markets, so that small units could continue to operate, not

7. Charles Jones, "The Broom Corn Industry in the Counties of Franklin and Hampshire, and in the Town of Deerfield in Particular," *History and Proceedings of the Pocumtuck Valley Memorial Association* 4 (1899–1904): 105–111; Gregory H. Nobles, "Commerce and Community: A Case Study of the Rural Broommaking Business in Antebellum Massachusetts," *Journal of the Early Republic* 4 (1984): 287–308.

8. McLane Report, pp. 310–311; U.S. Fifth Census, 1830, Population Schedules for Hampshire County, MCFL.

by competing with large producers, but by making essentially different products.[9] Both these factors played a part in shaping the pattern of rural manufacturing. However, two further sets of influences must be added to them: the availability and stability of capital and credit, and the supply of labor in an economy still strongly shaped by households' organization of farm production. The supply of capital and labor was influenced by social structure but helped in turn to shape the segmentation of markets within the constraints imposed by geography and transport.

Location and markets certainly helped determine variations between local firms. The size and flow of rivers influenced the location of textile mills as well as forges and turners' shops, which used waterpowered machinery. Because the Connecticut River was too broad and slow-moving in this part of the Valley to generate much power, these works were located at sites on tributary streams that had long been used for grist and saw mills. Competition for a restricted number of sites inevitably led to lawsuits over water rights, dams, and flowage.[10] The absence of a single big waterpower site kept large outside investments, such as those made by Boston merchants farther south at Chicopee, out of the area. Geography clearly played a role in shaping the structure of capital formation.

Moreover, as Atack pointed out, proximity to raw materials and supplies also helped encourage manufactures. The expansion of sheep raising, especially in the hills to the west of the Valley, provided relatively cheap raw materials for the woolen mills of Northampton, Williamsburg, and other towns. The availability of wood—cleared off land that farmers were improving—ensured supplies of building materials and fuel for metal forges, as well as raw materials for tools, ax handles, broom handles, and other wooden products. Broom making in the river towns was concentrated on or near the fertile meadow farms that raised broomcorn. Manufacturers used local exchange networks and practices to obtain many raw materials, offering products in exchange for lumber, rags, or partly completed materials. Knowles and Thayer used local exchanges of goods and work to build up their extensive carriage business. In 1832, for instance, Samuel Smith contracted to provide them

9. Jeremy Atack, "Firm Size and Industrial Structure in the United States during the Nineteenth Century," *Journal of Economic History* 46 (1986): 463–475, esp. pp. 474–475.

10. On water rights, see Morton Horwitz, *The Transformation of American Law, 1780–1860* (Cambridge, Mass., 1977), pp. 34–42, and Gary Kulik, "Dams, Fish, and Farmers: Defense of Public Rights in Eighteenth-Century Rhode Island," in *The Countryside in the Age of Capitalist Transformation: Essays in the Social History of Rural America*, ed. Steven Hahn and Jonathan Prude (Chapel Hill, 1985), pp. 25–50.

with wagon spokes at $1.33 per hundred, in return for a wagon, a wheelbarrow, other goods worth $51.00 and the same amount again in cash.[11]

Above all, manufacturers could rely on obtaining food and other supplies from farmers in the neighborhood of their works. Eleazer Cowles, for instance, provided carting, sledding, cider, and other labor for the Amherst Cotton Factory between 1815 and 1819. Local supplies provided a considerable proportion of the goods (or "truck") that many manufacturers used to pay part of their wages. The McLane Report valued the grain, butter, meat, firewood, and other goods that the Amherst mill raised or purchased for its workers in 1832 at $2,048. Assuming that the twelve men, thirty women, and three boys employed at the mill at average rates of 45, 30 and 25 cents a day worked a 300-day year, these supplies would have amounted to 45 percent of their wages (Table 11). Similar calculations for other mills at the same time suggest that "truck" payments varied, from 50 percent of wages at the Northampton Woolen and Satinet Manufactory and 52.6 percent at Wells and Bodman's, to about 25 percent at the Geres' woolen mill and a nearby metal and button works. The extent of "truck" payments implied in the statistics suggests that, roughly speaking, they were inversely proportional to skill. Factories and shops paying high average daily wage rates laid out a smaller proportion on truck payments than those paying lower rates.[12]

Market segmentation clearly played a role in variations in character between manufactories in similar locations and similar activities. The McLane Report indicates that neighboring textile mills often differed significantly in the materials they used, the type and quality of goods they produced, and the customers they aimed for—differences that related to the size and techniques of their operations. The three woolen mills, Northampton Woolen, the Geres', and Kingsley's, for instance, were quite dissimilar from one another. Kingsley acquired his wool from "the immediate vicinity of the factory." The Geres also used domestic wool, but from a wider area, including New York State and Vermont as well as Massachusetts. Three-quarters of Northampton Woolen's raw materials, on the other hand, consisted of Saxony wool imported from abroad. Kingsley specialized in producing a heavy, finely woven broadcloth that he valued at forty cents a yard. The Geres

11. Knowles and Thayer, Agreement with Samuel Smith, Amherst, Aug 13, 1832, BCJL.

12. McLane Report, pp. 298–324; for a discussion of the rural origins of payment in kind, see Christopher Clark, "The Truck System in Nineteenth-Century New England: An Interpretation," *Acadiensis* (forthcoming). Truck payments were widespread in the textile industry, for example, other than in the mills of the Boston Associates.

Table 11. Outlays on wages, food, and supplies by selected manufacturers, 1832

Firm and location	Product	Mean daily wage rates ($)			Outlays on food/supplies as percentage of wages
		Men	Women	Children	
I. & F. Gere, Williamsburg	Wool	1.00	0.40	—	25.0
J. & J. Hayden, Williamsburg	Metals, buttons	1.00	0.50	0.33/0.30	26.3
Amherst Cotton Mfg. Co., N. Amherst		0.45	0.30	0.25	45.0
Northampton Woolen & Satinet Mfry.		0.65	0.40	0.26	50.0
Wells & Bodman, Williamsburg	Satinet	0.75	0.33	—	52.6

Source: *Documents Relative to the Manufactures in the New England States*, 22d Cong. 1st sess., 1833, House Executive Doc. no. 308, 1:298–324.

also produced high-quality cloth on a smaller scale, possibly—given their high wage rates—using a good deal of hand labor. Northampton Woolen, however, made coarser, lighter cloth, worth twenty-nine cents a yard; its comparatively lower wage rates reflect the lesser skill and shorter time involved in spinning and weaving coarse yarns.

In the textile industry, quality and skill went with small-scale production. In the carriage and wagon trades, by contrast, they were associated with the largest producer. Knowles and Thayer expanded their Amherst carriage works rapidly in the 1830s by paying high hourly wage rates to large numbers of workmen. They produced high-quality carriages in batches for sale to wealthy urban purchasers, of whom there were 110 in Boston alone in 1834. The firm's owners revealed their political sympathies, publicizing their pride at having supplied carriages to both Andrew Jackson and Martin Van Buren. By 1835 Knowles and Thayer had evolved a minutely detailed and tightly controlled division of labor in the works, through which skilled tasks were specialized and costed. "Every person employed has his own particular branch of business, and no person works at two," reported the *Hampshire Gazette*; "the proprietors can tell, to a cent, the exact cost of every vehicle they manufacture." In much of the rest of the carriage and wagon trade, however, production was on a small scale, unspecialized, and of lower quality. Makers, many of whom worked part-time at other tasks, assembled wagons that they had fashioned themselves or contracted out for parts of, in the same way that Ira C. Goodale had done in the early 1820s. These rough, workmanlike vehicles found markets in and out of the region at prices in a few tens of dollars, in marked contrast to Knowles and Thayer's elegant carriages, whose cost easily ran into three, and sometimes four, figures.[13]

Such examples serve to validate Atack's market-segmentation thesis. Indeed, the Valley's experience in the 1830s suggests that it was also valid in the wider sense that local manufacturing was being drawn in to an increasingly articulated northeastern division of labor, in which certain types of goods were produced in large-scale factories, certain others in urban workshops and yet others in rural districts. The Valley's role in producing basic articles such as cloth was much smaller in the 1830s than it had been a quarter-century before. In 1810 "old" Hampshire County had produced all of Massachusetts' recorded output of tow cloth and one-quarter of the state's blended cloths. By 1837 the same region produced only 14 percent of the state's cottons and 12 percent of its woolens, while "new" Hampshire County proper, which included some big mills at Ware, produced only 1 percent of cotton and 7 percent of wool. The region's new importance was in furnishing more peripheral products, which served as accessories or adjuncts to basic industrial output. Its joiners' tools, brooms, buttons, and palm-leaf hats were shipped out on their way to distant consumers who now bought other goods from manufacturers elsewhere.[14]

However, markets were not the sole determinants of the structure or variety of local industries. Two further factors played important roles. The provision of capital and credit shaped the size and success of individual ventures, and the ability of manufacturers to secure labor continued to affect the way they ran their operations. These two issues were interrelated, insofar as they were each affected by the rural social structure, exchange practices, family patterns, and household strategies. Availability of credit, capital, and labor would, as we shall see, have a more powerful effect than geography or markets alone in reshaping rural industry between the 1830s and the 1850s.

Broom making provided the most direct example of the application of rural credit to manufacturing. At its simplest, where the trade was conducted by farmers who processed their own broom brush in their own workshops over the winter, "credit" was provided mainly within families and finished goods exchanged at the store or carried to distant markets for cash. But the evolution of the trade, especially the growth of larger broom workshops such as John Shipman's, depended on more complex networks of credit. By the late 1830s growing broomcorn and making brooms no longer remained mainly in the same hands. Makers

13. *Hampshire Gazette,* June 10, 1835.
14. Mass. Industrial Census, 1837.

bought brush from farmers, either paying cash from the avails of the previous year's sales or giving notes or store credit for payment in goods by a third party. Local merchants, such as William Porter of Hadley, became closely involved in the broom trade for a period in the mid-1820s, bringing in shipments of broom handles, twine, and wire to sell to broom makers and taking consignments of finished brooms to ship on their own account. But their involvement was not essential to the financing of the business. Even a large broom workshop required capital of no more than $2,000 or so, a minute fraction of that required for a substantial textile mill. Most craft trades were similar.[15]

Direct exchanges of goods and labor on book account, third-party payments of notes and accounts, store orders, and all the other paraphernalia of local exchange long underwrote much manufacturing, especially that on a small scale. Family and kin also provided sources of capital, or by endorsing notes and other paper helped to channel it into local hands. After William Edwards abandoned his Northampton tannery and went west about 1815, kinship helped determine the future of his establishment over the next two decades. It passed in 1817 to a relative, David Edwards, who may have been one of the backers to whom William owed debts. David entered a partnership to run it with his brother-in-law David L. Dewey. When Dewey died in 1820 his share was purchased by another brother-in-law, Leander Moody. David Edwards, in turn, died in 1829 and was succeeded by his son-in-law Horace Wright, who formed a new partnership with Moody. A few years later, they were joined in partnership by one of their apprentices from the 1820s, Benjamin B. Hoxie, another brother-in-law of David Edwards, to whom Moody then sold out. The tannery, which went through four reorganizations and was owned by members of at least five families, nevertheless changed hands in a definable kinship pattern.[16]

Family credit and support also lay behind several of the smaller textile mills operating in the 1820s. The trade fluctuations that followed the 1812 war had put a number of custom mills into difficulties. Declining household textile production, coupled with falling rates for carding—which halved between 1803 and 1819—made their business especially precarious, but manufacturers who had sought to expand out of the problem by installing spinning machines or looms also found themselves caught out by shifting markets and overextended credit. Firms

15. On Porter's involvement, see receipts in William Porter Papers, Boxes C–F, OSV. The separation between growers of broomcorn and makers of brooms was noted by Henry Colman, *Fourth Report on the Agriculture of Massachusetts: Franklin County* (Boston, 1841), p. 31.
16. David E. Hoxie, Manuscript Book, transcript, n.d., NHS, Archive Files.

like Bodmans of Williamsburg survived because the family had trading interests. Other mills were sold to new purchasers. Two of them, Nathaniel Sears of Williamsburg and the brothers James and Chester Cook of Northampton, were backed by family assistance. Sears slowly expanded his mill, financing it cautiously out of profits, over the next three decades. The Cooks, too, were successful for a decade on the same basis. Both firms weathered the reversals of the mid-1820s that put the Cooks' large neighbor, the Shepards' woolen mill, into bankruptcy. This seemed to underscore the wisdom of using tightly held family credit. But in the Cooks' case it was not enough to prevent disaster. When a fire destroyed their mill in 1829, trade conditions were such that it was not feasible for them to rebuild it with their limited capital. They went out of business.[17]

The combination of family and local sources of credit had the sociological effect of making entry into manufacturing feasible for artisans and others with suitable skills during the 1820s and 1830s. Although important firms such as the Shepards' had been financed directly by merchant capital, and though others, such as Wells and Bodman after 1824, were classic partnerships between merchant and skilled craftsman, the majority of manufacturing ventures were controlled by "mechanics" and received merchant backing through the less formal channels of local exchange. Even the outwork trades, which were to become important centers of mercantile influence in manufacturing, largely originated in the hands of nonmerchants. Samuel Williston, who gained effective control of the button industry after 1827, had started as a farmer. Leonard M. Hills, who played a leading role in establishing the palm-leaf-hat trade in Amherst, had previously moved from Connecticut to become one of Knowles and Thayer's first carriage workers. Only later did other merchants follow them into the business. Knowles and Thayer, indeed, provided a striking example of mechanics' success at expanding a manufactory while maintaining control of it. Needing to enlarge their works to keep pace with demand for their carriages in the early 1830s, they sought assistance from local traders and craftsmen. They issued notes to cover local debts for wages and supplies, having these endorsed by backers such as the palm-leaf-hat merchant Leonard M. Hills, their former employee. Since their urban customers could be expected to make substantial cash payments for carriages on delivery,

17. On the Bodmans, see Bodman Family Papers, SSC; on Sears, see Agnes Hannay, "A Chronicle of Industry on the Mill River," *Smith College Studies in History* 21 (1935–1936): 31; the Cooks' success and failure are described in William R. Bagnall, "Contributions to American Economic History: Sketches of Manufacturing Establishments," ed. Victor S. Clark, 4:2518–2519, HBS (typescript). On James Cook, see Bagnall, "Contributions," 2:1072–1080. Cook moved in 1830 to become a mill superintendent for the Middlesex Manufacturing Co., Lowell, Mass.

this practice appeared to be a good risk in the period of price inflation between 1834 and 1836.[18]

Knowles and Thayer's chief advantage from selling in a lucrative cash market, however, was in recruiting their sizable labor force. Only by offering skilled craft wages of up to one dollar a day were they able to overcome the difficulties that many other employers experienced in obtaining sufficient labor in the rural economy. Population growth in the 1820s eased some of the structural tightness that had affected the early-nineteenth-century labor supply, but as fertility declined and the reduction of net in-migration slowed growth again in the 1830s, employers resorted to other strategies to recruit labor. They sought more actively to attract women into manufacturing as household textile production declined, and they settled for temporary and part-time help to assist or substitute for full-time employees. In Northampton and Williamsburg textile and button-making companies, the number of women recorded as employed in workshops or factories rose by two-thirds, from 148 to 246, between 1832 and 1837.[19] Toolmakers, such as Truman Nutting in Amherst, employed about six workers at any one time in the 1830s. Some of these workers were men on annual contracts, but Nutting also employed neighbors and relatives for short stints or to complete specific orders, paying them largely in work, goods, store credit, or personal notes.[20] The expansion of the outwork system in the 1830s combined these two new approaches. The large networks of women on both sides of the Valley, who made button molds or palm-leaf hats at home, were both substituting for the decline of independent household manufacture and working part-time for entrepreneurs.

Letters from the family of the Amherst widow Judith Nutting in the 1840s, from which we saw earlier how outwork fitted into households' work schedules, also demonstrate how households with land and control of their own labor continued to regulate the terms on which they would participate in the labor market. Judith's son John played an important role in the family's economy, combining work on the farm with jobs as a stonemason and occasional stints in his cousins' or other local toolshops. But while John helped support his mother and sisters, they also supported him when he was unable or unwilling to work. In 1841 he hired himself as a mason in Easthampton but did not like the working conditions and quit. His sister Mary wrote that "he got 'his sixpence' . . . and has not been there for five weeks. The man he worked for was not satisfied with the number of hours in a day—and John didn't like him and wouldn't work any more so he came home." John's

18. *Hampshire Gazette*, June 10, 1835.
19. McLane Report; Mass. Industrial Census, 1837.
20. Truman Nutting, Account Books, Amherst, 1833–1851, BCJL.

unemployment, for three weeks until he found another job, obliged his mother and sisters to work harder—for instance, taking on more out-work—to make up for the loss of earnings.[21] A few years later another of John's sisters, now employed in an Amherst sewing workshop, expressed her determination to take a break from work, even though her employer had tried to insist that she stay. "I am not obliged to do *exactly* as he says. I know he wants my help very much this summer for several of his old sewers he cannot have."[22] Uncertainty of labor supply and difficulties in supervising the work of widely scattered outworkers had already encouraged Samuel Williston and other button merchants to invest in machine production during the 1830s, both to reduce labor requirements and to concentrate more work in a single place.

Rural Lives in Transition

Changes in markets, the availability of credit, and the supply of labor would substantially alter the balance of power in rural manufacturing between the mid-1830s and late 1840s. All the characteristics that I have stressed so far—the central role of artisans, the local sources of credit, and households' restraint on the labor supply—were modified by the emergence of new conditions. An illustration of the effects of these changes on different members of one family who lived through them may be seen in the lives of three sisters, Ann, Mary, and Sophronia Bullard, who grew up in Conway in the early nineteenth century. By the mid-1820s all were working as servants in farm households—Mary in South Deerfield; Ann in Conway, Ware, and Amherst; Sophronia in Colrain. They were among the last generation of rural women to under-take household textile production. Their adult lives touched on dif-ferent aspects of the transformation of rural manufacturing by the mid-dle of the century.[23]

Both Ann and Mary married. Ann's husband, Lewis Edwards of Northampton, was a small tavernkeeper and trader. He ran oyster stalls at cattle fairs and other events to help make a living, fell afoul of the license laws at least once, and appears to have fallen into debt during the late 1830s. The family moved from Northampton to Springfield in

21. Mary Nutting to Eli Nutting, Amherst, Sept 29, 1841, Nutting Correspondence, BCJL.

22. Maria Nutting to Eli Nutting, Amherst, Mar 12, 1848, Nutting Correspondence.

23. This and subsequent paragraphs are based on letters in Edwards Family Corre-spondence, MCFL. The sisters' movements in the 1820s can be traced in Mary Bullard to Sophronia Bullard, Deerfield, May 21, 1825; Mary Bullard to Ann Bullard, Buckland, May 28, 1826; Lucius Lyons to Ann Bullard, Bloody Brook, Sept 27, 1827.

1838, where during the 1840s Edwards managed a concert hall. In 1850 they moved again, to the "new city" of Holyoke, which was then being developed by the Boston Associates to house workers at their new textile and paper mills. Ann Edwards's household work, in addition to bringing up her children, included taking in boarders to supplement Lewis's sometimes precarious income. In Northampton, Springfield, and Holyoke, in turn, the Edwards were able to make a living providing services to a rapidly growing urban industrial population.[24]

Mary's marriage took her in a different direction. Her husband, Lucius Graham of Buckland, in Franklin County, was a shoemaker and small farmer. Like most relatively poor rural women, Mary Bullard Graham made do as often as possible without hiring help in the house. Her letters, and others referring to her, reflect the struggle that she faced during the 1830s. She gave birth to five children, ran the household, and contributed directly to its income by taking in outwork, helping out with farm chores, and working in Lucius Graham's workshop. Graham was, by all accounts, a competent shoemaker with sufficient work during the mid-1830s to employ apprentices or journeymen assistants at least part of the time. But as an independent producer, his position became increasingly precarious after 1837. Mary and the children worked hard at binding shoes and other tasks to help maintain income in the face of falling prices. After holding out for some years and wrestling to pay off debts, Graham decided in 1844, despite Mary's objections, to move the family to western New York. Reluctantly, Mary left the Valley, setting up housekeeping again on a smallholding, where Lucius continued to work at shoemaking. She never returned to Massachusetts. Lucius continued to foster hopes of obtaining cheap land in Wisconsin, which would allow him to become a full-time farmer and abandon his declining trade. But Mary was never to see that, either. In September 1847, during a visit to the Grahams in their new home, Sophronia Bullard wrote to Lewis and Ann Edwards to tell them that Mary had fallen ill and died.[25]

Sophronia, the third sister, never married. At first she continued the kind of life that she and her sisters had shared in the 1820s, hiring out as a servant to farm households in Franklin County, apparently in demand

24. References to Ann's boarders appear in Mary Graham to Lewis Edwards, Buckland, Feb 25, 1834; Sophronia Bullard to Lewis Edwards, Buckland, Aug 12, 1839; Emily Graham to Sophronia Bullard, Northampton, Feb 21, 1849. Lewis Edwards's stall is mentioned in Ann Edwards to Sophronia Bullard, Springfield, Nov 1844, and Aug 17, 1845; his position as agent of the Hampden Hall in Springfield, in ibid., June 28, 1846.

25. Mary Graham described life in Buckland in letters to Lewis Edwards, Apr 6, 1835, Feb 5, 1837, Feb 12, 1839. She expressed her objections to moving west most strongly in a letter to Lewis Edwards, Mar 3, 1844. Her death is reported in Sophronia Bullard to Lewis Edwards, Moscow, N.Y., Sept 26, 1847.

as a spinner among families that continued to produce yarn. She moved from job to job, "boarding around" in Buckland, Conway, Ashfield, and other towns. During the price inflation of 1835 and 1836, however, this work became scarcer and Sophronia found work for a while at a Williamsburg textile mill. It is possible that she lost this job in 1837, when the depression stopped many local mills. By the 1840s she had returned to her peripatetic existence working in rural households. But the nature of the work that she did changed. Few if any families spun yarn any more. Sophronia found less regular employment as a house-keeper or dairy hand. She contemplated returning to work in the mill but appears not to have done so. Still a domestic worker in the 1850s, she experienced some of the decline in status that occurred as "domes-tics" became proletarianized. Like her sister Ann, she was now looking after wage workers. She was, however, not the owner but the hired servant in a Whately boardinghouse for farm laborers, one of a growing number of women who depended on doing housework for wages for employers with whom there were no kinship or neighborhood ties.[26]

Problems of debt and shifts in work patterns, of the sort that altered the Bullard sisters' lives, touched broadly on rural manufacturing in the 1830s and 1840s. Lucius Graham's predicament was widely shared by independent artisans. As the eastern Massachusetts shoe industry, organized by dealers in Lynn and other centers, expanded, shoemakers in the Valley were squeezed. Some took on contract work for these dealers. Rufus Sackett, a Northampton shoemaker, was working in the early 1840s "supported by a connexion of his in Newburyport," and the Northampton merchant Christopher Clarke may also have put out work to local artisans on contract to outside dealers.[27] It is not clear whether Lucius Graham continued independent production or also worked on contract, but throughout the late 1830s he relied increasingly on his family's labor to maintain his rate of output. "L. and I have had to

26. Sophronia's movements can be traced in Emily Graham to Lewis Edwards, Buckland, Mar 30, 1841; Sophronia Bullard to Lewis Edwards, Buckland, Nov 25 [1844?]; Sophronia Bullard to Ann Edwards, Buckland, Apr 27, 1845; Sophronia Bullard to Lewis Edwards, Buckland, Sept 21, 1845; Ann Edwards to Sophronia Bullard, Holyoke, July 28, 1850, and Northampton, Feb 18, 1856. Her employment as a domestic servant is recorded in Wait Family, Account Book, Whately, 1855–1856, pp. 21–22, MCFL. By 1860, there were 302 "domestics" listed in the census schedules for the six towns, of whom 286 were women; Northampton had 179 and Amherst 65: U.S. Eighth Census, Population Sched-ules, 1860, Massachusetts, National Archives, Washington, D.C. (microfilm). Faye Dud-den, *Serving Women: Household Work in 19th Century America* (Middletown, Conn., 1983), discusses the increasingly "proletarian" character of hired domestic labor by mid-century.

27. Mercantile Agency credit reports on Sackett and Clarke, respectively, are in Massa-chusetts, vol. 46, p. 109 and p. 112, R. G. Dun and Co. Collection, Baker Library, Harvard University Graduate School of Business Administration, Boston (hereafter cited as MA 46, followed by a page number).

work as hard as we have been able," wrote Mary Bullard Graham in April 1835, "and a good deal harder than we wanted to." She had "had shoes aplenty to bind, from six to eight and twelve pairs in a week, and with all the rest have four as dirty, noisy, ragged children to take care of than any other woman." Two years later, even though the elder children could now help, another baby in the family and falling prices for finished work prompted a more urgent tone in Mary's letters. "I wish you would try to find me something to do," she wrote her sister, "for I have only five babies to take care of and shoes to bind." She had bound thirty pairs of shoes in under five weeks and signed the letter "Mr L Graham's wife and children all shoemakers." By 1839, "unusually crowded with work," Mary was spending even more time in the shop and doing a wider range of tasks: "I do the pegging hammer the leather and considerable of the fitting." But this self-exploitation did not prevent the Grahams from slipping into debt.[28]

Financial Crisis and the Role of Merchants

While shoemakers faced stiff competition and falling prices, other artisans experienced difficulties collecting debts owed to them, both during the inflation of the mid-1830s and the depression that followed. Indeed, the 1837 crisis disrupted the patterns of credit that had supported many rural manufacturers. Knowles and Thayer's strategy of obtaining local credit against the prospect of cash receipts from sales made the company an early and spectacular victim of the depression. The financial crisis in the cities caused its customers to stop payments. The subsequent collapse of the firm along with several others shook the town of Amherst. Leonard M. Hills was one of those eventually able to resume business, but Knowles and Thayer could not revive. Attempts to float a corporation to restart the carriage works never succeeded. When the company did reopen, under the ownership of Lorin Blanchard, a former employee, it was on a greatly reduced scale. By 1845 all four Amherst carriage makers combined had work forces equal to only 16 percent and capital equal to only 9 percent of Knowles and Thayer's at its peak. By 1847, Blanchard too was bankrupt and his property sold up at a sheriff's auction.[29]

28. Mary Bullard Graham to Lewis Edwards, Buckland, Apr 6, 1835, Feb 5, 1837, Feb 12, 1839.
29. On Knowles and Thayer's bankruptcy, see Carpenter and Morehouse, *History of Amherst*, p. 297, and Aron, "Minds of Hands," p. 39. Hills's difficulties lasted several years: see David Mack, Jr., to Joseph Lathrop, Amherst, Mar 14, 1843, BCJL, discussing Hills's prospects. John G. Palfrey, *Statistics of the Condition and Products of Certain Branches*

Many artisans had to obtain mortgages in order to stay afloat during the crisis. Even so, not all succeeded. Dexter Fox, an Amherst tool-maker who had to mortgage his tools in 1843 to raise credit, was still so heavily in debt three years later that his assignee put his farm up for sale to pay it off.[30] Probate records and credit reports suggest that many craftsmen's positions remained weakened. Of nine artisans in the six towns who died in 1850, for instance, only four owned real estate and only one possessed more than two hundred dollars worth of personal property. All had debts outstanding, requiring administration to settle. Some were insolvent when they died.[31] Even in trades such as broom making, where independent workshop production continued throughout the 1850s, market disruptions and competition created increasing difficulties. Of the seven Hatfield broom makers remaining in 1860, four were listed in Mercantile Agency credit records. None was recommended strongly.[32]

Manufacturers in financial difficulties after 1837 turned to various sources of help. They arbitrated with creditors, formed new partnerships, and sought the support of families and friends. Peter Ingram, proprietor of a small North Amherst mill, was rescued from bankruptcy during the crisis by relatives and connections. He mortgaged the mill for $5,000 to a physician from Greenwich and his own brother Ezra, who owned a woolen mill nearby. But Ezra was also in difficulties. His machinery was already mortgaged and he owed $1,500 to the Hadley Falls Company of South Hadley. Anxious to place his property out of the creditor's reach, he executed a second mortgage back to his brother Peter on the machines and on cloth he had shipped to Boston, Hartford, and New York just four days before a writ of attachment arrived from South Hadley. Through this mutual support the brothers survived the

of Industry in Massachusetts for the Year Ending April 1, 1845 (Boston, 1846; hereafter cited as Mass. Industrial Census, 1845), revealed the small scale of Amherst carriage making after Knowles and Thayer's collapse. Blanchard's firm advertised: *Hampshire Gazette*, Sept 19, 1843; the sale of his property was announced in *Hampshire and Franklin Express* (Amherst), Apr 1, 1847.

30. Amherst, Record of Personal Property Mortgages, vol. 2, 1837–1851, p. 74, Town Clerk's Records, series no. 1.15, Amherst Town Hall (hereafter cited as Amherst, Mortgages).

31. Hampshire County, Probate Records, 48:48–49 (John D. Osborne, Hadley); 48:145–146 (Roland S. Harris, Hatfield); 48:340–342 (Noah Edson, Hadley); 49:5–6 (Daniel S. Everett, Northampton); 49:41–42 (Melzar Burnell, Northampton); 49:44–46 (George Holmes, Williamsburg); 49:78–80 (David L. Brown, Westhampton); 52:12–13 (Eli Bangs, Amherst); 52:14–15 (Benoni Thayer, Amherst), Hampshire County Hall of Records, Northampton.

32. MA 46:78 (Alvin Sanderson, who failed in 1862); 46:93 (O. Marsh and C. S. Marsh, "very doubtful"); 46:93 (George Claghan, "not good"); 46:94 (S. Mosher, "as good as the average of broommakers; but slow pay").

immediate crisis. But, short of adequate capital in the long run, both their businesses eventually foundered.[33]

With family and other sources of credit stretched to the limit, it was inevitable that large and small manufacturers should also turn to merchants and other wealthy men for assistance. Although in Amherst only 16 percent of personal estate mortgages written in the early 1840s were in favor of merchants or traders, these men had a disproportionate share in bailing out artisans and mill owners. Truman Nutting executed several mortgages to the traders Pitkin and Kellogg; Luther Fox also raised more than a thousand dollars on a mortgage from the merchant and toolmaker James Kellogg. The papermaker Sylvester Roberts and Company mortgaged its machinery to merchants in Worcester. Other firms raised capital from large Amherst property owners such as John Leland and John Dickinson; from the hat merchant Leonard M. Hills; from Oliver Watson, a shoe manufacturer and merchant; and from Sweetser, Cutler and Company, the town's principal dry-goods dealers. Similarly, in Northampton, leading merchants and prosperous manufacturers such as J. P. Williston took a hand in providing finance to a variety of craftsmen and small manufacturers.[34] To avoid these conditions and maintain a sense of independence some craftsmen, like Lucius Graham, left the area. Once settled in New York State, Graham wrote to his Massachusetts relatives, "I am not 3 or 4 hundred dollars in [debt?] as I was there. . . . If we are prospered as well as we have been thus far I hope no Merchant will ever be able to say that I owe him."[35]

The aftermath of 1837 led to a significant shakeout and restructuring of rural industry. Capital invested in the six towns in 1845 was 23 percent lower than that reported in 1837.[36] Proportionate falls were greatest in Northampton and Amherst and were somewhat counterbalanced by increases in Williamsburg. Some hill towns at the edges of the Valley suffered crippling reverses. Migrants from Chesterfield, who had moved to Ohio and taken up farming in the late 1830s, urged relatives to follow them, writing that "if things are well they are better off there with nothing but their hands than they would be here with all the factories in Hampshire County." A Cummington man lamented the decline of manufactures there. Writing with some exaggeration that

33. Amherst, Mortgages, 2:4–5, 8. On the Ingrams, see Carpenter and Morehouse, *History of Amherst*, p. 291, and Fay C. Kaynor, "Peter Ingram, Nineteenth-Century Miller at 'The City,'" *New England Galaxy* 17 (Winter 1975): 52–59.
34. Amherst, Mortgages, 2:35, 195, 453 (Nutting), 165, 168, 265, 348, 400. W. A. Arnold and Co. to Assessors of Northampton, Jan 6, 1839, Town Papers Collection, 5.71, FL.
35. Lucius Graham to Lewis Edwards, Moscow, N.Y., Jan 18, 1845, Edwards Family Correspondence.
36. Mass. Industrial Census, 1837, 1845.

"that town was the first engaged in this state in manufacturing," he noted that "it has all run down excepting Leather." In Cummington, he concluded, people "are always ready to engage in new projects & they are always poor."[37] But the shift was not only geographical; it was also social. Merchants and other men with substantial capital resources and connections took an increasingly important hand in the Valley's manufacturing after 1840. When it expanded again after the depression, it bore the marks of their influence. Above all, they had the advantage that, with the influx of foreign-born workers to the region at the same time, it would be possible for them to overcome many of the restraints on labor supply the rural household-based economy had always exercised.

A New Industrial Structure

By mid-century, in a region that usually impressed visitors with its pastoral character, the presence of manufacturing and its impact on the surroundings were increasingly evident. Factories were visible: a guide to Northampton and environs recommended a visit to the new cotton mills at Haydenville, between there and Williamsburg. They were also audible: Sylvester Judd noted the constant noise from the fourteen triphammers of the Bay State Tool Company, which rang out across Northampton after the factory opened in 1855. This was the result of a new, more concentrated expansion of manufacturing. Between 1845 and 1850, capital investment in the six towns rose by 45 percent, much of it in Williamsburg and Northampton. From then until 1860 it rose another 68 percent, a slightly lower annual rate, but still impressive. New cotton, silk, and thread mills, machine works, and cutlery and tool factories joined the textile, button, woodenware, tool, furniture, hat, and shoe works already in the area, many of which had themselves expanded. The Mill River between the centers of Williamsburg and Northampton, in particular, took on the character of an industrial district. By 1860, there were about forty-nine mills and workshops along this five-mile stretch of the river. Settlements of from a few dozen to several hundred residents clustered around millsites at Thayerville, Searsville, Haydenville, Leeds, Florence, and Bay State and Paper Mill villages, housing factory owners and agents, storekeepers, overseers, and workers. Here, as in other parts of New England, the "factory village" had become a distinct social formation.[38]

The backgrounds of the entrepreneurs and investors who financed

37. Orren Bryant to Martin Bryant, Pittsfield, Aug 8, 1837; Richard Clarke to Orren Bryant, Chesterfield, Sept 4, 1839, both in Bryant Collection, MCFL, Box 6.

38. John Eden, *The Mt. Holyoke Hand-Book and Tourist's Guide for Northampton and Its Vicinity* (Northampton, 1851), pp. 38–39; Judd, "Notebook," vol. 7, Oct 1, 1855. Data on

these developments remained in many ways as diverse as those of previous groups of manufacturers. Of forty-two men active as proprietors or agents between 1845 and 1860 whose backgrounds could be traced, ten started out as skilled craftsmen and eight as farmers. Five other men, migrants to the Valley from other states or abroad, had previous careers in the factory system. But the largest single group, nineteen men, had mercantile origins. The prominence of merchants and traders in acquiring the capital and credit required for larger-scale manufacturing gave them an unprecedented degree of influence over it. In the largest local industries they supplanted the artisans who, before 1840, had held most positions of authority.[39]

Merchants' involvement in industry was not always successful. Luke Sweetser and some of his associates made investments during the 1840s in textile- and paper-manufacturing ventures at North Amherst. The paper mills survived the 1850s, but textile production proved no more successful then than it had in earlier decades. After several reorganizations and mill fires it ceased entirely before 1860. But in other cases it became clear during the period that connections between manufacturing and trade were more likely to succeed in a highly competitive regional and national market for manufactures than otherwise. Broadly speaking, the factories and workshops that survived the period from 1845 to the Civil War were those whose owners also had retailing or other business interests. Proprietors who were not diversified were more likely to fail.[40]

This was true in two well-established rural industries, shoemaking

---

capital invested is from Mass. Industrial Census, 1845; U.S. Seventh Census, Non-Population Schedules, 1850, Massachusetts: Manufactures, Massachusetts Archives, Boston, Mass.; and U.S. Eighth Census, Non-Population Schedules, 1860, Massachusetts: Manufactures, National Archives, Washington, D.C. (microfilm). See also Hannay, "Chronicle of Industry," passim. On factory villages in general, see *The New England Mill Village, 1790–1860: A Documentary History*, ed. Gary Kulik, Roger Parks, and Theodore Z. Penn (Cambridge, Mass., 1983). The discussion in this and subsequent paragraphs is congruent with the findings of Kenneth L. Sokoloff that it was the reorganization of capital and labor that primarily explained the increase in New England's industrial output in this period ("Productivity Growth in Manufacturing during Early Industrialization: Evidence from the American Northeast, 1820–1860," in *Long-Term Trends in American Economic Growth*, ed. Robert W. Fogel and Lance E. Gallman [Chicago, 1986], pp. 679–736). Judith A. McGaw, *Most Wonderful Machine: Mechanization and Social Change in Berkshire Paper Making, 1801–1885* (Princeton, 1987), traces the steady process of change in one industry.

39. Biographical information on manufacturers was collected from A. Forbes and J. W. Greene, *The Rich Men of Massachusetts: Containing a Statement of the Reputed Wealth of About Fifteen Hundred Persons, with Brief Sketches of More than One Thousand Characters* (Boston, 1851); *Northampton General Directory 1860* (Northampton, 1860); Carpenter and Morehouse, *History of Amherst*; Mercantile Agency credit reports.

40. On Sweetser's investments, see Thomas Jones to George Cutler, Amherst, Sept 7, 1844, Jones Family Papers, BCJL; Smith, Cutler and Co., Partnership Agreement, May 24, 1847, BCJL; Amherst, Mortgages, 2:348; Carpenter and Morehouse, *History of Amherst*, p. 291.

and broom making, both of which were subject to competition from outside the region. By 1850, for example, there were only two shoemaking workshops remaining in Amherst. One, belonging to Oliver Watson, employed fifteen people and turned out 6,000 pairs of boots and shoes a year, valued at $10,000. The other, a smaller shop owned by the brothers D. and H. Kellogg, employed four workers to make about $6,500 worth of goods annually. Both were hit by unremitting pressure from eastern manufacturers, which kept prices low. The Kelloggs' enterprise failed in the early 1850s. Watson, though he expanded output, apparently faced a squeeze on his profits as his firm's earnings per employee fell in 1855 to only 76 percent of their level in 1837. He was helped to stay in business by the fact that he had other interests, in land, lumbering, and shoe distribution. The same was true of surviving shoe manufacturers elsewhere in the area. Jonas Winter, who moved to Amherst from Franklin County in 1851 as a shoe dealer, had within four years moved into general retailing, becoming agent and president of the North Amherst branch store of the New England Protective Union.[41] Competition from the West similarly weakened the position of Hadley and Hatfield broom makers in the 1850s. At least one large workshop, Shipman's of Hadley, went bankrupt in 1857. Of men associated with the trade whose names were known to the Mercantile Agency, those with the best reports were Thaddeus Smith of Hadley and A. J. Jones of Hatfield, both landowners, who had begun dealing in western-grown broomcorn during the 1850s and so reduced their dependence on manufacturing alone.[42]

The advantages of diversification were further illustrated by the differing fortunes of rivals in the Amherst toolmaking trade, Truman Nutting and James Kellogg. Their workshops each employed about six men in the 1830s and expanded after the depression to provide work for up to twenty at a time. But by the early 1850s, Nutting was heading toward bankruptcy and Kellogg toward being one of Amherst's wealthiest citizens. Nutting, seeking to acquire new equipment in the late 1840s, raised capital from a number of backers in the town. In the process, according to the Mercantile Agency reporter, he overextended himself. In 1851, before Nutting could pay off much of his debt, three of his creditors died within a few months of one another. The calling-in of their loans probably hastened his failure the following year. He settled his debts at thirty-three cents on the dollar and moved to Minnesota in 1853.[43] Kellogg, on the other hand, had more resources to call on. He

41. MA 46:2 (Watson), 46:3 (Kelloggs), 46:7, 46:112 (Winter).
42. MA 46:95 (Smith, Jones).
43. On Nutting, see MA 46:6; on his creditors' deaths, see Hampshire County, Probate Records, 49:103–104, 128–131. A memoir of members of the Nutting family appeared in the *Springfield Sunday Union and Republican*, Apr 1, 1934.

had established himself as a merchant in East Amherst in 1819 and had not entered the tool business until later. He continued to run a store in Kelloggville, where he had located his tool shops. He also owned the boardinghouses in which his workmen rented rooms. These properties not only provided income and profit additional to that from the tool shops but were a source of goods and cash with which to pay for labor. Above all, they provided Kellogg with credit, both for his own business and to lend to others. Indeed, it was Kellogg who, by taking mortgages in the late 1830s, had helped keep his rivals—then the firm of Nutting and Fox—afloat. Diversification gave Kellogg not only a lead over his neighbors, but some direct power over them too.[44]

By 1856 the owners of one-third of all general stores in Hampshire County were also engaged in manufacturing.[45] Among them was the Amherst entrepreneur Leonard M. Hills, who had rebuilt his strong position in the palm-leaf trade and, joined by his son Henry, was now on the point of concentrating and mechanizing hat production on a large scale. In the 1840s the merchant David Mack, Jr., had installed new machinery in his Amherst palm-leaf workshop; the Hillses took this process a step further with profits from their store business. They installed pressing machines in their works in 1855; by the end of the decade they had built a new factory and had taken over old Amherst textile mills to handle the preparation, pressing, and shaping of hats, leaving only the braiding of palm leaf to outworkers. By 1862 they were employing up to two hundred men and women in their two works at the height of each season. The Hillses, like some others, used capital accumulated in trade to finance a progressive concentration of their manufacturing activities.[46]

The brothers Joel and Josiah Hayden of Williamsburg provided the most striking example of the success that diversification as manufacturers and traders could bring. Having grown up in Cummington, they both traveled to Connecticut in the late 1820s to work in a Waterbury metal works belonging to an uncle. Trained in making metal buttons, they returned to establish a factory in Williamsburg in about 1831. After some reverses, they were joined in partnership by Samuel Williston,

44. On Kellogg, see MA 46:1; Carpenter and Morehouse, *History of Amherst*, pp. 140, 294. Kellogg's potential power over his debtor and competitor Nutting was revealed in 1837. Kellogg had apparently taken possession of Nutting's account books. When Nutting allegedly entered Kellogg's house to reclaim them, Kellogg had him prosecuted for theft; see Commonwealth v. Nutting, Hampshire County Court of Common Pleas, Files, Mar 1837, Massachusetts State Archives, Boston, Mass., in which Kellogg was the complainant. The case was dropped, presumably after the two men reached an accommodation.

45. George Adams, *Massachusetts Business Directory for the Year 1856* (Boston, 1856), pp. 114–123.

46. Henry F. Hills to Adelaide Spencer, Amherst, June 19, 1862, in Isabelle Carlhian, "The Hills Houses in Amherst" (1973; copy in BCJL), appendix.

who by the mid-1830s was seeking to mechanize parts of his outwork button business. Williston's capital and the Haydens' skill contributed to a business that by 1837 was employing up to one hundred people and was becoming the nucleus of the factory village named after the brothers. After the company was halted by the panic that year, the partners sought to diversify. By the 1840s they were manufacturing pens, brass goods, and machinery. Before Williston withdrew in 1848 to concentrate his button-making activities in Easthampton, the Haydens entered another partnership to build a four-story cotton mill, which employed twenty-three men and fifty-four women by 1850, a quarter of the male and two-thirds of the female employment recorded in Williamsburg in the industrial census that year. During the 1850s Josiah Hayden entered a partnership with an iron founder. In addition to a retail store, the Haydens also had connections with a cutlery and hardware manufacturer and, later, a tobacco warehouse. On a slope near the village, each brother built a modest-sized but impressive Palladian-style villa, whose porticoed facades looked down toward the mill and brassworks on the riverbank.[47]

While the Haydens exemplified the advantages of diversification, they also took part in the concentration of capital and labor, which was the most important root of new manufacturing in the region. Joel Hayden's work toward mechanizing button manufacture in the 1830s formed the basis for a rapid shift from outwork to factory production in the trade. By the 1850s half a dozen button factories in Williamsburg, Northampton, and Easthampton were producing thousands of gross of articles a day, often on Hayden's machinery. Samuel Williston's Easthampton button works, employing mainly women workers, turned out japanned and cloth-covered buttons whose parts were cut or stamped out in batches by hand tools and assembled in larger batches by lever-driven and waterpowered machinery.[48]

Meanwhile, the Haydens had also become connected with a group of capitalists who invested heavily in reviving Northampton's manufacturing from the mid-1840s. The breakup in 1846 of an experimental community, the Northampton Association for Education and Industry, which had been set up in 1842 with silk production as its major activity, provided personnel for new manufacturing concerns. One group that

47. Biographical data on the Haydens is drawn from Phyllis B. Deming, comp., *A History of Williamsburg in Massachusetts* (Northampton, 1946); Edward Foster, "Giants in the Earth: The Hayden Family of Williamsburg" (1965; copy in WHS); entries in MA 46:108 (Hayden & Kingsley, Ironfounders), MA 46:60 (Joel Hayden, Jr.); and Forbes and Greene, *Rich Men*, p. 146, whose entry on Joel Hayden put his personal fortune at $150,000.

48. A report on Williston's Easthampton factories appeared in *Hampshire Gazette*, Feb 27, 1855. See also W. B. Gay, *Gazetteer of Hampshire County, Massachusetts, 1654–1887* (Syracuse, [1886?]), p. 237.

had left the community had already set up a silk works nearby in 1844. Prominent community members, George Benson and Samuel L. Hill, each headed companies to set up new silk mills. Local capital played an important role in establishing these firms. Hill was backed by the wealthy Northampton lawyer and financier Samuel L. Hinckley, Benson by J. P. Williston and others. When Benson failed in 1850, dragging Hill with him, these backers helped expand and reorganize the mills under corporate charters, getting rid of Benson and bringing in the Hayden brothers as partners in another new cotton mill, the Greenville Manufacturing Company.[49] In 1850 Northampton had work for 222 men and 295 women operatives in eight silk, cotton, wool, paper, and button factories, the largest of which employed more than 220 workers. By 1856 eleven mills, including two clothing manufactories, were employing about 287 men and more than 400 women. In addition, new machine works had jobs for 15 or more men in a trade that had previously only employed half a dozen, and a substantial tool works had also opened. The town's manufacturing population reached nearly 800 people in 1860.[50]

Even well-capitalized firms, however, faced the vicissitudes of trade, which could undermine apparent success. The depressions of 1854 and 1857 left business in these new mills slack for a period. When there were orders for goods, the Mill River did not always provide sufficient water to power the machinery to produce them. The Greenville mill was reported idle for a period in 1858 for this reason. By the end of the 1850s, after much foot-dragging, a group of manufacturers invested in a dam higher up the Mill River in Goshen to regulate the water supply. (Poor construction or maintenance of the dam would ultimately lead to tragedy. During a freshet in 1874, it collapsed, releasing a flood that drowned 136 people and destroyed 100 houses and factories along an eight-mile stretch of river.)[51] But while the larger, locally backed firms survived the fluctuations of the 1850s, others did not. An enameled-cloth works, set up by two merchant tailors early in the decade, failed in 1857. The crisis of that year also brought the failure of the outside-owned Northampton Woolen Manufacturing Company, which closed down entirely, with the loss of more than 200 jobs.[52]

49. On Northampton manufacturers, see Hannay, "Chronicle of Industry," pp. 68–70. Evidence on shareholdings is in Northampton, Assessors Records, Town Papers Collection, 5.75, FL.

50. U.S. Census, 1850: Manufactures; Adams, *Mass. Business Directory*; U.S. Census, 1860: Population.

51. On water supply, see MA 46:106. On the reservoir, see Williamsburg Reservoir Co., Record Book, MCFL. The Mill River Flood is described in Gay, *Gazetteer*, p. 475. If the reservoir company records contained entries for the period covering the flood, they have not survived: the pages following entries for 1872 have been torn out of the book.

52. The failure of White, Smith and Co., enameled-cloth manufacturers, is discussed later in this chapter. The demise of the Northampton Woolen Manufacturing Co. can be traced in MA 46:106 and the *Hampshire Gazette*, Mar 9, Sept 21, and Oct 26, 1858.

A New Labor Force

Manufacturers knew that their efforts alone were not the guarantee of profits. As Asahel Goodale of Belchertown put it while discussing venturing into manufacturing in the 1840s, "it must be done by employing other people to work for us."[53] Until then the conditions for securing industrial labor were largely dictated by the state of the rural economy and the demands of rural households. Especially in districts where agriculture remained successful, these demands frequently included intermittent or seasonal wage work that could be fitted in with other household tasks. The concentration and expansion of manufacturing depended on having labor readily available to work in larger mills and workshops. Immigration permitted entrepreneurs to avoid these constraints to some extent. They sought to create the circumstances for a stable supply of labor and steady work habits. To a degree they succeeded. But the continued instability of markets, together with other unpredictable effects on their operations, made their ideal hard to achieve. Meanwhile, of course, these conditions also shaped the experience of the men and women who worked in manufacturing.

The world of master craftsmen, journeymen, and apprentices had always been a step apart from the remainder of rural society. Not only the boys who went from outlying towns to serve apprenticeships in the craft shops of Northampton during the 1820s and 1830s, but those like Theodore Bliss whose home was only a few hundred yards from the bindery he worked in, were conscious of entering a distinct form of life and work. The same was true to a lesser extent in the scattered rural workshops that made tools, brooms, and other articles. Truman Nutting's tool shops in South Amherst, for instance, maintained close links with the work and exchange patterns of the surrounding countryside. As Nutting's business expanded in the 1840s to keep pace with rising demand for the tools he produced, he modified his employment strategies. Work in his shops became more specialized. He hired more men, sometimes on contracts lasting between one and three years. He paid a high proportion of these men's wages in cash. But he still relied on casual, intermittent hiring in the neighborhood to help out at busy times. Similarly, in the broom-making sections of Hadley and Hatfield, connections between farm and workshops remained strong.[54]

Factory villages, on the other hand, had always been regarded as

53. Asahel Goodale to Ira Chaffee Goodale, Belchertown, Oct 12, 1845, M. W. Goodell Collection, BCJL.

54. Theodore Bliss, *Theodore Bliss, Publisher and Bookseller: A Study of Character and Life in the Middle Period of the Nineteenth Century*, ed. Arthur A. Bliss (Northampton, 1941), pp. 36–37; Nutting, Account Books, Amherst, BCJL.

more separate places. Located often in hilly terrain less than ideal for farming, they had seemed remote to many rural people. Henry Gere, who grew up nearby, recalled the Northampton Woolen Manufacturing Company's village (later called Leeds) as markedly different from the rest of the town, with an "old and dingy" mill and "small one-story tenement houses . . . even dirtier." According to Rev. George Cooke, farmers among his parishioners in North Amherst saw little in common between themselves and the millworkers at Factory Hollow and North Amherst City, not conceiving, for instance, that doing factory tasks really constituted working for a living.[55] Factory villages were often populated by outsiders, men and women who had migrated to find work. The villages' cultural practices were different. When Northampton Woolen completed a new brick mill in 1847, it threw a dance to "dedicate it to the manufacture of woolen goods," in a manner more reminiscent of large mill towns than of rural villages.[56]

It was the factory village, rather than the rural workshop, that expanded more rapidly after 1840. Like Samuel Williston and the Hayden brothers when they set up their button works, manufacturers hoped to achieve a greater regularity of work patterns and a closer supervision of production than was often possible in rural areas. They sought to supplant the competing authority of rural household heads and hoped to instill more regular work discipline than farming and independent production had often demanded. A firm that opened in Amherst in 1837 advertised for filers "who can do first-rate work and who feel smart enough to do a day's work in ten hours, without raising higher pressure of steam than cold water will make, and can leave their long yarns until their day's work is done."[57] This particular business quickly failed, but owners and agents of new textile, button, and paper mills in the 1840s sought to achieve its ideal of regularity.

Where new investment was low, old labor and employment practices often remained. Amherst's manufacturing capital grew in the late 1840s but fell back again during the early 1850s as textile factories failed. The work force was overwhelmingly Massachusetts-born; in 1855 only 6.5 percent of the town's population were immigrants. Larger new investments in Northampton and Williamsburg, however, drew in outsiders in greater numbers. Capital in the two towns was 120 percent higher in 1860 than it had been in 1845. In 1855, 16.4 percent of people in Williamsburg and 23.8 percent of people in Northampton were foreign-

---

55. Henry S. Gere, *Reminiscences of Old Northampton: Sketches of the Town as It Appeared from 1840 to 1850* (n.p., 1902), p. 130; George Cooke, "Reminiscences of the North Parish, Amherst, Mass., from Oct 1838 to March 1858," part 2, p. 11, AAS (typescript, 1883).
56. *Hampshire Herald* (Northampton), July 6, 1847.
57. Morrill, Mossman and Blair, advertisement, *Hampshire Gazette*, Mar 8, 1837.

born, largely as a reflection of the expansion of manufacturing employment. In 1844–1845, for instance, the county common pleas court heard
sixty-three petitions for naturalization presented by Northampton residents, including twenty-one from Great Britain, twenty-five from Ireland, and fifteen from Germany. During the 1850s the pattern shifted;
fully 80 percent of petitioners were Irish. Industrial workers represented a significant proportion, especially of the first group. Of them
thirty-six (57 percent) worked in textiles, eighteen from Britain, eight
each from Ireland and Germany, and two from France. The flood of
workers searching for employment in the town's mills placed the region
for the first time within the scope of an international labor market and
gave manufacturers an opportunity to evade some of the constraints
under which they had so far been operating.[58] In Williamsburg over 26
percent of factory operatives were foreign-born in 1850. By 1860 the
proportion had risen to 58 percent. Among male workers the proportion rose from 41 percent to 61 percent. By then, more than 200 immigrant men, women, and children, many of them Irish, were working in
the town's mills.[59]

While immigrants swelled the numbers of local factory workers, they
did not supplant American-born operatives. The demand for labor was
sufficiently high in the 1850s that employers sought it from a variety of
sources. Williamsburg mills had employed at least 87 men and women
listed in the census in 1850. By 1860, their work force was 345. In both
years, roughly four groups of workers could be discerned. American
and foreign-born men constituted 47 percent of the group in 1850 and 63
percent of the much larger 1860 work force, which had grown in number from 41 to 217. Immigrant women aged twenty-five or under, many
of whom lived with their own families or in boardinghouses, were
rarely enumerated in the 1850 census, although 5 can be identified. By
1860, however, they formed nearly 16 percent of the group. Young New
England–born women, who had traditionally formed an important part
of mill labor forces since the 1820s, still constituted over 40 percent of all
workers in 1850 and over three-quarters of all women in the mills. Ten
years later, their numbers had risen slightly, although their proportion
of the whole work force was now under 11 percent. Finally, the number
of women over twenty-five, American- or foreign-born, only 11 in 1850,
rose to 26 during the decade.

58. The proportion of foreign-born workers is calculated from U.S. Census, 1860:
Population; capital investment from Mass. Industrial Census, 1845, and U.S. Census,
1860: Manufactures. Naturalization petitions were recorded in Hampshire County Court
of Common Pleas, Records, vol. 30, nos. 200–275 (1844), Hampshire County Courthouse,
Northampton, and Hampshire County Court of Common Pleas, Files, no. 359 (1845).
59. U.S. Census, 1850, 1860: Manufactures and Population, provided the data upon
which this and the following paragraphs are based.

Although the relative importance of immigrants and male workers increased, and that of New England–born women proportionately diminished, the absolute numbers in all groups increased. Manufacturers were tapping new sources of labor but continued to hire from among the groups that they had drawn from in the past. Up to 1860, at any rate, rural New England continued to be an important source of factory labor in the Valley. For while young women continued to seek work in textile mills, they also found it at a variety of other tasks, in merchant tailors' and hat makers' sewing rooms, at the ink factory in Northampton belonging to J. P. Williston and his son, and at Samuel Williston's Easthampton elastic and webbing factories. Button and palm-leaf-hat manufacturers also brought into factories some of the women who would previously have done domestic outwork for them. In Amherst during the late 1850s, L. M. Hills and Sons recruited hood makers for their newly enlarged palm-leaf works. Two boardinghouses accommodated fifty-six of them, all women, in the summer of 1860. Of the twenty-seven women at one house, all were Massachusetts-born except one, who came from Vermont. Their average age was 20.6. At the other lived twenty-nine workers, two from New Hampshire, the rest from Massachusetts. Their ages ranged from 14 to 28, but the average was just over 19 years.

Conditions in Rural Industry

The living and working arrangements of workers were as varied as their origins, reflecting their employers' need to maintain a disparate labor force and their own need to put together livings from the different resources at their disposal. Mills like those in Williamsburg and Northampton, small by the standards of major textile centers in mid-century, could not rely on single dominant housing arrangements, such as the boardinghouse system of the Lowell mills or the "family" system of Rhode Island and southern Massachusetts. Instead, workers lived in a mixture of circumstances. Of 336 Williamsburg operatives for whom living arrangements can be discerned from the 1860 census, 76 (23 percent) were household heads who had no other family members working in the mills and another 60 (18 percent) boarded with local families to whom they were not related. A total of 71 men, women, and child workers belonged to families in which there were at least two operatives—in other words, some variant on the "family" system in which parents either took children into the mills they worked in themselves, or sent them to work to supplement earnings from other sources. The largest group, 129 workers, lived in boardinghouses rented by mill owners to tenants who contracted to board operatives or laborers for them. There were seven of these houses in Williamsburg in 1860, varying in size from 9 to 31 boarders each. Nevertheless, although this was the single most important form of workers' housing, it accounted for less than 40 percent of the total number.

While these varied arrangements to some degree spoke of the flexibility of industrial work, and the availability of means by which workers could fit mill employment into their family circumstances, they also reflected the relatively weak position of both New England–born and immigrant laborers in the mill villages of the 1840s and 1850s. The depression following 1837, which reduced other employment opportunities, and the increased flow of migrants in the mid-1840s depressed real wages. Between 1830 and 1860 Massachusetts industrial wages rose by 21.3 percent, but food and drink prices rose by 56.1 percent. Workers found it harder to bargain for good wages or to obtain jobs on favorable terms. In March 1856 the Bodmans hired two men to work in their Charlemont scythe-snath works at fourteen to fifteen dollars a month. Three months later an old hand turned up to look for a job, evidently fortified by liquor; "he offered to work 2 months for $60 and would not work for any less." Leaving the house, wrote Edward C. Bodman, he "had to cross his legs to keep from tumbling over and that decided the case;" he was not hired.[60] In Amherst, Northampton, and Williamsburg textile mills, capital-to-labor ratios fell between 1837 and 1850 as employers took advantage of relatively cheap, easily recruited labor to expand their work forces. The lower costs of labor in turn encouraged mill owners to expend relatively expensive capital to employ it. Statistics available from the industrial censuses suggest that in good years their profit rates rose as a result.[61] But the evidence also suggests that workers did not generally share in these benefits. Conditions of employment were, for them, often precarious.

A substantial proportion of mill workers had to supplement their wages from other sources. A majority of operatives who were household heads either had children at work in the mills as well, took boarders into their families, or both. The principal exceptions were young married men who did not yet have children, whose household expenses would be lower than most, and whose wages could in any case

60. Wage levels and food prices are given in Mass. Bureau of Statistics of Labor, *History of Wages and Prices, 1752–1883* (Boston, 1885). The Charlemont workers are referred to in Amos Whitaker to Luther Bodman, Charlemont, Mar 13, 1856, and Edward C. Bodman to Luther Bodman, Williamsburg, June 7, 1856, Bodman Family Papers, Box 4, SSC.

61. Capital-to-labor ratios were calculated from Mass. Industrial Census, 1837, 1845, and U.S. Census: 1850, 1860, Manufactures. Crude operating profit rates were calculated business by business from the estimates of costs and returns provided in the industrial censuses.

be supplemented by their wives' paid or unpaid work. Under these conditions, it was hard for many workers to accumulate property. In this respect factory operatives were at a disadvantage compared with skilled workers in smaller, craft workshops. Whereas one-third of employees in eight Amherst craft trades owned real estate in 1850, and about one-half in 1860, only 2 percent of Williamsburg's male operatives had property in 1850. This rose to only 8 percent ten years later. A large majority of workers who were heads of household or who kept boardinghouses had to rent accommodations from their employers or other local landowners. The absolute number of propertyless male workers rose from 40 to more than 200. Immigrants and American-born workers were equally poorly off in this regard; the proportion of men in each group who owned real estate was virtually the same.[62]

Workers' poverty was connected with instabilities inherent in small rural manufactures. Some trades, including hat making, remained seasonal and employed large numbers of workers for only a few months each year. Even during the season, production difficulties could reduce hours and therefore wages. Hills and Company found itself with a large quantity of palm leaf too tender to weave easily in 1860; as a result, wrote Henry F. Hills, "we have not had work enough for the Girls all of the time which has made it very unpleasant."[63] Even well-capitalized mills were vulnerable to business fluctuations, as an observer implied in 1852, noting that the Northampton Woolen Manufacturing Company had "been for many years regarded as the best and most skilfully managed concern in the Country [that is, region] often doing successful or prosperous business when other companies were running at a loss or lying still." The depressions of 1854 and 1857 saw some local mills standing idle or working at a fraction of their capacity. Ironically, they included Northampton Woolen, whose employees were thrown out of work when the firm went bankrupt and its president was arrested for conspiring to remove property from the reach of the assignees.[64]

In addition to reductions in work hours and bankruptcy, workers faced other risks to their employment. Accidents were common; one of the worst, in 1859, killed several men when a boiler exploded at a Northampton machine works. Fire was a constant threat, especially but

62. U.S. Census, 1850, 1860: Population.

63. Henry F. Hills to Adelaide Spencer, Amherst, Sept 25, 1860, Hills Family Papers, Box 1, folder 3, ACA.

64. MA 46:106; on the firm's failure, see *Hampshire Gazette*, Mar 9, Sept 21, and Oct 26, 1858. It was alleged that, knowing the company to be insolvent, Thomas Musgrave arranged to sell some of its goods through a relative in New York, who would then claim for losses against the assignees: Commonwealth v. Musgrave, Hampshire County Superior Court Files, Criminal, Box 1, no. 26 (1858), Hampshire County Courthouse, Northampton.

not solely in wooden factory buildings. Few millsites or factory owners avoided having buildings destroyed at some point in their careers. There were at least eighteen factory fires in Northampton alone between 1840 and 1860. One site in North Amherst suffered repeated burnings; during a fire in 1857 that completely destroyed the mill, operatives, many of whom were women, had to jump out of second-story windows to escape the flames.[65] Greater than the risk of injury was the certainty that mills would close for considerable periods and workers would be forced to seek employment elsewhere.

When they were employed, workers were often under strong pressure to produce. Luther Bodman wrote of his scythe-snath business in 1852 that the "hands work like dogs this winter . . . 'holing away' . . . trying hard to do work to suit me." But the fluctuations and instabilities of manufacturing in practice tempered the effect of employers' efforts to enforce stricter work discipline on their workers. During the lumber boom of the 1840s and 1850s, some sawmills worked around the clock in the early spring of each year. J. Adams, an owner of extensive woodlands in Hadley, advertised in 1846 for "a man to tend Saw Mill . . . to saw nights and rest days until July next." But the diary of a young man who got a job in a sawmill and woodworking shop in 1853 shows that patterns of work varied considerably. From mid-March onward he worked mainly at the sawmill, with occasional breaks of up to a day for farm tasks. Regular mill and shop work, including midnight-to-midday stints at the sawmill, lasted until early May. From then until October, much of his time was taken up with work on the land; only after mid-October did he return to the mill and shop, with occasional half-days off for hog killings and other tasks.[66] Workers often had latitude, however, to set their own pace of work. The paucity of local factory records makes judgment difficult, but it appears that in many textile mills and other factories where goods were produced in batches, wages were paid by the piece. Otis Hill of Williamsburg, in diary references to work in his brother's button factory, suggested that his work rate varied by one-quarter or more from one day to the next.[67] A newspaper article on hat making remarked that "each girl knows it all depends on herself whether she will have good wages or not." This of course was only a partial truth. Reports appeared from time to time of workers' exceptional achievements at production. In 1849, for example, Mary Ann Hall, a weaver at the Amherst mill of Smith, Cutler and Company,

65. Reports of the boiler explosion at Hiram Wells and Co. were in the *Hampshire Gazette*, July 12, 19, 1859; reports of fires were drawn from various newspapers, 1840–1860.

66. Luther Bodman, Jr. to Joseph Bodman, Charlemont, Jan 25, 1852, Bodman Family Papers, Box 3; advertisement in *Hampshire and Franklin Express*, Jan 26, 1846; anon. diary for 1853 in Whitmarsh Family Papers, NHS Collection, FL.

67. Otis G. Hill, Diary, 1863, WHS.

wove 2,500 yards of cotton cloth in two weeks, averaging wages of six dollars a week. But while this was equivalent to a good day-laboring rate for a man, it was impossible to sustain over a long period and most women textile workers earned half that amount or less. It was, in any case, a small fraction of the sale value of the product. In this instance, assuming that cotton cloth sold for six cents a yard, Mary Ann Hall received just 8 percent of its value in wages.[68]

Instability and low wage rates shaped workers' resistance to the work discipline they were subjected to. As the historian Jonathan Prude has shown, workers in rural Massachusetts mill villages rarely in this period took collective action to protest against their employers or the conditions they faced. It is possible that Hampshire County women were among the workers who struck in protest at wage cuts by mills in Chicopee in 1843, but few if any similar incidents occurred in local factories. If anything, immigrant workers were more likely to act collectively. Twice in 1848 alone Irish construction workers struck for better pay and conditions; in one incident on the railroad near Northampton, strikers assaulted the sheriff sent to disperse them and dragged him off his horse.[69] Yankee and immigrant mill workers most often took individual action. When a fire burned down William Clark's paper mill in Northampton in 1860, putting seventy-five men and women out of work, a former employee was charged with setting it to settle a grudge. A workman in South Hadley even resorted to blackmailing his employer, allegedly threatening to spread stories of sexual misconduct by a fellow worker so that local parents would refuse to permit their daughters to work at the factory. But in the majority of cases of dissatisfaction, workers simply walked off the job, like John Nutting, who "took his sixpence" from Easthampton in 1841.[70]

Transiency and Permanence

Although the shortage of factory records prevents precise measurement of labor turnover rates, it is evident that factory workers were among the most geographically mobile of all people in the Valley. Edward Jenner Carpenter, a physician's son from Bernardston, worked in a North Amherst mill for a time in the early 1840s, when he was about sixteen, leaving again to work in Greenfield in 1842. Two and one-half

68. *Hampshire Gazette*, Mar 20, 1849.
69. Jonathan Prude, *The Coming of Industrial Order: A Study of Town and Factory Life in Rural Massachusetts, 1813–1860* (Cambridge, Eng., 1983), chap. 5; the construction workers' actions were reported in the *Hampshire and Franklin Express*, Jan 13, Mar 9, 1848.
70. *Commonwealth v. Maynard*, Hampshire County Superior Court Files, Criminal, Box 2, no. 3 (1860). The South Hadley case is in Hampshire County Court of Common Pleas, Records, 30:515–522.

years later, he went back to visit, but "did not find but three there that was there when I worked there." In 1859 Hills's hat factory in Amherst gave prizes to the ten best women workers that season. The next year only six of them were listed in the census.[71] Of sixty-two men who filed naturalization petitions in Northampton in 1844 and 1845, only fifteen (24 percent) were listed in the census of 1850. Of the textile workers, 76 percent had left. Of all men in their twenties when they filed their petitions, 83 percent had left. Very few of the factory operatives who worked in Northampton in 1850 were still there ten years later. Only one man of the eighty-seven men and women working in the Williamsburg mills in 1850 was still doing the same in 1860. All the rest had left town or turned to other occupations.[72]

High mobility and labor turnover did, in many instances, reflect the willingness of younger workers in particular to move from job to job in search of better wages or conditions. Factory work remained, for both sexes, predominantly a youthful occupation. Both in 1850 and 1860, nine out of ten women operatives in Williamsburg were under thirty, and few worked in the mills after marriage. High turnover rates gave workers with key skills the opportunity to play on employers' anxieties about sudden labor shortages to negotiate for better terms somewhere else.[73] Judith McGaw, however, in her studies of the Berkshire County paper and textile industries, has suggested that certain groups of workers opted for job security, when they could get it, in preference to high wage rates. The high proportion of workers who moved out of the region suggests that many of the Williamsburg and Northampton mills were chronically unable to provide this kind of stability, even to those who sought it.[74] Coupled with the inability of most workers to accumulate any property, it suggests that factory workers were in danger of slipping into a perpetually poor underclass, with transiency their only hope of altering their position.

That this condition was becoming more permanent during the 1850s is reflected in the swinging balance of age and gender among Williamsburg operatives. While at least 53 percent of them were women in 1850, by 1860, 63 percent were men. Census evidence shows that the average wage differential between men and women was narrowing, suggesting

71. Edward J. Carpenter, "The Diary of an Apprentice Cabinetmaker: Edward Jenner Carpenter's 'Journal,' 1844–1845," ed. Christopher Clark, *Proceedings of the American Antiquarian Society* 98 (1988), entry for Oct 9, 1844; for the Hills workers, see Aron, "Minds of Hands," p. 102.

72. Naturalization petitions, Hampshire County Court of Common Pleas, Records, vol. 30, nos. 200–275 (1844), and Hampshire County Court of Common Pleas, Files, no. 359 (1845); U.S. Census, 1850, 1860, Population Schedules.

73. U.S. Census, 1850, 1860: Population.

74. Judith A. McGaw, "'A Good Place to Work': Industrial Workers and Occupational Choice: The Case of Berkshire Women," *Journal of Interdisciplinary History* 10 (Autumn 1979): 227–248.

that men's wages were being depressed in the direction of the traditionally lower rates at which women's work was paid for. Moreover, although textile workers remained a youthful group, they were getting older. Women, who were twenty or twenty-one years old on average in 1850, now averaged twenty-three. Men, formerly twenty-four or twenty-five on average, were now over twenty-seven. Indeed, the proportion of men aged thirty or over rose during the decade from 24 percent to 35 percent of all male operatives. In absolute terms this meant that while Williamsburg in 1850 had only ten factory operatives aged thirty or more, ten years later it had seventy-seven. A growing proportion of people faced the prospect of insecure factory work for the rest of their lives.[75]

Population growth, wealth inequalities, and in particular the growth of propertylessness brought about a partial but significant shift in the functions the Valley's households fulfilled for the manufacturing sector. The early growth of rural manufactures had been fueled by households' search for "careers" for their offspring, something that they perceived as new activities undertaken within the existing frameworks of rural society. This made labor available for outwork, or to work in workshops and factories, but frequently on a seasonal or intermittent basis: irregular work patterns characterized broom making, the outwork trades, and other industries reliant on agricultural labor and raw materials. Even in trades such as shoemaking, subject to competition from outside the region, agricultural rhythms impinged on the work process; until shortly before he left Massachusetts, for instance, Lucius Graham of Buckland would take time off from his workbench each summer to go haying. The growth in the numbers of migrant workers, the new concentrations of capital and labor that this growth permitted, and the increasing proportion of the work force without property, for whom manufacture was a primary source of livelihood, meant that the function of many households was changing from the provision of careers for offspring to the provision of permanent wage laborers for capitalists. High labor turnover and migration rates meant that few individuals stayed for long in one place of work, but the proportion of the population who relied on such work increased markedly.

A New Economic Hierarchy

As wage labor increased, Northampton and nearby towns sported signs of commercial and industrial prosperity, which marked them off from the poorer hill towns. The completion of the Connecticut River

75. U.S. Census, 1850, 1860: Population.

Railroad through Northampton from Springfield to Greenfield in the mid-1840s placed many of the farms and factories in the bottomlands within easy reach of rail transport; the Amherst and Belchertown Railroad to Palmer, opened in 1854, would likewise connect the eastern side of the Valley with larger New England centers. Northampton's Main Street bore witness to the town's comparative wealth and influence. In 1849 the *Hampshire Gazette* praised the "spirit of enterprise and improvement" that had accompanied its new expansion, citing the evidence of a new town hall, a new bank building, newly constructed or refurbished stores, the large number of new, well-furnished houses, and "the outward adorning . . . generally prevalent." Five years later the paper reported the completion by the merchant S. C. Parsons of a new store building, whose three-story edifice was the first iron-fronted building in Hampshire County, and whose facade alone, complete with French plate-glass windows, was reputed to have cost $1,300.[76] This concern with outward signs of prosperity, especially on the part of merchants, revealed consciousness of Northampton's place in an economic hierarchy whose order had begun to shift rapidly with the opening of railroads and new accumulations of capital.

Northampton was able to assert an influence on the region around it more powerful than at any time since the late eighteenth century. The town's stock-in-trade, assessed at $281,000 in 1860, was not only far higher than that of any other in the county but represented a per capita concentration greater than that of any outlying town. As its stores grew in number and became more specialized, people of other towns were conscious of relying on services that only Northampton could provide. At the Hadley bicentenary in 1859 a speaker remarked that when a freshet had damaged the Northampton-Hadley bridge and forced its closure, the people of the smaller town had realized how often they used Northampton stores, banks, and lawyers' offices. Even Amherst's leaders, who conducted a fierce rivalry with the shire town, could not deny Northampton's preeminence. "Our men trooped to her banks while for years we had none," wrote Susan Gilbert Dickinson, "and our ladies pressed to her dressmakers or hung over the counter at Stoddard and Lathrop's in hope of some more distinctive elegance than Sweetser and Cutler could afford."[77]

This influence was shared to some extent among the prosperous towns in the center of the Valley. Sweetser, Cutler and Company, Amherst's leading store, drew three-fifths or more of its customers from

---

76. *Hampshire Gazette*, May 29, 1849, and Aug 29, 1854.

77. *Celebration of the Two Hundredth Anniversary of the Settlement of Hadley, Massachusetts, at Hadley, June 8, 1859* (Northampton, 1859), p. 88; Susan Gilbert Dickinson, "Two Generations of Amherst Society," in *Essays on Amherst's History* (Amherst, 1978), p. 169.

within the town, but the remainder were from sixteen other towns throughout a region stretching into Hampden and Worcester counties. By 1856 Northampton, Hadley, Amherst, and Williamsburg between them had a concentration of economic power unrivaled in the county. They had eight out of thirteen druggists, six out of eight booksellers, four of six watchmakers, four of five hardware stores and six of eleven milliners. They had an even stronger hold on the professions, with fifteen of twenty-two lawyers, five of seven insurance agents, the only architects, and the only brokers.[78]

Nevertheless, this hierarchy was also linked to an increasing degree to outside markets. One measure of this linkage was the extent to which credit reports were sought on local firms and individuals by subscribers to Lewis Tappan's Mercantile Agency and its successors; for Amherst new entries were made at an average rate of three each year from 1842 to 1849, four a year from 1850 to 1855, and seven a year between 1856 and 1860. Exports of local farm produce and manufactured goods and the increasing inward shipments of consumption goods of all kinds meant that Northampton and its vicinity were subjected to influences from cities and regions well beyond the Valley. They depended on significant quantities of imported basic foodstuffs and other items. As woodland was cleared and the price of firewood increased, some families started to use imported coal for cooking and heating. Dealers in shoes, furniture, stoves, and agricultural implements were by the 1850s less concerned with manufacturing and selling local products than with retailing those made elsewhere. After a protracted dispute among the directors of the Connecticut River Railroad, Northampton even lost its repair shops to Springfield. Concern about outside influences and competition was central to the consciousness of the area's traders, manufacturers, and craftsmen. When, in the late 1840s, a local newspaper published the advertisements of a Boston clothing firm, its editor faced the public disapproval of one of Northampton's leading merchant tailors.[79]

Wealth: Its Forms and Distribution

The growing control by entrepreneurs over business and labor meant that place in the wider economic hierarchy was associated with increasing local social division and inequality. These inequalities varied from

78. Adams, *Mass. Business Directory*, pp. 114–123.
79. Credit reports in MA 46:1–120, 1842–1861; Gere, *Reminiscences of Old Northampton*, p. 41.

town to town (Table 12). They were much starker in Northampton than in Amherst, for example, though there the contrasts were again greater than in a hill town such as Westhampton. But in all three towns, wealth was more unequally distributed than it had been early in the century. Even in Amherst in 1860 over 40 percent of the taxable population owned no real estate, and just over one-quarter were not taxed on property at all, whereas two generations before fewer than one in ten had been in this position. Fully one-half of Northampton's people had no taxable real or personal property. Wealth was concentrated particularly in the hands of the richest 10 percent. In 1859, 178 individuals were taxed on property of $5,000 or more. This was about 4.5 percent of Northampton's adult population, about one in ten of its families.[80]

Inequalities were evident in the quantity of property that people held, the forms that it took, and the ways they could use it. There were divisions between the propertied and the propertyless, but also between wealth holders themselves, whose access to the benefits of a more diversified, national commercial and financial marketplace varied greatly. There was a distinction between those who continued to rely on older patterns of family support and neighborhood assistance and those who participated in institutional forms and diversified property holdings.

Local, private networks of credit remained significant in the 1850s. The administrators' accounts of fifty-one individuals from the six towns who died early in the decade listed among their personal property a total of $112,000 worth of stocks, insurance policies, cash, notes, and book debts owed or owing. Of this total, over $53,000 consisted of debts and credits owed to or by individuals. Thirty decedents had outstanding notes worth a total of $38,480, an average of $1,282.67 each. Twenty-two had book accounts to be settled worth at least $15,000, an average of just over $680 each. Most of these notes and accounts were with other people within the region. Personal loans and credit run up in the course of business continued to play a substantial role in financing production and trade. They also played an important role in town finances. Am-

---

80. Amherst, Tax Valuation List, 1860, Amherst Town Hall. Westhampton, Tax Valuation List, 1855, Westhampton Town Hall. Northampton data are from Robert Doherty, *Society and Power: Five New England Towns, 1800–1860* (Amherst, 1977), pp. 47 and 51, tables 5.1 and 5.3. Gloria L. Main, "Inequality in Early America: The Evidence from Probate Records of Massachusetts and Maryland," *Journal of Interdisciplinary History* 7 (Spring 1977): 567, 574, tables 3, 4, gives Gini coefficients of the inequality of wealth distributed among inventoried men of .54 for the period 1750–1754 ("old" Hampshire County), .56 for 1829–1831 ("new" Hampshire County), and .69 for 1859–1861 ("new" Hampshire County), suggesting that inequality may have increased significantly in the three decades before the Civil War after a long period without much change.

Table 12. Percentage of taxable wealth held by each decile of population in Amherst, Northampton, and Westhampton, 1800/10–1855/60

	Population decile[a]									
	1	2	3	4	5	6	7	8	9	10
Northampton										
1800	50.0	18.5	12.5	8.5	6.0	3.5	1.0	0	0	0
1860	72.0	19.0	8.0	1.0	0	0	0	0	0	0
Amherst										
1800	30.9	19.3	14.0	11.0	9.0	6.9	5.0	2.4	1.4	0.1
1860	47.2	19.7	13.8	8.9	5.6	3.3	1.4	0.1	0	0
Westhampton										
1810	27.9	18.3	14.8	10.8	9.4	8.1	5.2	3.4	1.9	0.2
1855	32.3	18.7	15.4	12.2	8.0	6.0	3.9	2.8	0.7	0

[a]Decile numbers are from richest (1) to poorest (10).

Sources: Amherst, Tax Valuation List, 1860, Amherst Town Hall; Westhampton, Tax Valuation List, 1855, Westhampton Town Hall; Northampton data are from Robert Doherty, *Society and Power: Five New England Towns, 1800–1860* (Amherst, 1977), pp. 47 and 51, tables 5.1 and 5.3.

herst, for example, had no funded debt until 1860. It had relied instead on personal loans from townspeople to cover its outstanding obligations.[81]

A majority of traders and small manufacturers continued to run their businesses as family enterprises. Of thirty-six stores in Northampton in 1860, twenty-one were held by individual proprietors and another three by family partnerships. Only twelve, one-third of the total, were owned by nonfamily partnerships. The family firms included old businesses, such as that belonging to Ansel Wright and Sons. Formerly belonging to a partnership, Wright and Rust, this grocery and provisions store had been bought out by Wright so that he could take his two brothers into the business with him. By the late 1850s, the brothers in turn had relinquished their interest in the store, and Wright ran it with his two sons.[82] Other family-owned stores included two run by immigrants. Michael Williams, an Irishman in his fifties, accumulated real estate and other property worth up to $15,000 during the decade out of the profits of a flour dealership that expanded rapidly with the town's growing population. He, too, had sons as partners, and the 1860 census listed Williams's twenty-five-year-old daughter as a clerk in the store. Lewis

81. Hampshire County, Probate Records, vols. 48, 49, 52. On town debt, see Carpenter and Morehouse, *History of Amherst*, p. 589.

82. Data based on advertisements in the *Hampshire Gazette*, 1860. On Wright, see MA 46:102.

McIntire, who ran the town's other similar business, had started out in partnership with a local printer but in 1854 had bought him out and continued the business on his own.[83]

Still, these networks and businesses, though numerically common, did not account for the most prominent local concerns, either in trade or manufacture. The one-third of Northampton stores owned by non-family partnerships included most of those considered the "leading" businesses in town. William Stoddard, the most prominent dry-goods merchant, conducted his store from the 1830s to the 1850s in partnership with a series of other men. When, in 1856, he sought out a final partner to whom the business would pass when he retired, Stoddard chose his clerk Benjamin Lincoln, rather than a member of his own family. In Amherst, Luke Sweetser likewise sold out to his partners when he retired from trade in 1854, retaining no family interest in the concern he had run for nearly thirty years. For these men business was becoming separable from family finances.[84]

Larger businessmen also came to distrust the risks of relying on personal networks of loans and credit. We saw earlier how Truman Nutting's tool shops became vulnerable through the deaths of three creditors. Sweetser's own large loans in 1850 were predominantly to members of his family or to his business partners in whose affairs he had an interest. The hat business of L. M. Hills and Company weathered the financial crisis of 1857–1858, but not without some anxiety on the part of its owners. Just when its own bank was unable to discount notes, wrote Henry F. Hills, a rumor spread in Amherst that the firm had failed, and "several who had brought money for us to keep for them became frightened and came for it."[85]

Lenders to the Northampton firm of White, Smith and Company were not so lucky; in 1858 they received a sharp lesson in the dangers of personal loans. Founded in 1853 by three local businessmen, the most prominent of whom, Charles Smith, was a respected merchant tailor, this company manufactured enameled cloth for use on upholstery, railroad car seats, and other purposes. Having experimented with production techniques, the firm enjoyed two years' success after 1856. But with credit squeezed by the crisis, the partners suddenly discovered that their New York agent—another Northampton man—had run up $30,000 in debts from unauthorized discounts and cash unaccounted for and then had falsified accounts to hide them. The firm's collapse, which

83. For Williams, see U.S. Census, 1860: Population. For McIntire, see MA 46:110.
84. For Stoddard, see MA 46:102; for Sweetser, see MA 46:5.
85. Sweetser, Cutler and Co., Account Books, BCJL. Henry F. Hills to Adelaide Spencer, Amherst, Oct 28, 1857, Hills Family Papers.

quickly followed, brought difficulty to many Northampton lenders who "had loaned most of their available funds, in small sums ranging from $7,000 to $300, amounting in all to about $60,000." "Few if any disasters of the kind," noted the *Hampshire Gazette*, "have so seriously affected the community." After anxious creditors' meetings, assets amounting to $75,000—less than half the firm's liabilities—were liquidated. Even fifteen years later it was still rumored in Northampton that Charles Smith had signed property into his wife's name to place it beyond creditors' reach.[86]

Advantage under these circumstances rested with the small proportion of men who had sufficient wealth to diversify their property holdings. Several Northampton and Williamsburg traders and manufacturers, for example, owned farmland. William Clark, a paper manufacturer, held 320 acres in 1850, as well as interests in woodlands in partnership with a local merchant. Otis and Hiram Hill, Williamsburg button makers, owned more than three hundred acres between them. Thomas Musgrave, president of the Northampton Woolen Manufacturing Company, had seventy-five acres.[87] Wealthier men than they branched out into stocks, mortgages, and other paper holdings as well. Over $45,000 in corporate stocks, banks, and insurance policies enumerated in probate records in the early 1850s belonged to just two wealthy Northampton men. One of them, Samuel Lyman Hinckley, a lawyer and judge, had accumulated large holdings in railroad and bank stock, western land mortgages and titles, and other investments outside the region. At the same time, he owned local farm and house properties and lent funds to stores, workshops, and other businesses. He was in a strong position to do this. Unlike the creditors of White, Smith and Company, who put much of their available funds into the one enterprise, Hinckley and a handful of other men had sufficiently diverse holdings to make investments without undue risk.[88]

86. White, Smith and Co.'s activities were described in "The Manufacture of Enamelled Cloth," *Hunt's Merchant's Magazine* 36 (Feb 1857): 254–255; Smith's failure was reported by the *Hampshire Gazette*, Sept 28, 1858, whose notion of a "small sum" well exceeded a farm laborer's annual wages; creditor's meetings were noted in the *Hampshire Gazette*, Oct 26, 1858, and Ansel Wright, Diary, Northampton, entry for Jan 6, 1859, MCFL; see also MA 46:51 (Charles Smith).

87. Manufacturers' landholdings were identified from U.S. Seventh Census, Non-Population Schedules, 1850, Massachusetts: Agriculture, Massachusetts Archives, Boston, Mass. Credit reports are in MA 46:110 (Clark), 46:107 (Musgrave).

88. Samuel Lyman Hinckley's Account Book, apparently used by his executors to wind up his estate, listed his interests in two local manufactories, the bridge and railroad companies, his two farms, two stores and several houses and houselots, together with extensive holdings in Illinois land and in railroad and mining shares (Northampton, 1853–1861, NHS, A.A.18.67).

Financial Networks

The influence of Hinckley and others was especially significant in two spheres: financing local manufacturing and backing local banks and other corporate institutions. Fifty years ago, the historian Agnes Hannay identified the connections between what she referred to as the "Florence group" of manufacturers. They were the backers and managers primarily responsible for the revival and expansion of Northampton textiles in the late 1840s and early 1850s, which they based on a nucleus of silk mills in the factory village they named Florence. In ten firms organized or reorganized between 1846 and 1861, in six sets of buildings near the Mill River, a total of thirty-four partners' and directors' positions were filled by just seventeen men. Some, like Samuel L. Hill, a former textile mill manager and member of the Northampton Association for Education and Industry, obtained positions in charge of several firms, first as an organizer and later as a financial backer. By the late 1850s Hill had interests in the Florence general store and post office; a silk mill, the Nonotuck Silk Company; a button and daguerrotype-case manufactory, Littlefield, Parsons and Company; and a machine shop, the Wells, Littlefield Company, which became the Florence Sewing Machine Company in 1861. Others, like the Hayden brothers of Williamsburg, used their connections with this group to add to their already extensive manufacturing interests. Joel Hayden shared interests in the Haydenville store and the Florence cotton mill belonging to the Greenville Manufacturing Company with D. G. Littlefield, who was to become a leading figure in the button and machine shops. Behind these men stood investors such as Hinckley—who backed the Nonotuck Silk Company and Littlefield, Parsons and Company—and the manufacturers Samuel and John P. Williston, who invested in the Greenville Company. Although other men, including skilled machinists, were brought into this network of proprietors, financial backing for it was channeled by a small, identifiable set of investors.[89]

The stability that these men's backing could bring to their companies was reflected in their generally better fortune during the 1850s than that of factories outside the group. As we have seen, two of the latter, Northampton Woolen and White, Smith and Company, failed entirely in the late 1850s. The Florence group of mills and machine shops had periods of closure and reduced working hours, but it stayed afloat into the 1870s, sponsoring various reorganizations and improvements. Among the backers of the Williamsburg Reservoir Company in 1865, for

89. Hannay, "Chronicle of Industry," pp. 77–79. See also MA 46:113 (S. L. Hill); 46:114 (J.P. Williston); 46:116 (Greenville Mfg. Co.).

instance, were Samuel Hill and A. T. Lilly of the Nonotuck Silk Company; Joel Hayden of the Greenville Company; William Clark and Company; and A. P. Critchlow, a former partner with Hill and others in button manufacture.[90]

Unlike the members of Northampton's late-eighteenth-century elite, who sought to profit from activities such as road and bridge building that were still essentially marginal to the Valley's economy at that time, these men were investing directly in production. But Hinckley, the Haydens, and the Willistons also provided a connection between this network and another important group of Northampton investors, whose interests lay in running and financing the town's banks and emerging utility companies. By 1860 there were seven incorporated companies, whose fifty-four directors' and officers' positions were filled by just twenty-eight men, twenty-four of whom lived in Northampton. Prominent merchants, such as William Stoddard, and wealthy investors, such as Eliphalet Williams, J. H. Butler, and Judge Samuel F. Lyman, were key links in this network alongside Hinckley and the Willistons. Butler, Williams, and Hinckley had been directors of the Northampton Bank. Samuel Williston and Joel Hayden were on the board of the Holyoke Bank, its main rival. Lyman, Butler, Stoddard, and Hayden's cotton-manufacturing partner, A. D. Sanders, were directors of the Northampton Institution for Savings. In addition, Butler and Lyman served on the board of the Hampshire Mutual Life Insurance Company; Butler, Williams, and Hinckley had been directors or senior officers of the Connecticut River Railroad Company; and Williams and Butler were directors of the Northampton Bridge Company. On the board of the town's newest venture, the Northampton Gas Light Company, was Charles White, director and cashier of the Northampton Bank and a director of the savings bank and the bridge company.[91]

Their connections with banks and other institutions did not give these men complete power over operations. As in their manufacturing companies, they shared directorships with less prominent men, some of whom sat only on one board. But between them, these interlocking directorates concentrated economic power in relatively few hands. While manufacturing gave them profits from production, banks and insurance companies allowed these men to benefit from the expansion of the cash economy and the increasing use borrowers and lenders

90. Williamsburg Reservoir Co., Record Book, FL. On the social and philanthropic activities of members of the group, see Charles A. Sheffeld, *History of Florence, Massachusetts, Including a Complete Account of the Northampton Association of Education and Industry* (Florence, 1895).

91. Officers of these companies were identified in *Northampton General Directory* (Northampton, 1860).

made of financial institutions for credit. These institutions reflected and reinforced inequalities, not only because they were controlled by a small group, but because they channeled services and profits unevenly.

Shareholdings in Northampton corporations were held much more widely than the seats on their boards, but ownership was nevertheless largely restricted to particular groups. There were 118 Northampton residents who held shares in the two leading banks, the railroad company, and the gas company in 1860. This represented only about 3 percent of the town's adult population. Of these individuals, 56, or just under half, were men who owned property worth $5,000 or more—in other words, men from the richest tenth of the population. Another 31 shareholders were women, most of them also members of prosperous families. When the Connecticut River Railroad Company was established in the 1840s it had been criticized for distributing locally held shares too narrowly. As Amherst town leaders projected the Amherst and Belchertown Railroad in the early 1850s, lack of interest from outside investors obliged them to seek widespread local support. Share subscription lists were carried throughout the towns the road would cross, and several hundred people—many of them farmers and artisans—signed up for shares. By 1854, when the line opened, there were at least 110 stockholders in Amherst alone. But the road's fortunes were a discouragement from such widespread ownership of shares. The company, deep in debt, had to be reorganized in 1857. Of the original $300,000 capital raised, $195,000 was wiped off the value of its stock. By 1860, holdings in the company were much more narrowly distributed. By then only twenty-three Amherst taxpayers held its stock, barely a fifth of the previous number and a group barely larger than the twenty-one residents of the town who owned any other type of share that year.[92] Corporate capitalism was for the few, not the many.

This turned out to be true even of institutions trumpeted as pioneers of wider popular involvement in capitalism—savings banks. Like those in larger cities, the Northampton Institution for Savings had been founded to encourage small investors to save spare cash and to participate in the growing financial system. After reorganization in about 1853 the bank evidently fulfilled this role to some extent. Between 1854 and 1860 more than 1,200 people opened accounts there. If only half of them had lived in Northampton, this would have represented a group almost

92. Shareholdings were identified from returns and correspondence for 1860, Northampton Tax Assessors' Records, Town Papers Collection, 5.71, FL; see Thelma M. Kistler, "The Rise of Railroads in the Connecticut River Valley," *Smith College Studies in History* 23 (1937–1938): 56–60, 77–78, 88–89, for share subscriptions to the Connecticut River and Amherst and Belchertown companies. Share ownership in Amherst was measured from Tax Assessors' Records, 1854 and 1860, Amherst Town Hall.

six times larger than the local shareholders we just examined. Evidence from nine months of business after the bank reopened in 1854 suggests that depositors were varied in wealth and background. Members of prosperous Northampton families deposited money there, but the bank was also used by poorer people. Fifty-eight percent of individuals' accounts—as opposed to those held in trust—were in women's names. The first depositor was an Irish laborer, the second a young North-ampton domestic servant whose account was opened by her employer. Of the early depositors over one-quarter had Irish names. Among the first 137 depositors, at least 1 male and 13 females put marks rather than signatures in the signature book.[93]

While the bank's charter laid down firm guidelines for accepting deposits, it gave officers broad discretion to make loans and invest-ments. The bank's cash book allows us to trace who it extended its credit to. In 1860 this was a markedly different group from the depositors we have just examined. A total of 133 individuals and firms paid interest on loans that year. Of these 92 (69 percent) can be identified from census and other evidence. Only 4 were women. Few if any had Irish names. Of the 88 men about whom information was gathered, a total of 55 (62.5 percent) were partners in trading firms, bank officers or investors, merchants or storekeepers, or manufacturers with more than a handful of employees. Another 13 percent were farmers from Northampton or surrounding towns. Just under 10 percent were small craftsmen and another 10 percent were lawyers.[94] The bank was therefore borrowing money from a wide group, including women and poor people whose cash savings were often their only independent assets, and lending it to people—mainly men—who were already property holders in good credit. The savings bank maintained inequality, turning the poor into lenders and the prosperous into borrowers.

In Northampton, as in other New England business centers, bank loans were significant in the finance of entrepreneurial activity. Among the savings bank's borrowers in 1860 was the button manufacturer A. P. Critchlow, whose $1,250 credit from the bank was equivalent to 15.3 percent of the total wages and materials costs of his business that year. The hatter Nathan Dikeman borrowed $275, which was equivalent to 31 percent of his much smaller variable costs.[95] Without bank credit men

93. Northampton Institution for Savings, Signature Book, 1854–1869, held at the bank's offices in Northampton. I am grateful to Richard Wall and Richard Stewart of the Northampton Institution for Savings for permitting me to consult this and other docu-ments, and for making copies available to me.

94. Northampton Institution for Savings, Daily Cash Book, 1858–1863.

95. Wages and materials costs were taken from U.S. Census, 1860: Manufactures. On the importance of kinship and local connections in banking and the banks' role in

such as Critchlow and Dikeman would have had to turn to their neighbors and associates for assistance, something that experience had taught was a risky proposition. The bank gave a more stable source of credit to relatively prosperous men, many of whom would previously have arranged private loans to one another. Its credit was more stable because it drew on the resources of a broader segment of the population. Not merely capitalists but people from among the working poor now contributed capital to business. At the same time, bank officers exercised a greater degree of discipline over the local economy.

Rich and Poor

After listening to the sermon at Northampton's First Church one Sunday in January 1843, Sylvester Judd noted that the minister had "preached on the rich and the poor, and advanced the sentiment, commonly used, that all the distinctions in society were from God." Judd disagreed: "Many of the distinctions and inequalities among men come from the selfishness, avarice and ambition of those who call themselves upper classes, who have governed the world for their own benefit, and not for the advantage of the many." Twelve years later another minister, dismissed from the same church for doctrinal liberalism, drew attention in his final sermon to the divisions between rich and poor, "said some hard things against the rich, and spoke strongly in favor of the middling classes and poor." His departure may have contributed to Judd's own decision to leave the church in 1856.[96] But while the lines of economic division in the Valley were becoming clearer and the relative advantages and disadvantages of an emerging industrial capitalist and market system apparent for different groups, social and political divisions were not clear-cut. Society was being divided, not simply into rich and poor, but into more complex fragments. These shifts were apparent not only in the town centers and manufacturing villages, but also on the farms, which were at the heart of the rural economy.

channeling capital to industry, see Andrew A. Beveridge, "Local Lending Practice: Borrowers in a Small Northeastern Industrial City, 1832–1915," *Journal of Economic History* 45 (1985): 393–403, and Naomi Lamoreaux, "Banks, Kinship and Economic Development: The New England Case," *Journal of Economic History* 46 (1986): 647–667.

96. Sylvester Judd, "Notebook," vol. 2, Jan 31, 1843; "Notebook," vol. 7, Jul 15, 1855, and Oct 9, 1856.

Chapter 8

Farmers, Markets, and Society in Mid-Century

The divisions and inequalities traced in Chapter 7 also affected farming. Agriculture remained the single largest occupation in the Valley. In Hadley, Hatfield, and Westhampton it employed between 70 percent and 85 percent of the workforce in 1860. Even in the more industrialized towns of Amherst, Northampton, and Williamsburg, farming still occupied between 30 percent and 40 percent. Without agricultural change many of the shifts to cash dealing and manufacturing would not have been as rapid or far-reaching as they were. At the same time, though, the changing structure of the nonfarm population, together with the reorganized production and exchange of manufactured goods, profoundly affected the agricultural economy. Change on the land and in the nonfarm economy together propelled farmers and their households into a new economic world between 1830 and 1860. As greater quantities of agricultural produce were imported to the region or shipped out from it, and as farmers became increasingly dependent on outside markets for their livelihoods, exogamous influences on the rural economy were more important than ever.

Continuity and Change

On the face of it, some things altered little over this period. Patterns of local, noncash exchange between households persisted in farming districts. John F. Warner, who owned a 170-acre farm in Northampton, frequently swapped with neighbors and provided produce in return for work in the 1850s. During 1854 he provided boards and timber for Zenas Field, Jr., receiving ashes, a sled, candles, and an adjustment on a third party's account in exchange; Patrick Carran worked for him and took part of his pay in lard, corn, rye, and beef, together with an axhelve, a pig, and a turkey. The same year in Westhampton, Jared Bartlett gave Thomas Davenport pine boards worth $10.42 and later took in exchange six bushels of lime, a flatiron, and "a flute to balance." Long repayment periods and laxity in calculation could still be found. Estes Wilson took $1.16 worth of goods from the small store kept by his Belchertown neighbor Asahel Goodale in 1849. The next year, he gave Goodale a note for the amount. Goodale left it in his papers, endorsing it once for $0.75 when Wilson brought him some potatoes. Only in 1853, three and a half years after receiving the note did Goodale move to settle it. He agreed to take a barrel of cider from Wilson for $1.50. Since this now left him $1.09 in debt to Wilson, Goodale paid off a dollar Wilson owed another man and canceled the note. This of course left Wilson $0.09 out of pocket. But although he had effectively paid Goodale interest, at a rate of about 2 percent a year, neither man set this down as part of the calculation. It remained an unspoken part of the agreement they had negotiated.[1]

Internally, farm households also continued to rest on the gender and age divisions, interdependence, and cooperation they had used in the past. In a parade at the Hadley bicentennial celebrations of 1859, a float depicting manufactures of the past included women spinning yarn and weaving cloth. But as the watchers well knew, the passing of the domestic textile industry had merely shifted the character of women's household work. In addition to cooking, cleaning, and looking after children, women undertook the myriad tasks associated with preserving food, making and mending clothing, and keeping up their houses. Most farm families continued to make their own bread, for example, and many still made their own soap even after commercially produced lye became available.[2]

Women's work remained separate, functionally distinct from men's. A young Northampton woman expressed relief when enough snow fell to permit sleighing in 1852, so that the men on the farm could work in the woods "and we can do so much more when they are away and carry

1. John F. Warner, Ledger, Northampton, 1854–1861, MCFL; Jared Bartlett, entry in William and Solomon Bartlett, Account Books, Westhampton, 1704–1857, vol. 2, HBS; Note, Estes Wilson to Asahel Goodale, Belchertown, 1850, M. W. Goodell Collection, BCJL.

2. On breadmaking, see Mary Morton Hill, Diary, Mar 6, 1896, WHS. A young woman from eastern Massachusetts, who married into a Northampton family, noted when her mother-in-law made soap in 1850 that it was "the first time I ever saw any one making soap" (Mrs. John W. French, Diary, June 12, 1850, NHS, Archive Files [typescript]). Sylvester Judd, *History of Hadley, including the early history of Hatfield, South Hadley, Amherst and Granby, Mass.* (Northampton, 1863), p. 387, wrote (in a passage drafted in 1859) that "most families in Hadley still make their soap."

Table 13. Butter and cheese production in Amherst, Hadley, Hatfield, and Westhampton, 1860

	Amherst	Hadley	Hatfield	Westhampton
Butter output (lbs.)	72,159	96,310	47,328	34,645
Cheese output (lbs.)	37,030	900	0	2,560
Value of butter	$15,153	$20,225	$ 9,939	$ 7,275
Value of cheese	$ 4,258	$ 104	0	$ 294
Percentage of all farms producing				
butter	89.5	95.0	86.0	98.0
cheese	46.1	0.4	0	6.7
Mean value of butter, per farm producing it	$ 74.28	$ 88.70	$ 84.22	$ 81.75
Mean value of butter and cheese per dairy farm	$ 95.17	$ 89.13	$ 84.22	$ 85.10

Note: Dollar values are calculated for butter @ $0.21/lb. and for cheese @ $0.115/lb., prices reported for Northampton in Sylvester Judd, "Notebook," vol. 8, entry for January 1860, FL.

Source: U.S. Eighth Census, Non-Population Schedules, 1860, Massachusetts: Agriculture, National Archives, Washington, D.C. (microfilm).

their dinners."[3] But women's work was integrated in households' strategies of putting work together to make a livelihood. When Spencer Clark of Northampton was paid by his brother to take an elderly aunt to board on his farm, it was Clark's wife and family who did much of the work. When the aunt no longer lived with them, they took in other families to board instead. Similarly, Jared Bartlett of Westhampton contracted to board town paupers to eke out his household income; again this mainly involved women's work. In common with other farmers, Bartlett also hired out his son's labor in the neighborhood.[4]

Women and children also contributed directly to households' outside incomes. As we have seen, poorer households, as well as servants and unmarried women in more prosperous ones, made palm-leaf hats, button molds, suspenders, and other items, which they took out from local merchants and manufacturers. Much more widespread, however, was dairy production. Between 90 and 98 percent of farms kept cows in 1860. Of these the vast majority made butter or cheese (Table 13), responsibility for which lay with women and girls. Earnings from butter for the farms that produced it ranged from an average of $74.28 in Amherst, to $88.70 in Hadley. Factoring in the value of cheese made on the smaller number of farms that produced it raises the contribution of

3 Persis Clark to Charles Hillman, Northampton, Jan 6, 1852, NHS, A.L.18.37.
4. Spencer Clark, Account Book, Northampton, 1800–1856, NHS, A.A.18.21; Bartlett, Account Book, vol. 2.

women's dairy earnings to an average of $84.22 for Hatfield and $95.17 for Amherst. This was roughly equivalent to 40 or 45 percent of a fully employed laborer's annual wages, or between a tenth and a fifth of total farm earnings.[5]

The rhetoric of public speakers and editorial writers in praise of farming reflected this apparent stability. As they had done earlier in the century many continued to celebrate the republican simplicity and virtue of "yeoman freeholders" who remained, as one put it, "independent of the hazards and reverses to which commerce and manufactures are exposed." From the 1830s to the 1850s, farmers who read newspapers or listened to the speeches at agricultural fairs heard the "independence, quiet [and] comfort" of their way of life praised. Nothing did more to reinforce this view than the crisis of 1837 and its aftermath. In contrast to the upheavals faced by those engaged in commerce as a result of the panic, the *Northampton Courier* noted the "calm serenity and happy condition of the tiller of the soil."[6] Individuals thought the same. Chauncey Parkman Judd wrote in the summer of 1837, "I believe the people begin to think that agriculture is the only sure mode of getting a good living; they think that too many have left the plough for the workshop and the counter." Even after the depression was over the *Massachusetts State Record* continued to publish dire statistics of business failure as a warning to young men to stay in farming.[7] At an agricultural fair in 1845 Asahel Foote praised the moral superiority of the farmer who "receives . . . the substantial necessaries of life . . . *directly* from the hand of the Great Giver," and relies on "honest industry" rather than "the success with which he can drive a rival trade." Here, too, individuals concurred. Farms were families' property, not to be lightly traded away. "I am glad to hear that you have moved back to the *old* stand," wrote one man to a relative in 1840. "There you ought to live and die, it is a house your Father gave you and no trifling sum ought to tempt you to move out of it."[8]

The fact that most farmers raised many of the basic products required for subsistence reinforced the validity of these views. Farm production patterns maintained many of the characteristics of the subsistence-surplus strategies of early in the century. Evidence from Hatfield and Westhampton, the two towns with the highest percentage of farmers

5. U.S. Eighth Census, Non-Population Schedules, 1860, Massachusetts: Agriculture, National Archives, Washington, D.C. (microfilm).

6. *Northampton Courier*, July 19, 1837.

7. Chauncey P. Judd to Apphia Judd, Hartford, May 9, 1837, Judd Papers, 55-M1, Box 2, HCL; *Massachusetts State Record and Yearbook of General Information, 1848* (Boston, 1848), pp. 216–217.

8. Address to the Berkshire Agricultural Society, 1845, reprinted in *New England Farmer*, Jan 21, 28, 1846; Ezra Weeks to Hinckley Williams, Canaan, N.Y., Jan 17, 1840, BCJL.

Table 14. Percentage of farms raising certain produce in the six towns, 1860

	Amherst	Hadley	Hatfield	North-hampton	West-hampton	Williams-burg
Wheat	39.0	10.8	10.9	9.2	4.4	5.4
Corn	89.5	93.8	90.5	86.3	95.6	83.7
Rye	61.8	67.9	56.9	51.3	38.5	7.0
Oats	74.6	25.0	12.4	17.9	62.6	15.5
Potatoes	90.4	89.6	90.5	94.6	100.0	89.9
Dairy cows	93.4	93.3	90.5	93.8	95.6	96.9
Other cattle	64.9	30.0	38.0	37.5	84.6	66.7
Swine	75.0	80.0	74.5	73.3	91.2	72.9

Source: U.S. Eighth Census, Non-Population Schedules, 1860, Massachusetts: Agriculture, National Archives, Washington, D.C. (microfilm).

among their inhabitants, shows that in 1850 most farms, whether they were situated in the hills or on the floor of the Valley, were capable of providing many of their basic food needs. In both towns 97 percent of farmers grew corn. In Westhampton 100 percent and in Hatfield 97 percent grew potatoes. Rye was grown by 61 percent in Hatfield and 38 percent in Westhampton. All farms produced hay, the vast majority made butter, and over 90 percent slaughtered livestock in the year before the census enumeration.[9] In 1860 the position was substantially the same in most parts of the region (Table 14). Substantial proportions of farmers raised each type of product.

The diversified character of most farms is better expressed, however, by calculating the number of crops and types of animal each produced. Giving each farm a "score" of one for every separate product, excluding draft animals, and giving each group of "linked" animals and products (for example, dairy cattle and dairy produce) a score of one, it is possible to construct an index of the number of "activities" farms were engaged in. These activities are summarized in Table 15. Although Amherst farms were on the whole slightly more diversified than those in Hatfield, the difference was not great. The mean number of "activities" for Amherst farms was 8.3; that for Hatfield, 7.4.

Nevertheless, despite the rhetoric, the perpetuation of household gender roles and production patterns, the continued use of local exchange practices, and the maintenance of an impressive degree of agricultural diversity, it would be misleading to leave the impression that farming was little changed by the middle of the century. The evidence

9. This and the next paragraph are based on U.S. Seventh Census, Non-Population Schedules, 1850, Massachusetts: Agriculture, Massachusetts State Archives, Boston, Mass., and U.S. Census, 1860: Agriculture.

Table 15. Distribution of farms by number of activities, Amherst and Hatfield, 1860

	Number of activities											
	1	2	3	4	5	6	7	8	9	10	11	12
Number of farms,[a]												
Amherst	0	1	2	1	2	6	6	7	10	14	7	1
Number of farms,[b]												
Hatfield	0	1	2	1	1	9	20	23	6	4	2	0

[a]One-quarter random sample of Amherst farms.
[b]One-half sample of Hatfield farms.
Source: U.S. Eighth Census, Non-Population Schedules, 1860, Massachusetts: Agriculture, National Archives, Washington, D.C. (microfilm).

of apparent continuity is only partial. A closer analysis reveals that many of the things we have examined had in fact changed, more or less subtly. Above all, farmers, their households, and their production methods existed in an economic and social context entirely different from that of the early part of the century. The change in context alone altered the significance even of many things that themselves remained the same. In a whole range of ways the cattle-show rhetoric about farmers' virtue and "independence" came to have a hollow ring to it. At all events, it did not mean what it had once meant.

There were subtle but important differences in household production and local exchange patterns. Gradually after 1830 the proportion and regularity of cash dealings between neighbors increased. When Joseph Spear did day work for Marquis F. Dickinson in 1842 and 1843, for example, he took some of his pay in rye, corn, and broomcorn seed, but just over half of it in cash. Similarly many of John F. Warner's accounts a decade later included cash payments, along with the goods and services that he exchanged.[10] The point, however, is not simply that the proportion of cash increased but that it came to be used more often for purposes that at an earlier period would not have required it. Neighboring farmers and laborers demanded cash, or expressed frustration at not obtaining it, because they wanted it to conduct exchanges elsewhere. They were, in other words, more dependent on the rules of a wider market, and more determined to conform to its requirements. They needed cash more often because a significant proportion of their requirements were now met through long-distance trade.

Similarly, household production by women and children came increasingly to be valued in cash terms, and women to compare their

10. Marquis F. Dickinson, Account Books, 3 vols., Amherst, 1770–1842, BCJL; Warner, Ledger.

situation as household workers with that of women in the alternative employments more commonly available to them. After the 1820s, young women had opportunities that had formerly not existed for them. While household work had once been virtually their only option, they might now have the chance to take in outwork, travel to work in factories, or, as a small but increasing proportion did, become teachers. As several scholars have shown, a higher proportion of women remained unmarried in the middle decades of the nineteenth century than had been the case before. Although opportunity was unevenly apportioned and access to it usually determined by family circumstances and connections, work in a farm household became measurable against a variety of new standards. Joan M. Jensen, among other historians, has suggested that these circumstances provided a limited amount of autonomy for women, which "loosened the bonds" of an older rural patriarchy. But for women who remained on farms, activities such as butter making and outwork whose products were sold for consumption goods were means of maintaining household independence, not routes to individual advancement. They provided no control of property and little power beyond that over the work itself.[11]

Even the gradual retreat from household patriarchy had mixed benefits for women who worked away from home. In some respects it merely threw them up against the wider "social" patriarchy of male authority in the workplace and wider cultural undervaluing of women and their work. Just as women's wages in household work and manufacturing remained a fraction of men's, so "women's" products such as butter, cheese, and the results of rural outwork were "cheap" items, providing poor recompense for the labor and skill that were put into making them. Moreover, as cash prices became increasingly the operative measure of "value" in rural society, the work of women and children at unpaid household labor became relatively devalued in wider cultural terms. In the postrevolutionary period household manufactures had been treated with considerable respect, regarded (rhetorically at least) as essential bulwarks to the republic's independence. While women writers and editors of women's magazines stressed the value and importance of household work in the mid-nineteenth century, male pronouncements about it often suggested that they now regarded it as

---

11. Joan M. Jensen, *Loosening the Bonds: Mid-Atlantic Farm Women, 1750–1850* (New Haven, 1986), pp. 91, 107. On singlehood, see Lee V. Chambers-Schiller, *Liberty, a Better Husband: Single Women in America; the Generations of 1780–1840* (New Haven, 1984). For a clear theoretical exposition of women's position under changing economic circumstances, see Nancy Folbre, "The Logic of Patriarchal Capitalism: Some Preliminary Propositions" (Paper presented to the conference entitled "Rural Women in the Transition to Capitalism," Northern Illinois University, DeKalb, Mar–Apr 1989).

trivial. Cattle-show premiums awarded to "domestic manufactures" increasingly went to items of comfort and decoration rather than necessity. In the bottomland towns in particular, this reflected the activities of prosperous rather than poor households. The display of counterpanes, bedspreads, quilts, and "fancy articles" was a mark of prosperity, but it also permitted men to congratulate themselves on the importance of their own work compared with the "cultivation of the artistic and the beautiful," which they left to their womenfolk. By 1857 the Amherst Cattle Show abandoned the category of "Domestic Manufactures" altogether, grouping household articles under the general heading of "Fine Arts."[12] In many poorer rural families, meanwhile, the household labor of women and child members remained a cheap, exploitable item. It required little beyond the hidden overheads of board and lodging, whose costs were rarely calculated within families.

Production and Consumption

If the standards of a cash market economy had limited benefits for farm women, they nevertheless began to have a profound impact on farm strategies generally. We saw earlier, in Chapter 4, that rural consumption patterns shifted in the 1820s and 1830s toward a greater dependence on long-distance markets for certain necessary items, such as flour. This shift throws a qualifying light on the evidence just presented about diversified farm production and subsistence-surplus strategies in mid-century. Diversified agriculture was a response to the perceived risks of relying too heavily on market exchange for supplies, but evidence of increased farm output in the 1840s and 1850s suggests that the surpluses now attained by a significant proportion of farmers were sufficient to demand that they make regular use of "markets" to dispose of produce even when they were capable of supplying many of their own basic needs themselves.

Despite the rhetoric of farm independence, the price fluctuations of the 1830s and the crisis of 1837 had hit some farmers hard, especially in the hill towns, where much land was poor and growing conditions were marginal. The "calm serenity and happy condition" that the *Northampton Courier* celebrated in 1837 was not shared by several Westhampton farmers, whom Sylvester Judd wrote about a few years later. By 1841 Oren Kingsley, who had bought Judd's father's old farm in 1833, had been forced to sell it to assignees to pay off debts. Eleazer Judd was also running into trouble, "though he not sensible of it." Two

12. *Hampshire Gazette* (Northampton), Oct 20, 1857.

others had failed or assigned their property since the start of the crisis. All, remarked Judd, were "men who did not examine their affairs and would not believe they were going to ruin, but expected to come out well by some haphazard." They may have had virtue, but it was not rewarded: "The community are in danger of losing more by such honest men than by knaves." The *Northampton Courier* itself remarked that rural districts were no longer insulated from general market trends, and that "whatever may be the condition of things in the city, there is a sympathy at once felt in the country." Judd wrote of Kingsley: "A Westhampton farmer in debt almost 7000 dollars! Had he done not a stroke of work, but run in debt for his living since 1833, he would not have been more in debt than he now is." When Kingsley's farm was sold off, it fetched little more than half the value of his debts.[13] Although this was a serious case, many other farmers faced more or less difficulty during the depression of the late 1830s and early 1840s. Some lost money on mulberry trees when the bubble burst on that speculation in 1839. The long faces one observer noted on Amherst farmers in 1840 and 1841 derived from the low price of butter and other difficulties. In Amherst and Westhampton alone several dozen farmers had to mortgage personal property at a fraction of its value during this period in order to obtain loans to keep their heads above water.[14]

Maintaining a diverse crop output and preserving a degree of self-sufficiency was therefore a protection against the vagaries of a long-distance market that had proved dangerously capricious in the 1830s. Local self-sufficiency may actually have increased in the 1840s as farmers adopted a more cautious approach to production and consumption. After letting their dependence on imported flour build up, a significant number of Valley farmers took advantage of government bounties at the end of the 1830s to raise wheat, and many continued to do so even after the bounties ended. Especially on good land, wheat remained common in 1850. Nearly half the farmers in Hatfield raised it, for example. Although it went into general decline during the 1850s, the proportion of Amherst farmers growing wheat actually increased from about 5 percent to 39 percent.[15] The debate in agricultural journals about the relative wisdom of growing or importing foodstuffs continued with renewed intensity in the 1840s, spurred by the depression and the influence of publications such as Henry Colman's *Reports on the Agriculture of Massachusetts*, which had advocated regional self-sufficiency. A

13. Judd, "Notebook," 1, Apr 3, 9, 30, 1841; *Northampton Courier*, May 31, 1837.
14. Amherst, Records of Personal Property Mortgages, vol. 2, 1837–1851, Amherst Town Hall; Westhampton, Records of Mortgages of Personal Property, vol. 1, 1841–1877, Westhampton Town Hall.
15. U.S. Census, 1850, 1860: Agriculture.

letter to the *New England Farmer* in 1846, which expressed the view that "farmers had better, as a measure of economy, *put their hands in their pockets*, to get their flour . . . than to attempt the home production of it," prompted vigorous opposition from supporters of the alternative. "Let every farmer say, *I will raise my family's bread*," one insisted, "and, my word for it, he will succeed."[16]

One farmer who did "raise his family's bread" in the mid-1840s was Charles P. Phelps, whose fifty-eight improved acres in Hadley gave him one of the larger farms on the fertile intervale land east of the Connecticut River. A study by Karl Finison of Phelps's accounts for 1844 revealed the extent to which his family was able to supply its own food requirements in the period following the agricultural depression. Of Phelps's improved land, sixteen to twenty acres was devoted to tillage, twenty to twenty-five acres to mowing, and the remainder to orchards and pasture. His principal products were hay, grain, meat, and dairy produce. Finison estimated "energy flows" on the farm by converting recorded quantities of labor, crops, and supplies to kilocalorie equivalents (and thereby furnishing a standard measure, independent of price, for production, consumption, purchase, and sale). He estimated that small grains, corn, milk, butter, cheese, potatoes, and pork raised on the farm constituted as much as 92 percent of the family's diet that year, and that in kilocalorie equivalents Phelps purchased only 8 percent of his family's needs. The amounts of flour, bread, meat, cheese, sugar, and molasses purchased from stores were only small. In such cases, women's work at dairy production and food preservation helped keep down households' dependence on store-bought food. After the Civil War the Stoughton family, substantial farmers in Gill, near Greenfield, made their own cheese. "For two or three years mother discontinued making it," wrote Elizabeth Stoughton. "But fathers unnatural fondness of it— and the fact that he *would* keep himself supplied with the article from the stores . . . decided her to resume its manufacture."[17]

Other, smaller landholders similarly attempted to achieve a degree of self-sufficiency. Judith Nutting owned a farm in South Amherst that in 1845 supported a cow and at least three pigs, as well as producing 30 bushels of rye, 40 of buckwheat, 100 of corn, and 60 of potatoes, together with apples from an orchard. Letters suggest that these things formed the basis of the Nuttings' diet.[18] Another Amherst widow,

---

16. *New England Farmer*, Mar 1846.

17. Karl Finison, "Energy Flow on a Nineteenth-Century Farm," *Ecological Anthropology of the Middle Connecticut River Valley*, ed. Robert Paynter, University of Massachusetts, Department of Anthropology, Research Papers, no. 18 (Amherst, 1979), pp. 90–101; Sarah J. Stoughton, Diary, Gill, Mass., Aug 17, 1869, Manuscript Collection, AAS.

18. Hannah Nutting to Eli Nutting, Amherst, Nov 11, 1845, Nutting Correspondence, BCJL.

Elizabeth Shumway, also attempted to maximize her own self-support in the years before her death around 1850. Her estate inventory shows that, having been left cash but little land at her husband's death, she had chosen not to work for an income with which to purchase food but to use her slender resources to produce her own. She rented a house and a small pasture to keep livestock. When she died, there were a cow, a hog, and fifteen chickens. She lived off some of the meat, poultry, eggs, and milk, and traded the remainder with neighbors for grain and flour.[19]

But if the experience of price fluctuations and uncertainties had disposed farmers to look to their own food supplies, it did not prevent them from seeking out markets for their surplus produce, which by mid-century was growing in quantity. Finison's data on Charles P. Phelps's farm provides a striking example. Although the Phelps family supplied most of its own needs, its consumption accounted for only 36.3 percent of the foodstuffs the farm produced. This left 63.7 percent—including hay and grain fed to livestock that were sold—available for local exchange or to be sent to market.[20] Phelps's was a large farm, probably run in an unusually systematic manner. But cruder evidence from tax valuations and census data suggest that substantial surpluses were becoming more common after 1830. In 1831 total grain and hay production in Amherst, Hadley, Hatfield, and Northampton was running at most about 15 percent ahead of the needs of their population and livestock; in Westhampton and Williamsburg production was between 5 and 15 percent less than requirements. By 1850, population growth in Northampton and Williamsburg had outstripped local supply, but elsewhere surpluses had grown.[21] Data from Hatfield and Westhampton farms in 1850 suggest that the great majority produced more than their families' requirements and that, especially in fertile Hatfield, surpluses were considerable (Table 16). As shown in the table, 81 percent of Hatfield farms sampled and 60 percent of Westhampton farms exceeded their families' and livestock's food and feed requirements by at least one-third. In Hatfield, perhaps one in three farms matched or exceeded Phelps's achievement in producing two-thirds more than they needed for their own requirements.[22] So while Valley farms were still technically operating in a subsistence-surplus

19. Elizabeth Shumway, Inventory, Hampshire County, Probate Records, 48:366–367, and her Administrator's Account, 49:58–59, Hampshire County Hall of Records, Northampton.

20. Finison, "Energy Flow," figs. 1 and 4.

21. Mass., General Court (Committees), Aggregates of Valuations, 1831, 1850, Mass. State Library, Boston (microfilm).

22. Crop data from U.S. Census, 1850: Agriculture, were gathered for a one-third sample of Hatfield farms and a one-half sample of Westhampton farms. Corn equivalents were calculated using the following ratios: 1 bushel of wheat equal to 1.104 bushels of

Table 16. Estimated food surpluses on Hatfield and Westhampton farms,[a] 1850

	Farms in Hatfield (N = 31)		Farms in Westhampton (N = 35)	
Percentage of surplus	No.	%	No.	%
76+	8	26	0	0
51–75	13	42	6	17
31–50	4	13	15	43
11–30	3	10	10	29
0–10	2	6	3	9
Deficit	1	3	1	3
Total	31	100	35	101[b]

[a]Random samples.
[b]Total exceeds 100% due to rounding.
Source: U.S. Seventh Census, Non-Population Schedules, 1850, Massachusetts: Agriculture, Massachusetts State Archives, Boston, Mass.

framework, providing their own needs and maintaining diversified production, the "surplus" element in the equation was significantly bigger in mid-century than it had been a generation before. Most farmers were both ensuring their families' positions and making more produce available for sale and exchange.

Pressure toward Markets

A double set of influences on the Valley's farmers in mid-century worked both to push and to pull them into greater contact with and reliance on markets and the standards of long-distance exchange. One influence was at the level of their own motivation. Farmers were operating in an economy that, because of changes in the nonfarm sector, was generally more commercialized in mid-century than it had been before. This increased the desirability of obtaining sources of cash. In order to do this it was necessary to increase production, but the need for cash and credit to finance improvements also tended to reinforce the upward spiral. The other set of influences was from outside pressures on farmers. These, in turn, were of two types. One came from fluctuations in national and regional produce markets, which altered patterns of competition in the supply of many items raised on the Valley's farms. The

---

corn; rye, 1.050; corn, 1.000; barley, 0.866; oats, 0.433; potatoes, 0.220 (Roger L. Ransom and Richard Sutch, *One Kind of Freedom: The Economic Consequences of Emancipation* [Cambridge, Eng., 1977], p. 247, tab. E-2).

other, even more important, came from the region's social structure. As the nonfarm population grew and wealth inequalities widened, new local "markets" for farm produce were created. At each level, therefore, the influences motivating farmers were complex. They included, but were not limited to, "market" forces.

Ironically, although their experience of market fluctuations in the 1830s had taught farmers caution, securing their own food supplies placed them in a stronger position than they had previously been in to produce for markets without undue short-term risk to themselves or their families. But over the 1840s and 1850s they again changed their strategies sufficiently to renew their dependence on market exchange for their livelihoods, and took this dependence to an extent unprecedented in the past. By the end of the 1850s, for example, one-quarter of all new credit reports from Amherst to the Mercantile Agency in New York were on farmers.

Farm output expanded in all six towns between 1831 and 1850. In Hadley and Hatfield, overall production of grains and hay grew by about 90 percent during the period. Gains in the other towns were smaller, between one-quarter and one-third. Although the rate of increase was generally not as high, production of these crops continued to grow in the 1850s. Corn output rose by between 10 and 15 percent in Amherst and Hadley between 1850 and 1860. In Hatfield, it nearly doubled. Except in the hill towns, farmers brought about these increases in the face of continued population pressure on land. As they had done earlier in the century, many farmers continued to clear unimproved land to bring it into cultivation. The proportion of cultivated land to towns' total area continued to increase in Amherst, Hadley, Hatfield, and Northampton between 1831 and 1860 (Table 17).[23] In Amherst, for instance, whereas farmers' average total landholdings in the early 1820s had been about fifty-two acres, by 1860 the average farmer had more than forty-two improved acres alone.[24]

Apart from the continuous process of land purchase and transfer, by which individual farmers accumulated holdings, they extended total cultivable land in a variety of ways. Some continued to clear their unimproved holdings. Dan Huntington of Hadley reclaimed swampland adjacent to his farm in the 1830s, for example, and improved the drainage in some of his existing fields. Other farmers cut back and cleared the brush around fences to make lots larger, and reports from several towns suggest that it was common to find that farmers with land along highways had moved their fences outward, increasing the size of

23. Mass., General Court, Aggregates of Valuations, 1831, 1850, 1860.
24. Amherst, Tax Valuation Lists, 1820, 1860, Amherst Town Hall.

Table 17. Percentage of land under cultivation in Amherst, Hadley,
Hatfield, and Northampton, 1831 and 1860

	1831	1860
Amherst	28.9	38.6
Hadley	34.9	42.0
Hatfield	37.9	49.5
Northampton	26.8	35.3

Source: Massachusetts, General Court (Committees), Aggregates
of Valuations, 1831, 1860, Mass. State Library, Boston (microfilm).

their fields by encroaching on public land. The result of these incremen-
tal changes was to improve the overall quality of land. Sylvester Judd
traveled across Hatfield's south meadow in 1846 and noted that "there
is hardly a poor acre on it." These improvements to cultivable land were
one source of increased output.[25]

Changes in technique were another. Grain cradles for harvesting, still
comparatively rare in the 1820s, had become common two decades
later. Judd remarked in 1845 that "most rye is cut with a cradle nowa-
days. . . . Sickles are almost out of use. Seldom is one seen in the
meadow." A few farmers on the better bottomlands were also beginning to use seed drills, horserakes, and mowing machines by the early
1850s.[26] But the most important technical contribution to increased
output was the more systematic use of manure on many farms. After
falling during the depression of the late 1830s, the number of cattle kept
in the six towns rose by almost 10 percent between 1841 and 1850.
Farmers who had once confined manure spreading to homelots were
carrying it out each spring into tillage and meadows. Collecting, storing, and spreading manure became a substantial chore, demanding as
much time as plowing, sowing, and other preparation of the land. But it
became essential to maintaining and improving output, especially in an
agricultural regime that still did not include systematic crop rotation.

Behind the general rise in output, however, were two important
trends. First, it resulted from a further tendency toward intensive,
rather than extensive, farming methods. At the turn of the century,
farmers had raised output largely by expanding pastures and extensive
livestock raising at the margins of the Valley. From the 1830s onward,

25. Dan Huntington to Hampshire, Franklin, and Hampden Agricultural Society,
Hadley, 1837, and Frederic Dan Huntington to Edward P. Huntington, Amherst, Mar 27,
1837, both in PPHH; Judd MS, "Hatfield and Deerfield," 2:66, contains notes made in
Hatfield, Apr 10, 1846.
26. Judd, "Notebook," vol. 3, July 14, 19, 1845.

however, rising output was concentrated on the region's most fertile land. While the number of cattle in Westhampton and Williamsburg fell or ceased rising between 1830 and 1860, livestock increased and became more concentrated in the older towns. Similarly, the earlier expansion of pastures largely ceased, especially in the hill towns. The largest proportionate increase in pastureland between 1831 and 1860 occurred in Hadley, as farmers there sought to increase their livestock holdings and use a greater proportion of the manure for spreading on their own fields.[27]

Second, as output rose and farming became more intensive, there were renewed signs of specialization. Although, as noted earlier, farmers continued to raise a wide range of produce during the 1850s, they did not increase output evenly across the range. They raised food supplies for themselves, but they were not seeking systematically to supply the region with all its needs. While Amherst, Hadley, and Hatfield farmers increased their corn and hay production, for example, largely in order to feed livestock, they reduced their rye crops by between 3 and 18 percent.[28]

Both trends were the result of market changes. Western farm production increased and transportation improvements helped bring vast quantities of cheap farm produce into eastern urban markets. Local merchants, including members of the Bodman family of Williamsburg, who organized substantial trading connections in Ohio and Illinois in the 1840s and 1850s, contributed to this process by shipping livestock, wool, and other produce into the Valley. Competition with local farmers stiffened. They found themselves with increasing surpluses but depressed prices on the distant markets they had traditionally consigned their surpluses to.[29]

The pressures of competition were felt first in the hill towns. Increased western supplies of wool, together with upheavals in local textile manufacturing during the economic depression, sharply reduced demand for the wool produced by local sheep raisers. In the towns that had had the largest flocks, sheep raising stagnated in the 1830s and fell off precipitately in the 1840s (Table 18). This decline, disrupting as it did

27. Mass., General Court, Aggregates of Valuations, 1831, 1860.
28. U.S. Census, 1850, 1860: Agriculture.
29. The Bodmans' activities can be traced in letters in Bodman Family Papers, Box 3, SSC; shipping horses: Oliver Bodman to Elam Bodman, Williamsburg, Oct 1849; hogs: Lewis Bodman to Joseph Bodman, Newark, Ohio, Nov 21, 1852. See also Lewis and Luther Bodman, Account Book, Aug 11, 1843, and agreement of July 18, 1849, attached to p. 1, on shipping wool, MCFL. Data in Winifred B. Rothenberg, "A Price Index for Rural Massachusetts, 1750–1855," *Journal of Economic History* 39 (1979): 984–985, suggest that overall farm produce prices fell 31 to 36 percent between 1836 and 1844 and did not achieve their predepression levels again until 1854.

Table 18. Number of sheep in Northampton, Westhampton, and
Williamsburg, 1831–1850

	1831	1841	1850
Northampton	3,096	2,674	562
Westhampton	2,079	1,351	945
Williamsburg	4,238	2,416	107

Source: Massachusetts, General Court (Committees), Aggregates
of Valuations, 1831, 1841, 1850, Mass. State Library, Boston (microfilm).

older subsistence-surplus and farm-labor strategies in the hill towns,
was a major cause of the decline in farm population after 1830, especially in Williamsburg, whose sheep flocks fell in size to a mere 2.5
percent of their 1831 level.

Competition also gradually affected patterns of production in the
more fertile Valley towns, even after the opening of the Connecticut
River Railroad in 1846 gave farmers near it easier access to urban markets. Their two major income-earning products, broomcorn and fat
cattle, were both under pressure. Cattle raising did not substantially
decline, but stagnant demand during the middle of the decade, especially in the Boston market, encouraged larger farmers to concentrate
their production to cut costs. Local broomcorn production was progressively affected by western competition from the mid-1840s onward.
First, shipments of cheaper Ohio broom brush began to enter the Valley. Second, during the 1850s increased broom production in Pennsylvania, Ohio, Indiana, and other states undercut the market for Hadley
and Hatfield brooms, sending a number of manufacturers to the wall.
Either way, farmers found themselves producing broomcorn for fluctuating and insecure markets.[30]

Local Markets

Valley farmers had their fat pulled from the fire by demographic
changes in the region. The rapid growth of the nonfarm population,
especially in manufacturing towns after the end of the depression in the
mid-1840s, radically altered the structure of local demand for farm

30. On cattle markets, see *Hunt's Merchant's Magazine* 38 (Feb 1858): 252; of cattle sold in
the Cambridge market in 1857, only 6.1 percent were from Massachusetts. The *Hampshire
Herald* (Northampton), June 1, 1847, reported sales in the Valley of low-priced western
broom brush.

produce and created a real local "market" for the first time. Commentators had long predicted that this would happen. W. Buckminster, writing in the *New England Farmer* in 1838, had urged farmers not to worry about western competition for their major crops: "If more fertile regions can supply our cities with grain at a cheaper rate than we can, let us not lament. We shall find full employment in furnishing what cannot so well be transported from a distance. Fresh meats, butter, hay and the small market vegetables, must be supplied by the farmers of New England." The reopening and expansion of factories in Northampton and Williamsburg, the influx of migrants, and similar developments elsewhere in the region helped turn this expectation into a reality a decade later. Northampton's population rose by 81 percent between 1840 and 1860, an increase of more than 3,000 people. Williamsburg grew by more than 700 people, or 60 percent, in the same period. Most of these increases were outside agriculture. The official report of the first Amherst Cattle Show in 1849 referred to the Boston Associates' mill developments downriver, which were rapidly creating the new city of Holyoke with its town dwellers and factory workers: "Their cry for food will soon come up from the rising city as music to the farmers of the Valley."[31]

This structurally induced demand had widespread effects. More farmers directed produce to local sale, or raised new, perishable goods. William A. Nash of Williamsburg sold quantities of fresh meat to local customers, including the Haydenville mill store of Hayden, Wells and Company. John F. Warner, like an increasing number of farmers, supplied apples. Another pair of Northampton farmers made vinegar from fallen apples in their orchards. By 1860 there were 1,142 acres of orchards listed in the six towns' tax valuations, including 400 acres in Amherst alone. In addition, some farmers began to supply soft fruit. Theodore G. Huntington, for instance, was picking up to fourteen boxes of strawberries a day on his Hadley farm during the season of 1858. Vegetable output also rose. In 1859 the storekeeper and farmer Ansel Wright raised in his garden lot peas, potatoes, onions, beets, squashes, cucumbers, lettuce, carrots, buck beans, sweet corn, parsnips, and turnips.[32]

---

31. Buckminster quoted in Lester E. Klimm, *The Relation between Certain Population Changes and the Physical Environment in Hampden, Hampshire and Franklin Counties, Massachusetts, 1790–1925* (Philadelphia, 1933), p. 76. The Amherst Cattle Show report was printed in the *Hampshire and Franklin Express* (Amherst), Nov 2, 1849.

32. William A. Nash, Account Books, 2 vols., Williamsburg, 1840–1886, WHS. Warner, Ledger. Acres of orchard were reported in Mass., General Court, Aggregates of Valuations, 1860; Huntington's strawberries in Edward T. Fisher to Elizabeth Fisher, Hadley, June 22, 1858, PPHH; Ansel Wright, Diary, Northampton, 1859, MCFL.

Owners of dairy cattle, especially in and near Northampton, began to supply increasing quantities of fresh milk to families in the town, through at least two and probably more specialist milk dealers. John F. Warner sold 817 quarts of milk to one dealer in October 1859 alone, receiving $24.51 for it at $0.03 a quart. The dealer would have then sold it to customers at $0.05, a 60 percent markup.[33] During that year Sylvester Judd and his family consumed a total of 245 quarts of milk. Had that been typical in the town, total demand would have exceeded 300,000 quarts by 1860. In any event, Judd's records of his family's consumption between 1846 and 1859 suggest both an increasing variety of foodstuffs and a shift in balance, toward types of food produced locally and away from those obtainable only from a distance. While 56 percent of Judd's expenditure in 1846 was on locally available items, the proportion had reached 63 percent by 1859.[34]

These supplies took forms increasingly distinct from older patterns of local and intraregional exchange. It is possible to speak of the expansion of a local "market" because transactions came to follow "market" rules rather than those of neighborhood exchange. Certainly, direct swaps of goods and services facilitated the supply of farm produce to the towns, but a significant proportion of the business was now done in cash. Nor was this just a technical adjustment. It reflected a real shift in the social geography of exchange relations. Many of the middle-class townspeople or factory workers whom farmers supplied were themselves directed toward the distant markets for which they produced goods and from which they received cash payments. They were local people not enmeshed in the patterns of reciprocal exchange arrangements that had previously crisscrossed the countryside.

Uplands and Lowlands

An effect of the growth of local markets was to arrest the decline of farming in the nearby hill towns. Westhampton's population, which fell by 34 percent between 1830 and 1850, rose again slightly before 1860. The number of farms counted in the agricultural census for the town rose from seventy-six to ninety-one during the 1850s, as fewer farms were abandoned than in previous decades and some land returned to cultivation. A similar process occurred in Williamsburg. Production of hay, corn, and other crops expanded again after a period of stagnation.

33. Warner, Ledger, account with E. Fitts; Sylvester Judd recorded purchases of milk at an average of five cents per quart in 1859; see Judd, "Notebook," vol. 8, Jan 1860.
34. Judd, from "Notebook," vol. 3, Jan 1, 1846, to "Notebook," vol. 8, Jan 1860, made annual estimates of his family's food consumption for the previous year, and its cost.

Table 19. Acres assessed as woodland in Northampton, Westhampton, and
Williamsburg, 1831–1860

	1831	1841	1850	1860
Northampton	4,425	5,625	4,508	2,498
Westhampton	2,281	2,391	1,843	1,754
Williamsburg	1,661	1,925	1,807	1,395

Source: Massachusetts, General Court (Committees), Aggregates of
Valuations, 1831–1860, Mass. State Library, Boston (microfilm).

Rye output grew eightfold in Westhampton, though from a very low
base in 1850. Part of this revival was prompted by the opportunity to sell
hay and other feedstuffs to larger farmers in the river towns, but there
were also direct suppliers of grain, meat, and dairy produce to customers and storekeepers in the manufacturing villages. One Westhampton farmer, Allyn Winchell, grew grain on his own small landholding and collected produce from neighbors to peddle around the
factory villages of Northampton and Williamsburg. Hill farmers also
supplied seed and other items to Valley producers through "market
fairs," which became annual events in towns such as Hadley in the late
1850s.[35]

This revival came at a price, however. Although demand existed for a
range of products, the hill towns' most valued resource was lumber.
Population growth prompted a massive requirement for building materials and firewood. Much of this was satisfied by the progressive stripping of upland woodlots during the 1840s and 1850s, by farmers who
just at that point were seeking to replace income they had lost from the
decline of sheep raising. The timing and extent of the clearances are
demonstrated in Table 19. Woodland expanded during the 1830s but
after 1841 began to be cleared rapidly and at an increasing rate. Together
the three towns lost 1,783 acres of woods between 1841 and 1850 and
another 2,511 acres in the following ten years. "Thousands of farmers in
Massachusetts," wrote Sylvester Judd, "could not live from their farms,
if they did not sell wood and timber."[36] Families such as the Bartletts of

35. On Allyn Winchell, see Samuel L. Wright, "Westhampton Local History," 3 vols.,
compiled 1892–1905, 2:70 FL (typescript). An announcement in the *Hampshire Gazette*, Apr
3, 1860, for a Market Fair in Hadley Town Hall urged hill-town farmers to bring samples of
potatoes, wheat, and oats, "as the valley farmers buy largely of those articles from the
hills."

36. Judd, incomplete draft letter to the editor of the *New England Farmer*, n.d., Judd
Papers, MCFL, Oversize File. Arthur H. Cole, "The Mystery of Fuel Wood Marketing in
the United States," *Business History Review* 44 (1970): 339–359, discusses the small impact
of wood on distributive institutions, given its economic importance. Farmers were not the

Westhampton became reliant on their own and their neighbors' timber-lands. Several members of the family entered a partnership in 1848 to build a sawmill on a water privilege they owned. Farmers could earn significant sums from cutting and selling lumber. William A. Nash received nearly $170 from sales of softwood and green hardwood to local customers in Williamsburg in the winter of 1854–1855, while the same year John F. Warner sold over $325 worth, four-fifths of which represented straight profit over the labor costs of cutting and carting the wood.[37]

But if stripping the woodlands helped prevent the decline of upland farming, it was a temporary solution because the process occurred faster than trees could regrow. Judd noted "rapid . . . destruction of timber" in Northampton in the late 1840s and "sawmill yards and the highways and open places around . . . filled with logs." Already much of this timber was small, because it came from land that had previously been cleared only two decades before. The Bartletts' sawmilling venture came almost too late. Westhampton lumber production fell off in the 1850s, as supplies became exhausted. Logs delivered to sawmills were getting "smaller and more inferior each year." When big logs did appear, according to Judd they were "crooked and knotted," of a sort that "would not have been sawed a few years since." Farmers' incomes from their woodlands threatened to decline; "the time seems not very distant," Judd concluded, "when many farmers not only will have no wood to sell, but none to use."[38]

Farmers' attempts to satisfy their immediate needs had longer-term economic and ecological costs. Although the Valley could continue to supply firewood and low-grade lumber, it became increasingly dependent on imports of building lumber, shingles, and other wood products, some of which might have been available locally had fewer trees been cut down in the 1840s and 1850s. Moreover, timber cutting laid bare much of the upland landscape, leading to soil erosion and a renewal of the struggle to wrest livings from land that had often been poor to begin with. It also made water runoff and river levels variable and unpredictable. Poor flowage in the Mill River forced Northampton and Williamsburg manufacturers to build the Goshen dam and reservoir to

only owners of woodland, though; merchants and other townspeople also owned and traded woodlots as the lumber boom got under way: see Charles P. Huntington to Edward Huntington, Northampton, [Dec 1838?], PPHH, seeking a purchaser from Cabotville for forty-one acres of woods on Mount Tom.

37. Bartlett, Account Book, vol. 2, contains records of work done in the construction of the Bartletts' sawmill, largely by family members. Nash, Account Book, vol. 2; Warner, Ledger.

38. Judd, "Notebook," vol. 4, Feb 2, 1847; "Notebook," vol. 6, Apr 12, 1851; "Notebook," vol. 7, Apr 1, 1853; the final quotation is from Judd, draft letter to the editor of the *New England Farmer*.

control it in the 1850s. The collapse of this dam in 1874 exacted, as noted earlier, an appalling toll in human life.[39]

The stripping of the woodlands symbolized the fragility of the upland economy, which was also evident in more immediate ways. Among those responsible for expanding farm production in Westhampton and other hill towns in the 1850s were Irish immigrants who, for the first time, moved in to rent or purchase land to farm. But the fact that they were able to do this reflected the widening differential in land prices between hill and bottomland districts. Whereas good land in the hill towns had doubled in price between 1800 and the 1850s, prime mead-owland in Hadley, Hatfield, and Northampton could fetch three, four, or five times what it had cost half a century earlier. In 1851 the average price of land without buildings listed in probate administrators' accounts was $26.18 per acre in Westhampton and Williamsburg, and prices as low as $14.00 were common. Hadley and Northampton land, by contrast, averaged more than $100.00 per acre. Meadowland sold during a price boom in 1853 and 1854 changed hands for more than $200.00 an acre.[40]

Evidence on farmers' property holdings from U.S. census schedules confirms this bifurcation between the Valley and the hill towns. The average value of the real estate owned by Hatfield farmers in 1850, at just under $4,000, was nearly twice the average holdings of farmers in Westhampton. During the 1850s the differential widened slightly. However, these differentials reflected not only the better quality of land near the river, but the high expectations of income from farming in an increasingly commercialized region. Of Westhampton men who owned farms both in 1850 and in 1860, 38 percent were able to increase the value of their real estate faster than the general rise of property values in the town, but in Hatfield the comparable proportion was 67 percent. Moreover, the 1860 census made it clear that, on average, lowland farmers had been able to accumulate more than real estate; their holdings of personal property were three times greater than those of West-

39. For purchases of wood outside the region, see Josiah Ayres to David Sumner, Amherst, Oct 2, 9, and 17, 1850, BCJL. Ayres, clerk to Amherst's first parish, sought 55,000 shingles from Sumner, a supplier in Hartland, Vt. "In relation to the further sale of your shingle[s]," wrote Ayres, "we would say, that a large quantity are wanted at this place, and if you prove as good as you recommend we think you may sell many." On the 1874 flood, see Chapter 7. This discussion of upland ecological change draws on Peter Thorbahn and Stephen Mrozowski, "Ecological Dynamics and Rural New England Historical Sites," in Paynter, *Ecological Anthropology*, esp. pp. 131–133, which used data from Middlefield, Mass., where a dam also collapsed in 1874.

40. In "Westhampton Local History," 1:345–349, 2:51, 54, 57, Wright cites several Irish settlers in the town in the 1850s. Overall land prices were reflected in Mass., General Court, Aggregates of Valuations, 1850, 1860. Administrators' accounts were drawn from Hampshire County, Probate Records, vol. 52. The boom in valley land prices was noted in Judd MS, "Miscellaneous," 16:102–103.

hampton farmers. In the upland town, the ratio of personal to real estate holdings, at just over one to five, was little greater than it had been half a century earlier. For many farmers in the bottomlands, though, the land had brought a measure of comfort and material prosperity, as well as family security.

However, this prosperity was not achieved in mid-century by cultivating traditional crops, despite the fact that the expansion of grain and hay production and the opportunities to supply produce to local markets were both greater than in the hills. These activities were subject to the same market fluctuations that had affected the sale of surpluses outside the region and were therefore not devoid of risks for farmers. There were "a large number of sufferers" in 1859 when a Williamsburg gristmill, to which farmers had consigned grain on contract, failed before they received payment. One of the losers, David B. Phelps of Southampton, had delivered his whole 300-bushel rye crop to the mill, expecting to receive cash on the spot.[41]

Accounts kept by an anonymous small farmer in the late 1850s reveal how he discovered that intensifying the production of traditional crops did not pay if price changes intervened. In 1856 he tilled 6.75 acres of land in five lots, planting two of them to corn and one each to wheat, oats, and potatoes. He reckoned that his total income from these was $285.07, which, when set against his costs, represented a net return of $89.36 or a mean of $13.24 per acre. Three years later he had 11.75 acres under crops. These now included, in addition to what he had previously grown, rye, winter wheat, and turnips. But 1859 was a tricky year. Part of the corn crop failed and the rest yielded only two-thirds of a normal crop. Prices for small grains were low. The farmer sold oats at a loss, and eventually earned net returns of $85.38, 4.4 percent less than he had obtained three years previously. But because he was tilling more land, his returns per acre were actually 55 percent lower than in 1856.[42] He had had to run harder just to stand still. Conditions such as this, and uncertainties about incomes from cattle fattening and especially broom-corn, encouraged many farmers on the best land in the Valley to seek new sources of earnings in the 1850s. Doing so, they increased their dependence on distant markets even further.

Tobacco: A New Cash Crop

For farmers on land fertile enough to grow it, tobacco was by far the most important new source of income. It had been grown on a small

41. *Hampshire Gazette*, Feb 1, 1859.
42. Farm Account Book, 1856–1874, Manuscript Collection, AAS.

scale in the eighteenth century but remained of little significance. By the 1840s, however, tobacco had become increasingly successful in Connecticut. In 1843 a Whately farmer grew some, and in the following few years it was adopted by more farmers there and in other towns. During the late 1840s small patches of tobacco could be seen on scattered farms in Hatfield, Hadley, and parts of Amherst and Northampton, but the crop made little showing in the 1850 agricultural census. Total Massachusetts production reached 138,000 pounds that year, but the contribution of Hampshire County farmers to that was small.[43]

As demand for broomcorn became more uneven, however, interest in tobacco-growing sharpened considerably. During the 1850s an increasing number of farmers in Hadley and, particularly, in Hatfield adopted the crop. By 1860, when Massachusetts tobacco output reached 3.2 million pounds, these two towns alone contributed about one-third of the total. That year the crop was raised by a handful of farmers in Westhampton and Amherst, by 16 percent and 19 percent respectively, of Williamsburg and Northampton farmers, by just under one-third of those in Hadley, and by no less than 82.5 percent of farmers in Hatfield. As Sylvester Judd wrote in the late 1850s, "Tobacco for the first few years was a bonanza. The profits were large and people thought they were going to get rich in a year or two."[44] In fact, as we shall see, only a few farmers were to achieve substantial prosperity by 1860, but the returns on tobacco in a good year were indeed high.

The expansion of tobacco farming in the 1850s occurred in three phases. A price boom in 1850 and another in 1852 apparently encouraged many Hadley farmers to adopt the crop, and it was claimed that by 1853 as much as three hundred acres of land in the town was planted to it. Optimistic published estimates of yields and profits suggested that even at a relatively low selling price of $0.08 a pound, farmers might expect to clear $90.00 or $100.00 on each acre they grew. This compared favorably, for example, with the maximum earnings per acre achieved by the small farmer discussed earlier of $31.65 for a crop of potatoes in 1856.[45] A fall in prices to 1855 seems to have driven many farmers out of tobacco growing. The Massachusetts census returns that year suggest that only about fifty-seven acres were now under the crop in Hadley and another fifty-four in Hatfield. After this, however, more farmers entered the business. Another price boom from 1855 to 1857 saw prices rise to $0.35 or more per pound. At this point there was another col-

---

43. Elizabeth Ramsey, "The History of Tobacco Production in the Connecticut Valley," *Smith College Studies in History* 15 (Apr–July 1930): 133–134.

44. U.S. Census, 1860: Agriculture; Judd, *History of Hadley*, p. 468.

45. Ramsey, "History of Tobacco Production," p. 143, gives a rough guide to tobacco prices and, on p. 139, a discussion of yields.

lapse. Prices fell to $0.14 or $0.15 for good-quality tobacco leaf and to only $0.06 or $0.08 for poorer leaf. Some farmers abandoned the crop again. But by 1860, especially after a number of larger farmers entered the business for the first time, production was exceeding one million pounds of leaf per year.[46]

The prospect of fresh earnings and the booms and slumps in prices both helped determine when farmers entered and left tobacco cultivation in the 1850s. Even in 1858, after prices had fallen and some producers were caught out, large tobacco growers made substantial returns. A newspaper reported that one Hatfield farmer had received $4,200 for his crop from ten or twelve acres of land, though if that were so it was the result either of exceptionally good yields or of high prices for the year. Nevertheless there were at least two Hatfield farmers who earned $3,000 or more in 1860, and net returns after costs probably amounted to $60,000 in Hatfield alone that year. As the *Hampshire Gazette* remarked, not only did the town "possess . . . some of the best lands in the Connecticut Valley," but "her enterprising farmers know how to use them to the best pecuniary advantage."[47]

However, the desire for income and the pattern of price movements do not entirely explain the adoption of tobacco or the extent to which it spread. The first boom, up to 1853, coincided with a period of particular uneasiness in the broomcorn market. Imports from outside the state were rising, prices were fluctuating and at least one Hadley dealer failed at this point. That uncertainty may have persuaded farmers to go in for tobacco. But it seems likely that many of them tried either to grow too much at once or to raise the crop on soil that was not ideally suited to it. After 1855 expansion of tobacco production was much faster in Hatfield, so that by the end of the decade there were proportionately more than twice as many growers there than in Hadley. Contemporaries attributed this to better soil conditions, but it is also likely that the relative fortunes of the broom industry in the two towns played a part. Hatfield's broom production fell quite rapidly in the 1850s, whereas a significant number of small broom makers continued to work in Hadley. Local demand for broom brush may have kept more Hadley farmers out of growing tobacco despite the fact that potential earnings from the new crop were higher.[48]

46. Judd MS, "Hadley," 3:184–185, reproduced the census takers' crop returns for 1855. The revival of production was reflected in U.S. Census, 1860: Agriculture.

47. *Hampshire Gazette*, Feb 1, 1858. Net returns were calculated from reported earnings in U.S. Census, 1860: Agriculture, and estimated costs given in Ramsay, "History of Tobacco Production," p. 139.

48. U.S. Census, 1860: Agriculture, reported tobacco on 82.5 percent of Hatfield farms and 32.5 percent of Hadley farms. In Hatfield there were seven broom makers; in Hadley,

Farmers with the right type of land adopted tobacco as it came to suit their particular strategies and circumstances. Analysis of the growers suggests that they fell into three broadly distinct groups, that these groups were in turn divided between men who put greater or lesser reliance on it, and therefore that motivations for adopting tobacco could vary considerably from farm to farm.

One group consisted of smallholders who owned twenty acres or less of improved land. They had in fact been among the first to take up tobacco in the late 1840s and early 1850s. Noah Edson of Hadley, who had five hundred pounds of tobacco in store when he died in 1851, owned only seven and one-half acres of workable land. His tobacco, assuming it was his whole crop from the 1850 season, would have been the product of a quarter-acre lot, of the sort that observers noted was common at this period. Edson's farm was too small to grow the food his family would have needed. That he probably worked to earn supplies is suggested by the fact that his inventory listed cabinetmakers' tools. His tobacco, worth about $70 at the 1850 harvest, would have provided more exchange value than any of his other crops or activities. Selling it for cash at the right moment would have enabled him to avoid taking "store pay" or some other swap for work he did in the neighborhood. Smallholders such as Edson accounted for about one-quarter of Hatfield tobacco growers in 1860. Their earnings from the crop would not have exceeded $150, and in some cases would have been rather less than that.[49]

Also among early tobacco growers had been middling farmers like Horace Smith of Amherst, who raised small amounts of tobacco on his forty-acre farm before he died in the early 1850s. By 1860 over two-fifths of Hatfield growers fell into this category, owning between twenty-one and fifty acres of improved land. A farmer in this group was one of the two in Hatfield who grew enough tobacco to earn him about $3,000 that year, and two more grew about $1,600 worth. But most middling farmers earned between $200 and $400 from the crop. Similarly to smallholders like Edson, they grew relatively modest amounts of tobacco on small proportions of their farms, in the same way that they had grown

---

twenty-nine. There were a few large farmers in both towns, however, who handled both tobacco and broomcorn. Thaddeus Smith of Hadley was a tobacco dealer by 1860 but also raised and dealt in broomcorn and was, with eight employees, now the town's largest broom manufacturer. In partnership with A. J. Jones of Hatfield he had earlier bought broom brush in the West. Jones, by 1860, was Hatfield's third largest tobacco producer. Both farmers were the subject of credit reports in Massachusetts, vol. 46, p. 95, R. G. Dun and Co. Collection, Baker Library, Harvard University Graduate School of Business Administration, Boston.

49. This and subsequent paragraphs are based on data from U.S. Census, 1860: Agriculture.

the broomcorn that it largely replaced. Nearly two-thirds of Hatfield growers raised less than three acres of it (Table 20). Only one in seven of the middling farmers devoted more than 15 percent of their improved land to the crop. Most grew it in two- or three-acre lots and took modest supplements to their incomes from it. Even smaller farmers did not usually commit themselves heavily to tobacco. Only eight out of twenty-eight used more than a quarter of their land for it, and only one man used half of his improved acreage. This farmer clearly perceived tobacco as a route out of the constraints of smallholding and used income from it to buy many of his family's needs. But he was rare in making this kind of calculation. Most farmers fitted tobacco in alongside existing production strategies. At least in 1860 the households of tobacco growers also seem to have maintained their work patterns. All of the Hadley and Hatfield tobacco farms that also kept livestock produced butter that year, suggesting that tobacco income was used not to substitute food purchases for the products of women's or children's labor but for other purposes.

Large farmers, with more than fifty acres of improved land, tended to enter the tobacco business later than some of their poorer neighbors. With plenty of land at their disposal, they could afford both to maintain diversified crop strategies and to raise considerable quantities of tobacco without disturbing them. By 1860 nearly a third of Hatfield growers had over fifty acres of land and nine of them had over one hundred acres. After early hesitation, large farmers in the town now accepted tobacco with enthusiasm. Over 80 percent of all Hatfield farms with forty acres or more of workable land grew it. Several large farmers were earning incomes in excess of $1,000 from it by 1860. But only one became more or less a tobacco specialist. There and in Northampton, large farmers conducted tobacco production in conjunction with their other activities. The largest producers also tended to be the largest cattle fatteners, who had access to substantial quantities of manure with which to fertilize the crop. Nevertheless tobacco often became their most lucrative product. A statement of income from a large Northampton farm in 1864 showed earnings of over $3,000 from tobacco, nearly three times as much as from beef cattle and 65 percent of its total income.[50]

However much it fitted into farmers' existing strategies, though, the adoption of tobacco marked a departure in the Valley's agriculture. It was, in many respects, the region's first "cash crop," raised solely and specifically for market sale. It provided, for the towns in which it became established, the staple export crop that had been absent since

50. Memoranda for Estimate of Farmer's Income, 1864, NHS, A.m.d.18.69.

Table 20. Acres per farm devoted to tobacco, Hatfield, 1860 (*N* = 113)

Acres of tobacco	Percentage of all tobacco farms
less than 1.5	34.5
1.5–2.99	29.2
3.0–5.99	22.1
6 or more	14.2
Total	100.0

Source: U.S. Eighth Census, Non-Population Schedules, 1860, Massachusetts: Agriculture, National Archives, Washington, D.C. (microfilm).

the decline of wheat in the eighteenth century. Unlike hemp, or teasels, which had been tried earlier in the century, it was grown by large numbers of farmers, sometimes in substantial quantities. Unlike the mulberry trees grown during the silk craze of the 1830s, tobacco was raised on prime land. Moreover, unlike mulberry, it was to become a successful crop, the established staple of the Valley for the next hundred years or more.

Most significantly, tobacco was grown solely to be sold. Farmers had sold produce for decades, but they had always raised things that had a variety of uses. Grains, cattle, wool, and dairy produce could be used at home, exchanged in the neighborhood, sent to local manufactures, or sold in distant markets. Even broomcorn, which in many respects preceded and prepared the ground for tobacco, fitted into a variety of local production patterns. It could be grown for its brush—a raw material for local manufacture—or allowed to run to seed and used as cattle feed. Tobacco had none of this flexibility. It had one function, and was grown almost exclusively for markets in large cities such as New York. Indeed, the best tobacco grown in the Valley was not even a complete product. High-quality leaf was sold for cigar wrappers, to be assembled in the cigar factories of New York, Baltimore, and other cities with filler tobacco from Virginia or the Caribbean. At no time before had Valley farmers committed so much energy to an enterprise of which they were only a part, whose success rested on an industry entirely beyond their control.[51]

They quickly found that selling and shipping tobacco followed pat-

51. Ramsey, "History of Tobacco Production," pp. 133–144; on leaf for wrappers, see also pp. 126–130. E. R. Billings, *Tobacco: Its History, Varieties, Culture, Manufacture, and Commerce* (Hartford, 1875), pp. 311–314, attributed the success of Connecticut Valley tobacco growers to their concentration on the crop; it was not the only crop they grew but, according to Billings, they invested much of their effort and expertise in it.

terns different from most other crops. Sales in the 1850s were usually made directly from the farm to traveling dealers, many of them Connecticut-based agents of Hartford, New York, or Baltimore tobacco merchants. Gradually local growers also set up as dealers to market their own and neighbors' crops. Tobacco growers' commercial links almost completely bypassed existing local merchants. Dealing with itinerant dealers, as most of them did, farmers faced various risks, especially as prices could fluctuate as rapidly within a season as they did from one season to the next. The Hartford dealer D. M. Seymour, who spent the 1850s attempting to establish a centralized warehouse system of purchasing through town growers' associations, repeatedly warned farmers about the dangers from "speculators." In November 1856, predicting that prices were about to rise, he urged farmers not to sell tobacco "at *any price*" and warned that dealers would use "every artifice . . . to blind and deceive you."[52] By the following year, a few Massachusetts growers had joined the warehouse system, but direct sales to dealers remained most common. The *Hampshire Gazette*, reporting in 1860 that some prices were rising, warned that "sharpers are about seeing whom they may devour in a friendly way," and advised, "Let the motto be 'Cash down and few words.'" The *Springfield Republican* remarked that dealers could take substantial markups on the prices they had negotiated with farmers: "The manner in which tobacco is prepared for market after it reaches second hands is an enigma to most growers. By some wonderful hocus-pocus, it increases very rapidly in value, so that the same article that to-day was sold for 12 cents by the producer, tomorrow is repacked and sold for from 25 to 50 cents. Tobacco speculators make money even in hard times."[53]

Although many farmers evidently regarded the risks as worthwhile, the character of tobacco and its economic implications created a strong current of moral objection to it. As Sylvester Judd noted, "some citizens fought shy of tobacco. They thought the use of it was vicious and the raising of it scarcely less so." At the Hadley bicentennial in 1859 President Stearns of Amherst College urged farmers to return to raising broomcorn "so that [they] need not be constrained to sacrifice their luxuriant and lovely meadows to the growth of a narcotic."[54] Almost as soon as its cultivation expanded in the 1850s, antitobacco campaigners such as Rev. George Trask of Fitchburg began to circulate tracts and

52. Seymour's advertisements appeared in *Hampshire Gazette*, Nov 11, 1856 (from which the quotation comes), Feb 10, Oct 20, 1857, and Nov 8, 1859.

53. *Hampshire Gazette*, Oct 9, 1860; *Springfield Republican*, quoted in *Hampshire Gazette*, Sept 7, 1858.

54. Judd, *History of Hadley*, pp. 468–469; *Celebration of the Two Hundredth Anniversary of the Settlement of Hadley, Massachusetts, at Hadley, June 8, 1859* (Northampton, 1859), p. 81.

other propaganda against "the loathesome crop." Trask, organizing his attack along the lines of the temperance movement and making many of the same arguments, condemned tobacco as conducive to ill health, waste, idleness, and poverty. Like the temperance groups who campaigned against liquor sellers, Trask took his argument to the producers of tobacco, attempting in several tracts to dissuade Connecticut Valley farmers in particular from growing it. In addition to spelling out the consequences they brought upon the consumers of their crop, he drew attention to the economic risks they faced from growing it. Tobacco exhausted the soil. High returns tempted farmers to make heavy expenditures, which they could not pay for when prices collapsed. Trask had a fictitious Hadley farmer proclaim in one tract: "I am a poorer man today than when I began. . . . My notes are in the bank, I have injured all my choice lands; and I should have been far better off had I stuck to my old crops."[55] Judd, who held an old-fashioned republican suspicion of "extravagance" in any form, condemned tobacco growing as "a kind of intoxication." Farmers "were bewitched with the new crop, and with the money flowing in built big barns, and bought recklessly many things they never thought of needing before." Writing after the 1858 collapse in tobacco prices, he was hopeful that this reversal had put an end to the farmers' folly. His hope was quickly proved to be a vain one.[56]

That year the *Northampton Courier*, reporting a plea that farmers not raise tobacco because of its "injury to body and mind," wondered "if any body will forego the profits of the crop for any such reasons as these?" Clearly, the unprecedented returns from tobacco may have caused many farmers to put aside their scruples and grow it. Antitobacco campaigners condemned the lure of profit that tempted growers toward evil. But it is worth asking why their arguments failed to stem the spread of tobacco growing, when exactly the same arguments, made to the same people, were at the same time successfully curbing the free sale and use of alcohol? One answer, of course, is that farmers who had never supported the temperance movement would hardly be swayed by antitobacco tracts. However, there were protemperance farmers who grew tobacco. Ansel C. Marshall, for instance, one of the small number of Amherst tobacco growers in 1860, had once taken his

55. Quoted in Ramsey, "History of Tobacco Production," pp. 151–153. I have not been able to locate a copy of the tract from which this quotation was drawn (George Trask, *The Tobacco Crop a Curse to the Connecticut Valley* [Fitchburg, n.d.]), but Trask published numerous other pamphlets in the 1850s and 1860s, some of which singled out Connecticut Valley farmers for criticism. On the range of arguments against the crop, see also Stephen Sewall, *Alarming Effects of Using Tobacco* (Winthrop, Me., 1870).

56. Judd, *History of Hadley*, p. 468.

zeal against liquor so far as to appear as an informant against a man prosecuted for illegal selling.[57] Part of the explanation lies in the web of economic connections in which farmers were entangled by 1860 and the role tobacco could play for them in controlling their new circumstances.

Compared with the height of the popular temperance movement of the 1830s and 1840s, farmers were more likely to be dependent on stores for goods they needed and more likely to require cash (or the promise of cash) to purchase them. Other income-producing activities, such as raising broomcorn or fattening cattle, were becoming uncertain or less lucrative. Dairy production and outwork were paid for at pitifully low rates in comparison with potential earnings from tobacco, which could also be accommodated within the mixed-farming strategies by which farmers had always sought security. Moreover, growing tobacco entailed obligations that made it hard to relinquish. As a crop that took a toll of the soil it was grown in, it required heavy applications of fertilizer. These demands rapidly outran the supplies of manure available to many farmers. Increasingly they were obliged to buy guano, superphosphates, and other commercial fertilizers that were being stocked in increasing quantities by local merchants. A tobacco-growing manual of the early 1860s asserted that "no farmer can fail to see that he impoverishes his farm by the annual exportation of his tobacco crop. Hence he cannot fail to see that if he can import and use to advantage a commercial fertilizer, he should do it."[58] The need to raise income to pay for these fertilizers was one of the hooks by which farmers were caught in a progressively complex dependence on outside markets.

Contemporaries and agricultural historians alike noted the enthusi-

57. *Northampton Courier*, Mar 9, 1858; Ansel C. Marshall, recorded as a tobacco grower in U.S. Census, 1860: Agriculture, had been a complainant in the case of Commonwealth v. Upson, Hampshire County Court of Common Pleas, Records, 32:274–279 (1849), Hampshire County Courthouse, Northampton, in which a Southampton man was prosecuted for selling liquor illegally at the Amherst College commencement; he was found guilty, but the prosecution was dropped on appeal.

58. [William L. Bradley], *Bradley's Manual of Growing and Curing Tobacco: Containing Interesting and Valuable Statements of His New Tobacco Fertilizer, Important to All Growers of the Weed* (Boston, 1864), p. 25. When Otis G. Hill planted tobacco on his Williamsburg farm in 1864, for example, he ordered phosphate of lime from the Northampton merchant Lewis McIntire (Hill, Diary, Williamsburg, May 20, 31, 1864, WHS). It was precisely this point on which critics of tobacco growing focused. A writer in the *Hampshire Gazette*, Apr 5, 1858, warned farmers that tobacco demanded so much "care and *manure*" that they might neglect the rest of their crops, while George Trask, in "An Appeal to a De[a]con Who Raises Tobacco on the Banks of the Connecticut," asked his subject how he kept his fields "fat and fertile in spite of this exhauster," tobacco. "It is a fundamental principle *that your farm should fertilize itself*," claimed Trask. "Instead of this do you not rely on foreign manures? Do you not rob your potato and corn patch and impoverish neighbors?" (*Tobacco and Hard Times: An Appeal to a Poor Man to Give Up Tobacco* [Fitchburg, 1859], unpaginated).

asm for cash crops evident among many farmers in new farming regions in the West.[59] New Englanders, even on the most fertile land,
seem to have been more cautious in their approach. Even the returns
from tobacco did not prompt most of them to alter their strategies
radically. Only a few small farmers became specialists in the crop. The
majority incorporated the cash crop into their existing mixed-farming
regimes, using its income to cushion them against the continued pressure of population increase in a densely settled district.

This kind of adaptation to new conditions exemplifies the argument
that farm households retained a degree of independence and self-
determination throughout the period of this study; among the things
that tobacco farmers could contemplate was the splitting even of relatively small farms between heirs or siblings. Even in prosperous Hatfield, nearly three farmers out of five had movable property of less than
$1,000 in 1860; they were, aside from their land holdings, no better off
materially than 85 percent of farmers in poorer Westhampton.[60] Nevertheless, tobacco helped some of these small farmers maintain their
households with fewer resources than might otherwise have been necessary. For the majority, the cash crop was not a route to wealth, but in
good years it was a guard against poverty. The context in which farm
households operated changed significantly.

For a substantial minority tobacco helped provide more than an ability to maintain a livelihood. By 1860 nearly one-quarter of all Hatfield
farmers had accumulated movable property valued at $2,000 or above,
more than any Westhampton farmer owned. The price rises of fertile
Valley lands, the ability to build or improve houses and barns, the
accessibility of consumer goods, all reflected the prosperity that a few
farmers were able to derive from local and distant markets. As the
greatest prosperity came from tobacco, the crop least geared to local
needs and most dependent on fluctuations on distant markets, the
farmers best placed to benefit from it were those with the means to hire
labor to grow it. Their prosperity rested on a growing division between
farmers and laborers, which put the former for the first time in the
position of "capitalists" in the widest sense.

---

59. Paul W. Gates, *The Farmer's Age: Agriculture, 1815–1860* (New York, 1960), p. 403.
60. Wealth data in this paragraph and the next are from U.S. Eighth Census, Population Schedules, 1860, Massachusetts, National Archives, Washington, D.C. (microfilm).
An excellent discussion of the material culture of successful farmers in the mid-nineteenth
century is in Thomas C. Hubka, *Big House, Little House, Back House, Barn: The Connected
Farm Buildings of New England* (Hanover, N.H., 1984), chap. 1 and passim. Hubka shows
how many farm families modified their houses and outbuildings, partly to meet the
demands of commercial farming and partly to improve standards of domestic comfort,
but also to continue the practices of diversified farm production.

Farm Labor

Among the connections that farmers had developed by 1860 was a new relationship with labor. Tobacco required careful tending and labor-intensive cultivation. The soil had to be prepared and fertilized, seedlings planted, and the young crop hoed several times to keep down weeds and pests. Harvesting had to be done quickly and the leaf hung up in barns to dry before being sorted and packed for shipment. Tobacco was, as one contemporary put it, "a full crowded summer crop." The average cultivation cost was reckoned to be 50 percent higher per acre than that of corn, mostly because of the extra labor involved.[61] Growers could handle small tobacco crops on their own, or with family labor, but the larger crops that became common in the 1850s were possible only because a larger pool of hired labor was available in the Valley towns than had been the case earlier. The rise of tobacco was one consequence of the growth of a more permanent agricultural proletariat in mid-century, the emergence in farming of many of the conditions that we already observed in manufacturing.

We saw in Chapter 3 that hiring labor was a normal, frequent part of farmers' strategies before 1820, but that most wage work was done in small amounts, intermittently, and by people who had other things to do as well. Most households preferred to rely on their own labor whenever possible, hiring help or swapping work in the neighborhood when they had to. It was this aim, "to do with as little labor as possible," that Josiah Quincy had condemned in his speech to the Massachusetts Agricultural Society in 1819. But old practices lasted a long time. Many smaller farmers continued to avoid hiring if they could. Ira Chaffee Goodale wrote in 1847 that "I expect Father will overdo himself as he is to[o] anxious to get along without hiring any body to help him do his spring's work." In 1850, even during the summer, 55 percent of Hatfield farm households had no live-in hired help. Letters and diaries continued to reflect the importance of exchanging work and intermittent hiring. Polly Cathcart of Williamsburg noted how the men in her household worked at neighbors' chores, traveled to Hatfield to do a day's work, or went to work off an obligation on someone else's land the same day that a neighbor came to work for them. Just as intermittent hiring continued, so did the attitudes that went with it. Many people continued to regard farm laboring as a temporary expedient, undertaken by young men who had prospects of obtaining land of their own. It could even facilitate this advancement: in 1854 an Amherst woman sent advice to a nephew who was renting land but wanted to buy his

61. The tasks involved in growing tobacco are described in Billings, *Tobacco*, chap. 13.

own farm to "sell his stock this spring, and stay on the farm . . . as a hired man, and only for the summer—Then in the fall he will be at liberty to look up a place."[62]

Quincy had argued in his speech that "labour [is] the root and spring of all profit." Despite the persistence of older practices, more and more farmers were coming to appreciate this as clearly as manufacturers in the 1830s and 1840s. There was a progressive increase in contract hiring of farm labor for five, six, or seven months each summer and, in fewer cases, for a year at a time. William Nash, for instance, Williamsburg's largest farmer, hired at least one laborer for the summer season in March or April of each year during the 1840s. He also employed a man over three winters, on two occasions merely extending the contracts of his summer workers and on the third hiring afresh. The extent of these practices varied, however. Whereas in Hatfield there were 113 men identifiable as farm laborers in 1850, equivalent to almost one for each farm, in Amherst there were only 53, about one for every five farms in town.[63]

Why did the view that hiring should be avoided if possible give way to the notion that it was a normal and regular part of farm life? One explanation lay in the increase in farm output, which clearly demanded more labor than in the past. Up to the 1840s, households often increased output by "self-exploitation" in the face of labor shortages. No help was available to pick apples on the Grahams' land in Buckland in 1835, so Mary Bullard Graham did it herself. "I have been out and picked up as many as sixty bushels," she wrote. "Do you think I shall *turn to a man bye and bye?*" Judith Nutting's daughters also did farm chores when her son was away and there was no help to be hired.[64] However, as falling fertility rates and migration to other occupations reduced the numbers of children available to help on farms, larger landholders like Nash relied increasingly on hired labor to get work done and used term

62. Ira C. Goodale to Moses and Susanna Goodale, New York, May 18, 1847. Hatfield data are drawn from U.S. Seventh Census, Population Schedules, 1850, Massachusetts, National Archives, Washington, D.C. (microfilm); farm laborers include the following: those designated "laborer" or "farm laborer" and those who gave their occupation as "farmer," but who neither owned real estate nor shared the family name of the head of their household. Polly Cathcart Tilton, Diary, Williamsburg, Jan 22, Apr 24–26, July 7, Aug 7–8, 20, 27, Sept 23, Oct 29, 1839, PVMA. The advice was in Mary [?] to Mrs. Pliny Spaulding, Amherst, Mar 16, 1854, BCJL.

63. On contract hiring, see Winifred B. Rothenberg, "The Emergence of Farm Labor Markets and the Transformation of the Rural Economy," *Journal of Economic History* 48 (1988): 537–566; William A. Nash, Account Book, vol. 1, WHS. U.S. Census, 1850: Population.

64. Mary B. Graham to Lewis Edwards, Buckland, Nov 17, 1835, Edwards Family Correspondence, MCFL; Harriet Nutting to Eli Nutting, Amherst, Aug 29, 1848, Nutting Family Correspondence.

contracts to arrange it. New techniques, especially on larger farms, were not always directed to labor saving but to using hired labor more intensively so as to spread out some of the seasonal unevenness of the work. Northampton farmers, for example, were having their corn cut near the ground by the early 1840s, partly to increase the amount of fodder from the crop and partly to clear fields for fall plowing. The consequence was more work during corn-husking, "but this can be done when there is time."[65]

As hiring increased during the period of labor shortage, real wages probably rose. Monthly wages for summer work increased by about 50 percent between 1820 and 1837, at least keeping pace with the rise in food prices after 1829. Wage levels did not fall back suddenly during the depression; they remained almost as high in 1840 as they had done in 1836. Even during the 1840s, William Nash's laborers were able to negotiate hard with him over wages and other terms of employment. Their contracts varied from year to year, as their cash wages were adjusted against differing agreements over the provision of board, laundry, tools, and Sunday lodging. But several factors were altering the situation by the mid-1840s, some temporary and others more permanent or structural. Unemployment and dislocations during the depression encouraged more young men to stay home on their parents' farms, rather than leave. The *Northampton Democrat* noted in 1844 that "the dull times through which we have passed, lately, have opened their eyes to the fact that after all there is nothing like a farmer to stand through all times." What did not stand, as a result, were wages. Monthly wage rates appear to have collapsed during the early 1840s. By 1844 they were 20 to 30 percent lower than they had been four years earlier. Although rates were to fluctuate over the next fifteen years, this collapse marked the beginning of a period of relative labor abundance during which there emerged an agricultural proletariat larger than at any previous time.[66]

Two factors helped the temporary effects of the depression become more permanent. One was the rapid influx of foreign-born migrants to the Valley in the 1840s. Young French-Canadian *habitants*, encouraged to leave the land by the weaknesses of the Quebecois peasant economy, traveled south into New England, often just for the season, to seek work on farms or in broom shops. The English and Irish-born factory workers who sought out jobs in the mills during the early and middle years of the decade were followed to the Valley by the laborers, many of them Irish, hired to build the Connecticut River Railroad from 1845 to

65. Sylvester Judd, "Notebook," vol. 1, Oct 26, 1843.
66. Nash, Account Book, vol. 1. *Northampton Democrat*, Jan 23, 1844.

1847. Some of these men settled in the area, were joined by their families, sought work, and became a local nucleus for further migration. In the 1850s, they were in turn to be followed by German craftsmen and farm laborers.[67]

Second, as foreign immigration promised to solve farmers' labor shortage, structural circumstances also increased the potential New England–born work force. Property distribution was increasingly uneven. In Amherst, where 79 percent of taxpayers had held real estate in 1820, only 57 percent had any by 1860. Among landowners, moreover, inheritance practices were more inegalitarian than early in the century. About 1800 over three-quarters of testators with more than one heir divided their land between them. After 1850, fewer than half were doing so.[68] Opportunities to remain on the land were more constricted than ever in the middle of the century. Although the lack of opportunity contributed to further outmigration and shifts from farming to other occupations, it also meant that as Valley farmers offered more laboring jobs there were local men available to fill them.

Patterns of farm labor in the 1850s reflected these factors. The number of hired workers increased in all six towns, but the differentials between bottomland districts and those away from the river became smaller. Hatfield's wage-labor force grew from 113 to 188 between 1850 and 1860, a rise of 66.4 percent, but Amherst's more than tripled, from 53 to 179. The six towns together had 1,156 farm laborers by 1860, almost exactly one-fifth of all occupations recorded in the census. In Amherst and Westhampton they accounted for 17 percent of the working population, but in Hatfield the proportion was 38 percent. This expansion, which had started before 1850, was accompanied by the stagnation of wage rates. Although food prices rose in the late 1840s, monthly wages failed to follow. At least until the mid-1850s, rates even for "good" hands seem not to have risen more than 10 or 15 percent. The farm prices of food crops were generally falling during this period, but the cash value of farm output, especially on tobacco farms, rose substan-

67. Naturalization Petitions: Hampshire County Court of Common Pleas, Records, vol. 30, nos. 200–275 (1844); Hampshire County Court of Common Pleas, Files, no. 359 (1845); Mass., Supreme Judicial Court, Hampshire County Files, Box 11 (1851–60), both in Massachusetts State Archives, Boston, Mass.

68. Amherst, Tax Valuation List, 1860. Inheritance data, drawn from wills for the six towns in Hampshire County, Probate Records, vols. 20–21 and 52, were as follows:

	1800–1803	1851–1855
Number of wills	29	43
Real Property divided (%)	69	49
Real Property undivided (%)	31	51

tially. The Massachusetts average farm wage of $15.34 a month with board, reported by the census of 1860, was no higher than the rates paid by William Nash fifteen years before. To farmers with rising incomes, this meant that labor was significantly cheaper in real terms than it had been. To laborers, it meant comparative poverty and dependence.[69]

Data on farm laborers from the 1850 and 1860 censuses suggests not only that their numbers were growing but that their condition was becoming more permanent. This was especially evident in Hatfield, which had the largest concentration of farm workers in its population. Laboring was becoming less a young man's occupation. The average age of Hatfield farm workers rose from 23.9 years to 28.4 during the 1850s, while the proportion aged over 30 rose from 11 to 36 percent. Both in 1850 and in 1860 just over half the laborers were immigrants. But while at the beginning of the 1850s over three-quarters of these immigrant workers were French-Canadians, many of them young summer migrants, by 1860 seven out of ten were Irish or German immigrants who were more permanently settled and less likely to move seasonally. The fastest-growing segment of the work force, however, was local. The number of Massachusetts-born laborers increased by three-quarters, from forty-eight to eighty-five men, 45 percent of the whole group in 1860. On farms, just as in industry, the number of American-born wage workers grew along with the immigrants.

Moreover, an increasing number of Hatfield laborers were household heads. During the 1850s the proportion who boarded with the farmers they worked for fell from 77 percent to 46 percent. By 1860 over half lived with their own families or in boardinghouses such as the one in Whately owned by the Wait family, in which Sophronia Bullard worked as a servant. Laborers' living arrangements increasingly came to resemble those of factory workers, with a marked increase in segregation between employers and employees. But if this represented for some a degree of independence, it was not a particularly lucrative one. Some farm laborers owned real estate, and the proportion increased over the decade. But the number was pitifully small, only seventeen (9 percent) in 1860. Even among those who were household heads, only one-fifth owned property. Most laborers were poor. They lived in one of New England's most prosperous agricultural towns. By their work in the tobacco fields they were contributing notably to its farmers' increasing comfort. But they were a distinctively underprivileged group, sepa-

69. The data in this and the next two paragraphs are from U.S. Census, 1850, 1860: Population, using the definition of laborer described above, in note 62. Mass. Commissioner of Labor, *Sixteenth Annual Report*, Mass. Public Doc. 3, no. 5 (Boston, 1885), reported a widening differential between unskilled farm laboring wage rates and those for skilled workers between 1840 and 1855.

rated by poverty, residence, and prospects from the farmers who employed them.

Farmers in Rural Society

Farmers and their households inhabited a social landscape that by 1860 was significantly different from that of two generations earlier. They were no longer the sole symbols of a republican social order. They shared a more varied and divided terrain with lawyers, traders, manufacturers, factory workers, and their own laborers. While they still controlled their own households' production; bought, sold, and passed on property to children; and looked to their offsprings' future provision, their influence over these things was reduced. Many of them were more prosperous, but they were tied to distant markets, reliant on income to provide comforts and necessities. Some even hired foremen to manage their farms and oversee workmen, introducing a formal hierarchy to the work process that had become normal in factories. But for the majority who remained independent farmers, working on their own account with the cooperation of their families, the networks of outside connections were different from those of the past. They relied less on neighbors, more on laborers, stores, and banks. They needed cash, as much as credit, to arrange the work and supplies that farming required.

Although landowning farm households remained at the center of the agricultural economy, farmers ceased to enjoy the respect that had once been preeminently theirs. Achieving prosperity and control over labor did not prevent farmers from suffering losses in social status. An article by J. G. Holland in 1858 criticized the narrowness and drudgery of farm life, accusing farmers of a single-minded, boorish concentration on work and accumulation.[70] Farmers even found parts of the rural world divided against them, just as their status and prosperity divided them from their laborers. They faced encroachments on old privileges by new groups and interests in the countryside, and they found themselves increasingly put at a distance by the merchants, lawyers, and other middle-class people who controlled the center villages they traded in.

Hadley farmers, for instance, faced two examples of encroachment in the 1850s, neither of which they were able to prevent. Like many colonial towns, Hadley had granted water privileges to millers on condition that they provide custom milling to the neighborhood. The mill on Fort River near the center of Hadley had received such grants in the

70. J. G. Holland, "Farming Life in New England," *Atlantic Monthly* (1858): 335–341.

seventeenth and eighteenth centuries. In 1850, however, when the mill changed hands, the deeds made no mention of the town's rights. The Hadley Manufacturing Company, which now owned it, built a paper mill alongside the gristmill. In 1854, when dry summer weather lowered the water level in the river, the company decided to concentrate on papermaking and refused to operate the gristmill to grind corn for customers. Farmers, already troubled by falling tobacco prices and difficulties in the broomcorn trade, voted in town meeting to choose a committee to restore their rights. Failing to achieve a compromise, the town sued the company, arguing that in refusing to honor the conditions of the town's grant it had forfeited its water rights. When the case was completed two years later, Chief Justice Lemuel Shaw ruled for the company, finding that in the absence of a specific provision "that they should grind for customers, rather than for market," the matter had been "left to be regulated by the usages of the country." Presumably, he reasoned, the grantors had relied on the millers' "own self interest to accommodate the neighborhood."[71] The custom of the country had changed. The social structure of a diversified rural economy no longer left room for assumptions that private and public interests would coincide.

In another case, Hadley farmers also found private property rights acting against them. Since the seventeenth century they had taken recreation and grazed their livestock on the steep wooded slopes of the Holyoke Range, which formed the town's southern boundary. In 1821 a group of up to three hundred men, women, and children had walked up the mountain to frame and raise a shelter at the summit on what was still legally common land. By 1850, however, the land had passed into private hands. A Northampton bookbinder, John French, backed by local capital, took over the property, enclosed it, and built a larger summit house to attract the growing Valley tourist trade. By the late 1850s, these actions had brought him into conflict both with local people who resented the enclosure of the land and attempts to charge admission to it and with farmers whose cattle were now excluded from grazing on the mountain. The mutual bitterness of this dispute is reflected in French's diary for November 1, 1857, when he wrote that "The Hoccanum *Thieves* have turned 20 head of cattle on to my home lot this morn."[72] Farmers faced similar opposition in a constant series of attempts in various town meetings to curb the roaming of livestock to

71. Inhabitants of Hadley v. Hadley Manufacturing Co., 70 Mass. Reports (4 Gray): 140–145 (1855); the background to the case is sketched by Ellen E. Callahan, "Hadley: A Study of the Political Development of a Typical New England Town from the Official Records (1659–1930)," *Smith College Studies in History* 16 (1930–1931): 25.

72. "Mount Holyoke Register," Nov 1, 1857, NHS Archive Files (typescript).

feed on highways and wasteland. Northampton by the 1850s, for example, permitted animals to browse only under the supervision of keepers, requiring farmers to employ a child or hired laborer to accompany them.[73]

It was in Amherst, rather than Hadley, that the most striking instance of a symbolic and physical exclusion of farmers from the center of town life occurred. By 1830 Amherst's west parish had secured its disputed position as the principal center of trade in the town. Stores sprang up at the north end of its common, while to the south lay the now successfully established college. The common became the location for what passed as public entertainment in this still tight-laced community. Above all, it featured the college commencement each August, an event that drew crowds from towns throughout the Valley. After 1849, when Amherst first formed an agricultural society, the common also became the site for an annual cattle show. In addition to farmers and their families, the crowds of onlookers, and the "Oyster-Booths, Auction-stands, gingerbread and cider carts" that dotted the common, the show attracted rival teams of oxen from the neighboring towns, which competed to assemble the longest, most impressive drove. In 1851, for instance, Belchertown sent 101 yoke of cattle drawing a car carrying 181 people, the town band, and a collection of banners and agricultural implements. Farmers and farm laborers celebrated their work and skills in the geographical center of the town.[74]

However, in the 1850s indications began to appear that they were not to maintain this presence. Complaints had been voiced for years about the common's scruffy appearance. When the Amherst and Belchertown railroad was opened, the town newspaper successfully campaigned to have sidewalks laid near the stores at the common's northern end. A nucleus of prominent village residents set out to continue the process. The Amherst Ornamental Tree Association, formed in 1857 and led by a group of lawyers and college professors, gained effective control of the common and mounted a campaign of tree planting and tidying-up that occupied the village for several years. This group had close links with the leaders of the agricultural society, most of whom were not farmers, but merchants, and persuaded them to further its purpose. Earmarking land for a permanent showground east of the town center, the agricultural society's leadership obtained approval to purchase it at a poorly attended meeting in December 1859. By the time more than three hun-

73. Northampton, Town Meeting Warrant, *Hampshire Gazette*, Mar 9, 1858.
74. On the widespread popularity of commencement, see Nash, Account Book, accounts with William Miller, 1843, and Thomas M. Jones, 1847, noting laborers leaving work to travel from Williamsburg for the day; on the cattle show, East Hampshire [from 1851, Hampshire] Agricultural Society, Records, BCJL.

dred of the society's ordinary members could petition to protest this action, the purchase contract was in force and they were left with no choice but to accept it. Subsequently the annual cattle show moved from the common to the new site away from the village. During the Civil War, Amherst College also removed its commencement activities from the common, withdrawing onto the college grounds and turning what had once been a holiday for farming people into a private event.[75]

Conflicts between farmers and other groups in the Valley had also spilled over into politics. It was in the predominantly farming towns of Hadley, Hatfield, and Westhampton that support for the dying Whig party remained most loyal in the early 1850s, whereas votes in the towns with larger manufacturing populations had already begun to swing toward Free Soil and its temporary coalition with the Democrats. The farming towns, too, remained resolutely opposed to the constitutional convention, which, when it eventually met in 1853, did, as expected, shift the balance of representation in the General Court away from agrarian and toward industrial centers. As Whiggism collapsed, many farmers temporarily transferred their allegiance to the Know-Nothing movement. Only in the later 1850s did these men come to support the Republican party, which was to become the new dominant political alliance in the Valley.[76]

Growing opposition to the expansion of slavery, and later to slavery itself, became the uniting political force in an otherwise fragmented field. As Eric Foner pointed out, the issues of free soil and free labor, which the Republicans addressed, appealed to a wide range of northern voters. In a rural area that had sent thousands of migrants to the West and which was, in the 1850s, still sending families and individuals to seek new farmland there, strong support for the principle of free soil could be expected. When a local minister said prayers during the violent struggle between pro- and antislavery settlers in Kansas, "for the afflicted people on our western border, meaning the persecuted people of Kansas," Sylvester Judd noted that some of them had emigrated from Southampton.[77] Farm laborers and factory operatives, insofar as they remained in the Valley long enough to have an impact on elections, saw

75. Polly Longsworth, "The Growth of Civic Consciousness," Essays in Amherst's History (Amherst, 1978), pp. 144–147, describes the Ornamental Tree Association, which had among its purposes "laying out and ornamenting the common." The proposal to move the cattle show, the purchase of the new site, and the disputed meetings to approve it were reported in Hampshire Gazette, Mar 20, and Apr 6, 1860.

76. Election reports and returns in Hampshire Gazette, Nov 12, 1850; Nov 9, 1852; Aug 1, Nov 14, 1854; Nov 6, 1855; Nov 4, 1856; and Nov 3, 1857; Minutes of Know-Nothing Convention, Williamsburg, Oct 11, 1854, Nash Papers, WHS. See also John Mulkern, "Western Massachusetts in the Know-Nothing Years: An Analysis of Voting Patterns," Historical Journal of Western Massachusetts 8 (Jan 1980): 14–25.

77. Eric Foner, Free Soil, Free Labor, Free Men: The Ideology of the Republican Party before the Civil War (New York, 1970); the quotation is from Judd, "Notebook," vol. 7, Nov 9, 1856.

in slavery the threat of oppression that they were seeking to resist in their own employment. The freedom to move and to bargain for terms and conditions of work, while no guarantee of equality or wealth, was an essential part of their strategy for survival in a divided social structure. Finally, free-soil ideology appealed strongly to small businessmen, manufacturers, and farmers, who formed the backbone of local political campaigns; it was a guarantee of "equal rights" against overweening privilege. These strands linked highly disparate groups together.[78]

The alliance against slavery obscured the rifts in rural society and reflected the emergence of social conditions markedly different from those of the early republic. The image of a republic whose independent freeholders upheld its virtue was displaced by the vision of an ordered, separated social structure where property rights conveyed private but not public privileges. Farmers, many of whom made significant financial advances in the new order, nonetheless found themselves and their families in a distinct social sphere. Links of interdependence still ran within households and between neighbors and kin within the sphere, but their influence and significance had become constrained. Meanwhile, the links of interdependence between classes and groups, farmers, traders, manufacturers, and laborers, had become invisible, mediated by cash rather than by debt and obligation. Rural people found themselves both richer and poorer for it.

Commercial farmers could subscribe to the free-soil, free-labor ideology of the new Republican party, sharing the viewpoint of other small businessmen and capitalists. Still, they found that in the ideology of market capitalism, they no longer merited the special place that the older republican ideology of independence had given them. Sylvester Judd, pondering Hadley farmers' newfound dependence on the market for tobacco, looked back to an earlier period when their obligations had seemed different, more closely related to town and neighborhood. With other early historians of New England, Judd misread the contrast that he perceived between dependence and an older sense of independence, and helped lay the basis for the myth of self-sufficiency that has dogged rural history ever since.[79] The history of the countryside was not one of a decline from earlier virtue, but a profound shift in the terms of interdependence on which its society rested. Household organization, exchange patterns, and production all changed. Market and industrial capitalism were the result.

---

78. Alan Dawley, *Class and Community: The Industrial Revolution in Lynn* (Cambridge, Mass., 1976), makes a comparable point, that the Civil War created a degree of political unity across social divisions in the shoemaking town of Lynn, Massachusetts.

79. Judd, *History of Hadley*, pp. 367, 468.

PART V

CONCLUSION

Chapter 9

The Connecticut Valley
in Perspective

Both at the beginning and the end of the period covered by this book
the people of rural Massachusetts were at war, against the British in the
1770s and 1780s and against the Confederacy in the 1860s. Yet the men
who went to fight in the two wars did so on very different conditions;
the contrast illustrates the extent of rural social change in the interven-
ing decades. Eighteenth-century soldiers were recruited from a household economy that required them for farm labor as well as to fight. Their
vital role in rural production made colonial and revolutionary militia-
men notorious for preferring short-term enlistments and being reluctant to remain far from home for long periods. To conduct the revolutionary war Congress came to rely heavily on a Continental army
recruited from among the young, poor, and marginal, for whom fight-
ing conflicted less with other pressing obligations. By the Civil War,
things were different. Massachusetts farm laborers, mechanics, factory
operatives, and clerks enlisted in such substantial numbers—prepared
to serve for considerable periods, hundreds or even thousands of miles
from their homes—that the war was two years old before conscription
became necessary. Population growth, immigration, and the emergence of a wage-labor market had made individual young men less
essential to the survival of the rural economy. They could be replaced at
their work, or could (if their families had the means) buy substitutes for
military service.[1]

1. On colonial militia, see Fred Anderson, *A Peoples' Army: Massachusetts Soldiers and
Society in the Seven Years' War* (Chapel Hill, 1984); on the Civil War, see Phillip Shaw
Paludan, *A Peoples' Contest: The Union and Civil War* (New York, 1988), pp. 18–19.

The Processes of Economic Change

The route from one type of society to the other was complex. The social structure of the mid-nineteenth century resulted not from a single "transition" from a set of interactions broadly divisible into two phases but from several types of change working in parallel. Demography, land shortage, the "market," household strategies, or capital accumulation were not single, outstanding motors of change, but came together, taking different forms at different periods, to alter the character of rural New England profoundly and relatively rapidly. Agriculture, manufacturing, education, and other activities were not separable; it was together that they gave rural people livelihoods and means of providing for the future. The search for livelihoods and security was a crucial driving force for change.

In the first, "involutionary" phase of the process, roughly from the 1780s to the 1820s, the household system was the framework for a dynamic rural expansion. Inequalities, land shortage, and demographic growth prompted households to intensify production and seek out new occupations. The gender and age divisions within households and the practices of local reciprocal exchange provided much of the framework for this expansion before 1820. The existing social structure, based on household organization, broadened and deepened. Household and local needs dictated the expansion of markets for farm produce. There were few bases for capital accumulation by entrepreneurs. Pressure for change came largely from within the rural economy; up to the 1820s, change was not caused primarily by the imposition of outside forces on it.

There were reasons, of course, why this pattern should have been particularly followed in New England, whose eighteenth-century rural economy was unusual in various respects. Though unequally distributed, freehold property was widely held, and compared with the mid-Atlantic colonies, there were few households wholly or permanently dependent on renting land. Unlike the middle colonies and the tidewater South, interior New England had no staple export crop and was a relatively small market for imported manufactured goods. Labor was largely provided by family members, or swapped between households; again, compared with other regions, servanthood was rare or temporary, slavery insignificant. For these reasons and others, which were explored in Chapter 2, elites were weak. The social and economic structures for concentration and control of production were largely lacking in the eighteenth century, and the process of rural involution left them weak well into the nineteenth.[2]

2. Distinctions between the major American colonial regions are outlined in Gary B.

Household independence, in the sense that we have defined it, remained a feasible basis for securing livelihoods and other needs. Visitors unused to New England's peculiarities sometimes found this hard to understand. One traveler in the 1820s was apparently entirely puzzled; he found "not much improvement in husbandry . . . though the people have a strange look of property and comfort." Farms swarmed with children, but "how they are fed God only knows; for not a thousandth part of the soil is properly cultivated, and it is a very difficult thing for a farmer to sell enough . . . to pay his yearly taxes." By the standards of commercial farming, the region did indeed fall short, but household production and local exchange provided sufficient that, as the same writer remarked—still scratching his head—"one never saw, or heard of, so happy a people."[3]

There were reasons why the increase in rural production from the 1780s to the 1820s was largely successful. Clifford Geertz, who introduced the concept of "agricultural involution" over a quarter-century ago, and other scholars who have followed him, have stressed that such internally generated intensification of effort has rarely led to rural economic expansion. Marginal returns to labor tend to decline; effort becomes "self-exploitation" by families constrained within ecological and economic limits to higher output. However, the social and economic conditions of late-eighteenth-century New England exempted many rural households from these constraints, at least for a while. Large reserves of unimproved land, the expansion of livestock raising, and the more systematic use of family and exchange labor all permitted increases in labor productivity.[4] Local exchange, population growth, and households' aspirations helped keep demand in pace with the increased supply of produce and manufactures. As a result, the Valley achieved levels of comfort and household consumption that, while not extravagant, nevertheless ensured that rural expectations were raised; they would help propel the economy into a new phase.

Both the success of intensified rural production and the strains that it imposed led to an outward turning of the economy from about 1810 onward. Farm output increased, but so did the number of young men and women seeking "careers" outside farming. Local noncash ex-

---

Nash, "Social Development," in *Colonial British America: Essays in the New History of the Early Modern Era*, ed. Jack P. Greene and J. R. Pole (Baltimore, 1984), pp. 233–261.

3. Quoted in *Hampshire Gazette* (Northampton), Mar 5, 1828.

4. Clifford Geertz, *Agricultural Involution: The Process of Ecological Change in Indonesia* (Berkeley, 1963); Philip C. C. Huang, *The Peasant Economy and Social Change in North China* (Stanford, 1985) Winifred B. Rothenberg, "The Emergence of Farm Labor Markets and the Transformation of the Rural Economy," *Journal of Economic History* 48 (1988): 537–566, presents evidence of increased labor productivity in the late eighteenth and early nineteenth centuries.

change imposed burdens of debt and obligation from which individuals started to seek outlets when they could. The duties of household production and reproduction fell disproportionately to women, who began to shift their strategies to ease the burdens on them. Reducing fertility and seeking certain goods from distant markets, they altered the labor and consumption patterns of their households. Ready to capitalize on this shift were the local merchants and manufacturers whose numbers had expanded as young people searched for "careers" in the late eighteenth and early nineteenth centuries. Gradually, merchants extended their influence over local exchange, inserted themselves between households and between the producers and consumers of goods, and, in some cases, sought and obtained control of household labor for outwork production as well.

While successful merchants and manufacturers invested accumulated profits in new factories and machinery to employ permanent wage labor, farmers with the means to do so also employed labor more regularly to grow the produce that now had to be exchanged at stores for household necessities. This second phase in the transition of the rural economy, the period of "concentration" from about 1830 to the 1860s, resulted in a new, more complex social structure in which households and capitalism coexisted. Households producing largely with family labor continued to function, especially on the land, but there were now, in addition, many factories and farm households that relied on hired workers; poorer households, in turn, depended on this wage work in order to survive. Accompanying this structural shift was an increasing emphasis on cash transactions and the curtailment of credit, which would restrict, but not destroy, older practices of neighborhood exchange. This change in the conduct of transactions had, as we have seen, social and cultural as well as simply economic effects.

"Independent" households, pursuing their own ends, had therefore helped bring into existence a rural capitalism in many ways antithetical to their own older values and practices. The period of capitalist "concentration" brought the countryside much more readily under the sway of outside economic pressures. The processes of accumulation and reorganization of production and labor had much more in common by the mid-nineteenth century with those of other American and Western European regions that also experienced a transition to capitalism. Household and regional independence became less important, both ideologically and in reality.

Rural Massachusetts as a Case Study

A case could be made that the processes outlined in this book were unique to the rural interior of New England, that the region's distinctiveness in the eighteenth century gave it a starting point unmatched elsewhere, and that it must stand as an exception to the broader patterns of economic transition traceable in other parts of the world in this period. Indeed, the thrust of the argument here has been that only in the nineteenth century did the Massachusetts countryside become subjected to powerful economic influences not generated from within its own social structure. Other parts of rural America, heavily engaged in exporting staple crops; exploited for furs, wood, fish, or minerals by outside agencies; or reliant on imported manufactures, were presumably more under the sway of outside commercial influences, which helped determine whether local capitalist expansion took place or whether a state of relative dependency was maintained.[5] However, for three sets of reasons, it is not adequate simply to regard New England as a special case; the processes of change traced here have wider implications.

First, New England would itself play such a significant role in American economic development that an explanation of change in its own rural economy has important ramifications. The energy generated by rural households' confrontation with scarce resources in the late eighteenth century sent migrants to frontiers, farming regions, and towns across America, especially to the Midwest; the importance of New England emigration has been recognized ever since the process itself was taking place. But recent scholars have made clear that emigration was not merely the result of rural decline; in many instances, it was the opposite—the outgrowth of economic and demographic dynamism.[6] The countryside itself, as it underwent the transitions outlined in this book, contributed to the commercial developments and capital accumulation that sent New England people, products, and power far and wide in the nineteenth century. The shifts in household consumption strategies about 1820, for example, not only released labor for employment in the growing textile industry but provided a significant "home market" for factory textiles close to points of production. The persistence of agriculture in fertile regions like the Connecticut Valley meant that this

5. H. Veltmeyer, "The Capitalist Underdevelopment of Atlantic Canada," in *Underdevelopment and Social Movements in Atlantic Canada*, ed. Robert J. Brym and R. James Sacouman (Toronto, 1979), pp. 17–35; Pete Daniel, *Standing at the Crossroads: Southern Life in the 20th Century* (New York, 1986), refers to the intrusion of capitalist rice farming in Louisiana (pp. 10–11) and the development of mining in the Appalachians (pp. 16–17).
6. The classic account of the effects of New England migration was Lois Kimball Mathews, *The Expansion of New England: The Spread of New England Settlement and Institutions to the Mississippi River, 1620–1865* (Boston, 1909); Daniel Scott Smith addresses this cultural expansion in " 'All in Some Degree Related to Each Other': A Demographic and Comparative Resolution of the Anomaly of New England Kinship," *American Historical Review* 94 (Feb 1989): 44–79. See also Hal S. Barron, *Those Who Stayed Behind: Rural Society in Nineteenth-Century New England* (Cambridge, Eng., 1984).

effect remained important throughout the nineteenth century and beyond.[7]

Second, although rural Massachusetts displayed an unusual *combination* of economic characteristics in the late eighteenth century, most of its facets were not unique in themselves. Over a decade ago Robert Brenner, in a seminal article, argued that the social structure of early modern English agriculture, with its class divisions between landowners, capitalist tenant farmers, and wage laborers, explained England's rapid industrialization in the eighteenth and nineteenth centuries. France, by contrast, with its rural economy of peasant smallholders, remained comparatively slow to industrialize. Since Brenner wrote, scholars have demonstrated that there were numerous exceptions to his thesis that agricultural smallholding retarded capitalist development. Certain combinations of access to land, population growth, and household production led to manufacturing developments in various regions; fertile agricultural districts, for instance, supported outwork networks in France, the Low Countries, and other parts of Europe. Widespread property holding could support independent household manufacture, as in the woolen districts of West Yorkshire in the eighteenth century. Different land, population, and household work patterns led to considerable variations in manufacturing organization and its evolution. Sharing more characteristics with France, where the average late-eighteenth-century landholding was about thirty acres, than with England, where the average was about one hundred acres, New England may be said to belong to this pattern of exceptions. The Connecticut Valley, indeed, supported a sequence of different forms of activity, each with a counterpart in other regions.[8]

In America, too, virtual freehold landholding had already given rise to an expansion of agricultural output in colonial Pennsylvania; we need more parallel studies to determine whether similar patterns of rural stimulus for manufacturing played as important a role in the mid-Atlantic region as it did in the New England interior.[9] We also know, of

7. For a general discussion of this issue for a later period, see John Ermisch and Thomas Weiss, "The Impact of the Rural Market on the Growth of the Urban Workforce: The United States, 1870–1900," *Explorations in Economic History* 11 (Winter 1973–1974).

8. See T. H. Aston and C. H. E. Philpin, eds., *The Brenner Debate: Agrarian Class Structure and Economic Development in Pre-Industrial Europe*, (Cambridge, 1985); Gay L. Gullickson, *The Spinners and Weavers of Auffray: Rural Industry and the Sexual Division of Labour in a French Village, 1750–1850* (Cambridge, Eng., 1986); Patricia Hudson, *The Genesis of Industrial Capital: A Study of the West Riding Wool Textile Industry, 1750–1850* (Cambridge, Eng., 1986). For an important comparative discussion, see Jean H. Quataert, "A New View of Industrialization: 'Protoindustry' and the Role of Small-Scale, Labor-Intensive Manufacture in the Capitalist Environment," *International Labor and Working-Class History* 33 (Spring 1988): 3–22.

9. James T. Lemon, *The Best Poor Man's Country: A Geographical Study of Early Southeastern Pennsylvania* (Baltimore, 1972).

course, that familial values and household organization were central to the opening of much of the Midwest in the nineteenth century. Indeed, even as wage labor was growing in Massachusetts, extensive use of family labor remained characteristic of new farming regions in various parts of the world. As slavery and serfdom were destroyed or discredited, family members became the chief sources of labor where land was plenty and people scarce.[10] Rural households elsewhere would also, in places, eventually be drawn into providing wage labor for manufacturing, as they had been in New England. Textile firms that moved to the South in the late nineteenth century recruited labor from farm households by means not dissimilar from those they had originally used fifty years and more before.[11] New England was not so unusual, after all.

Finally, perspectives adopted in this book will be relevant for other studies of economic transition. Five points are particularly worth stressing: the relative autonomy of rural social developments; relationships between economic practices and social structure; the cultural and moral dimensions of the exchange process; household strategies under different demographic conditions; and the role of household organization in the emergence of capitalism.

The absence of staple-crop exports in the late eighteenth century and the relative autonomy of independent farmers meant that sources of economic change in rural New England were those internal to the rural economy. In the early phases at least, markets and capitalism were not imposed from somewhere else. It is no longer acceptable to portray rural people simply as passive victims of "the extension of the market," that "broke down family-based household structures." Under many circumstances, they could shape the terms on which they agreed to deal with developments taking place elsewhere. Sometimes, as in parts of the upland South, this capability appears to have led to a shunning of commercial contacts for a considerable period. In New England, as we have seen, a generation of families tried to expand production without surrendering their local independence; only over time did the internal contradictions of the household economy bring them more under market influences. That this was so, in turn, implies that rural economic life

10. John Mack Faragher, *Sugar Creek: Life on the Illinois Prairie* (New Haven, 1986), esp. chap. 19, and Jon Gjerde, *From Peasants to Farmers: The Migration from Balestrand, Norway, to the Upper Middle West* (Cambridge, Eng., 1985), esp. chap. 8, both stress the importance of family labor. For its wider relevance, see the important article by Harriet Friedmann, "World-Market, State, and Family Farm: Social Bases of Household Production in the Era of Wage Labour," *Comparative Studies in Society and History* 20 (1978): 545–586.

11. Ronald D. Eller, *Miners, Millhands, and Mountaineers: The Industrialization of the Appalachian South, 1880–1930* (Knoxville, 1982), esp. pp. 120–127; Cathy L. McHugh, *Mill Family: The Labor System in the Southern Cotton Textile Industry* (New York, 1988).

should be understood as dynamic, not static. Scholars have in the past debated whether independent household production retarded or promoted capitalist development. I have suggested in this book that it did both at different times.[12]

The notion of an active, dynamic rural culture is connected with my emphasis on social structure as a determinant of the process of change, because social structures shape the context in which people seek livelihoods. Even in economies where capital and markets are much more directly intrusive than was the case in late-eighteenth-century New England, local property distribution and the organization of work obviously play a critical role in deciding how they will be received or reacted to. In the kind of relatively autonomous household economy discussed here, familial concerns and household strategies were as important in determining the supply of labor or commodities for the market as, for example, purely demographic factors or density of population. A focus on social structure may, indeed, throw light on the long-drawn-out debate over labor supply and early American industry. Constraints imposed by the household system helped maintain effective labor scarcity until the second quarter of the nineteenth century. Equally, the release of some household labor for employment by merchants and factory owners from 1815 onward provided the basis for industrial expansion even as emigration and declining fertility rates reduced growth in the New England population as a whole.[13]

In this book I have also regarded exchange practices as cultural processes, connected with social structures, rather than as economic institutions of purely technical significance. Local exchange, based on face-to-face transactions, and a network of obligations at first embodied the independence of rural household production. Ethical considerations as well as actual practices distinguished these personal networks from those of long-distance traders; the clash between the two ethics, as at the time of Shays's Rebellion, could provoke severe conflict. In time, instabilities within local exchange encouraged some rural people to avoid it and seek other, less personal, means of dealing. These shifts, as we have seen, had moral and ideological as well as economic implications. Partly because it entailed disentangling economic concerns from the social fabric of rural life, the shift to cash transactions was slow, uneven, and incomplete, and only in mid-century did they become very common. Although dealings of the type associated with local exchange continued to take place, they became confined to particular circum-

---

12. The quotation is from Michael Paul Rogin, *Fathers and Children: Andrew Jackson and the Subjugation of the American Indian* (New York, 1975), p. 251.

13. See Alexander James Field, "Sectoral Shift in Antebellum Massachusetts: A Reconsideration," *Explorations in Economic History* 15 (Apr 1978): 146–171.

stances. They no longer remained, as they had once been, the norm for a wide range of transactions. But more research is needed to identify the ethical bases of exchange in other contexts, including the rapidly growing towns and cities of the nineteenth-century United States, where neighborhood and kinship played as important a role in the lives of many people as they had done in the countryside. What were the relationships there between cash and noncash forms of exchange, and how did these help shape economic activity and social structure?[14]

The spring that drove the intensification of rural output in the late eighteenth century was the confrontation between families' aspirations and the prospect of scarcities under the prevailing conditions of land distribution, production, and exchange. Far from explaining away familial ambition as an economic issue, the modern debate on early American rural society has merely focused attention on it, and this book has sought to suggest some of its implications. It is likely, though, that this approach will have wider applications. Research being done into living standards, inheritance practices, and family and household organization suggests the possibility of a deeper understanding of the connections between household strategies and resources and their role in shaping economic structures. Such research would apply to urban as well as to rural areas. If questioning the old assumption that rural people were passive receptors of urban economic and cultural influences has been of value to the current debate, then it follows that the economies of towns need to be examined along lines similar to those developed by scholars of rural life. Towns, indeed, were often populated by rural people, whose experiences of organizing livelihoods in the countryside may have profoundly influenced their approach to the same problem in their new homes.

The focus on household strategies, in turn, lies close to an issue that has been of central concern to social historians for some time: the relationship between families or households and the early development of industrial capitalism. Two assumptions that dominated discussion in the 1970s have repeatedly been criticized by recent scholars. One is that there was a shift from "traditional" to "modern" forms of social organization and behavior in which attachment to familial values gave way to individualism. The other is that capitalists were primarily motivated by

14. Good studies of the fabric of urban economic culture include Barbara Clark Smith, "Markets, Streets and Stores: Contested Terrain in Pre-Industrial Boston," in *Autre Temps, Autre Espace, An Other Time, An Other Space: Etudes sur l'Amérique pre-industrielle*, ed. Elise Marienstras and Barbara Karsky (Nancy, 1986), and Christine Stansell, *City of Women: Sex and Class in New York, 1789–1860* (New York, 1986), especially chaps. 1 and 3. Jonathan Prude suggests the need to integrate urban and rural studies in "Protoindustrialization in the American Context: Response to Jean H. Quataert," *International Labor and Working-Class History* 33 (Spring 1988): 26.

the search for profits. Work on rural-urban migration, on attitudes to property ownership, and on the conduct of business has suggested that family aspirations helped govern strategies and decisions by rich and poor, men and women alike. Family and household concerns indeed played a central role in capitalist development; perhaps it was only after family security had been achieved that thoughts of profits and individual interests could develop in the minds of members of the successful middle classes.[15] For millions of men and women who remained on the land, household organization remained the central concern. But, whether they were in declining or prosperous regions, hired labor or did their own work, they found a social and economic context far different in 1860 from the one their grandparents had faced at the end of the colonial period. Recent scholars have revived the old observation that farming had two sides to it; it could be regarded as a business or as a way of life. But for the farmers who faced it, this dilemma was something relatively new in the mid-nineteenth century. For many, less fortunate, farming remained what it had always been—a struggle.[16]

I have emphasized social structure and the contexts of economic practices in the hope of grasping the richness of the transition process. Life did not change for Sylvester Judd and his contemporaries because there was a clear-cut shift "from subsistence to commercial agriculture" or "from household labor to wage labor" but because the balance of these things altered within a broad social and cultural context. Household production, local exchange, and other institutions important in the late eighteenth century had not been swept aside by the mid-nineteenth, but their relative significance was very different. The emergence of rural capitalism embodied a new set of practices, forms of organization, and rules within which people now tried to make their livelihoods. I have tried to trace not only the structural changes this transition entailed, but peoples' efforts to come to terms with them.

Epilogue: The Connecticut Valley in the Late Nineteenth Century

After the Civil War, the success of Valley families in securing their needs rested heavily on the markets many of them now relied on. How

15. On the continued influence of family values on migrants, see Louise A. Tilly and Joan W. Scott, *Women, Work, and Family* (New York, 1978), and Thomas L. Dublin, "Rural-Urban Migrants in Industrial New England: The Case of Lynn, Massachusetts, in the Mid-19th Century," *Journal of American History* 73 (Dec 1986). See also Richard L. Bushman, "Family Security in the Transition from Farm to City," *Journal of Family History* 6 (1981): 238–256. Lee Davidoff and Catherine Hall discuss the importance of family values in early industrial capitalism in *Family Fortunes: Men and Women of the English Middle Class, 1750–1850* (London, 1987).

16. Jeremy Atack and Fred Bateman, *To Their Own Soil: Agriculture in the Antebellum North* (Ames, Iowa, 1987), chap. 15.

did they fare? Inevitably, the answer is mixed. For hill farmers less able to compete in produce markets, the 1860s marked a resumption of their long decline in fortunes. Hill-town populations became markedly older between 1850 and 1870 as young people left to earn their livelihoods elsewhere. In the 1850s farmers in the hills to the west of the Valley had recognized that their problems and interests were different from those in more prosperous areas and formed the Pontoosuc Agricultural Society to reflect them. While trees remained, hill farmers lived from lumbering and switched what resources they had into dairy cattle for butter, and—later—milk production. Population decline and outmigration meant that they had to rely mainly on family labor to get work done; wage labor again became as scarce and intermittent in the uplands as it had been earlier in the century.[17]

By contrast, commercial farming expanded on the fertile lowlands in the 1860s and early 1870s. Population continued to grow as well; more people lived in Hadley and Hatfield in this period than at any other time in the nineteenth century. Although grain and beef output declined, the value of tobacco production more than tripled between 1860 and 1870; dairy, fruit, and vegetable output for local markets increased too. As the wage-labor force continued to expand, so did the number of young people and immigrants. Prosperity pushed up land prices to record levels. But, as Margaret Pabst's study of Hadley and Hatfield agriculture clearly shows, all these factors were tied to success in the marketplace. When demand for Connecticut Valley tobacco fell in the 1870s, and markets were depressed, the two towns experienced their worst reversals in fortune in the whole nineteenth century. For nearly two decades, until tobacco markets revived again in the 1890s, population and land values fell back.[18] It must have seemed to farmers as if they might share the economic decline faced by their cousins in the hills.

The process of becoming dependent on markets had altered some of their strategies and attitudes. Until the 1840s Hadley and Hatfield farmers had grown corn because it was part of a mixed-crop strategy. From then on, many of them curtailed corn production because it was cheaper to import than to grow. With the profits from tobacco and other crops during the boom years of the middle of the century, they acquired new tools and implements. In the 1870s, when tobacco prices fell, many resumed corn production because, with improved methods, it was now

---

17. Margaret Pabst, "Agricultural Trends in the Connecticut Valley Region of Massachusetts, 1800–1900," *Smith College Studies in History* 26 (1940–1941): 34–36, 42–43. The *Hampshire Gazette*, Nov 3, 1857, reported on a meeting of the Pontoosuc Agricultural Society, in the hill town of Huntington (formerly Norwich). On labor and farming strategies in declining districts, see Hal S. Barron, "The Impact of Rural Depopulation on the Local Economy: Chelsea, Vermont, 1840–1900," *Agricultural History* 52 (1980): 318–335.

18. Pabst, "Agricultural Trends," pp. 52–61.

cheaper to grow than to buy.[19] Just as their predecessors had done, most farmers grew corn in the late nineteenth century, but their reasons for doing so were now much more closely geared to the dictates of price.

The experience of boom and depression also altered many farmers' attitudes toward their land. As late as the mid-1850s, Sylvester Judd interviewed a Hadley farmer who insisted that, despite having been offered an unusually high price for it, his land was not for sale. By the end of the century, fewer of his successors held to this position. As produce markets improved again in the 1890s, and tobacco and onion production in the meadows expanded, more and more farmers leased and later sold land to in-migrants, many of them Polish families whose offspring have retained it ever since. Even farm operation and ownership, once the mark of regional independence, was now part of an international division of labor.[20]

Manufacturers and their workers, too, faced fickle markets after a period of continued expansion in some parts of the Valley following the Civil War. New factories tended to be concentrated in Northampton; metal, cutlery, and machinery works opened there in the 1860s and early 1870s, and the town's silk industry remained strong throughout the ensuing depression. Between 1860 and 1920, Northampton's factory work force would increase more than fourfold, as American-born and immigrant workers continued to flock to the town. So many British and German families lived in Bay State Village in the 1870s that it became known for a while as "Victoria-Bismarck." Outside Northampton, however, signs of weakness were evident. Although palm-leaf-hat and tool works remained in Amherst, they employed scarcely more workers than they had done before the Civil War. The depressions of the 1870s led to bankruptcies and reorganizations. Leonard M. Hills's hat company had to be reorganized after his death in 1872, and his son Henry went bankrupt again in 1883. Even before the Mill River flood of 1874, Williamsburg's manufacturing was stagnating, and the construction of a branch railroad into the town did little to change the situation. Having rebuilt their works after the flood, the Hayden family got into difficulties in 1878, and their firm went into outside hands. So did some of the mills of the "Florence group" in Northampton. By the end of the century, Valley manufacturing had lost many of the distinctive qualities it had displayed in 1860. The most successful large firms were owned and controlled by people outside the region.[21]

19. Ibid., pp. 16–17.
20. Reluctance to sell land was noted by Sylvester Judd in Judd MS, "Miscellaneous," 16:102–103, after interviewing a Hadley farmer in 1855; reproduced in SPJM, p. 342. Polish settlement and farm purchases were noted in the *Hampshire Gazette*, June 17, 1898, and Apr 25, 1910.
21. Agnes Hannay, "A Chronicle of Industry on the Mill River," *Smith College Studies in History* 21 (1935–1936): 93–94, 106–109. Hills's difficulties are referred to in Hills Family Papers, ACA.

Whereas household production had fostered a widely diffused farming, trading, and manufacturing economy in which functions and occupations were intermixed, rural capitalism brought about a repolarization of the Valley's economic structure. Manufacturing and major trading activities became concentrated again in and around Northampton, now a small city and once again a "central place" with an importance to the countryside around it comparable to that of the eighteenth century. The farming districts and the outlying towns lost much of their manufacturing activity, other than that to do with agriculture. On the poorer uplands, trees once again began to grow on land that had been tillage or pasture for little more than a generation. Railroads connected the Valley towns with larger centers; in the late nineteenth century trolley lines would be laid out through Northampton and Amherst. The towns became suburbanized. The countryside became "ruralized" again. Through photography, tour guides, and travel literature, the image of a rusticated rural New England would become fixed in the popular imagination.[22] But this image was formed too late to capture the countryside in its most vibrant, most distinctive, and most influential phase. One of the purposes of this book has been to rectify that misfortune.

22. Quataert, "A New View of Industrialization," pp. 10, 12, discusses regions and households that move from manufactures to agriculture. Photographs of the Valley at the end of the century are in Alan B. Newman, ed., *New England Reflections, 1882–1907: Photographs by the Howes Brothers* (New York, 1981). Guides to the region that dwelt on its rusticity included the numerous works of Clifton Johnson.

Appendix

Population of the
six towns, 1790–1860

	1790	1800	1810	1820	1830	1840	1850	1860
Amherst	1,233	1,358	1,469	1,917	2,613	2,550	3,057	3,206
Hadley	882	1,073	1,247	1,461	1,686	1,814	1,986	2,105
Hatfield	703	809	805	823	893	933	1,073	1,337
Northampton	1,628	2,190	2,631	2,854	3,613	3,750	5,278	6,788
Westhampton	683	756	793	896	918	759	602	608
Williamsburg	1,049	1,176	1,122	1,087	1,236	1,309	1,537	2,095

Sources: U.S. Census Office, *Return of the Whole Number of Persons within the Several Districts of the United States* (Philadelphia, 1791); *Return of the Whole Number of Persons within the Several Districts of the United States* (Washington, D.C., 1801); *Aggregate Amount of Persons within the United States for the Year 1810* (Washington, D.C., 1811); *Census for 1820* (Washington, D.C., 1821); *Fifth Census; or, Enumeration of the Inhabitants of the United States, 1830* (Washington, D.C., 1832); *Sixth Census or Enumeration of the Inhabitants of the United States . . . in 1840* (Washington, D.C., 1841); *The Seventh Census of the United States, 1850* (Washington, D.C., 1853); *Population of the United States in 1860, Compiled from the Original Returns of the Eighth Census* (Washington, D.C., 1864).

Index

Accidents at work, 257–258
Account books, 26, 30, 33–37, 65–67, 70, 164–165, 219–220, 224
Administrators' accounts, 35, 64–65, 68, 264
Agricultural societies, 93, 96, 121, 276, 280, 289, 304, 311
Agriculture. *See* Farming
Albany, N.Y., 102, 151, 175
Allen, Samuel C., 154, 207
Allmendinger, David, 115–116
American Revolution, 4, 6, 43, 67, 195–196, 317
Amherst, Mass., 7, 39, 57, 145, 247, 329; farming in, 74–77, 311; fertility rates in, 135–139; outwork in, 183, 185–190; trade in, 159, 170, 174, 262; wealth in, 22, 307
Amherst and Belchertown Railroad, 262, 270, 311
Amherst College, 115–117, 209, 311–312
Amherst Cotton Factory, 111–112, 234
Amherst Ornamental Tree Association, 311–312
Anti-Masonic party, 204, 207
Apprenticeship, 94, 99, 111–112, 114, 252
Arson, 213–214, 259. *See also* Factory fires
Artisans. *See* Craft producers
Atack, Jeremy, 232–236

Baltimore, Md., 102, 299–300
Bancroft, George, 207–209
Bankruptcy, 126, 162, 200–201, 208, 217–218, 280–281, 294. *See also* Debt
Banks, 159, 269–272. *See also* Northampton Institution for Savings

Bargaining, 36, 70, 213, 220, 223–224
Barre, Mass., 185, 189
Barter, 34. *See also* Local exchange
Bartlett family, 32–35, 62–63, 92, 274, 291–292
Bay State Tool Company, 246
Belchertown, Mass., 184, 188–189
Bidwell, Percy W., 12
Billings, John, 47
Bills of exchange. *See* Commercial paper
Bliss, Chester, 127–128
Bliss, Theodore, 87, 252
Boardinghouses, 241–242, 249, 254–256, 308
Bodman family, 111, 171, 183, 186, 221; as manufacturers, 231, 234–235, 238, 256
Bogin, Ruth, 196
Boltwood, William, 34, 66, 72–74, 89–90, 92, 97
Boston, Mass.: investment from, 113; marketing in, 28, 31, 68, 77, 82, 102, 175, 288
Bottomlands, 7, 83, 293–299
Braiding. *See* Palm-leaf-hat making
Brenner, Robert, 322
Brissot de Warville, Jacques-Pierre, 33–34
Brooke, John L., 47
Broomcorn, 83, 85, 148–150, 288
Broom dealers, 248
Broom making, 83, 100–103, 148, 176, 230, 232, 236–237, 248
Brown, Abner, 66–67, 71
Bullard, Sophronia, 240–242
Burke family, 226–227
Button making, 181–182, 240
By-employments, 72–73, 110

Canals, 10, 53–54, 151

Capital: accumulation, 190; in manufacturing, 16, 228–231, 245–246, 250–251, 256

Capitalism: defined, 14; discussed, 7–9, 12, 15–17, 318–326; restrained, 111–113. *See also* Transition to capitalism debate

Careers, 22, 57–58, 63–64, 94, 101, 113–116, 160–163, 229–230

Carpenter, Edward J., 259–260

Carriage making, 231–233, 235–236, 243

Cash: social implications, 33, 67–69, 224–227; sought after, 198–199; spread of, 199, 221, 278–279; at stores, 164–167, 171–172, 195, 221–224; wages, 252

Cash crops, 17, 84, 150, 294–303

Cattle, 77–78, 287; dairy, 145, 290; fattened, 82–83, 148, 152–153, 288

Cattle shows. *See* Agricultural societies

Chesterfield, Mass., 50

Children: provision for, 27, 38, 62, 71–72, 88–89, 129, 161–162; work by, 24–25, 78, 305

Churches, 6–7, 51, 116–117

Cider, 83, 98–99, 123

Civil War, 317

Clapp, Oliver M., 202

Clark, Olive Cleveland, 23, 97

Clark, William, 214, 259, 267

Clarke, Joseph, 35, 73

Clarke, Samuel, 173

Clothing, 24, 26, 96, 98, 144

Cole, Thomas, 109–110

Coleman, Peter J., 50

Colman, Henry, 121–122, 152–154

Commercial paper, 31–32, 59, 67–68

Connecticut River Railroad, 220, 261–263, 269–270, 288

Connecticut River Valley: climate and growing season, 25; in-migration, 8, 39; landscape, 7; white settlement, 39

Consumption goods, 28, 68, 85. *See also* Households, consumption by; Stores

Cook, Caleb, 72, 97, 110

Cook, James and Chester, 238

Cowles, Simeon, 88–89, 92, 131–132

Craft producers, 30, 41, 93–95, 99–100, 126, 186, 230–231; control of production by, 238; squeezed, 242–246

Credit, 31–33, 71, 82, 128, 195, 214–220, 264–267; and inequality, 226–227; in manufacturing, 236–239; short-term, 32, 222–223; at stores, 163–169, 197. *See also* Debt

Credit reports, 215–220, 225, 263

Crops: prices, 149–150, 152, 200, 287, 290, 294–296; yields, 81, 294

Dairying, 78, 86–87, 145, 275–276, 290

Debt, 33–38, 49–50, 56, 64–65, 122–128, 164, 208–209, 280–281; imprisonment for, 45, 123, 206, 220; lawsuits for, 37–38, 123–128, 166–167, 199–203, 225; and Shays's Rebellion, 44–48, 50. *See also* Bankruptcy; Credit

Deerfield, Mass., 28–29, 78–79

Dickinson, Asa, 69, 90, 98

Dickinson, Charlotte, 187

Dickinson, Edward, 203, 213, 219, 225

Dickinson, Emily, 203

Dickinson, Hannah, 88, 96, 115

Dickinson, Levi, 83, 100, 102–103

Dickinson, Rebecca, 21–22, 56, 75, 97–98, 123

Ditz, Toby L., 27, 91–92, 129

Division of labor, 24–26, 95, 99, 122, 132

Dry goods, 28–29, 142, 170–171

Dwight, Timothy, 30, 39, 54

Dwight and Partridge, 164–165, 169

Easthampton, Mass., 40, 181, 184

Eastman, Joseph, 66–67, 108–110

Education, 89–90, 94, 114–116, 162

Edwards, Ann Bullard, 240–241

Edwards, David, 237

Edwards, Lewis, 240–241

Edwards, William, 54, 113, 237

Elections, 49–52, 153, 205, 207

Elites, 38–44, 48–54

Emigration, 8, 53, 63, 121–122, 241, 248

Evangelical revivals, 117, 191, 196–197, 208–211, 213

Exchange: ethics of, 31–38, 44–50, 69–70, 122–124, 195, 215–220; of labor, 25, 30, 66, 72–74, 87, 98–99, 304. *See also* Local exchange; Trade

Factory fires, 238, 247, 257–258

Factory system: conditions in, 255–261; constrained, 111–113; criticized, 207; growth of, 228–229, 246

Factory villages, 246, 252–253

Factory workers, 146, 251, 252–261, 328; age and gender, 112, 260–261; women as, 112, 146, 239, 242, 251, 254–255

Family, 21, 56; businesses, 262–263; disputes, 129–132; labor, 21, 23–26, 38–40, 106–108, 274–276, 304–305; life-cycle, 89–90; size, 26, 137–138; tension with neighbors, 88

Farmers: prosperity, 293–294, 303; status, 6–8, 23, 309–313

Farm foremen, 309

Farming, 8, 24–25, 71–87, 146–150, 273–309; extensive, 80; intensive, 80–83, 286–287; mixed, 75–76, 85–86, 147,

276–278; rhetoric about, 276; risks of, 149, 280–281, 294; techniques, 286, 306; tilled acreage, 80–81, 285–286
Farm laborers, 304–309; age, 308; numbers, 307
Farm output, 74–75, 81–82, 147–148, 282–285, 294
Farms, division of, 60–63, 307; improvement of, 63, 73–74, 80–82, 91, 285
Farm size, 62, 80, 285, 297–299, 322
Farm surpluses, 75–77, 151–152, 283–284; marketing of, 86–87, 147–148, 283
Federalism, 51–52, 95, 116
Female Education Society of Amherst, 115
Fertility rates, 134–139
Fertilizers, commercial, 302
Flax, 75, 145; processing, 140
Florence group, 268–269, 328
Folbre, Nancy, 92, 106, 129, 134
Foodstuffs, shipped into region, 75, 151–152, 263
Forward, Rev. Justus, 36, 109
Fruit growing, 83, 123, 289

Gender roles, 24–26, 78, 132–134, 305
Gere, I. and F., 230, 234–235
Goodale, Asahel, 252, 274
Goodale, Ira Chaffee, 101, 107, 115, 127–128, 304
Goodale, Moses, 90, 92, 146, 156
Graham, Lucius, 241–243, 245, 261
Graham, Mary Bullard, 56, 133, 188–189, 240–243, 305
Grain, 56, 74–76, 81–82, 85–86, 147, 286. *See also* Wheat
Greenville Manufacturing Company, 268–269
Greenwich, Mass., 47
Gross, Robert A., 59
Grout, Esther, 144–145

Hadley, Mass., 7, 21, 39, 46, 148–149, 232; farmers in, 309–311, 327–328; fertility rates in, 135–139; trade in, 29, 157–160
Hadley Manufacturing Company, 310
Hale, Rev. Enoch, 48–49
Hall, Arethusa, 96, 107
Hall, Mary Ann, 258–259
Hampshire County: divided, 174
Hampshire County Temperance Society, 211
Hampshire Homespun Society, 178
Hannay, Agnes, 268
Hartford, Conn., 28–29, 32, 175–176, 300
Hatfield, Mass., 7, 39, 47, 122, 232; farming in, 293, 295–299; farm laborers in,

307; trade in, 159; wealth in, 22, 293, 303
Hayden, Joel and Josiah, 182, 249–251, 268–269
Haydenville, Mass., 246, 250, 289
Henretta, James A., 11–12, 26
Hill, Samuel L., 268–269
Hills, Henry F., 249, 257, 266, 328
Hills, Leonard M., 182, 202, 238, 243, 245, 249, 266, 328
Hill towns: decline of, 290–294, 327; farming in, 82–83, 287–288
Hinckley, Samuel L., 267–269
Hogs, 84–85
Holyoke, Mass., 241, 289
Holyoke Range, 310
Horwitz, Morton, 224
Household economy, 13, 15–17, 38–39, 71, 84–87, 229, 274–275, 303, 318–320; and capitalism, 52, 111–113, 229; labor in, 105–113, 239–240; and social structure, 41, 44, 52, 56–58, 60, 93
Households, 21, 55–56; consumption by, 28, 139, 142, 151–152, 290; control of production, 87–92; independence of, 4, 23–27, 38, 56, 129, 204, 279, 303, 319; manufactures abandoned by, 141–142, 180, 242; manufactures in, 64, 72–73, 75, 95–100, 114, 140, 144. *See also* Clothing; Housework; Outwork; Textile production
Houses, 41–42, 55–56
Housework, 24, 26, 132–134, 139–146, 241–243, 274–275
Hoyt, David, 78
Hoyt, Epaphras, 121–122
Hudson, Patricia, 179–180
Huntington, Dan, 68, 109, 115, 131, 148, 285; as merchant, 162, 171, 198
Huntington, Edward P., 162, 182, 203, 213
Huntington, Theodore G., 289

Immigrants, 8–9, 214, 252–254, 306–308, 327–328
Industry. *See* Factory system; Manufacturing
Inequality. *See* Property distribution
Ingram, Peter, 244
Inheritance, 27, 60, 62, 91–92, 129–132, 307
Interest, 31–32, 35, 37, 67, 221–224, 274
Interlocking directorates, 268–270
Involution, economic, 15–16, 60, 318–319
Itinerant workers, 57, 97–98, 242

Jensen, Joan M., 145–146, 279
Jones, Douglas Lamar, 56

Judd, Apphia Hall, 5, 142–143
Judd, Chauncey Parkman, 201–202, 211, 276
Judd, Jonathan, Jr., 43, 50–51, 212
Judd, Sylvester (1752–1832), 4–5, 51, 79, 82, 313
Judd, Sylvester, Jr. (1789–1860): as editor, 5–6, 208; on family consumption, 290; as farmer, 81–82, 90–91; on hill towns, 281, 291–292; as historian, 3, 7, 87; on inequality, 272; as merchant, 4–5, 145, 158, 161–162, 165, 170; on religion, 6–7, 208; republican values of, 4–6; and temperance, 210; on tobacco, 300–301; visits Ohio, 5, 122
Judd, Sylvester, III (1813–1853), 163

Kellogg, Daniel, 57–58
Kellogg, James, 127–128, 175, 231–232, 245, 247–248
Kerber, Linda K., 114
Kingsley, Edwin, 219–220
Kingsley, Joseph, 95, 98–99, 130, 161, 166, 168
Kinship, 30, 87, 202–203
Knowles and Thayer, 231–233, 235–236, 238–239, 243

Labor: and profits, 116, 252; shortage of, 38–41, 75–78, 246, 252, 305; turnover, 239–240, 259–260. See also Factory workers; Family; Farm laborers; Household economy; Outwork; Servants; Women: work
Land: accumulation of, 73–74, 88–91; price of, 60–61, 293, 303, 327; scarcity of, 60–61, 74–75; speculation in, 52–54. See also Property distribution
Liberal ideology, 195–197, 227
Liquor, 65, 87; distilleries, 83, 85–86; laws, 210–214; retailed, 212–213. See also Cider; Temperance movement; Total-abstinence societies
Livestock, 76–83, 310–311; in local exchange, 88; and manufactures, 99, 233. See also Cattle; Hogs; Sheep
Local exchange, 27–38, 64–74, 76, 195–196, 273–274, 324; difficulties of, 197–199; and economic change, 71, 82; and manufactures, 98–105, 233–234; merchants in, 163–169; nonmarket character, 12, 27, 70–71; and redistribution of surpluses, 76, 88; transformed, 223–224, 309
Lyman, Rev. Joseph, 48–51

McGaw, Judith, 260

Mack, David (of Middlefield, Mass.), 69, 160
Mack, David, Jr., 213, 249
McMahon, Sarah F., 76
Manufacturers: diversified, 247–251; social origins of, 238, 247
Manufacturing, 93–105, 176–190, 228–261; location of, 101–102, 105, 233–234, 245–246, 328; and markets, 102–103, 232–236; raw materials for, 233–234; structure of, 229–240. See also Factory system; Households: manufactures
Manufacturing hamlets, 231–232. See also Factory villages
Markets: competition in, 287–288; contemporary debates about, 152–154, 281–282; historical debate about, 11–14, 27, 59–60, 70, 84; land, 59, 63, 88–90, 92; local, 288–289, 327; pressure toward, 284–288; produce, 59, 77–80, 84–87, 147–148, 156, 283–288, 327–328
Marriage, age at, 135–138
Marshall, Ansel C., 301–302
Marshall, Chester, 107
Martin, Margaret E., 172–173
Meat, 77–79
Mendels, Franklin F., 179
Men's work, 24–26, 78
Mercantile Agency. See Credit reports
Merchants, 29, 37, 156–191; criticized, 162–163, 166, 168; and household manufactures, 99, 175–176; investors in manufacturing, 238, 245–249; and labor, 176–191; in rural economy, 52–55, 65, 163–174, 189–191; and surpluses, 79; and temperance movement, 211–213. See also Outwork; Stores
Merrill, Michael, 11–12, 31
Milk, 290
Miller, John, 48, 52, 56
Millinery, 230
Mill River, 246; flood of 1874, 251, 292–293, 328
Mills, custom, 103–104, 309–310
Money supply, 221
Moral economy, 195–196
Mortgages, 37, 91, 154, 202–208, 244–245, 267, 281
Mulberry trees, 154–155, 202

Nash, William A., 289, 292, 305–306, 308
Neighborhood, 30, 48, 57–58, 87–88, 101, 128, 206
New England: compared with other regions, 17, 71, 93, 179–180, 190, 303, 318–326

New York City, 151, 175, 181, 215, 219, 299–300
Nims, Seth, 102, 203
Noncash exchange. *See* Local exchange
Northampton, Mass., 6–7, 29, 39–40, 52–55, 78–79, 329; buildings in, 174, 262; farmers in, 61–62, 306; manufacturing in, 99, 246, 250–251, 268–269, 328; trade in, 29, 157–160, 169–170, 221–223, 262; wealth in, 22, 99, 263–267
Northampton Association for Education and Industry, 250–251, 268
Northampton Cotton and Woolen Manufacturing Company, 112
Northampton Institution for Savings, 270–272
Northampton Temperance Association, 210
Northampton Woolen and Satinet Manufactory, 230, 234–235
Northampton Woolen Manufacturing Company, 251, 253, 257, 267
Nutting, Harriet, 188
Nutting, John, 239–240
Nutting, Judith, 145, 188–189, 239–240, 282, 305
Nutting, Truman, 239, 245, 248–249, 252

Occupational structure, 8, 72, 94, 105, 228, 230, 273, 307
One-price policy, 223
Orders against third parties, 68, 124
Outwork, 146, 176–189; earnings from, 184, 187–189; and rural households, 184–185, 241–242; textile production, 176–179. *See also* Button making; Palm-leaf-hat making
Outworkers, 185–189

Palm-leaf-hat making, 181–190, 249, 260
Palm-leaf merchants, 182–184
Panic of 1837, 200–202, 243, 280–281
Parker, William N., 88
Parsons, Enos, 217, 225
Parsons, S. C., 262
Pasture, 81, 287
Patriarchy, 25, 51–52, 106, 114, 228, 279
Paxton, Mass., 45
Pelham, Mass., 39, 46–47
Pettengill family, 130–131
Phelps, Charles, 41, 61, 68–69, 109, 111
Phelps, Charles P., 147–149, 155, 282–283
Phelps, Elizabeth, 26
Politics: county, 42–43, 51–52; state, 44; town, 51, 161, 312–313. *See also* Elections; *entries for individual parties*

Population, 8, 40, 60, 160, 228, 288–289, 331
Porter, William, 29, 108, 157, 165–170, 175–177, 183, 237
Potash, 29
Poverty, 56–58, 139, 163, 226–227, 265, 272, 308–309; and education, 115–116
Price: in book accounts, 70–71, 171–172; convergence, 59, 84; movements, 86, 281
Privacy, 225
Profit and loss: calculated, 70, 145, 155, 190, 294
Promissory notes, 29, 37, 65–68, 124–125. *See also* Commercial paper
Property distribution, 22–23, 61, 263–267, 293, 307; of factory workers, 257; of farm laborers, 308; of outworkers' families, 187
Protoindustrialization theory, 179
Prude, Jonathan, 259
Pruitt, Bettye Hobbs, 74, 76
Prutt, Caesar, 57
Putting-out system. *See* Outwork

Railroads, 10, 153, 205, 261–263, 270, 288, 311, 328–329
Reciprocal exchange. *See* Local exchange
Reddy, William M., 227
Religion. *See* Churches; Evangelical revivals
Reproduction. *See* Fertility rates; Gender roles
Republican party, 312–313
River Gods, 41–43
River transport, 28–29, 53–54, 151
Roads, 10, 53–54, 174
Rothenberg, Winifred B., 11, 13, 59, 77–78, 84, 92

Savings banks. *See* Northampton Institution for Savings
Scott, Sarah, 177
Sears, Nathaniel, 238
Seasonal work, 25–26, 96–97, 99, 104, 110, 230, 261
Self-control, 211, 214
Self-exploitation, 242–243, 305, 319
Self-sufficiency, 12, 23–27, 281–283, 313; regional, 84–87, 146–147, 151
Servants, 35, 39–41, 105–108, 186, 241–242
Settlement of accounts, 35, 45–46, 49, 68, 124, 224
Shareholding, 264, 267–270
Shays, Daniel, 48
Shays's Rebellion, 44–50

Sheep, 81, 85, 233, 287–288
Shepard, James, 159
Shepard, Levi, 29, 31–32, 49, 52, 112, 158, 178
Shepard, Thomas, 159, 178
Sheriffs' auctions, 45–46
Shipman, John, 100, 148, 232, 236
Shoemaking, 72, 97–98, 231, 241–243, 247–248
Shumway, Elizabeth, 283
Slavery, 38–39, 41; opposition to, 312–313
Smith, Adam, 95
Specialization: in manufacturing, 229, 236; in retailing, 222, 262
Springfield, Mass., 39, 240–241, 262–263
Staple crops, 28–29, 38, 42–43, 85–86, 324. *See also* Cash crops; Wheat
Stoddard, William H., 173, 190, 214, 223, 266, 269
Storekeepers. *See* Merchants
Store orders, 68, 108, 168–169. *See also* Orders against third parties
Stores, 85, 157, 169–170, 220–227, 262; diffusion of, 158–160, 175
Strikes, 199, 259
Strong, Caleb, 48, 51–52, 56
Strong, Hezekiah Wright, 166, 170–173
Subsistence-surplus strategies, 28–29, 74–80, 84–87, 121, 154–155, 276–277
Surplus. *See* Farm surpluses
Sweetser, Cutler and Company, 183, 186–187, 245, 262–263
Sweetser, Luke, 170, 173, 190, 202, 247, 266

Tanning, 5, 98, 113, 237
Tappan, Benjamin, 53–54, 159, 166, 263
Tappan, Lewis, 54, 215–220, 225
Taxation, 44, 50
Temperance movement, 209–214, 300–302. *See also* Liquor; Total-abstinence societies
Tenancy, 39, 63, 73, 149–150, 154, 283, 304, 318
Textile production: in factories, 233–235; in households, 72–73, 96–98, 132–133, 140–142. *See also* Dry goods; Outwork
Thomas, Robert B., 35–37
Tobacco: in cultivation, 294–303, 327; and broomcorn, 295–296; farming strategies, 297–299; income from, 295–296, 303; marketing, 299–300; opposition to, 300–302; output, 295–296
Toolmaking, 99, 232, 239, 246, 248–249
Total-abstinence societies, 210–212
Trade, 27–29, 151, 157–158, 175; dis-

rupted, 96; in manufactured goods, 102–103
Traders. *See* Merchants
Transiency, 57, 259–261
Transition to capitalism debate, 9–15, 318, 322
Trask, Rev. George, 300–301
Truck system, 234

Uplands. *See* Hill towns
Urbanization, 9, 325
Utility companies, 269–270

Vegetables, 289
Vickers, Daniel, 38, 106

Wage rates, 25, 40, 200, 234–235, 256, 258–259, 306–308
Wage workers, 59–60, 105–106, 146, 251–261, 304–309; skilled, 231–232, 234–235, 239
Wagonmaking, 101, 127–128
Wait, Benjamin, 92
Warner, John F., 273–274, 289, 292
Warning-out, 56–57
Watson, Oliver, 219, 248
Wealth, 22, 263–267, 293, 303. *See also* Property distribution
Wells, Amasa, 164–165, 169
Westhampton, Mass., 4–5, 7, 40, 48–51, 62–63, 290–294; trade in, 159; wealth in, 22, 293, 303
Wheat, 42, 281
Whig party, 204, 207, 312
White, Smith and Company, 266–267
Whitney, David S., 173, 213
Williams, Israel, 41–43
Williams, Joseph, 177
Williamsburg, Mass., 7, 29, 39, 79, 290–291, 328; in American Revolution, 43; crafts in, 99; factory workers in, 255–257, 260–261; outwork in, 181, 184; trade in, 159
Williamsburg Temperance Reform Society, 211
Williston, John P., 173, 190–191, 213–214, 220, 268–269
Williston, Samuel, 181, 238, 240, 249–250, 268–269
Women: in churches, 117; and education, 114–115; in manufacturing, 239, 242; and temperance movement, 211–212; work, 24–26, 72–73, 78, 98, 274–279. *See also* Clothing; Dairying; Fertility rates; Housework; Outwork; Servants
Wood, J. S., 59

Woodenware, 28, 94–99, 102–103, 233
Woodland: ecological costs of stripping,
   292–293; lumbering, 24–25, 291–292
Work-discipline, 253, 258

Workers' protests, 259
Workingmen's movement, 5, 204–209
Wright, Ansel, 226–227, 265, 289
Wright, Solomon, 72–74

Library of Congress Cataloging-in-Publication Data

Clark, Christopher, 1953–
    The roots of rural capitalism: western Massachusetts, 1780–1860 / Christopher Clark.
        p.   cm.
    ISBN 0–8014–2422–4 (alk. paper)
        1. Massachusetts—Economic conditions. 2. Massachusetts—Industries, Rural—
History. 3. Capitalism—Massachusetts—History. 4. Households—Massachusetts—
History. 5. Agriculture—Economic aspects—Massachusetts—History. 6.
Massachusetts—Social conditions. I. Title.
HC107.M4R66 1990
330.9744'203—dc20
                                                                              89–46177